PRE-TRIAL
CRIMINAL PROCEDURE

PRE-TRIAL CRIMINAL PROCEDURE

A Survey of Constitutional Rights

By

MARC WEBER TOBIAS

and

R. DAVID PETERSEN

With a Foreword by

Richard E. Shugrue, A.B., J.D., Ph.D.

Creighton University School of Law
Omaha, Nebraska

CHARLES C. THOMAS · PUBLISHER

Springfield · Illinois · U.S.A.

Published and Distributed Throughout the World by

CHARLES C THOMAS • PUBLISHER
BANNERSTONE HOUSE
301-327 East Lawrence Avenue, Springfield, Illinois, U.S.A.

© 1972, by **CHARLES C THOMAS • PUBLISHER**
ISBN 0-398-02613-0

Library of Congress Catalog Card Number: 72-81719

Printed in the United States of America
C-1

To

Dr. Manuel L. Weber

and

Carl J. Worgren

FOREWORD

A CRITICAL problem facing American society is attaining an
even-handed administration of justice. The typical citizen
has his earliest encounter with the system of law when confronted
by a law enforcement officer with a charge of wrongdoing. Whether that charge will result in a dismissal, conviction, fine, jail term
or one of the other sanctions of American justice, it is imperative
that the police are well trained in the basic rules of constitutional-
criminal law and procedure.

It is a truism that police are expected to possess a vast reservoir
of knowledge on subjects ranging from first aid and psychology to
scientific investigation. In no field is the possession of up-to-date
information more important than in law and the processes surrounding it. There can be little doubt that vast changes have
taken place in criminal law and procedure within the past dozen
years. The Warren Court has been charged with handcuffing the
police and making criminal convictions more difficult. However,
in a constitutional system in which basic guarantees of freedom
are as old as the nation and for that matter, the underlying cause
of establishing the country, a scrupulous regard for the rights of
the individual is essential.

The police officer is charged with many duties, including keeping the peace, apprehending the criminal suspect and preserving
evidence vital to the state's case against the accused. Each of these
responsibilities must be carried out within the framework of the
constitutional system. When fundamental rights of the citizen are
shunted aside in the name of efficient administration, organized
society becomes the loser. When the state can obtain a conviction
without preserving due process of law (so vital in the American
scheme of things), disrespect for the law is generated and the rationale for a nation of free men breaks down.

It is a prerequisite for the preservation of a nation of laws, and
not of men, that the first line of societal protection—the law en-

forcement agencies—be the best trained in the world. The myriad of rules in the field of criminal law and procedure makes this a tremendously difficult task. Decisions (requiring instant judgment on the part of the police officer) made at the scene of a crime or in a hostile neighborhood are simple to criticize after the fact.

It is obvious that a significant part of the continuing training of the professional law man must be in the fields of criminal justice and constitutional law. The "fruits" of an unconstitutional search, formerly admitted into evidence at trial, are now banned. An unwarranted arrest may result in dismissal of the complaint against the accused. A confession coerced from a suspect may not be used to make the task of the prosecutor easier. Careless methods of suspect identification are now prevented by the requirement that counsel be present during a lineup. All these rules emerge directly from the constitutional mandates found in the American Bill of Rights and in no agencies should protection of those rights be more diligently observed, than by the police forces of the nation.

The seeming dilemma faced by police departments can be resolved by excellent training programs for the officers. This book is designed to provide a storehouse of knowledge for law enforcement officers, as well as for lawyers who desire an accessible collection of basic rules.

This book accomplishes three important tasks. First, it is a thorough, accurate statement of the law with sufficient illustrative material to cover the many contingencies which a law enforcement officer is likely to encounter. It sets down the rules of law without oversimplifying them—a task absolutely vital in a field where simplification can result in a miscarriage of justice.

Second, the text is organized in such a way that in the hands of a professional educator it will be an outstanding teaching tool in courses relating to police practices and the law. It does not attempt to make excuses for the rules of law nor does it provide questionable loopholes for avoiding the high standard of constitutionality demanded by all levels of American courts of the professional.

These two accomplishments alone commend the book to the student of criminal procedure, yet there is a third task which the book performs. Many individuals criticize the work of the courts without understanding what the tribunals have done. This book offers the reader an opportunity to become involved in the actual case decisions by explaining the rather mystifying system of legal citations which are second nature to the attorney and judge. In this respect, the book encourages independent study and research by personnel of law enforcement agencies so that they may understand the reasons behind the decisions which have altered the practices of criminal procedure.

There are longer studies of criminal procedure; there are volumes for the attorneys which emphasize fine points of evidence; and there are books which examine highly technical issues of constitutional law in extreme detail. Yet there is probably no better statement of the current law status for the individual charged with day-to-day administration of society's rules than is found in this text. Mr. Tobias and Mr. Petersen have provided a genuine service to the continuing task of raising the level of professionalism for the first line of America's criminal justice system—the law enforcement officer.

RICHARD E. SHUGRUE

INTRODUCTION

"THE Constitution in its words is plain and intelligible, and it is meant for the homebred, unsophisticated understanding of our fellow citizens." In spite of this statement by former Vice President George M. Dallas, different interpretations and new understanding seem to be a daily occurrence with the United States Constitution.

In the past few years, the Supreme Court has given an expanding, liberal interpretation to the Constitution. A suspect demands his "constitutional rights" or an accused claims that his "rights" were violated. If the court agrees, the evidence in the case may be thrown out, or the lower court conviction reversed. Accordingly, a continuing education in recent Supreme Court case law is a necessity, particularly to those in the law enforcement field.

This book is intended to acquaint law enforcement personnel, law students studying constitutional law and criminal procedure, and students in law enforcement curriculums with pre-trial criminal procedure as implemented by the law enforcement officer and experienced by the accused, under the guidelines of the United States Constitution as viewed in the light of current court decisions.

The topics are chosen according to their frequency of occurrence in the field and at the stationhouse. The text should aid law enforcement agencies in the training of cadets, and in the continuing education of the experienced officer in the area of pre-trial police procedures.

The book is divided into three major parts; the first contains a brief history of the "law," the concept of the "criminal sanction," and the meaning of "due process."

The second part deals with the role of the officer and the rights of the accused under the fourth, fifth, and sixth amendments to the Constitution. To aid in the understanding of court

xi

rulings, actual case examples are presented throughout this section. At the end of each chapter are key cases, quoted in part, which are generally considered as turning points in criminal procedure.

Part three is devoted to a discussion of bail, pre-trial detention, and the basic functions of the courts.

M. W. T.
R. D. P.

Marc Weber Tobias
5820 E. 1st Avenue
Denver, Colorado 80220

R. David Petersen
Box 3911
Omaha, Nebraska 68103

LEGAL CITATIONS

MOST states publish the decisions of the highest court in the state, for example, the Supreme Court of the State of Nebraska, in "official reports." Some states however, such as Florida, have discontinued the publication of official reports, and hence one must look to the "unofficial" reports. The West Publishing Company publishes unofficial reports of both the states and the federal court systems.

The state reports are contained in regional reports such as the *North Western Reporter* and are grouped by geographic regions.

When a citation to a case is given, it tells where the case may be found.

The following is a citation to a decision written by the Supreme Court of the State of Iowa—*State v. Mullin,* 349 Iowa 10, 85 N.W.2d 598 (1957). The opinion appears both in the "official" and "unofficial" reports. The "official" citation 349 Iowa 10, indicates that the case may be found on page 10, volume 349 of the Iowa State Supreme Court Reports. The "unofficial" citation, 85 N.W.2d 598, indicates that the same decision may also be found on page 598, of volume 85 of the 2nd series of the *North Western Reporter.* The year the decision was handed down is 1957.

Abbreviations used for the state reporters are as follows:

P.	Pacific
N.W.	North Western
S.W.	South Western
N.E.	North Eastern
A.	Atlantic
S.E.	South Eastern
So.	Southern
Cal. Rptr.	California Reporter
N.Y.S.	New York Supplement

xiii

The national reporter system by the West Publishing Company also includes the following: a) the Supreme Court Reporter, which reports the decisions of the Supreme Court of the United States; b) the Federal Reporter, which among other courts reports the decisions of the United States Court of Claims and the United States Court of Appeals; c) the Federal Supplement, which among other courts, contains decisions of the United States District Courts since 1932; and d) the Federal Rules Decisions, which contains reports of the United States District Courts which do not appear in the Federal Supplement and which involve the Federal Rules of Criminal Procedure since 1946 and the Federal Rules of Civil Procedure since 1939.

United States v. Wade, 388 U.S. 218 (1967) is found on page 218 of volume 388 of the *United States Reports.* This is a United States Supreme Court decision handed down in 1967.

Cortez v. United States, 337 F.2d 699 (1964) is found on page 699 of volume 337, of the *Federal Reporter,* 2nd series. This is a United States Court of Appeals decision handed down in 1964.

Johns v. Smyth, 176 F. Supp. 949, 1959, is found on page 949 of volume 176 of the *Federal Supplement.* This is a United States District Court decision handed down in 1959.

United States v. Reid, 43 F.R.D. 520 (1967) is found on page 520 of volume 43, of the *Federal Rules Decisions.* This is a United States District Court decision handed down in 1967.

ACKNOWLEDGMENTS

THE authors are indebted to a number of persons who supplied materials for certain sections of the text.

The United States' Attorney's Office, Omaha, Nebraska and a number of agents of the Federal Bureau of Investigation were most helpful in the preparation of the chapter dealing with searches and seizures.

I appreciate the assistance of the Denver Police Department and Harry D. Taylor of that department. Appreciation is also expressed for the help provided by Chief Ben Roach, Jr., Lieutenant Mary Ruth Norris, Detective Jack P. Baldwin, and Jeff Grazi, all of the Commerce City, Colorado, Police Department.

Gratitude is also expressed to the Omaha Police Division for their assistance.

A special note of thanks to the Gorgen family: Tom, Twink, Barbara, and Floyd, for their encouragement and friendship.

The advice and direction of G. L. Kuchel, Director of the University of Nebraska Law Enforcement Department, and that of Theodore Clements, Professor, Creighton University School of Law, must be acknowledged.

We would also like to express our respect to Dr. James Reinhardt, Lincoln, Nebraska.

Finally, without the stenographic efforts of Jane A. Petersen and Michael Charles Tobias, a great deal more time would have been required to complete the text.

M. W. T.
R. D. P.

SUMMARY OF CONTENTS

CONTENTS

xvii

PART II. CONSTITUTIONAL GUIDELINES

PRE-TRIAL
CRIMINAL PROCEDURE

PART I

OVERVIEW OF THE
CRIMINAL PROCESS

CHAPTER I

BUILDING BLOCKS OF JUSTICE

Section I. THE CRIMINAL JUSTICE SYSTEM IN DEVELOPMENT

THE first division of this text outlines the foundation and component parts of our modern legal system. The brief discussion which follows presents a look at several interrelated concepts which, taken as a composite, make up "the law" as we know it today. It was felt that an overview tracing the development of our legal framework would furnish a logical beginning for a text dealing with specific rights and immunities provided by our form of government.

1.1. Law as a Concept

The term "law" is often used incorrectly as a synonym for "crime," which is to say, a system of controls placed upon members of society to limit, alter, deter, or encourage certain forms of behavior; however, the concept of law goes much deeper, and in order to fully understand its many facets, it becomes necessary to examine the term "law" and to probe the underlying reasons for its development.

Law can mean many things to many people. To a natural scientist, the law differs considerably from what it means to a philosopher, attorney, or police officer. A beginning definition of law might be "the enforcement of justice among men."

Three general theories or rationale have evolved, all of which attempt to explain the law with respect to its different facets and periods of history. These are the Natural Law Theory, the Imperative Theory, and the Historical Theory.

1.2. Natural Law

Natural law stresses the interrelation between justice and morality. Its supporters consider the basis of law to lie in Right and Reason, that is to say, man is a moral, rational being. In essence,

5

the moral element predominates the legal process in the Natural Law theory.

1.3. Imperative Law

This school of thought places emphasis on the relation between law and political power. It considers the origin of the law in the Will of the State, meaning the law consists of the commands of the highest political authority, backed by coercive sanctions. The Imperative theory sees the law as a body of technical rules and concepts to be analyzed (hence analytical jurisprudence).

1.4. Historical Law

The Historical model sees law in the perspective of the development of man and state. Proponents of this theory consider the law as a product of tradition and custom, interbound with the mind and spirit of the people. The law, it is said, develops in custom, and is then solidified by juristic activity. A society's laws represent an expression of the common conscience of the people at a given time; a complex of ideas, institutions, and techniques, all in a state of continuing development.

Each of the three legal theories contributes to an understanding of our modern legal system. In the formative era of Western legal thought, the eleventh to the fifteenth century, legal thinking was based on the Natural Law model, expounding such definitions as "a theory of *right* and *wrong*," "an art of the good and equitable," and "reason unaffected by desire." Other definitions during this period related to human nature and the Divine law. In this context, Sir Thomas Aquinas, Roman philosopher, defined law as "nothing else than an ordinance of reason for the common good, made and promulgated by him who has care of the community."

A case tried on the Common Bench (England) in 1345 stated the feeling of the day saying the law is not just the "will of the justices, but that which is *right*."

By the sixteenth century, as nations were developing, the Imperative theory of law came to the fore, and by the nineteenth century, predominated. Hobbs wrote, "Law properly is the word of him, that by right hath command over others." A leading English jurist of the nineteenth century wrote, "Law is a command proceeding from the supreme political authority of a state, and addressed to the persons who are subject to that authority." Justice Holmes said that law was "a statement of the circumstances under which the public force will be brought to bear on persons through the courts."

The nineteenth century saw the beginning of the Sociological School of Jurisprudence, which was a combination of Historical and Imperative theories. The Sociological theory sought to explain society's legal rules as the balancing of various interests. Each legal decision thus becomes a balancing of social consequences and interests.

Each of the three schools of legal thought help explain the modern legal concepts that our society accepts, yet they are not a complete definition of "the law."

At this point in our discussion, it might be well to consider the function of the law; what does it strive to accomplish? Basically, the law seeks to perform three broad tasks.

1.5. Functions of the Law

1.5.1. EQUILIBRIUM. The law seeks to maintain and restore social equilibrium when disturbed, as for example, in the resolving of disputes. By the resolution of disputes, the law serves as an alternative to private vengeance, self help, and the employment of brute force. This first concept becomes vitally important when speaking of the criminal law, to be discussed.

1.5.2. PREDICTABILITY. The law allows the citizen the ability to calculate the consequences of his actions. This provides for reliability in action and sets forth precise obligations and related sanctions for violations. Legal predictability facilitates the regulation of social conduct, rationally and efficiently. It assists in accomplishing things, and at the same time, permits one to accurately predict what others will do.

1.5.3. EDUCATION. The law teaches right beliefs, right feelings, and right action. It forms and molds legal attitudes and concepts of society. The legal goals of equilibrium, predictability, and education are universal to all legal systems. In addition, Western law has sought to maintain historical continuity.

In summary, our legal system is a formal process, definite and deliberate, to a) resolve disputes, b) facilitate and protect voluntary arrangements, c) mold moral and legal conceptions of society, and d) maintain historical continuity.

1.6. The Development of the Law

The reader may well be asking at this point, just where did our law come from? From the common law, a constitution, statutes, or possibly from legislative bodies?

The law, in fact, is derived from all of these areas, and more. Before exploring the roots of our law, however, it becomes necessary to point out not only that our law developed from a number of sources, but that our law is also subdivided into a number of different areas, developed to fulfill different needs of society. Accordingly, as our discussion of the law progresses, we will also consider the present legal divisions found within our system.

The Latin phrase *lex non scripta* simply means law without a writing, or unwritten law, as contrasted with statute law, which is set forth in a writing. The common law or unwritten law is said to be the primary source of our modern legal system. But what is the common law, and where did it come from?

The basis of the common law lies in reason, conscience, honor, conventions, morality, customs, and religion. The common law developed as the needs of society called for it. It is a continuing expression of a conception of justice by each generation subscribing to it.

The common law, which initially guided the Royal Courts in England, set forth certain procedures, rules, and remedies to adjudicate disputes. The Royal Courts were the "law" courts, primarily concerned with criminal matters, contrasted with the later developed Chancellor Courts, or courts of conscience, which dealt with equity problems. The common law was a law made by judges, rather than a lawmaking body such as Parliament. The common law is found by reading the decisions of the courts.

An 1817 judicial decision in discussing the unwritten law stated,

No just government ever did, nor probably ever can, exist without an unwritten or common law. By the common law, is meant those maxims, principles, and forms of judicial proceedings which have no written law to prescribe or warrant them, but which, founded on the laws of nature and the dictates of reason, have, by usage and custom, become interwoven with the written law, and by such incorporation, form a part of the municipal code of each state or nation, which has emerged from the loose and erratic habits of savage life, to civilization, order, and a government of laws. (*Ohio v. Lafferty*, C.P. (5th Cir. 1817.))

(The reader will note the reference to the Natural law theory discussed earlier in the chapter.)

The unwritten law is preserved and evidenced by court decisions. The decisions, however, are not "the law" nor is legal authority to be derived from the decisions. Rather, they merely reflect the current trend in legal thinking relative to a certain point.

Sir James Stephen, a nineteenth century English jurist and author, said of the unwritten law,

It is not till a very late stage in its history that law is regarded as a series of commands issued by the sovereign power of the state. Indeed, even in our own time and country, that conception of it is gaining ground very slowly. An earlier, and to some extent a still prevailing view of it is that it is more like an art or science, the principles of which are at first enumerated vaguely, and are gradually reduced to precision by their application to particular circumstances. Somehow, no one can say precisely how, though more or less plausible and instructive conjectures upon the subject may be made, certain principles come to be accepted as the law of the land. The judges held themselves bound to decide the cases which come before them according to those principles, and as new combinations of circumstances throw light on the way in which they operated, the principles were, in such cases, more and more fully devolved and qualified, and, in others, evaded or practically set at naught and repealed. Thus, in order to ascertain what the principle is at any given moment, it is necessary to compare together a number of decided cases, and to determine from them the principle which they establish. (1 Stephen, Criminal Law, viii.)

The common law, developed in England, is the primary source of our United States criminal law. Said Judge Tappan, in *Ohio v. Lafferty*,

But although the common law, in all countries, has its foundation in reason and the laws of nature, and therefore is similar in its general principles, yet in its applications it has been modified and adapted to various forms of government; as the different orders of architecture, having their foundation in utility and graceful proportion, rise in various forms of symmetry, and beauty, in accordance with the taste and judgment of the builder. It is also a law of liberty, and hence we find that when North America was colonized by emigrants who fled from the pressure of monarchy and priestcraft in the old world, to enjoy freedom in the new, they brought with them the common law of England, claiming it as their birthright and inheritance. In their charters from the Crown, they were careful to have it recognized as the foundation on which they were to erect their laws and governments: not more anxious was Aeneas to secure from the burning ruins of Troy its household gods, than were these first settlers of America to secure to themselves and their children the benefits of the common law of England. From thence, through every every stage of the colonial government, the common law was in force, so far as it was found necessary or useful. When the revolution commenced, and independent state governments were formed; in the midst of hostile collisions with the mother country, when the passions of men were inflamed, and a deep and general abhorrence of tyranny of the British government was felt; the sages and patriots who commenced the revolution, and founded those state governments, recognized in the common law a guardian of liberty, and social order. The common law of England has thus always been the common law of the colonies and states of North America; and indeed in its full extent, supporting a monarchy, aristocracy, and hierarchy, but so far as it was applicable to our more free and happy habits of government.

1.7. Branches of the Law

Our system of law is further divided between civil and criminal, constitutional, statute, administrative, and canon law.

1.7.1. CIVIL LAW. The civil side of our law is mainly composed of the law of Contracts, the law of Torts, and the law of Property. The term *civil,* as contrasted with *criminal,* indicates a legal basis founded on personal disputes or controversies, where private rather than public interest predominates. In the area of contracts, for example, the main interest is the protection of private contractual rights. The criminal law, on the other hand, is primarily interested in the good of the state and the population of society as a whole.

Tort law allows the aggrieved individual a compensatory remedy, usually in the form of monetary damages. Tort law involves all of those injuries arising exclusive of contract, and is the civil counterpart of criminal law. Whereas the prosecution of an action in tort, for example, of assault and battery, will allow the plaintiff an award of damages; the same action, brought in the name of the people, rather than the individual, would not give the plaintiff any compensation, but would render justice to all those involved. The civil law allows the individual to obtain compensation and redress, while the criminal law protects the good of the state.

1.7.2. CRIMINAL LAW. The "criminal law" is a collection of rules or norms, both unwritten (common law) and written (constitutional, statute, case) which have developed to protect society from various harms. The criminal law is founded on a) the public policy to be served in preventing injury to life and property, b) to deter interference or destruction of government processes or functions, and c) to guard vital institutions other than governmental.

The criminal law is derived originally from the law of Tort, where its principal goals were vengeance and reimbursement to the injured party. As law developed, the emphasis changed from allowing a private remedy such as vengeance, to the protection of the general public, the state. Thus, the distinction between tort and criminal law became more clearly defined.

The purpose of the criminal law, said Oliver Wendell Holmes,

> is to induce external conformity to the rule. All law is directed to conditions of things manifest to the senses. And whether it brings those conditions to pass immediately by the use of force, as where it protects a house from mob by soldiers, or appropriates private property to public use, or hangs a man in pursuance of a judicial sentence, or whether it brings them about mediately through men's fears, its object is equally an external result. In directing itself against robbery or murder, for instance, its purpose is to put a stop to the actual physical taking and keeping of other men's goods, or the actual poisoning, shooting, stabbing, and otherwise putting to death of other men. If these things are not done, the law forbidding them is equally satisfied, whatever the motive. (Holmes, *The Common Law*, p. 42.)

1.7.2.1. *Goals*. The criminal law strives to achieve a number of goals, chief among which are to recognize and define certain forms of conduct considered harmful to the state. Basically, the first set of criteria to be considered in proscribing conduct would be the following: a) Is the conduct injurious to the public? b) Is the activity immoral, to the prejudice of the community? c) Is the conduct or result of such conduct against sound public policy?

After defining the prohibited conduct, the law must set up appropriate machinery to empower the state to commence action against the individual. This would encompass the legislative function, that of lawmaking, the executive function, that of enforcing the laws made by the legislature, and the judicial function, that of determining whether individual conduct in question falls within that prohibited or commanded by law.

In addition, the criminal law must a) be reliable in its process of determining guilt, b) preserve the right of the accused, and c) promote effective law enforcement.

1.7.2.2. *State and Federal.* The common law of England, and the United States Constitution form the basis of our system of criminal law. The Constitution allows both for the Federal judiciary system, and the Federal lawmaking function, the Congress. The Constitution provides for the states to rule themselves and set up the necessary legislative, executive, and judicial machinery, however, the United States government is held supreme and independent from the states. The common law, with its definitions of crime, is accepted by approximately half the states today. The other half rely strictly on statutory law to define and punish crime.

1.7.3. FEDERAL LEGISLATION. The United States Constitution grants power to Congress to define and punish crime falling within specified categories. Its power is limited to that either expressly given or implied by the Constitution. Unlike the state legislature, Congress has no inherent power to make law. There are *no* common law crimes within the federal system. All crimes must be specifically set forth, as must be the punishment for said crimes.

Congress may legislate in such areas as treason, commerce, currency, piracy, and the broad area of protection and promotion of the public safety, health, and welfare. Congress may also make laws to protect the rights, privileges, powers, and immunities as set forth in the thirteenth, fourteenth, fifteenth, and nineteenth amendments. Federal crimes are set forth in the United States Code, Title 18.

1.7.4. STATE LEGISLATION. Except for the specified areas in which Congress may legislate, the states have been vested with the general power to form their own legislatures and to make laws that are consistent with the Constitution. Thus, states may declare, define, and punish crimes, subject to the qualifications that a state may not make or enforce laws which abridge the privileges or immunities of United States citizens, nor deprive citizens of life, liberty, or property without due process of law, nor deny any person within the jurisdiction equal protection of the laws. Laws enforced by state governments may come from the state constitution, from the common law, or from statutes.

Once the state legislature has enacted a law, and made certain conduct criminal, the courts may not question the authority of the lawmaking body to enact the particular legislation, with the exception of examining the constitutional validity of the law. Since the time of the French Revolution, the legislature has jealously guarded the power to define what is criminal and to prescribe the limits of punishment. Prior to the Revolution, judges *and* lawmaking bodies had equal power to declare crime and punishment. Although today judges do not, in fact, make the law, they do interpret it and thus share with the lawmakers the responsibility of the creative development of criminal law.

Section 2. CRIME

A crime may be defined as: The commission or omission of an act which the law forbids or commands under pain of punishment to be imposed by the state, proceeding in its own name. In cases of crime *mala in se,* the law will also require the element of unlawful intent.

2.1. The Commission or Omission of an Act

Some act or failure to act is always required. The act must be committed by human agency (the accused), rather than by natural occurrence. Some minor crimes require only an act, how-

ever, as the seriousness of the crime increases, intent, in addition
to the act, becomes important.

The requisite act may be simple, complex, or a series of acts.

1. A *simple act* may be all that is required. Such would be
   the case of striking a person to constitute battery.
2. A *complex act* may require several interwoven actions such
   as (1) possession of (2) stolen property.
3. A *series of acts* may be needed to meet the statute such as
   the case for burglary, where breaking + entering + dwelling
   house + intent is required.

The actor may be liable for the consequences of his acts if
harm is the result. For example, a simple battery may, in time,
become murder if the injured party dies.

2.1.1. CAUSATION. A determinant relation must exist between the
act of the accused and the prohibited result constituting the
crime. The act must be the *proximate cause* of the injury. An
act is said to be the proximate cause of the injury if: a) the injury is the natural and probable consequence of the act, b) the
injury is reasonably foreseeable from the act, and c) the act is sufficiently connected with the injury to show causation. (Distance
in time and space between the act and injury is immaterial.)

2.2. Proximate Cause of Crime

A *concurrent act,* where two persons commit a crime, can
produce a single injury, where each contributing cause may be
considered the *proximate cause* of the injury. When one's act
combines with another person's act, and both contribute to the
injury, both actors may be liable. The accused act need not be
the sole cause of the injury, if it be the proximate cause. For example, actor A inflicts a mortal wound to X. Actor B then comes
along and *also* delivers another mortal blow to X. Whether A
and B were acting in concert, or independently, both A and B
may be held for homicide, even though either's actions alone
would have produced the death of X. Each act is said to be the
proximate cause of the injury.

The defendant's act may be the proximate cause of the injury,
even though alone it would have been insufficient to produce the
injury. Such is the case when the act is an *intervening* cause.

Thus, when the defendant sets in motion an outside force, or chain of events which produce the unlawful result, he is held for the act. For example, where the decedent had a preexisting illness, and the combined act of the defendant with the illness produced death, he will be held, even though death probably would not have occurred but for the decedent's weakened condition.

If the defendant is engaged in an unlawful act and produces unexpected or unintended results, his acts may still be the proximate cause of the injury, and he will be held liable.

2.2.1. NEGLIGENCE. If the defendant's act was the proximate cause of the injury, the fact that the act was negligently done is immaterial, except to possibly show a lack of intent. If, however, the injury would have occurred with or without the defendant's negligent act, then in most instances, the actor will not be held liable.

2.2.2. ACCIDENT. If the defendant's act is accidental, as where a reasonable man could not have avoided the injury, there will be no criminal liability, regardless of causation. The law does not demand absolute perfection in action.

2.2.3. LAWFUL ACT. Where illegal conduct results from the doing of a lawful act, the actor is not held if there is no unlawful intent.

2.2.4. CORPUS DELECTI (the body of a crime). The corpus delecti governs rules of evidence which determine what proof is necessary for a particular crime. Ordinarily, there are four basic elements which are required to be proved in every criminal action, plus the specific elements peculiar to the crime. The four elements are as follows:

An injury has occurred
Which is a declared crime
Which was committed by a human agent
The human agency was the defendant.

2.3. Nullum Crimen Sine Lege

In the case of felonies and some high-grade misdemeanors, the act must be prohibited or commanded by competent legal authority. Certain minor crimes do not require a statute, such as those against public morals. Where a statute is required, certain criteria must be met. These include the following:

1. The law must be in force at the time of the act.
2. The measure of punishment must be in effect.
3. The law must be in effect when the defendant is to be punished.

In addition, the statute must be sufficiently definite for persons to understand; be understood by those of average intelligence; the act must come within the intent of the statute; and the statute must give "fair notice" to the public of expected conduct.

2.4. Why Statutes?

As noted in above, the purpose of a statute is to precisely define criminal conduct. The rationale behind a statutory system of laws is aptly discussed by one author,

> In England and in several of the states, the common law prevails in the punishment of crimes; and many acts are punished from precedent which have never been made so by legislative provision. But the manifest evil of this doctrine is, that the majority of men, unskilled in law, cannot be supposed to know beforehand, whether a given act will be criminal or not. In fact, the accumulation of precedents through the lapse of centuries must render it difficult for the most consumate lawyer to be able to pronounce at once with certainty on the subject. And yet it is absolutely necessary to act upon the well-known maxim that ignorance of the law is no excuse for its violation, because, otherwise, ignorance would always be pretended. This consideration alone is sufficient to demonstrate the importance of requiring every offense to be defined by the legislature, together with its punishment, and accordingly it has become a fundamental doctrine in the federal courts and in some state courts that they have no common law jurisdiction of crimes; and cannot treat any act as an offense, until the proper legislature has declared it to be such, and meted out the punishment. With regard to the federal courts, this doctrine, though sometimes doubted, rests upon the absence of any power in the federal constitution to punish crimes except in certain specified cases—thus on a few pages of the statute books may be found enumerated all the offenses which can be punished by the Federal or state government, and the measure of punishment annexed to each. So that the only use now made of the criminal part of the common

law is to furnish the outline of criminal procedure and define the terms employed in the statutes. If there be any evil to be apprehended from this doctrine, it is that such cases may arise in which men cannot be punished, though they richly deserve it, because the legislature has not anticipated their offense; but this objection weighs hardly a feather against the inestimable privilege of having every offense, for which punishment can be inflicted, distinctly and accurately defined, instead of being left to be collected from doubtful precedent established in a very different state of society, and scattered at remote intervals, through the reported decisions of seven or eight centuries. (Walker, *Introduction to American Law,* Philadelphia (1837) art. 447.)

2.5. Ex Post Facto Laws

The Constitution prohibits the passage of a law after the commission of an act, which changes the legal effect of the act to the detriment of the wrongdoer. Included in the prohibition are the following laws:

1. Every law which makes an act, which was innocent when committed prior to passage, criminal after passage, and punishes the act.
2. That law which aggravates a crime.
3. That law which alters punishment and makes it different or more severe.
4. That law which changes the rules of evidence so as to require less proof for conviction.

2.6. Construction of Statutes

The statute must be construed strictly against the state and in favor of the accused. The offense may not be one created by inference or implication nor extended by implication. The legislature must specifically spell out the prohibited conduct. The judiciary does have the prerogative of going by the intent or spirit of the statute when the act in question does not fall precisely within its prescription.

2.7. Repeal of Statute

Where a statute is repealed, with no substitute enacted, the previously applicable law will apply.

2.7.1. UNDER PAIN OF PUNISHMENT. The sanction, or punishment must

1. Involve pain or other consequences normally considered unpleasant.
2. Be for an offense against legal rules.
3. Be imposed on actual or supposed offenders.
4. Be intentionally administered by human beings other than the offender.
5. Be imposed and administered by an authority constituted by a legal system against which the offense is committed. (Packer, *The Limits of the Criminal Sanction*, p. 21)

2.7.2. IMPOSED BY THE STATE PROCEEDING IN ITS OWN NAME. As stated above, the State, rather than private individuals, must inflict the punishment.

2.7.2.1. *Intent.* In the preceding definition of crime, it was noted that intent was an integral part of the more serious offenses (felonies). *Act* and *intent* were *both* required to prove all common law crimes because one of the grounds for imposing liability was the finding of a guilty mind; hence, if one had no criminal intent, one could not be held responsible for the commission of a criminal act. But just what is *intent?* A simple, general definition would be the particular state of mind of the accused preceding and during the commission of a particular act.

Intent or *mens rea* (guilty mind) is difficult to define. *Bouvier's Law Dictionary* defines the term as "a design, resolve, or determination of the mind." Other sources have explained intent as "fact or facts of intending or purposing intention, purpose (formed in mind)." Furthermore, the word is used synonymously with "purpose, willful, malice, knowingly."

2.7.2.2. *Motive V. Intent.* Motive is not intent and it is not essential in proving the crime. Motive must be shown, however, to establish other elements which are required, such as malice. One author states that motive is the desire or inducement which stimulates a person to do an act, whereas intent is the purpose or resolve to *do* the act. (Miller, *Criminal Law*, p. 54.)

2.7.2.3. *Degrees of Intent.* Intent may be classified into three categories:

1. General intent.
2. Specific intent.
3. Constructive intent.

The requisite intent is presumed automatically from the commission of certain crimes. This is based on the theory that a person is presumed to intend the natural and probable consequences of his voluntary actions. The above definition of *general intent* presumes that a) the defendant has the capacity to commit a crime (not insane or below the age of reason); and b) the defendant is acting without justification or excuse. A general intent is all that need be shown for most misdemeanors. It can be stated that general intent is sufficient for all crimes which do not require a specific intent.

It should be noted at this point that *intent to commit a criminal act* is not the controlling criteria, but rather the intention to commit the *act itself*, whether the actor knew it was criminal or not, is controlling.

In cases where *specific intent* is required, the crime consists not only of the performance of the act, but of having an intent to do the particular act. The intent will not be presumed from the mere commission of the crime, but must be shown to have existed in the mind of the accused. Specific intent differs from general intent in that the actor is required to know and intend the unlawful act. For example, the common law crime of burglary consists of (1) breaking and (2) entering of a (3) dwelling (4) of another (5) in the nighttime, with (6) *the intent to commit a felony therein*. The intent to commit a felony must be shown.

Constructive or transferred intent refers to those cases where a series of interrelated crimes are committed in one time frame, all part of one transaction, in which the actor can be shown to have had the required specific intent to commit the initial crime, but possibly not the succeeding crimes. In this situation, where the first act is usually Malum in Se, the actor's intent is said to transfer, or carry over, to the subsequent crimes. The doctrine usually applies only to later crimes which require only a *general intent*. For example, where a party, in the commission of a bank robbery, kills one of the tellers, he is said to have had the intent to commit the homicide, as well as the robbery. The intent present in the act of robbery transfers to the act of murder, as if the defendant had planned the killing from the outset.

2.7.2.4. *Negligence and Intent.* Negligence is the failure to use reasonable care, as may be required by law, for a particular situation. Where the law commands or sets a duty of care, the failure to meet that duty will constitute intent to violate the law. Simple negligence will supply only a *general intent* (*never* specific intent).

In order for negligence to form the basis of intent, several elements need be shown:

1. The defendant must owe some legal duty of care to persons injured or to a class of persons.
2. The defendant must know of his duty and be capable of meeting it.
3. The defendant has failed to perform the owed duty.
4. The defendant's failure to perform his duty was the proximate cause of the injury.

2.7.2.5. *Concurrence of Act and Intent.* Where an intent is required as part of the corpus delecti, act and intent must occur at the same time. Hence, in certain instances, where the actor repudiates his intention to commit the crime, he may not be held responsible. Such is the case where a party enters a store intending to rob its owner, then decides to abandon his plan. He is not liable for the mere planning of the crime, as there was a lack of intent to commit the act. Similarly, the mere desire to commit a crime is not intent in the legal sense.

2.7.2.6. *Liability: Civil V. Criminal.* In the case of the violation of a criminal law, neither the guilt nor contributory negligence of the injured person will relieve the defendant of his liability; nor will the fact that the injured party condones the defendant's actions, or accepts money damages to compensate for the wrong. However, in certain areas of the civil law, the acceptance of damages, or condoning of the act, or contributory negligence on the part of the plaintiff, *will* relieve the defendant of any future liability to the plaintiff.

2.7.2.7. *Intent and Statutory Construction.* By proper interpretation of a particular statute, one may determine whether the law requires a general or specific intent. In this connection, a number of key words have become common to statutory language. These terms are set out below, followed by a brief definition.

2.7.2.8. *Malice.* Although simple malice does denote a general intent, it also reflects a state of mind *more inclined* toward harm or injury than does just a general intent. Malice may indicate a wrongful act done: a) intentionally, without excuse, which the actor knows will injure another, b) which is done with a willful disregard of the rights or safety of another, c) is the expression of a wicked or depraved heart. A wanton act may be one that is willful, reckless, and/or unrestrained.

2.7.2.9. *Feloniously.* The term feloniously indicates an intent to commit the crime for which the defendant is charged. For example, in robbery, feloniously would mean the intent to take the money or goods from the victim, for the purpose of stealing them.

Crimes are classified as either *felonies* or *misdemeanors,* depending on a number of factors. The list below sets out the more important distinctions between the two concepts.

Felony	*Misdemeanor*
1. Punishable by death or imprisonment.	1. Fine or jail sentence in other than prison, usually for less than one year.
2. Serious crimes such as murder, rape, arson, burglary, robbery.	2. Minor crimes such as motor vehicle violations, shoplifting, larceny, etc.
3. There may be accessories.	3. All actors are principals.
4. Arrest is justifiable where it would not be for misdemeanor. Examples, arrest for on-sight, or reasonable belief/probable cause to believe defendant has or is about to commit felony. Citizen may also arrest in above circumstances.	4. Arrest only by warrant, or where action on sight. In some jurisdictions a police officer may arrest if probable cause to believe defendant has committed misdemeanor. Citizen may not arrest unless on-sight.
5. Taking of life may be justified in preventing or in effecting arrest for felony.	5. Taking of life in preventing occurrence of, or in arresting defendant, is *not permitted.*
6. Prosecution usually initiated by grand jury indictment or information.	6. Prosecution can be started by information or complaint.
7. Defendant has right of peremptory challenges of jurors during trial.	7. No challenges allowed.
8. Defendant must have an arraignment.	8. No arraignment, ordinarily.
9. Defendant must be present during trial.	9. Defendant need not be present to be convicted.
10. All crimes not felonies are misdemeanors.	

2.7.2.10. *Mala in Se V. Mala Prohibitum.* *Mala in se* crimes are those acts which are criminal by their inherent nature, such as murder, rape, and robbery. *Mala prohibitum* crimes are those acts which are wrong simply because the law says they are wrong, such as the prohibition of going through a red light without first stopping. The division between *mala in se* and *mala prohibitum* is of little importance today, and some jurists have even advocated an end to the distinction.

CHAPTER 2

THE CRIMINAL SANCTION

Section I. MEANING AND PURPOSE

THE *Criminal sanction* is a term given to the problem of attempting to control antisocial behavior by punishing individuals found guilty of violating criminal statutes or the common law. The purpose of the criminal sanction is to reduce, or ideally, eliminate, conduct which does not conform to established norms determined by society. Integral to the concept of the criminal sanction is the lawmaking function (legislative), the courts (judiciary), and law enforcement agencies (executive).

In forming a rationale for the criminal sanction, one may ask: Why do we define certain activities as criminal? What is the law, and how can we effectively, if at all, enforce it? Why do we want to punish those who are found guilty of violating the law? Are we justified in what we are trying to do?

The primary purpose of the criminal law is the prevention of crime. In achieving this goal, one encounters three contrasting variables which must be carefully balanced in a democratic society, namely, freedom of the individual, justice to the individual and society, and efficiency of law enforcement. Since the imposition of the criminal sanction tends to limit the freedom of the individual, and since one is not sure that punishment for a crime does more good than harm, one should invoke it sparingly in controlling behavior which really poses a threat. One should ask, what other means are there for controlling undesirable conduct, before imposing the criminal sanction.

Four classifications of sanctions have been generally recognized: regulation, compensation, treatment, and punishment. *Regulation,* such as the issuance of a driver's license, involves the testing for certain minimal skills in a given area, and the issuing of a license upon satisfactory demonstration of those skills. Regulation also involves compliance with standards set by the legislature, such as in federal inspection of beef. *Compensation*

23

involves the payment of money to an injured party with the thought of restoring him to his original condition prior to the injury. *Treatment* of the convicted individual involves the curing of diseases and mental disorders which may be present, such as narcotics addiction or aberrant sexual behavior. Finally, there is *punishment,* which generally consists of the confinement of a person, against his will, resulting from the commission of an act which society chooses to call criminal.

The astute reader may see yet a fifth classification, that of doing nothing. Indeed, when society finds that it does not have the resources to effectively impose any of the first four sanctions noted, it may resort to the policy of doing nothing. Doing nothing may be manifest in one of two ways, by not enforcing a certain law or by simply removing the crime from the books and accordingly no longer recognizing the conduct as criminal.

Section 2. WHAT CONSTITUTES A CRIMINAL ACT

The amount of crime we have is determined, in part, by what acts we decide to call criminal. Crimes that are real and create an immediate threat are most readily adapted to the criminal sanction (such as those recognized by the common law), however, enforcement becomes more difficult and freedom of the individual appears as a fading memory when acts that are called crimes, are possibly more immoral than they are harmful. This is not to say that immoral acts should not be made crimes, but merely that the act should be more than immoral to constitute criminal conduct.

It has been suggested that criminal conduct should be both immoral and create a risk of harm to others. When the bulk of society already thinks that certain conduct is immoral, it is easier to obtain the cooperation of society in the prohibition of such conduct. Note that the majority of society must consider the conduct immoral or the sanction will be *weakened* instead of strengthened. Secondly, if the prohibited conduct presents a risk of harm to others, the sanction is strengthened, as members of society seek to minimize activity which has the potential of causing harm to them personally.

When certain conduct is called criminal, and it is in fact, neither immoral nor harmful to other members of society (in other words there is no readily apparent reason for prohibiting such conduct other than some lawmaker did not like the particular activity) laws respecting such conduct are not only difficult to enforce, but very costly. Accordingly, resources of law enforcement should be directed away from such conduct to more immediate and harmful activities.

In deciding whether to call a certain activity criminal or not, one should consider if the conduct is injurious to society to such a degree that those who engage in it should be subject to the criminal sanction. Secondly, it must be agreed that law enforcement agencies will, in fact, enforce the prohibition of the activity. Once one has decided that it is in the best interest of society to call certain conduct criminal, one should attach a degree of punishment to the commission of such crime which offsets the gain a criminal would achieve from engaging in such conduct. When the gain derived from criminal conduct is less than the punishment inflicted for engaging in such conduct, the punishment is called *deterrence*. As the degree of punishment is increased, the appeal of the particular criminal conduct is decreased.

The more remote the connection between prohibited conduct and risk of harm, the more difficult becomes the job of the law enforcement officer in detecting the prohibited act and apprehending those that engage in it. When an act is difficult to detect, possible suspects must be kept under strict surveillance in gathering evidence of commission of the prohibited act; in maintaining surveillance, freedom can be limited or denied the suspect. The question to be asked is, how much freedom are we, as a people, willing to give up in order to enforce certain laws which may be very difficult to detect when broken, due to the limited harm done. It is elementary that increased difficulty in detection places an increased burden on law enforcement officers, and unchecked in the long run, either freedom or efficiency suffers.

Section 3. DETERRENCE

The law abiding citizen is affected most by the power of deterrence, for he is socialized enough to associate guilt feeling with antisocial conduct. Contrastingly, deterrence is not a threat to someone whose existence is depressed beyond hope, for he has the attitude of, "What do I have to lose by breaking the law, I couldn't be much worse off than I am now?"

A delicate balance must be struck so that the punishment for committing a prohibited act is not so great as to make an individual more antisocial after punishment than before punishment, and yet, severe enough to limit such future conduct. Interestingly, studies have shown recidivism in general to be *less* among those released on parole than those subjected to greater or longer punishment before release.

Section 4. PUNISHMENT VS. TREATMENT

Two theories which have been recognized with respect to the criminal sanction are as follows: a) The *Retributive Justice Theory,* which says that a man is rewarded when he does right, and punished (retribution) when he does wrong; and that the intensity of the suffering imposed is directly proportional to the "wrongfulness" of his act. In other words, a man that commits murder is made to suffer more than a man that commits larceny. b) Opposed to the Retributive Justice Theory is the *Behaviorist's Theory,* which deals with the prediction and control of human behavior. Under this view, when one commits a crime, he is not punished but is treated so that he does not commit future crimes. Those that commit acts against society should undergo scientifically controlled treatment to modify their personality so that they will no longer commit such acts. Psychologists and psychiatrists generally subscribe to the Behaviorist Theory. The behaviorist does not advocate a sentence for someone who has committed an antisocial act (a crime), rather that he be turned over to correctional experts for as long a period of time as is necessary to "cure" him.

What does one accomplish by prescribing the sanction of punishment as opposed to the sanction of treatment? Punishment imposes unpleasant feelings on the recipient for an offense that he has committed. It looks to his past antisocial behavior, and makes him suffer for it. Furthermore, it prevents future antisocial behavior by associating the unpleasantness of punishment with wrongful conduct. On the other hand, treatment does not look to antisocial conduct and impose suffering but is aimed at helping the individual. The antisocial act committed by the individual is not a guideline to determine punishment but is merely a signal that the person needs help. In summary, punishment looks to the act and its prevention; treatment looks to the individual and his betterment.

The criminal law provides an acceptable means of imposing punishment on wrongdoers within society. When one talks of punishment in the framework of the criminal sanction, one speaks mainly of imprisonment. This makes a strong argument for the Punishment Theory, that is to say, incapacitation of the offender during the time period of his punishment. It is axiomatic that one in a jail cell cannot rob a bank.

To morally justify the theory of punishment, one must show that the threat of punishment and the punishment that is imposed will cause less harm than the crimes it is (theoretically) preventing and punishing for. Punishment that is unjust causes more harm in the long run than no punishment at all. Individuals must be able to live according to certain announced standards which have been set up by society, without fear that criminal punishment will be unjustly and indiscriminately imposed. However, the system must not be so rigidly structured so that law enforcement efficiency replaces freedom of the individual.

Those that follow the Treatment Theory must ask, how well will the wrongdoer respond to treatment, and how soon will his personality be favorably changed so that he will not repeat his antisocial act? Probably the most important question to be answered is, how much should one human being be allowed to change the personality of another without sacrificing the individual's autonomy.

Section 5. PREFERRED DIRECTION OF THE SANCTION

What is the relationship between the seriousness of a crime and the degree of punishment and/or treatment? Ideally, each offender should be treated on an individual basis; however, the cost of such a system would be prohibitive. Possibly the next best alternative would be a system which provided just enough punishment to act as a deterrent, in addition to treatment generally suited to the class of offenders in question. The degree of punishment would be allowed to vary within limits predetermined by the type of crime. The legislature could define the limits of punishment for the offenses; the court would determine the sentence in each case, within the limits set by the legislature; and the authorities at the correctional institution would decide, within the limits set by the legislature and the guidelines of the court, when the wrongdoer should be released in the light of observation and rehabilitation; thus, the basis of the *indeterminate* sentence.

Through the judicious application of the criminal sanction, freedom of the individual will flourish but, as with any powerful force, if its direction tends toward oppression, under the guise of efficiency, the individual citizen will disappear in a faceless mass of humanity.

CHAPTER 3

DUE PROCESS OF LAW

No person shall . . . be deprived of life, liberty, or property, without
due process of law . . .

Fifth Amendment

. . . nor shall any State deprive any person of life, liberty, or property,
without due process of law . . .

14th Amendment, Section 1

THE same meaning is usually given to the guaranties of due
process of law as found in both the fifth and fourteenth
amendments. The due process clause of the fifth amendment
limits the powers of the Federal Government and the due process
clause of the fourteenth amendment limits the powers of state
government.

In order to determine what due process is, one must look to
two sources, the United States Constitution and the fundamental
principles of judicial procedure that existed in England and
America before the adoption of the United States Constitution,
in other words, the common law.

When conduct is complained of, the courts initially check to
see if the act violates provisions of the United States Constitution;
if not, they then look to the common law. This is the constitutional guarantee of due process of law.

The guaranty that no person should be deprived of life, liberty or property without due process, was incorporated in the common law of America before its adoption in the fifth and fourteenth amendments to the Constitution. The origin of the due
process principle can be traced back at least as far as 1215, when
it was part of the Magna Charta in England. The original purpose of the principle was to prevent the Crown from acting
against an individual that was not under the protection of the
law.

Due process of law is the framework upon which the system
of ordered justice is built, and without it the right to private

29

property would not exist as it does today. It encompasses the making, the administration, and the enforcement of law. It is the fundamental basis of justice and liberty as it exists in our society. It insures the fair administration of the laws with respect to disturbance of life, liberty or private property ownership.

Whenever a right in the Federal Constitution is of such a nature that denying it would violate the principle of liberty and justice, it is probably embraced by the due process clause of the fourteenth amendment and made binding upon the states.

There is no set definition of the term "due process of law" that would be applicable to every situation; even the United States Supreme Court has avoided giving a precise definition of it (*Bute v. Illinois,* 333 U.S. 640 (1948)). The definition depends upon the relationship between the law allowing the act and the law which limits the power of the legislature. Due process of law is not a rule of law but an essential element of justice itself. Generally, if a proceeding is found to be arbitrary, unjust, and oppressive, it will most likely not meet due process requirements. Determination of due process depends on past court decisions, history, reason, and the time, place and facts of the particular situation.

The courts have said, in general, that due process of law is the administration of established court justice in the protection of private rights. When a law conforms to the concept of applying the rules of rights to all people equally, due process requirements are met. In *Dartmouth College v. Woodward,* 4 Wheaton 518, 1819, 4 L.Ed. 629, due process of law was defined by Daniel Webster as "a law which hears before it condemns; which proceeds upon inquiry, and renders judgment only after trial."

Due process of law has been said to be identical with the phrase, "the law of the land" cited in the Magna Charta. The "law of the land" embodies not only the existing law of the Federal Government, and the common law, but the law of the particular state in which a proceeding is brought.

The constitutional guaranty of due process assures that no person will be deprived of life, liberty or property for reasons that are arbitrary. It is a *standard of reasonableness.* Due process protects the citizen against arbitrary actions of the government just as due process protected the Englishman against arbitrary action of the Crown. It not only looks to the present exercise of power but also looks to the future in limiting legislative power, by excluding laws that would arbitrarily deprive a person of life, liberty or property. The primary purpose of the due process guaranty is to protect the private rights of the individual. However, just because a law works a hardship does not mean it violates due process if the law operates on *all classes* of people equally, without discrimination. For example, due process of law is denied when any member of a class or community is individually singled out for the imposition of restraints of law not applied to the class or community as a whole. When an act denies one person in a community of private rights and privileges which have no bearing on the general community, the act is said to be more in the nature of a punishment than it is a law.

Due process of law applies not only to all citizens of the United States, but to all persons that are within the jurisdiction of the United States.

Some of the essentials of due process are the following: notice, a hearing, counsel, defense, evidence, and a fair and impartial court.

NOTICE

When a judicial proceeding is pending, the citizen whose rights are to be affected must be informed of the matter so that he may choose what course of action to take. Proceedings that affect the life, liberty or property of a citizen must require notice or they will be held unconstitutional. The notice requirement simply means that a person involved in a proceeding must be brought into it, but not that he be informed at each successive step of the proceeding.

Notice must be adequate and reasonable to satisfy the requirements of due process of law. The defendant must be given enough time to prepare and present a defense. Furthermore, just because a person happens to know of the proceeding against him does not satisfy the due process requirement of official notice. Notice must be officially given to all parties whose rights are affected by a proceeding. When actual notice is not practical, *constructive* notice may suffice. For example, if a person cannot be located for personal service, then *publication* of notice in the manner authorized by the legislature will suffice. The notice must come from the court that has jurisdiction over the subject matter in the proceeding. In addition, notice must be given so that there is sufficient time for the parties involved to appear before the court. For example, it would be unreasonable and a violation of due process to serve a person with notice minutes before the proceeding is to begin where it is physically impossible for the defendant to travel to the court in less than six hours.

If a person may be affected by a judgment or order of the court, then that person is entitled to notice of the proceeding. Generally, if a proceeding takes place without notice to those affected by it, such proceeding will be void.

The reason that a person is entitled to notice is that he must be given an opportunity to be *heard* on the charges or claim against him. He must be given opportunity to tell why the judgment sought should not be rendered against him. If a person voluntarily appears in a proceeding and has not been served with notice, the fact that he appeared does away with the requirement of notice, as it is no longer necessary. Such a voluntary participant in a proceeding cannot be heard to say that he was denied the constitutional right of notice under due process of law.

HEARING

The second essential element of the due process of law is the opportunity for a hearing. This right comes out of the common law, where it was said that no man should be punished without an opportunity to be heard. In other words, a person must be allowed his day in court. The defendant must be allowed to contest the issues against him in law and in fact. If a person is given a hearing, but the hearing is oppressive, harsh and biased, it will be said that the defendant was denied his right to a reasonable hearing in violation of due process of law. On the other hand, if a person is given the opportunity for a hearing but through lapse of time fails to take advantage of it, the right to a hearing may be lost.

The hearing must be fair and orderly and the defendant must be allowed to defend and protect his rights. No fixed procedure is required; it is sufficient that it adapts to the particular case, according to the decided case law, in a judicial court that has competent jurisdiction. The court may not be arbitrary in its determination of the case, nor may it apply a standard of law to the particular individual that it does not apply to the community in general under similar fact situations.

COUNSEL

Anyone that might be affected by a proceeding has the right not only to be present, but to be represented by counsel. If either a state or federal court denies the defendant the right to be represented by counsel, he is denied due process of law. Note, however, that if the defendant has been given notice of the proceeding, his presence is not required.

DEFENSE

Under due process of law, the defendant has the right to present a defense and raise such issues as are pertinent to the cause. If the defendant has no defense to the action against him, he still has the right to be heard in his own behalf. Many times, due process will require that the defendant be allowed to confront his accusers and cross-examine them.

With respect to the time of the presentation of the defense, due process of law is met when the defendants have an opportunity before final judgment to be heard. Generally, the concept of due process does not embody delay by the court in allowing the defendant to present his defense and/or to be heard.

EVIDENCE

When evidence is introduced at trial, due process of law forbids the unfair use of such evidence. The defendant must be afforded an opportunity to show that the evidence submitted is untrue. Furthermore, a defendant has the right to establish and prove any facts in evidence that would involve protection of his life, liberty or property. The defendant must be given an opportunity to know of, examine, and refute the evidence that has been introduced against him.

"Proceeding" has been used in the sense that it is the exercise of governmental power, as permitted by the rules and sanctions of law that serve to protect the individual rights of life, liberty, and private property. A proceeding is not necessarily a judicial proceeding such as a trial, it may be a commission, a board, an administrative officer, or even a private body. That which is appropriate within the due process of law depends on the particular circumstances of the case.

PROCEEDING

Under the requirements of due process of law, the proceeding must be impartial and fair. No member of the proceeding may have a direct pecuniary interest in the outcome.

REHEARING

Under due process, a rehearing is usually not necessary if, in the first hearing, a fair opportunity was available to the defendant to present his defense in an impartial, objective atmosphere. If the defendant has been allowed to present all evidence and arguments that he considers pertinent to his cause, due process of law is satisfied.

APPEAL

Usually, allowing an appeal is not an essential element to due process. In state courts, the appellate procedure is left for determination by the individual state.

SELECTIVE INCORPORATION

A minority of the justices on the United States Supreme Court believes that the Bill of Rights (the first eight amendments) *Should* be binding upon the States through the due process clause of the Fourteenth Amendment, however, a majority of the United States Supreme Court has adopted the method of *selective incorporation,* on a case-by-case basis, involving the procedural guarantees of the first eight amendments. The court determines which of the guarantees of criminal procedure are to be incorporated and made applicable to the state courts. Remember, all the guarantees of criminal procedure in the first eight amendments are binding on the *federal* court system. The United States Supreme Court has, from time to time, announced certain standards that are used to ascertain if the constitutional guarantee should be made binding on the states: Some of the standards are fundamental fairness in the concept of justice; principles which are basic to liberty; principles which are at the base of the political and civil structure of our nation with respect to justice and liberty; and the fundamental principles of justice which, if denied, would shock the conscience of the nation.

In summary, then, due process of law means the exercise of powers by the government in a particular case as the decided case law provides and permits, under whose sanction the rights of the individual, such as life, liberty, and the ownership of private property, are protected. Due process protects each individual in the jurisdiction of the United States from the arbitrary exercise of governmental power at the state and federal level, which would tend to deprive him of life, liberty, and the ownership of private property. It assures that all those in a given class and community are treated equally by the law in similar fact situations. It not only protects against the arbitrary use of power by the courts today, but against the arbitrary use of power by the legislature tomorrow. Due process of law is a fundamental concept which is the cornerstone of Anglo-American justice and liberty.

PART II

CONSTITUTIONAL GUIDELINES

CHAPTER 4

THE FOURTH AMENDMENT

Section I. INTRODUCTION

The right of the people to be secure in their persons, houses, papers, and effects, against unreasonable searches and seizures, shall not be violated, and no warrants shall issue, but upon probable cause, supported by oath or affirmation, and particularly describing the place to be searched, and the persons or things to be seized.

FOURTH AMENDMENT

THE requirements of the fourth amendment to the United States Constitution appear deceptively simple at first glance. It guarantees seemingly precise assurances: The right of the people to be secure in their houses, persons, papers, and effects against unreasonable searches shall not be violated; and, no warrant shall issue but upon probable cause, supported by oath or affirmation, particularly describing the place to be searched, and the persons or things to be seized. To the astute reader, several questions are apparent on first reading. Precisely, what is the right that is protected by the amendment? What does secure mean? What do the terms houses, persons, papers, and effects encompass? What is an "unreasonable" as contrasted with a "reasonable" search? What are the consequences if the amendment is "violated"?

What type of warrants does the amendment refer to? Who issues the warrants? What is "probable cause"? What type of oath or affirmation is required? What may be taken in a search? The list would appear to be without end.

Because of the *Mapp* decision in 1961, which made the requirements of the fourth amendment applicable to state criminal proceedings, the standards discussed throughout the chapters are basically those of the federal courts and federal rules of criminal procedure. It must be borne in mind that the individual states may require more stringent requirements of their law enforcement officers. Under the federal rules of criminal procedure, the validity of search and arrest is governed by

39

state standards, as long as those standards meet the minimum federal requirements. In other words, a state may adopt stricter requirements than the Constitution regarding searches and seizures, but it may not operate with lesser requirements than those promulgated by the Constitution.

With the above introductory comments in mind, we are now ready to proceed with a discussion of the fourth amendment.

The thrust of the fourth amendment is to guarantee that minimum standards are adhered to by persons acting under color of law when seeking evidence of criminal conduct or when making arrests. The requirements of the fourth amendment insure the integrity of the evidence collected which in turn, lessens the possibility of innocent parties being convicted. The amendment sets forth guidelines which, if followed, allow the "fruits" of a search and seizure to be admitted in evidence against the accused. The amendment prohibits evidence obtained by an unreasonable search and seizure. Hence, in the following material, situations will be presented detailing what courts considered to be both reasonable and unreasonable searches, within the meaning of the amendment.

Section 2. RIGHTS

The fourth amendment was inserted in the Constitution by our founding fathers to guarantee the fundamental right to privacy and security of the citizens of the United States. Based on the common law, the amendment was written as a response to the English use of General Warrants and Writs of Assistance. However, the amendment was drafted with greater protection of personal liberty than the pervasive English Writs.

The rights guaranteed in the fourth amendment must always be construed in the light of reasonableness and public interest. The rights must also be considered in connection with fifth amendment guarantees against self-incrimination. That is to say, the unreasonable seizure or compulsory production of an individual's private papers, property, or effects to be used in evidence against him amounts to a violation of the self-incrimination clause, of the fifth amendment.

Our constitutional form of government recognizes the right to be free from unreasonable searches and seizures as fundamental, while at the same time maintains a balance between the public interest in searches and seizures versus personal rights.

The underlying purposes of the Amendment are to forbid and prohibit oppressive action on the part of the government in making exploratory searches (*U.S. v. Silverman*, 166 F. Supp. 838 (1958)) and to guard against unwarranted intrusions into the privacy of the individual (*Jones v. U.S.*, 357 US 493 (1958)).

The right to privacy and personal security is the very cornerstone of constitutional liberty in our government. The amendment serves as a precautionary statement in respect to rigid restrictions placed on the invasion of personal privacy by officials and governmental agencies.

In summary, the goal of the fourth amendment is to eliminate the use of oppressive methods against individuals (including the guilty), while at the same time, not interfering with the reasonable means under utilization by law enforcement officers to detect and deter crime. The sanction imposed for the violation of the amendment is that any evidence seized will not be admissible in evidence.

The right to be free from unwarranted governmental intrusion applies equally to executive, legislative, and judicial action.

The right is considered a *personal* one, giving standing only to those persons with a right to object to a search or seizure. Standing which is based on a possessory or proprietary interest is discussed in detail later in the chapter. Suffice it to say that the right to be free from unreasonable searches and seizures is personal and hence may only be claimed by a party actually aggrieved by governmental conduct.

The right extends to all persons, and guarantees both freedom against unreasonable searches, as well as arrests. All citizens, civilian and military, within the United States are protected, as are corporations, aliens, and deportees. The right does not, however extend to United States citizens outside of the United States.

The amendment provides that the right will be invoked upon an independent, judicial inquiry, and not merely upon a determination made by government agents.

In summary, the right to be protected from unreasonable

searches and seizures is personal, extends to all persons, within any area of the United States, and at all times. The right may be waived under the proper circumstances, when certain formalities are met. The rights secured under the fourth amendment are considered implicit in the constitutional system, and may not be violated, even in the interests of crime detection.

Section 3. FREEDOM FROM INTRUSION

The amendment guarantees to all citizens that they shall be free from the threat of unreasonable search or seizure of constitutionally protected areas. Furthermore, persons need not fear governmental use of evidence in criminal proceeding against them which was obtained in violation of the fourth amendment.

Security may be considered both a mental and physical right, that is, an individual in our society must be totally at ease and feel perfectly insured from unreasonable intrusions by government agents.

In *Boyd v. U.S.* the court said, "It is not the breaking of his doors, and the rummaging of his drawers that constitutes the essence of the offense; but it is the invasion of his indefeasible right of personal security, personal liberty, and private property."

Section 4. HOUSES, PERSONS, PAPERS, AND EFFECTS

Only property of the type specified within the constitutional guarantee against unreasonable searches and seizures is protected, namely the broad categories of "persons," "houses," "papers," and "effects." These divisions are continually being given an ever-widening construction, as is evinced by the listing of protected areas to follow.

The terms "possessions" and "effects" are interrelated definitionally; however, "possessions" has been construed to include both real and personal property, actually *possessed* or *occupied* by the individual seeking fourth amendment protection. Further portions of dwellings included in the term "possessions" are houses, buildings, businesses, vehicles, etc. "Possessions" does not extend to land not used in connection with dwellings, wild land, waste land or lands located some distance from the dwelling. However, it has been held to cover land located within proximity of the dwelling, which could be used for residential purposes.

"Effects" include all personal property within the possession or proximity of the person.

"Papers" include mail, letters, packages, contracts, checks, documents, books, etc.

The term "person" extends to the body of the person, while living, as well as the actual integrity of the body, i.e. the organs and fluids within the body. "Persons" also includes aliens, corporations, and minors.

A general list of protected areas is set forth to give the reader an idea of the extent of the protection. Subsection **5.3** elaborates on these protected areas and cites, where necessary, specific case examples in which the validity of searches were determined. The reader is cautioned that the latest court cases should be consulted for new developments, as the list of protected areas is increasing.

Persons:
Aliens
Arrested persons
Convicts
Corporations
Guests
Minors
Persons
Parolees and probationers
Persons crossing borders

Commercial Property Open to the Public:
Common areas of curtilage
Dry cleaning shop
Dwellings
Evidence discovered in plain view
Fire escape
Garage
Garbage and trash
Home as business
Hospitals
Hotel and motel rooms

Leased and rented premises
Lockers
Offices
Open areas adjacent to house
Open lands or fields
Prisons
Private office as home
Public corridors
Public premises
Public streets
Public toilets
Rest rooms
School dormitories
Service stations
Social clubs
Storage rooms
Telephone booths
Tenant of building
Trailer home
Trash can
Urban and rural areas
Vacant buildings within curtilage
Vacant wooded areas

Houses	*Effects:*
Places of Habitation:	Clothing of accused
Apartments	Conversations
Barns	Contraband
Barber shop	Diaries
Buildings within curtilage	Foot lockers
Businesses and offices	Forfeited property
Bus station lockers	Game
	Mail matters
	Nonvisible contents of automobile
Papers:	Papers
Abandoned papers	Parcel or package
Attorney files	Private papers
Bank records	Records
Bankruptcy files	Safe deposit box
Books and papers	Telephone booth
Corporate books	Telegrams
Federal income tax returns	
Mail matters	*Transportation:*
Public mail	Airplane
In prison	Car
Private papers	Car in pursuit
Public records	Visible articles

Section 5. SEARCHES AND SEIZURES

5.1. Reasonable vs. Unreasonable Searches

The fourth amendment only prohibits "unreasonable" searches and seizures, it does not define it. What constitutes a reasonable or unreasonable search or seizure, in each case, is solely a judicial question.

5.1.1. TESTS OF REASONABLENESS. Neither courts nor the Constitution have set out exact criteria to determine whether a search is reasonable or unreasonable. The Constitution merely says that all unreasonable searches and seizures are forbidden. It can be said that the *reasonableness* of a search or seizure, whether or not there is a search warrant, is the ultimate constitutional test of the lawfulness of search or seizure (*White v. U.S.*, 271 F2d 829, 1959). Unless the search is (1) needed to arrest, (2) by consent, (3) made for contraband, instrumentalities of crime or fruits of a crime, (4) for other evidence connecting the accused with specific criminal conduct, (5) to protect the officer or others present from the immediate threat of harm or (6) in case of exigent circumstances, the search will be held unreasonable.

The amendment extends to both searches and seizures, and covers persons, houses, papers, and effects. Among the factors to be considered in measuring the reasonableness of a search are (1) whether a warrant was obtained, and if not, (2) was there time to reasonably obtain a warrant, (3) was the search conducted during the day or night, (4) was entry on enclosed or unenclosed land surrounding a dwelling or business, (5) the object or place that was subjected to the search, (6) the scope of the search, (7) whether or not the search was effected by force or coercion, (8) definiteness and type of information that caused the officers to enter the land, (9) the time elements involved in entry, search, arrest, and seizure, (10) the purpose of the search, (11) the character of articles taken, and, (12) the nature and importance of the crime suspected.

The reasonableness of a search must be determined from the particular facts of the case. Although a search can never be justified by what it turns up, one must not close his eyes to the realities of the situation at the time of search. Hence, implicit in the judicial decision of reasonableness is the precise situation at the time of search (*People v. Smalls,* 311 N.Y.S.2d 354 (1970)).

The Court said in *Giacona v. U.S.,* 257 F2d 450 (1958), the fourth amendment protects against "unreasonable" searches and seizures. Reasonableness is often a question of degree, when the right of privacy must reasonably yield to the right of search (see also *Johnson v. U.S.,* 333 U.S. 10 (1948)).

"What is a reasonable search is not to be determined by any fixed formula. The Constitution does not define what are reasonable searches, and, regretably, in our discipline, we have no ready litmus-paper test. The recurring question of reasonableness of searches must find resolution in the facts and circumstances of each case" (*Go-Bart Imports Co. v. U.S.,* 282 U.S. 344 (1931)).

What may be unreasonable in a search of a man's house may be entirely reasonable in a search of his place of business (*Harris v. U.S.,* 331 U.S. 145 (1947)).

In dealing with probable cause, the court has said, "we are dealing with probabilities. These are not technical; they are the factual and practical considerations of everyday life on which reasonable and prudent men, not legal technicians, act. The standard of proof is accordingly correlative to what must be proved" (*Brinegar v. U.S.*, 338 U.S. 160 (1949)). One test of reasonableness is whether there was the requisite "probable cause" which would be necessary to satisfy a neutral and detached magistrate, rather than a zealous officer acting under the stress of ferreting out crime (*U.S. v. Bell*, 126 F. Supp. 612 (1959)).

A final note relative to the reasonableness of a search deals with the fact situation in which a warrant might have been obtained, but was not. The court stated in *U.S. v. Rabinowitz*, 339 U.S. 56 (1950), the relevant test is not whether it is reasonable to procure a search warrant, but whether the search was reasonable.

5.2. Searches Without Warrants

Searches may be conducted *without* a search warrant within the framework of the fourth amendment, under the following circumstances only:

1. Contemporaneous with, or immediately after (subject to exigent circumstances) a *valid* arrest.
2. During emergency conditions such as fresh pursuit.
3. By consent.
4. Where probable cause exists to indicate the presence of contraband, fruits, instrumentalities, or evidence of specific criminal conduct.

Limited searches may be conducted during the following:

1. Stop and frisk.
2. Health and safety inspections.
3. Enforcement of certain statutes such as Motor Vehicle Laws.

5.2.1. Stop and Frisk. (*Terry v. Ohio*, 392 U.S. 1 (1968) and *Sibron v. New York*, 392 U.S. 40 (1968)).

Although police departments have employed "stop and frisk" techniques for quite some time, it is only since 1968 that the court has laid down specific guidelines for the admissibility of evidence seized in such encounters.

This section presents the two major problems inherent in "stop and frisk" situations and the criteria which must be met for the admission of evidence so seized. The section concludes with four case examples involving stop and frisk situations with analysis of each.

Three major questions must be answered in relation to the "stop and frisk" situation: a) What is the protection afforded by the fourth amendment to the stop and frisk situation; b) when does it apply; and c) what rules govern the admissibility of evidence which is the product of a stop and frisk?

5.2.1.1. *Protection of The Fourth Amendment: Extent.* Is a person entitled to the protection of the fourth amendment when walking down a street? If so, to what extent? The court, in *Terry v. Ohio,* held that, unquestionably, the amendment did apply to the stop and frisk situation. But when? Must there be, as many claimed, an actual search of this person to bring that person within the amendment's protection? Is a "pat-down" the same thing as a search? The Court dispensed with the argument that a "stop" was something less than an "arrest" (seizure) and a "frisk" was short of a "search" within the contemplation of the amendment. Proponents of the "technicality" argument reasoned that the "stop and frisk" amounts to a mere minor inconvenience and petty indignity, which can properly be imposed upon the citizen on the basis of a police officer's suspicion in the interest of effective law enforcement. The Court, however, took the view that whenever a police officer accosts an individual and restrains his freedom to walk away, he has seized that person. Further, it is a serious intrusion upon the sanctity of the person, which may inflict great indignity and arouse strong resentment, and is not to be undertaken lightly. The Court thus rejected any notion that the fourth amendment did not come into play at all as a limitation upon police conduct if the officers stop short of something called a "technical arrest" or a "full-blown search." Thus, *any time the individual is accosted on the street, his fourth amendment rights attach fully.*

5.2.1.2. *Admissibility of Evidence.* In order for evidence derived from a search or seizure to be admissible in criminal proceedings, that evidence must have been the product of a reasonable search. Thus, the question relating to stop and frisk is when and under what circumstances is the stop and frisk search reasonable?

To appreciate the ramifications of the question, one must remember that the goal of the fourth amendment in excluding certain evidence, has been to deter and discourage lawless police conduct. If the courts were to allow all items taken in stop and frisk situations to be admitted, it would, in effect, be putting its stamp of approval on possible lawless police conduct.

The heart of the fourth amendment is a severe requirement of specific justification for any intrusion upon protected personal security, coupled with a highly developed system of judicial controls to enforce upon the agents of the state the commands of the Constitution. Acquiescence by the courts in the compulsion inherent in the field interrogation practices at issue here, it is urged, would constitute an abdication of judicial control over, and indeed an encouragement of, substantial interference with liberty and personal security by police officers whose judgment is necessarily colored by their primary involvement in the often competitive enterprise of ferreting out crime (*Johnson v. U.S.,* 333 U.S. 10 (1948)).

The problem becomes one of balancing the governmental interest in allowing officers to conduct their investigations on the streets by stopping and perhaps searching persons, against the right of such persons to be left alone.

So then we come to the reasonableness question: when is an officer justified in (1) stopping, and (2) searching an individual. Furthermore, what is meant by "search" in this regard, and what limits must be imposed?

The amendment requires the belief that "probable cause" exists when criminal conduct is being engaged in, in order to justify a search. Is it always unreasonable for a policeman to seize a person and subject him to a limited search unless there is probable cause for an arrest? The court, in *Terry v. Ohio,* stated that when the officer is conducting a "limited" search for weapons, he may be justified in his actions. It should be remembered that the Constitution only prohibits *unreasonable* searches. It is recognized that often, when an officer reasonably suspects that the party in question may be in the process of committing a crime, the officer may be taking a grave risk in approaching the party, unless he can rapidly ascertain whether the suspect is armed and capable of injuring himself or others. The Court thus held that in the interest of safety, and effective crime prevention and detection, the officer may conduct limited searches when certain criteria are met.

The Court further stated that, there must be a narrowly drawn authority to permit a reasonable search for weapons for the protection of the police officer, where he has reason to believe that he is dealing with an armed and dangerous individual, regardless of whether he has probable cause to arrest the individual for commission of a crime. The officer need not be absolutely certain that the individual is armed; the issue is whether a reasonably prudent man in similar circumstances would be warranted in the belief that his safety, or that of others, was in danger. In determining whether the officer acted reasonably in such circumstances, due consideration must be given, not to his suspicion or "hunch" but to the specific, reasonable inferences which he is entitled to draw from the facts in light of his experience.

Would the facts available to the officer at the moment of the seizure or the search, warrant a man of reasonable caution in the belief that the action taken was appropriate? Good faith on the part of the arresting officer is not enough. The sole justification for the search must be the protection of the police officer and others nearby, and it must therefore be confined in scope to an intrusion reasonably designed to discover guns, knives, clubs, squirting acids, swords or other hidden instruments for the assault of the police officer. General exploratory searches may not be conducted.

5.2.1.3. *Criteria.* In order for evidence taken during a stop and frisk situation to be admitted, the officer's action must a) be justified at its inception, and b) reasonably relate to the circumstances which justified the interference in the first place.

In the case of (a), the officer must be able to point to the particular facts from which he reasonably inferred that the individual was armed and dangerous. There must be something at least in the activities of the person being observed or in his surroundings that affirmatively suggest particular criminal activity, completed, current, or intended.

By (b) is meant that the search must be reasonably limited in scope to the accomplishment of the only goal which might justify the stop, the protection of the officer by disarming a potentially dangerous man.

The four case examples to follow present the fact situations present in the major "stop and frisk" decisions decided. A brief analysis of each example will point out whether stop and frisk criteria were met, and why, or why not.

> 5.2.1.4. *Case Example.* A plainclothes police officer of thirty-nine years experience was patrolling the downtown area at approximately 2:30 in the afternoon, when his attention was attracted by two men, who were standing on the corner of a busy street. He had never seen the two men before, and was unable to say precisely why he noticed them. He explained in court that for thirty-five years he had been assigned to patrol the downtown vicinity for shoplifters and pickpockets and that he had developed routine habits of observation over the years and that he was feeling "the two men in question just didn't look right to him."
>
> The officer thus took up a surveillance position to observe the pair. He saw one of the men leave the other one and walk past some stores. The man paused for a moment and looked in a store window, then walked on a short distance, turned around, and walked back toward the corner, pausing once again to look in the same store window. The man's friend and he then rejoined and conferred briefly at the corner. Then, the second man went through the same series of motions, strolling down the street, looking in the same store window, walking on a short distance, turning back, peering in the store window again, and returning to confer with the first man at the corner. The two men repeated this ritual alternately about five or six times apiece, roughly a dozen trips total. At one point, a third man approached the two and spoke with them.
>
> The officer felt that the pair was "casing the store for a stick-up" and considered it his duty to investigate further. The officer approached the three men, identified himself as a police officer, and asked for their names. The man mumbled something in response to his inquiries. The officer then grabbed one of the men, spun him around between the other two, and patted down the outside of his clothing. In the left breast pocket of the overcoat, the officer felt a pistol. He reached inside the coat pocket, but was unable to remove the gun. At this point, he marched all three of the men into a store, and patted down all three, finding an additional weapon. The officer

testified that he only patted the men down to see if they had weapons, and that he did not put his hands beneath the outer garments of either of the men until he felt the weapons. Was the officer justified in stopping and searching the suspects?

Yes. Accordingly the weapons found were admissible in evidence. Although the Court stated that the officer had no probable cause to arrest the suspects, he had observed circumstances that would reasonably lead an experienced, student policeman to believe that the suspects were possibly about to engage in burglary or robbery. His justifiable suspicion afforded a proper constitutional basis for accosting the suspects, restraining their liberty of movement briefly, and questioning them. In addition, the officer confined his search strictly to what was minimally necessary to learn if the men were armed, and to disarm them once he discovered the weapons. He did not conduct a general exploratory search. The criteria of reasonableness of the stop, and reasonableness of the search were met (*Terry v. Ohio*, 392 U.S. 1 (1968)).

5.2.1.5. *Case Example.* An officer testified that while he was patrolling his beat, in uniform, he observed a party "continually from the hours of 4:00 PM to 12:00 midnight, in a certain vicinity." He stated that during this period of time he saw the party in conversation with six or eight persons all of whom he knew, from past experience, to be narcotic addicts. The officer testified that he did not overhear any of the conversations, and that he did not see anything pass between the men. Late in the evening, the suspect entered a restaurant. The patrolman saw the suspect speak with three more known addicts inside the restaurant. Once again, nothing was overheard and nothing was seen to pass between suspect and addicts. The suspect sat down and ordered pie and coffee, and as he was eating the officer approached him and told him to come outside. Once outside, he said to the suspect, "You know what I am after." According to the officer the suspect "mumbled something and reached into his pocket." Simultaneously, the patrolman thrust his hands into the same pocket, discovering several glassine envelopes, which turned out to contain heroin. Were the narcotics taken in the search admissible as evidence?

No. The officer lacked solid, concrete reasons to believe that criminal conduct was taking place. "The suspect's mere act of talking with a number of known narcotic addicts over an eight hour period no more gives rise to reasonable fear of life or limb on the part of the police officer than it justified an arrest for committing a crime. Nor did the officer urge that when the suspect put his hands in his pocket, he feared that he was going for a weapon and acted in self-defense. His opening statement to the suspect, "you know what I am after" made it clear that he sought narcotics, and his testimony at the hearing left no doubt that he thought there were narcotics in the suspect's pocket. The court held that the search was not reasonably limited in scope to the accomplishment of disarming the suspect. Hence, the narcotics were inadmissible (*Sibron v. New York,* 392 U.S. 40 (1968)).

5.2.1.6. *Case Example.* The defendant was convicted of possession of burglary tools, which were seized from his person at the time of his arrest. The officer testified that he was home in his apartment on the day in question. He had just finished taking a shower and was drying himself when he heard a noise at his door. His attempt to investigate was interrupted by a telephone call, but when he returned and looked through the peephole into the hall, the officer saw "two men tiptoeing out of the alcove toward the stairway." He immediately called the police, put on some civilian clothes and armed himself with his service revolver. The officer testified that he had lived in the 120 unit apartment building for twelve years and that he did not recognize either of the men as tenants. Believing that he had happened upon the two men in the course of an attempted burglary, the officer opened his door, entered the hallway, and slammed the door loudly. This precipitated a flight down the stairs on the part of the two men, and the officer gave chase. He apprehended the defendant one floor below his apartment. He grabbed the suspect by the collar, and continued down another flight in an attempt to catch the other man.

The defendant explained his presence in the building to the officer by saying that he was visiting a girl friend. However, he declined to reveal the girl friend's name on the ground that she was a married woman. The officer patted the defendant down for weapons and discovered a hard object in his pocket. He stated at the hearing that the object did not feel like a gun, but that it might have been a knife. He removed the object from the defendant's pocket. It was an opaque plastic envelope containing burglars' tools. Were the burglars' tools admissible evidence?

Yes. The officer had reasonable grounds to stop the defendant, on the basis that he believed a crime was about to be committed. His belief was based on his observation of the defendant and of the defendant's flight. The frisk made after the stop was a limited one and was constitutionally permitted to insure the officer's safety.

The fact that burglars' tools were turned up will not bar the State from admitting them as evidence.

> 5.2.1.7. *Case Example.* About 2:50 AM a police sergeant in the vicinity of a business district observed the defendant walking. The officer stopped the defendant and inquired about his identity and purpose for being out so late, as there had been several burglaries in the area recently. The defendant identified himself and stated that he was walking to visit a friend. When further questioned as to the route he was taking, the defendant replied that he had felt like taking a walk. Observing that the defendant was carrying a sack, with the name of "Mals Department Store" on the outside, the officer asked if he might examine its contents, and the defendant readily assented. The bag contained new articles of clothing consisting of underwear and socks, and a sales slip bearing the date of June 28. The defendant informed the officer that he had purchased the articles on the preceding day, July 1. Since the items of clothing were apparently not of the defendant's size, the officer became suspicious and frisked him to determine if he was carrying any weapons. The frisk consisted of the officer quickly running his hands over the surface of the defendant's clothing. He discovered a screwdriver in the small of the defendant's back, tucked under his shirt and belt. It had a shaft which was seven inches long, it was not new and had paint marks on both the shaft and handle. The defendant said he had bought the screwdriver along with the clothing at the department store. The defendant was arrested, and taken to the police station, where a thorough search was made. He was charged with possession of burglary tools. Was the screwdriver admissible in evidence?

Yes. The officer was justified in his suspicions. The court considered the presence of the defendant in the area, carrying a bag, at an unusual hour of the morning, where a number of burglaries had recently occurred, his unlikely story given to the officer, the articles contained in the bag, which were revealed voluntarily, that apparently were not the defendant's size, and the variance between the date on the sales slip and that which the defendant gave. All of these factors contributed to giving the officer justification for believing that a crime had been committed, and that he could reasonably fear for his safety.

In summary, where a police officer observes unusual conduct which leads him reasonably to conclude in light of his experience that criminal activity may be afoot and that the person with whom he is dealing may be armed and presently dangerous, where in the course of investigating this behavior he identifies himself as a policeman and makes reasonable inquiries; and where nothing in the initial stages of the encounter serves to dispel his reasonable fear for his own, or others', safety, he is entitled to conduct a carefully limited search of the outer clothing of such persons in an attempt to discover weapons, in the protection of himself and others in the area. Such a search is a reasonable search under the fourth amendment (*Terry v. Ohio,* 392 U.S. 1 (1968)).

5.2.2. ARREST. This section deals with arrest as contemplated within the fourth amendment under "seizure" and as applies to searches. It has been held that without a warrant, an arresting officer may search a person arrested in order to remove any weapons that the latter might seek to use in order to resist arrest or effect an escape. In addition, the officer may search for and seize any evidence on the arrested person. Finally, he may search any area into which the arrested person might reach to grab a weapon or destroy evidence (*Chimel v. California,* 395 U.S. 752 (1969).

A discussion of arrest, grounds for arrest, searches incident to arrest, place and scope of search, articles subject to seizure, and limitations on arrest and search is presented in the following pages.

Arrest is depriving a person of his liberty (i.e. taking the person into custody) so that he is available to answer criminal charges brought in the name of the state. An arrest may be made by a *police officer* in the following circumstances:

1. With an arrest warrant.
2. Where he has reasonable grounds to believe that a felony has been committed, and the person arrested committed.

There are a number of types of statutes to be found in the various states authorizing an arrest for a felony:

1. Common law rule, that arrest may be made by an officer where he has probable cause.
2. On a charge made, upon a reasonable cause, of the commission of a felony by the party arrested. At night when there is reasonable cause to believe that he has committed a felony.

3. On a charge, made upon reasonable cause, of the commission of a felony by the person proposed to be arrested.

4. Officer may, at night without a warrant, arrest any person whom he has reasonable cause for believing to have committed a felony, and is justified in making the arrest, though it afterwards appear that a felony had been committed, but that the person arrested did not commit it.

5. Where it is shown by a satisfactory proof to a police officer, upon the representation of a credible person, that a felony has been committed, and that the offender is about to escape, so that there is not time to procure a warrant, such peace officer may, without a warrant, pursue and arrest the accused.

With regard to arrest for a misdemeanor, there are two different rules laid down in the statutes:

1. An officer may arrest without a warrant for a breach of the peace committed within his presence. Presence has been interpreted to mean what the officer sees, hears, or smells.

2. An officer may arrest without a warrant for any misdemeanor committed in his presence.

In the case of arrest for a misdemeanor, the arrest must be made immediately or shortly after fresh pursuit.

A *civilian* may generally make a "citizen's arrest" for felonies committed within his presence. Statutes may allow a citizen to arrest for a felony:

1. Not committed in his presence, but where he knows the arrested person committed it, and he in fact did commit it.

2. Not committed in his presence, but where he had reasonable grounds to believe it was committed, although the arrested person in fact, it is later proved, did not commit the crime.

The private person may arrest for a misdemeanor only when committed in his presence. There are four different rules, depending on jurisdiction as to when an arrest may be made for the misdemeanor committed in the citizen's presence:

1. The citizen may not arrest for any misdemeanor.

2. May arrest for petit larceny.

3. For breach of the peace committed in his presence.
4. For any misdemeanor.

In each of the above cases, the question arises as to when a search may be made relating to the arrest and what is the permissible scope of that search. This section will outline the grounds for arrest without a warrant, presenting a detailed discussion of arrest by warrant in Part VI.

The constitutional guaranty of freedom from unreasonable searches and seizures does not apply to searches conducted *incidental* to a lawful arrest. However, the ability to conduct an incidental search is closely defined.

5.2.2.1. *Grounds for Arrest.* As noted, there are a number of grounds to justify an arrest.

1. *Felony.* If a police officer or private person has probable cause arising from the facts and circumstances within the person's knowledge of which he has reasonably trustworthy information and are sufficient in themselves to warrant a man of reasonable caution in the belief that an offense has been or is being committed, an arrest may be made (*Ker v. California*, 374 U.S.23 (1963)). An arrest may always be justified when its purpose is to apprehend a person known a) to have committed a felony, b) to be presently committing a felony, or c) to be about to commit a felony.

2. *Misdemeanor.* An officer or private citizen may arrest for a misdemeanor committed in his presence. Also, an officer may arrest for a misdemeanor not committed in his presence if there is probable cause to believe that, in fact, a misdemeanor has been committed, and the party in question is responsible. However, the officer may be precluded from a night arrest for a misdemeanor not committed within his presence. There is a split of authority as to whether a private person may arrest for a misdemeanor not committed in his presence.

Some state statutes (Nebraska, for example) authorize arrests on other grounds such as a) upon reasonable information that a person stands charged in the court of any state with a crime punishable by death or imprisonment; b) a child may be taken into custody when such child is endangered in his surroundings, and immediate removal appears necessary; and c) where there is reasonable ground to believe that the child is a runaway.

5.2.2.2. *Probable Cause Requirements for Arrest.* In order to arrest without a warrant, or to obtain an arrest warrant, probable cause must be shown, see **5.2.2.1.**

The probable cause requisite is the same for a search or arrest warrant (*Spinelli v. U.S.,* 393 U.S.410 (1969)). Probable cause does not mean the possession of evidence sufficient to convict. It may be based on hearsay, the training and experience of the officer, or other evidence which possibly would not be admissible at trial (*Brinegar v. U.S.,* 338 U.S.160 (1949); *Henry v. U.S.,* 361 U.S.98 (1959); *Wong Sun v. U.S.,* 371 U.S.471 (1963)). See subsection **5.2.**, generally, on probable cause.

Probable cause, simply stated, consists of the facts and circumstances known to the officer which would warrant a prudent man in believing that an offense is being, or has been committed, and that the person before him committed it (*Bell v. U.S.,* 254 F.2d.82 (1958)). Good faith on the part of the arresting officer is not enough to establish probable cause; nor is mere suspicion. Note that an arrest can *never* be justified by what a subsequent search discovers.

In order to establish probable cause, the source of the officers' information must be demonstrated. The officer may see criminal activity first-hand, as was the case in *Bell v. U.S.,* supra, where officers observed two men drive several blocks in a business area with their headlights out at 3:00 AM. Upon being stopped, the men failed to give an adequate explanation of what they were doing. This coupled with (1) the view by the officers of cartons in the car, (2) knowledge that burglaries were frequent in the area, and (3) one of the men reached under the seat, justified the officers in their belief that the crime of burglary had just occurred. The men were arrested, and the evidence secured by a subsequent search was admitted.

Facts may come to an officer from other officers to form the basis for probable cause. Stated the court in *Miller v. U.S.,* 356 F.2d.63 (1966), "The police department of a large metropolitan area does not and cannot operate on a segmented basis with each officer acting separately and independently of each other, and detached from central headquarters. There must be cooperation, coordination, and direction with some central control and exchange of information."

Probable cause may also come to the officer by way of an informant or through hearsay. It should be noted that hearsay may form the basis of a showing of probable cause, either in an application for a warrant, or for a nonwarrant arrest. Hearsay, conversely, may not be used to prove guilt in a criminal trial, except under certain exceptional circumstances.

> 5.2.2.2.1. Case Example. A federal narcotics agent stationed in Denver (with twenty-nine years experience) was receiving information from a special employee (informant) of the Bureau of Narcotics. On all occasions, the information supplied by the informant was accurate and reliable. On September 3, 1956, the informant told the agent that the defendant had recently taken up residence in Denver, and was peddling narcotics to several addicts in the area. Four days later, the informant advised the agent that the defendant had gone to Chicago and was going to bring back three ounces of heroin to Denver either on the morning of the eighth or ninth of the month. He also gave the agent a physical description of the defendant's clothing, and stated that he would be carrying a tan zipper bag, and walked "real fast."
>
> On the morning of the ninth, the agent, along with Denver police officers, observed a party having the exact physical characteristics, wearing the precise clothing described, walk briskly from the train which had just come in from Chicago. He was carrying a tan zipper bag in his right hand. The man was accosted, arrested, and searched. Two envelopes containing heroin were found in his pocket. The question presented on the facts was whether the knowledge of the facts and circumstances gave the agent "probable cause" and reasonable grounds within the meaning of the fourth amendment to believe that the defendant was committing a crime. If it did, the arrest, although without a warrant, was lawful, and the search valid.

The court held that the arrest was based upon probable cause, and hence was valid. The defendant claimed a) the information given by the informant to the agent was "hearsay" and hence, should not have been considered by the agent in assessing probable cause, and b) the information did not justify the agent in believing that a crime was being committed.

The court noted that the rules for hearsay are not the same for showing probable cause, and for proving guilt (Rule 4, Federal Rules of Procedure).

As to the second contention, the court found a) previous information had always proved reliable from the informant, b) the information was personally verified when the defendant alighted from the train, meeting the precise physical description given by the informant. All that remained for the agent to verify was that in fact the defendant was carrying narcotics (*Draper v. U.S.*, 358 U.S. 307 (1959)).

Quaere: Simply because an informant has been correct in nine out of the past nine cases, does this mean he will be accurate in the tenth case? Should this fact alone be determinative of probable cause? Was there in fact any real verification of anything in *Draper?* The reader is directed to see the dissent in *Draper,* and also to see *Stanley v. State,* 186 A.2d.478 (1962).

5.2.2.3. *Ability to Obtain a Warrant.* The measure of probable cause is the same, whether a warrant is procured or not. If the situation requires immediate action, the fact that an officer fails to obtain a warrant of arrest will not invalidate the arrest. This is so, even if there was time to obtain a warrant in fact. In the case of "on sight" crime, the court has stated, "Warrants of arrest are designed to meet the dangers of unlimited and unreasonable arrests of persons who are not at the moment committing any crime. Those dangers, obviously, are not present where a felony plainly occurs before the eyes of an officer of the law at a place where he is lawfully present. Common sense then dictates that an arrest in that situation is valid despite the failure to obtain a warrant of arrest." (*Trupiano v. U.S.,* 334 U.S.699 (1948)).

Although the practicability of obtaining a warrant is not the controlling factor as to whether the arrest and subsequent search are reasonable, the courts seem to be moving to the position that if it is possible to obtain a warrant, one should be obtained before acting. See also *Ker v. California,* 374 U.S.23 (1963) and *U.S. v. Rabinowitz, supra.*

Certain situations may make it possible to obtain an arrest warrant, but not a search warrant, i.e. where officers know who committed the crime, but not what evidence of the crime may be found. Under these circumstances, the arrest will justify the subsequent search without a search warrant. See *State v. Chinn, infra.*

Where an arrest is sought to justify a subsequent search, the arrest, whether it be with or without a warrant, must be lawful. This means that if there was not probable cause for the arrest, anything taken in the search will be inadmissible in any proceedings.

> 5.2.2.3.1. Case Example. On the afternoon of November 10, the defendant was driving his automobile in Cleveland, Ohio. Police officers accosted him, identified themselves, and ordered him to pull over. The officers did not possess either an arrest or search warrant. After placing the defendant under arrest, they searched his car and found nothing of interest. He was then taken to a nearby police station, where they searched his person and found an envelope containing a number of clearing house slips "beneath the sock of his leg." The defendant was subsequently charged in the Cleveland Municipal Court with the possession of clearing house slips in violation of an Ohio state statute. Was the search incident to a lawful arrest?

No. The arrest was not lawful. The constitutional validity of the *search* was dependent on the validity of the arrest. The record reflects only meager facts which gave the officers probable cause. The facts were as follows: a) the officers had a mug shot of the defendant, b) the officers knew that the defendants had some sort of record in relation to clearing houses and games of chances, and c) the officers had some "information" and had heard reports. There was no evidence what these reports were, nor who gave them. They testified that they perceived nothing that gave them grounds for belief that the defendant had acted, or was then acting, unlawfully.

The court noted that with the scant facts presented, no probable cause could be found. Further, "it was incumbent upon the prosecution to show with considerably more specificity what the (informer) actually said, and why the officers thought the information was credible. We may assume that the officers acted in good faith in arresting (petitioner). But good faith on the part of the arresting officer is not enough. If subjective good faith alone were the test, the protections of the fourth amendment would evaporate, and the people would be 'secure in their persons, houses, papers, and effects' only in the discretion of the police." *Beck v. Ohio,* 379 U.S.89 (1964). See also *Giordenello v. U.S., infra.* It must be noted again that regardless of what a search may turn up, if the arrest in the first instance was not lawful, that is, not based upon probable cause, the resulting evidence seized may not be used in court.

5.2.2.4. *Search Incidental to Arrest.* What is incidental? A search may be justified as incidental to a lawful arrest when it is not remote in time or place from the arrest. This means, for example, that a suspect cannot be arrested at his home, with a subsequent search being made of his place of employment, in the absence of a warrant. The reason is, the search sought to be justified, as incidental to arrest, is not sufficiently connected to the place of arrest. Likewise, when a person driving his car is arrested, taken down to headquarters, booked, and several hours later a search is conducted of his car, the search may not be justified because of the intervening passage of time. The search was not "incidental" to the arrest in time (*Preston v. U.S.,* 376 U.S.364 (1964) and *Chimel v. California, supra*).

The court has determined five criteria to consider when questioning the *reasonableness* of a search incident to arrest. These are the following:
1. Nature of crime for which an arrest is made.
2. Character of articles seized.
3. Criminal record of suspect.
4. Opportunity to obtain a warrant of search.
5. Necessity of search.

In addition, the test of reasonableness as to *time* of search and *space* need be considered.

In commenting on the above criteria, (1) would refer to the type of crime. Obviously, a more detailed search would be justified in the case of a homicide than one relating to a larceny. In the *Chinn* case example, *infra,* although a warrant of search might possibly have been obtained prior to the arrest of the defendant, the officers had no idea of what to look for, and thus would not be able to meet warrant requirements of "particularly describing" items to be seized. The court held in *Chinn* that the search was valid, even though they looked around the apartment and gathered up various items. The court took into

account the nature of the crime, i.e. rape, in determining to
what extent the search could be conducted and still held reasonable.

As to (2), again citing the example, the articles were reasonable with respect to the crime.

Item (3) involves the necessity of protecting the officer, by allowing him to "look around" to make sure he will not be subject
to attack from other parties not discovered in the immediate
area of arrest. In addition, he has a right to insure that there are
no weapons lying around which may be available to the arrestee.

Items (4) and (5) have previously been discussed.

As noted in above (**5.2.2.4.**), a search may be conducted as
incident to a lawful arrest. We will consider searches in the following time frames:

1. Search preceding arrest.
2. Search contemporaneous with arrest, and incidental thereto.
3. Search shortly after arrest.
4. Search delayed after arrest.
5. Continuation of search.

Generally, the rule is, "a search without a warrant may be
made incident to a lawful arrest, if reasonably related in terms
of time and space." A derivative problem may appear with respect to the precise time of the "arrest," and its relation to the
accompanying "search." In other words, was the search incidental to the arrest, or was it conducted prior to the arrest? We
have noted previously that a search may never justify an unlawful arrest. Hence, it becomes critically important to determine
whether a lawful arrest occurred *prior* to the search. The following case example demonstrates the problem of whether arrest followed search, and the attempt to justify the arrest in
terms of the evidence secured in the search.

5.2.2.4.1. Case Example. At about 10:00 PM, two police officers dressed
in plainclothes, riding in an unmarked car, observed a taxicab in the
parking lot of an apartment house. The neighborhood had a reputation for "narcotics activity." The officers saw the defendant look up
and down the street, walk across the lot and enter the cab. Neither
officer had seen the defendant before, had any idea as to his identity,

nor had any information to suggest that he was engaged in criminal conduct. They had no arrest or search warrants.

The taxi drove away, and the officers followed for a distance of two miles. When the cab stopped for a traffic light, the officers left their car and approached the taxi. One of the officers identified himself as a policeman. The cab door was opened, and the defendant dropped a recognizable package of narcotics to the floor. As one officer retrieved the package, the other drew his weapon. There was confusion as to the exact sequence of events at the moment the officers approached the cab. The officers claimed that the defendant dropped the package only after one of the officers had opened the cab door. The driver claimed that one of the officers drew his weapon and "took hold of the defendant's arm while he was still in the cab."

The package of narcotics was turned over to federal authorities, which resulted in a subsequent prosecution and conviction for unlawful possession and concealment of the drugs. Was the evidence taken in a search incident to a lawful arrest?

No, said the Supreme Court. The government attempted to justify the evidence as the fruit of a search incident to a lawful arrest. However, the court felt that there was no showing of probable cause at the moment the officers alighted from their car and approached the taxi. If, therefore, the arrest occurred when the officers took their positions at the doors of the cab, then nothing that happened thereafter could make the arrest lawful, or justify a search as incident to it. The validity of the search turned upon the question of the time of arrest. The court held that the case should be remanded for a new trial, to determine the question.

The dissent concluded that the arrest was lawful, in that the defendant had dropped or had thrown the narcotics to the floor, and had therefore given up possession thereof. The fact that it was then within plain view of the officers gave them probable cause to arrest for possession, as one of the officers was a veteran of the narcotics detail, and recognized the package as containing narcotics (*Rios v. U.S.,* 364 U.S.253 (1960)).

Although, generally, a *search preceding an arrest* is held to be invalid, there are occasions where a search may immediately or remotely precede arrest, and be held valid.

5.2.2.4.2. Case Example. Sometime during the day of October 2, 1960, a twelve-year-old girl was reported as missing. Upon her return to her mother the next day, she said she had been taken to a given address in Portland and there subjected to sexual abuse by a man known only as "Ray." The child next described the events to the city police. An officer thereupon obtained a warrant for the arrest of "John Doe, whose true name is unknown." No search warrant was sought or obtained. The officer then went to the reported address. As no one was home, he kept the apartment under surveillance from 2:00 until 6:00 PM. Shortly thereafter, the officer was joined by another officer. After about twenty minutes of waiting together, the officers saw two men enter the apartment. The officers knocked on the door and were admitted. The occupants of the apartment stated that neither of them was Ray. With permission, the officers looked around the apartment for the defendant. Although they observed various objects, they took no steps to take anything into custody. The victim had reported that she had been given beer, and that Ray had taken her picture. The officers asked their temporary hosts if Ray had a camera. They were told that he had. A camera was visible on a shelf in Ray's room, as was a six-pack of empty beer bottles on the floor. The officers looked into a closet and observed some bed sheets. The men then sat down to watch television and wait for Ray's return. When the man answering to the name of Ray entered the apartment, he was immediately placed under arrest. The officers then proceeded to gather up the objects they had noticed earlier in the evening. These objects included the empty beer bottles, camera, and linen. Some of the bottles turned out to have latent prints of the victim. The film, when developed, showed the victim on defendant's bed. Should this evidence have been admitted?

Yes. The court stated a) there was a lawful entry for the purpose of arrest, b) the arrest was based on probable cause, c) the probable cause for the arrest was independent of any evidence discovered, and d) there was no exploratory search, or ransacking of the premises. The search, although in fact preceding the arrest, was *not unreasonable* (*State v. Chinn*, 373 P.2d 392 (1962)).

In *Holt v. Simpson*, 340 F.2d 853 (1965), the court held that when probable cause for arrest exists independently of what the search may produce, the fact that the search precedes the formal arrest is immaterial when the search and arrest are nearly simultaneous and constitute, for all practical purposes, one transaction. The reader is also directed to *U.S. v. Boyster*, 204 F. Supp. 760 (1961).

A police officer may, *contemporaneous with, and incidental to, a lawful arrest, conduct a limited search* of the person arrested in order to remove any weapons he might have. In addition, he may search for, and seize a) any evidence *on* the arrestee, and b) any in the area into which the arrestee could reach in order to grab a weapon or destroy evidence. Within the limits outlined above, an officer in conducting his search, is not prevented from seizing "mere evidence" of the crime, instrumentalities, fruits, or contraband *(Warden v. Hayden, supra)*.

A *search* may still be considered as "incidental" to arrest, although conducted *a short time after the arrest* has been effected. The criterion is reasonableness. Depending on the crime in question, varying times of search will be held reasonable. For example, in a burglary case, a fifteen-minute search may be held reasonable which is conducted during the hour after the arrest of a suspect at his home. Or, in the case of an arrest for homicide, a longer and more *intense* search may be deemed reasonable. Contra where the defendant is arrested and several hours later his car or home is searched, without a warrant *(Preston v. U.S.,* 376 U.S.364 (1964)).

As the length of time between arrest and search increases, the finding of reasonableness of search in the absence of warrant decreases. This is for the following reasons:

1. The search is not necessary to protect the officer.
2. The search is not required to prevent the possible destruction of evidence.
3. There is more time to obtain a search warrant.

The controlling factor is reasonableness under the circumstances, always keeping in mind the connection between time of arrest and search. It should be noted in discussing reasonableness, that a delay of several hours between arrest and search *may* be justified, where the circumstances simply will not allow an earlier search. These types of cases may arise in connection with vehicle stops on public roads, where the car is immediately taken into custody, but not searched because of more pressing necessities. Another case may be where the suspect is to be thoroughly searched, but such search is impossible at the scene of arrest. However, when the elapsed time extends into many hours, or days, one can see that the reasonableness di-

minishes to a vanishing point, absent extreme circumstances. See
People v. Jones, 163 N.W.2d 22 (1968).

5.2.2.5. Place and Extent of Search. Chimel v. California, supra,
sets out the limits as to where the officer may search when making an arrest, and to what extent. "When an arrest is made, it is
reasonable for the arresting officer to a) search the person arrested in order to remove any weapons or seize any evidence on
the arrested person to prevent concealment or destruction, b) to
search the area within his immediate control (meaning where
the arrestee might go to gain possession of a weapon or destroy
evidence)." Thus, searches incident to arrest are limited to those
areas *under the immediate control* of the arrestee.

Where an individual is lawfully *arrested while in a motor vehicle,* officers have a right without a search warrant to make a
contemporaneous search of the person and the things under the
arrestees' immediate control *(Preston v. U.S., and Chimel v. California, supra).*

In addition, as noted, the search of a motor vehicle may be
made without a warrant where the officer has probable cause to
believe that the motor vehicle is being used a) in the commission
of a felony, b) for the purpose of transporting contraband, or
c) to house articles that the officers are entitled to seize. Such
searches may be made even though the officer may not have
probable cause to arrest the driver or occupants *(Carroll v. U.S.;
Brinegar v. U.S.; Henry v. U.S.; Rios v. U.S., supra;* also, *Chambers v. Maroney,* 399 U.S. 42 (1970)).

The Supreme Court has recognized several exceptions to the
rule requiring a search warrant when searching an automobile.
These exceptions are the following:

1. Search incident to valid arrest.
2. Probable cause for search.
3. Search of an impounded car which is being held for forfeiture.
4. By consent.
5. Exigent circumstances.

Several criteria have been developed by the courts in testing
the validity of the vehicle search.

5.2.2.6. Reasonableness and Place, Extent, and Time of Search.

The validity of the search depends upon reasonableness, as determined from the facts and circumstances of each case (*Cooper v. California,* 386 U.S.58 (1967); *Preston v. U.S., supra*).

As noted, the incidental search must be the result of a lawful arrest. See *Henry v. U.S., Chambers v. Maroney, Brinegar v. U.S., Rios v. U.S.,* all *supra.* In addition, *Gambino v. U.S.,* 275 U.S. 310 (1927) and *Scher v. U.S.,* 305 U.S.251 (1938).

If the place and time of the search are so remote from the place and time of the arrest, the search will be held invalid.

In *Preston v. U.S., supra,* the occupants of an auto were arrested for vagrancy (for want of a better charge at the time). The car was towed to a garage at the direction of the arresting officers. Shortly after booking the defendants, the car was searched and evidence was obtained which was used to convict the defendant of bank robbery. The search was held invalid, as being too remote. The court noted that once a defendant is *under arrest* and *in custody,* any search made at another place, without a warrant is not incident to the arrest. Even assuming the police had the right to search the car at the time of arrest, it does not determine the reasonableness of the search at a latter time and place. There was no danger to the officers, nor was there the possibility of evidence being destroyed by the defendants.

In *Dyke v. Taylor Implement Mfg. Co.,* 391 U.S.216 (1968), the court likewise held that where the defendants were arrested, apparently for reckless driving, and taken to a jail, with their auto being parked outside the jail; the search of the car after the defendants were in custody in the jail was too remote in time and place to be incidental to arrest. See also *Chambers v. Maroney, supra.*

As noted, the search incident to arrest must be restricted to those areas under the immediate control of the arrestee. The Supreme Court has not defined just what may be considered as under the arrestees control in a motor vehicle, i.e. a locked glove compartment or a trunk.

It is an interesting consideration that in cases involving automobile searches as incident to arrest, the suspect is usually ordered out of his car prior to arrest. Once removed from the car, it would seem difficult to justify a search of the interior, for nothing in the car could be within the arrestees' grasp. Nelson, *Chimel v. California: A Potential Roadblock to Vehicle Searches,* 17 U.C.L.A. L. Rev., 626, 647 (1970). The reader is also directed to the previous discussion of vehicle searches.

Note that the court has recognized a constitutional distinction between probable cause to search an auto and probable cause to search a fixed, permanent residence. Recognizing in both cases, exigent circumstances which may negate the requirement for a search warrant, see *Agnello v. U.S.,* 269 U.S.20 (1925); *Johnson v. U.S.,* 333 U.S.10 (1948); *Preston v. U.S.;* and *Cooper v. California, supra.*

5.2.2.7. *Impounded Vehicle.* The Supreme Court has ruled that the search of an automobile without a warrant is constitutionally justified where the car had been impounded and is being held for forfeiture. See *Cooper v. California, supra.* In *Cooper,* the defendant was arrested for narcotics violation, and his car impounded, as per state and federal law. The car was searched one week after the arrest. The court held it would be unreasonable under the circumstances not to permit a search of the vehicle, even without a warrant. The question was one of reasonableness under the fourth amendment.

However, where the car is not impounded for forfeiture, as in *Dyke v. Taylor, supra,* the search was held invalid as unreasonable, as it was too remote, plus the fact that the officers were under no duty to keep or control the car (as they were in *Cooper*).

One may waive his fourth amendment rights by a valid consent to search *(Chambers v. Maroney, supra).*

5.2.2.8. *Abandonment of Automobile.* An abandoned or wrecked vehicle may be checked by an officer to protect its contents and to determine the owner. Also, a car, reasonably believed to have been used in the commission of a crime, may be searched to learn the identity of the criminal. See *Fagundes v. U.S.* 340 F.2d 673 (1965); *Caldwell v. U.S.,* 338 F.2d 385 (1964); *Kimbrough v. Beto,* 412 F.2d 981 (1969); and *U.S. v. Gibson,* 421 F.2d 662 (1970).

5.2.2.9. *Objects in Plain View.* As noted in *Evidence in Plain View,* section 4., *supra,* if items are observed in plain view by an officer, who is lawfully in a position to observe those items, the mere observance of such objects does not constitute a search, and hence does not fall within the fourth amendment. See *Harris v. U.S.,* 390 U.S.234 (1968).

5.2.2.9.1. Search of Automobile Trunk. The trunk of a car may be searched incident to arrest for a crime when the officers *reasonably believe* that instrumentalities, fruits, or evidence of the crime are concealed in the vehicle.

In *Kriz v. U.S.,* 301 F. Supp. 1329 (1969), a postal inspector arrested the defendant for theft of gold from the mails, immediately after the defendant had loaded the believed stolen goods into the trunk of his car. The subsequent search of the trunk was held valid. The court said, "This was a search reasonably calculated to discover the stolen gold involved in the offense under investigation, was contemporaneous with the arrest, and was confined to the immediate vicinity."

5.2.2.10. *Pretext Arrests.* An arrest may not be used simply as a pretext in order to legitimize a search incident thereto. "Pretext arrests" are most prevalent where the party to be searched is stopped while driving a motor vehicle. In such arrests, there is an incidental search of the person and the auto immediately after arrest.

In *Amador-Gonzalez v. U.S.,* 391 F.2d 308 (1968), the court set out five guidelines governing arrests and incidental searches thereto:

1. The arrest must be lawful.
2. The arrest must not be a mere pretext for an otherwise illegitimate search.
3. The search must have some relation to the nature and purpose of the arrest.
4. The search incident to a lawful arrest is unreasonable if there is a lack of relationship between the search or scope of the search and the offense for which the arrest was made.
5. Absent special circumstances, the lawful arrest of an auto driver for a traffic offense provides no lawful basis for the search of the driver or his car. See also *Taglavore v. U.S.,* 291 F.2d 262 (1961).

An excellent summary as to the laws of arrest and searches relating to motor vehicles is presented in the November, 1967
F.B.I. Law Enforcement Bulletin, Searches of Motor Vehicles
(9th of series).

> The search incident to arrest must be confined to fruits, instru-
> mentalities, contraband, and mere evidence of the crime for which
> the arrest was made, and to weapons of injury or escape. The arrest
> merely serves the function of a search warrant for things seizable in
> connection with that particular offense. *Papani v. U.S.,* 84 F.2d 160
> (1936) . . . . Obviously, a search cannot be made where there is no
> tangible evidence connected with the arrest offense. That is usually the
> case where violations of motor vehicle codes are involved. With the
> exception of driving while under the influence of alcohol or narcotics,
> there are few traffic offenses in which any object other than the vehicle
> itself can be considered evidence of the crime (*Thompson v. State,*
> 398 S.W.2d 942 (1966). For this reason, the search incident to a traf-
> fic arrest is not permitted in most jurisdictions. *State v. Michaels,* 374
> P.2d 989 (1962). A search of the automobile could reveal nothing
> useful in establishing the offense for which the defendant was arrested
> —failure to signal for a left turn—and there was no reason to suspect
> that he would attempt to flee with the aid of something that might be
> found in the trunk of his car (*Barnes v. State,* 130 N.W.2d 264
> (1964)). There are no fruits or instrumentalities connected with the
> offense of driving a vehicle with a defective tail light (*U.S. v. One
> 1963 Cadillac Hardtop,* 224 F.Supp.210 (1963)). In the case of a stop
> sign violation there is no fruit of the crime. The means whereby the
> crime was committed is the vehicle itself (*U.S. v. Tate,* 209 F.Supp.
> 762 (1962)). There are no fruits of speeding.

5.2.2.11. *Pursuit of Fleeing Suspect.* The criteria set forth in
Amador-Gonzalez will apply also to searches made incident to
an arrest which is the result of a hot pursuit situation. Obviously, the crime for which the fleeing suspect is sought will be determinative of the scope and permissibility of a search. In the
case of a fleeing motorist one can either presume the party is
merely driving fast, or that he is a fugitive, or has just committed
a criminal act. Unless information is available to the officer which
gives him probable cause to believe the latter, it is doubtful if a
search of the vehicle would be justified beyond that which is
necessary for the protection of the officer, and that which is in
plain view.

See *Warden v. Hayden, supra,* for an amplification of searches relating to hot pursuit. In that case, within a few minutes after a bank robbery, the police chased a suspect into a residence near the site of the robbery. The ensuing search and seizure of the suspect and items in the house was held justifiable due to the circumstances. Note that if the fleeing party was simply believed to be a drunk driver, the search of the premises for fruits or instrumentalities of a crime would have been invalid, for the reason that (1) there would be no probable cause to suspect that the party had committed a crime, and hence (2) there would be no fruits, evidence, or instrumentalities, save the vehicle which the defendant would be driving.

5.2.2.12. *Search of Premises Incidental to Arrest.* Whether an incidental search of an arrestee's premises is reasonable within the meaning of the fourth amendment, is a determination which must be made on the facts and circumstances of the particular case. It has been held that to validly search a premises without a warrant as incident to the arrest, the search must be contemporaneous with the arrest in time and space. Thus, as has been noted previously, a search cannot be justified as incident to an arrest where the arrest occurred, for example, in a different locality, or a few blocks away, or even, in some cases, a few feet from the search.

The manner and extent of the search is also important in determining the validity of an incidental search. Searches of a general exploratory nature have been held not justifiable as an incident to arrest. In addition, the search must be closely limited to the area from which the arrestee might obtain either a weapon or evidence. Thus searches of an entire house or other area have been held not justified as incident to an arrest.

5.2.2.12.1. General Principles. The following general principles may be deduced from the cited cases, regarding premises searches, as incidental to lawful arrests:

1. Search incidental to a valid arrest is consistent with the fourth amendment's protection against unreasonable searches and seizures (*Harris v. U.S.,* 331 U.S.145 (1947) and *Chimel v. California, supra*).
2. The mere fact that there is a valid arrest does not automatically legalize a search or seizure without a warrant

(*Trupiano v. U.S.*, 334 U.S.699 (1948); *U.S. v. Rabinowitz*, 339 U.S.56 (1950); and *Chimel v. California, supra*).

3. An arrest cannot be used as a pretext to search for evidence. See **5.2.2.10**. *U.S. v. Lefkowitz*, 385 U.S.452 (1932).

4. The validity of a premises search as incidental to arrest depends mainly on whether the search is unreasonable under the fourth amendment.

5. Reasonableness depends on the facts and circumstances of the particular case. *Go-Bart Importing Co. v. U.S., supra*.

6. Stricter standards of reasonableness may apply to searches of dwellings than to businesses or other premises (*Harris v. U.S., supra*).

5.2.2.13. *Time and Place Relationship Between Arrest and Search.* A search, to be justified as incidental to arrest, must be substantially contemporaneous with the arrest and confined to the immediate vicinity of the arrest. In the cases cited below, the court held that the search was too remote in time or place as to be incidental.

1. *Agnello v. U.S.*, 269 U.S.20 (1925). Defendant and codefendants were arrested at the residence of codefendant. As the suspects were being taken to headquarters, other officers searched the home of the defendant. In that search they found cocaine which was used in evidence to convict. The conviction was overruled. *Rationale:* The defendants' home, where the search took place, was several blocks away from the home in which the arrest occurred.

2. *Preston v. U.S.*, 376 U.S.364 (1964). A search without a warrant which is remote in time and place from the arrest, where the accused is in custody, is simply not incidental to the arrest.

3. *Stoner v. California*, 375 U.S.483 (1964). A search was made of a hotel room in California as incidental to an arrest made in Las Vegas, Nevada, two days before. The search was completely unrelated to the arrest, both as to time and place. The conviction was reversed. *Rationale:* The search could be incidental to an arrest only where it was contemporaneous with the arrest and was limited to the immediate vicinity of the arrest. The permissible bounds of an incidental search do not extend to a

search of a house substantially removed geographically from the place of arrest, or from the time of arrest.

4. *James v. Louisiana,* 382 U.S.36 (1965). Defendant was arrested on a street corner two blocks from his home. The officers then drove the defendant back to his residence, where they broke down the door and conducted an intensive search for several hours, which yielded the narcotics equipment and morphine tablet which formed the basis of the conviction of the defendant. Conviction reversed. *Rationale:* The search was not incidental to arrest in time or space.

5. *Shipley v. California,* 395 U.S.818 (1969). Police officers arrested the defendant as he jumped from his car, which was parked fifteen to twenty feet from his house. They conducted a search of his house immediately thereafter. Evidence found in the house was used in a robbery conviction. Reversed. *Rationale:* The search extended beyond the place in which the defendant was arrested without reasonable justification, and hence could not be upheld under the fourth and fourteenth amendments as incidental to the arrest. The court stated that the Constitution had never been construed to allow the police, in the absence of an emergency, to arrest a person outside his home and then take him inside for the purpose of conducting a warrantless search. It has always been assumed that one's house can not be lawfully searched without a search warrant except as incident to a lawful arrest therein.

5.2.2.14. *Manner and Extent of Search.* The scope of a search which is supposedly conducted as an incident to a valid arrest must be narrowly limited. A search which is of a general exploratory nature cannot be justified as an incident to an arrest.

Chimel v. California, supra, has indicated that in order for a search to be justified as incident to a lawful arrest, the search must be limited to the area from which the arrestee might gain possession of a weapon or destroy evidence. The court noted that there was no justification for routinely searching rooms other than that in which an arrest occurs, or for searching through all the desk drawers, or other closed or concealed areas in the room of the arrest itself.

In the following cases, the court has reversed convictions where evidence was derived from incidental premises searches. In all of the cases, the court referred to the extent of searches as controlling their decisions.

1. *Chimel v. California,* cited in subsection 8.1, *infra.* The defendant was arrested in his home for burglary of a coin shop. After arrest, the three-bedroom house of the defendant was searched, including the attic, garage, and small workshop. In some of the rooms, the search was quite extensive.

2. *Go-Bart Importing Co. v. U.S., supra.* Defendants were arrested for the sale of liquor in violation of federal statutes. The office of defendant was thoroughly searched, with the seizure of numerous papers, books, files, etc.

3. *U.S. v. Lefkowitz, supra.* Agents searched an office ten by twenty feet, opening all the drawers of two desks in the room, examining their contents, and taking various books papers, and other articles.

4. *Von Cleef v. New Jersey,* 395 U.S.814 (1969). The defendant was arrested on the third floor of a sixteen-room house in which she and a codefendant lived. After the arrest, several policemen searched the house from top to bottom for three hours.

5.2.2.15. *Quantity of Items Taken.* A mass seizure of many and varied items, or of the entire contents of a place cannot be justified as an incidental search.

1. *U.S. v. Lefkowitz,* above.

2. *Kremen v. U.S.,* 353 U.S.346 (1957). After the arrest and search, the officers seized and carried away several thousand items, including books, magazines, catalogs, mailing lists, private correspondence, photos, drawings, and film.

4. *Abel v. U.S., supra.* Conviction *upheld,* where agents searched the hotel room of defendant for weapons and documents connected with the defendant's status as an alien. The person making the search did not seize the entire contents of the room, but only relatively few items.

5.2.2.16. *Necessity of Obtaining a Warrant.* If the arresting officers have sufficient time and information to enable them to obtain a search warrant, where a search is conducted which goes beyond the time and space limitations announced in *Chimel,* then a search conducted in the absence of a warrant will be held unreasonable. *Taylor v. U.S.,* 286 U.S.1 (1932).

As pointed out in 23 L. Ed. 2d 966, at 989,

> Law enforcement officers should be forewarned that if they are concerned about the possible presence of weapons or evidence in areas of the premises beyond the reach of an arrestee, they should not make a nonconsensual search without a warrant, but should remove the arrestee from the premises or handcuff him immediately after arresting him, and, while keeping the premises under close surveillance, should obtain a warrant.

5.2.3. EXIGENT CIRCUMSTANCES. Often, valid searches may be justified in the absence of a warrant, when exigent or emergency circumstances are present. Such may be the case when a vehicle is stopped, and the officer has probable cause to believe that contraband is being transported, or that the occupants are in the act of committing a felony. Under such circumstances, searches may be held valid.

The exceptional circumstances under which a reasonable search may be made without a warrant are generally limited to searches as an incident to arrest, search of a movable vehicle, or searches which may be justified under rare circumstances to prevent threatened destruction or removal of contraband (*Walker v. U.S.,* 225 F.2d 447 (1955)).

The question the courts must ask is, considering the circumstances immediately preceding the arrest or stop, was it impracticable to obtain a warrant? There must be compelling reasons to justify a search in the absence of a warrant. If at all possible, a warrant must be obtained prior to a search.

5.2.3.1. *Instruments of Transportation.* Generally, the problem of searching without warrants in times of exigent circumstances occur regarding the stopping and searching of vehicles. This is so because of the mobile and transitory nature of the vehicle. A car may be stopped, and if the officer believes that there is probable cause that contraband is being transported, or that a crime is taking place, he may be justified in searching the automobile. "A search warrant is not required under the fourth amendment for an automobile because of the impractability of the warrant's timely procurement, but reasonable or probable cause for search is still demanded." (*U.S. v. Cotter,* 80 F. Supp. 590 (1948).)

The United States Supreme Court, in *Carrol v. U.S.,* 267 U.S. 132 (1925), noted the distinction between the necessity of procuring a search warrant in the searching of a private dwelling and for an automobile. The Court said that if search and seizure without a warrant is made upon probable cause (that is, upon a reasonable belief, arising out of circumstances known to the officer that the automobile contains that which is subject to seizure by law) the search and seizure are valid. This relates to a vehicle on a public road. If the car is located on private property, a warrant for the premises or for the car must be obtained.

> 5.2.3.1.1. Case Example. State troopers received a call from a city police department detective that certain parties would be driving a certain car on a particular interstate highway during specified night hours, and that the parties would possess narcotics, in violation of the law. An officer observed the suspect vehicle on the interstate some twenty-five minutes later. A warrantless search was made of the vehicle. Narcotics were found and the defendant was convicted. Should the narcotics have been admitted?

Yes. The officer had sufficient information to furnish the requisite probable cause. Although the issue was raised by the defense that the officer had time to get a warrant, and by not obtaining it, fourth amendment provisions were violated with regard to unreasonable searches and seizures, the court stated that each case must be judged on its merits. The basic question involving moving vehicle searches is, whether it is practical to obtain a warrant or not. The court, relying on *Carrol v. U.S.,* held the search reasonable. In the above circumstances, it would not have been practical to obtain a warrant, and the officer was acting with probable cause to believe a crime was being committed (*Commonwealth of Pennsylvania v. LaValle,* 220 A.2d 399 (1966)).

> 5.2.3.1.2. Case Example. Officers observed a number of persons gathering at the estate of a person who had been under investigation for syndicate activities. A number of out of state and rented vehicles were observed on the grounds which led the officers to believe that a

major meeting of persons involved in syndicate operations was taking place. The police officers proceeded to set up a road block check point outside the estate, on a public road. All persons coming out of the estate were stopped, and directed to the police department for a driver's license and identification check. No one was kept for more than a half hour. The stop was used to identify all parties attending the gathering. Subsequently, information gathered by the police was used in prosecution for conspiracy against the defendant, one of those attending the meeting. Was the stop valid?

Yes. The court held that immediate action on the part of the police was absolutely necessary in this case, for if they had taken the time to get a warrant, all of the parties would probably have left the area. "Police activity without a warrant may be more reasonable in the case of an automobile which if not stopped is not likely to be seen again, than in the case of a fixed abode. There are exceptional circumstances which, on balancing the need for effective law enforcement against the right of privacy, it may be contended that a magistrates' warrant for search may be disposed with." *Johnson v. U.S.,* 333 U.S.10 (1948).

"On the basis of the facts presented, it is clear that the procedures utilized by the police officers in and around Apalachin on the day in question did not constitute an invasion of the liberty of any individual which would compel suppression of evidence procured. There was no 'raid.' There was no police brutality, nor coercion, or even pressure of any kind. There was a reasonable act on the part of law enforcement officers whereby they placed themselves into a position to question persons about a subject of legitimate police interest, with the least possible inconvenience to the persons questioned. Indeed, in this case we are not dealing merely with a nebulous concept like "legitimate police interest," but with a reasonable belief that a crime might have been committed which demanded immediate investigation (*U.S. v. Bonanno,* 180 F.Supp. 71 (1960))."

5.2.3.1.3. Case Example. An officer of the Alcoholic Beverage Control Board of Virginia pursued a car driven by a known bootlegger. After a chase, which climaxed in the defendant wrecking the car, the driver was arrested and the car searched. Alcoholic beverages were found. The defendant moved to suppress the evidence taken from the car, as a violation of his fourth amendment rights. His motion was denied and he was convicted of concealing and removing one hundred gallons of distilled spirits with intent to defraud the United States of tax. Should the evidence have been suppressed?

Yes. The officer had no probable cause to believe a crime was being committed, or that contraband was being concealed. He merely saw a known bootlegger driving a car. Although under exigent circumstances, a vehicle may be stopped and searched, there still must be the requisite probable cause; here, none was shown. "A reputation without more is not reasonable or probable cause for search and seizure." If otherwise, a citizen who once violated a law would thereafter forego the protection of the Fourth Amendment.

5.2.3.1.4. Case Example. The defendant was operating his automobile on a Chicago street around noon when he was stopped by two police officers. The officers informed the defendant that his rear license plate was missing and asked to see his driver's license. The license was produced as was a valid registration card showing that he had previously purchased front and rear plates. The officers took the defendant to the rear of the car and showed him that the plate was missing. The officers noted that the defendant behaved in a nervous fashion, moving his hands around and looking about. Because of his behavior, the defendant was asked if he had any weapons. When he said that he did not, the officers searched him. No weapons were found, but as the officers were still suspicious, they decided to take him to the police station to "check him out." Before leaving for the station, one of the officers searched the automobile and found a bag containing a white powder. The powder, later identified as heroin, was the evidence which the defendant moved to suppress in court. The motion was denied. Was the ruling correct?

Yes. The court held that there was not probable cause for arrest, in that the arresting officers testified that aside from his "nervous" behavior, they had no reason to suspect the defendant of having committed anything more serious than driving without a rear license plate. The Court noted that in *People v. Berry*, 161 N.E.2d 315 (1959), the total absence of license plates could reasonably suggest a serious violation of the law for which a search could be made. But distinguishing the present case from *Berry*, the court noted that in *Berry*, the defendants had neither front nor rear plates, nor a city vehicle sticker. In contrast, the case example indicates that the defendant was only missing the rear plate, and that he had valid registration and identification. Further, the Court cited *People v. Zeravich*, 195 N.E.2d 612 (1964), to the effect that when circumstances reasonably indicated that the police may be dealing not with an ordinary traffic violator, but with a criminal, the search of the driver and his vehicle is authorized to insure the safety of the police officers and to prevent an escape of the "might be" criminal. However, here the so-called "nervous" behavior of the defendant did not justify the search of the defendant's automobile, and bring it within the rule.

5.2.3.2. What Constitutes Search of Vehicle. The distinction between a search within the confines of the fourth amendment, and mere "looking," not constituting a search, can be a fine one. The Court has held that a search suggests looking into hidden places, for objects which may be concealed from plain view. (*U.S. v. McKendrick*, 266 F. Supp. 718 (1967).) Accordingly, merely drawing a curtain aside, or looking into a vehicle, or flashing a light into a car, does not constitute a search. Likewise, it is not a search merely to check serial numbers on vehicles in order to more accurately identify the automobile, but this right to check would be limited to those cases, in which there is a legitimate reason to do so.

When a policeman or federal agent, having jurisdiction, has reasonable cause to believe that an automobile has been stolen, or any other legitimate reason to identify the car, he may open a door to check the serial number. He need not obtain a warrant before doing so where the automobile is already otherwise lawfully available, or one under suspicion, to him (*Cotton v. U.S.*, 371 F.2d 385 (1967)).

In addition, it is not a search to look at the outside of a car unless the opportunity to do so is obtained by an unlawful entry upon protected premises. What an officer can see within the car, he may use as evidence. The court has expressed no opinion as to whether the car may be broken into or not, if locked, when the officer has probable cause, as outlined above.

5.2.3.3. Probable Cause. The requisite of a search warrant for a motor vehicle on a public highway *may* be dispensed with. The reason being, there is a higher probability that evidence will disappear which is in a motor vehicle, due to its highly mobile nature, than when it is in a dwelling. *Carrol v. U.S.* liberalized the rule regarding searches of a moving vehicle. It, however, relaxed the requirements for a warrant on the grounds of necessity, though it did not dispense with the need for probable cause.

The concept of probable cause relating to instruments of transportation and their search, must, of necessity, be ill-defined because of the great variety of situations which the law enforcement officer encounters each day. Various definitions have been advanced by the courts, to wit: "A reasonable ground for belief of guilt," "less than evidence which would justify conviction," "more than bare suspicion," and "the facts and circumstances within the officers' knowledge and of which they had reasonably trustworthy information are sufficient in themselves to warrant a man of reasonable caution in the belief that an offense has or is being committed."

The Court in *Brinegar v. U.S.*, 338 U.S. 160 (1949), in speaking of probable cause in relation to the vehicle search said,

> These long prevailing standards seek to safeguard citizens from rash and unreasonable interferences with privacy and from unfounded charges of crime. They also seek to give fair leeway for enforcing the law in the communities' protection. Because many situations which confront officers in the course of executing their duties are more or less ambiguous, room must be allowed for some mistakes on their part. But the mistakes must be those of reasonable men, acting on facts leading sensibly to their conclusions of probability. The rule of probable cause is a practical, nontechnical conception affording the best compromise that has been found for accommodating these often opposing interests. Requiring more would unduly hamper law enforcement. To allow less would be to leave law abiding citizens at the mercy of the officer's whim or caprice. The troublesome line posed by the facts (vehicle search cases) is one between mere suspicion and probable cause. That line necessarily must be drawn by an act of judgment formed in the light of the particular situation and with account taken of all the circumstances.

In *Henry v. U.S.*, 361 U.S.98 (1959), the court stated that common rumor or report, suspicions, or even strong reason to suspect was not adequate to support a warrant for arrest. Even the smell of opium coming from a locked room has been held not to support an arrest and search without a warrant, on the basis that no probable cause has been shown. The problems of probable cause relating to vehicle searches can seem especially perplexing, for the reason that one must of necessity make a rapid decision whether to stop a vehicle or not, and then another instant judgment whether or not there are grounds to search the driver and/or vehicle.

5.2.3.3.1. Case Example. At about 1:45 AM, the defendant stopped at a tavern on a major highway between New York and New Jersey. The defendant parked next to the curb and walked across the street to a tavern which closed at 2:00 AM. Two town police officers who saw the defendant noted that they had not seen him before. One of the officers watched the defendant through a tavern window, while the other searched his car and subsequently found a concealed shotgun. The defendant was arrested as he left the tavern. The weapon was used in evidence to convict the defendant of having a concealed weapon. Was there probable cause for the search?

No. There was no prior contact between the officers and the defendant which would arouse their suspicions. The officers stated that they were merely "suspicious." The car had New Jersey plates and there was nothing unusual in the appearance or demeanor of the defendant. There was no probable cause for the search. It was mere suspicion unsupported by facts. In the absence of a warrant, it was a violation of the defendant's rights. (*State v. Valentin*, 181 A.2d 551 (1962).)

5.2.3.3.2. Case Example. The defendant, while driving his car at night without lights, was stopped by police officers. As the defendant got out of the car to show his registration card to the officers, the dome light in his car disclosed articles which had been reported stolen from another auto in the area. The defendant did not give an adequate explanation of how he acquired the items. Should the articles have been admitted in evidence against the defendant at trial?

Yes. The circumstances called for prompt police action before the occupant of the car had opportunity to escape or to dispense of the articles. The officers accordingly took the suspect and the articles to the precinct station for further identification and investigation. Probable cause for the arrest having been found, it was sufficient to support the search and seizure of the reportedly stolen articles (*Campbell v. U.S.*, 289 F.2d 775 (1961)).

5.2.3.3.3. Case Example. Officers on patrol observed two male parties sitting in a car in "lovers' lane." As the officers approached the car to investigate, the men took flight, squealing tires, and left at a high rate of speed. The officers overtook the pair, ordered them out of the car and ordered them to put their hands on the roof of their vehicle. A bag was spotted in the car which later proved to contain marijuana. The two were convicted of possession. Were the drugs correctly admitted as the product of a "legal search"?

Yes. The search of the car was reasonable. The officers had probable cause to believe that a crime was being committed from the suspicious presence of the two men and their subsequent flight (*People v. Martin*, 293 P.2d 52 (1956)).

In summary, the requirement of a search warrant may be relaxed in the case of exigent circumstances, for example, when a motor vehicle on a public highway is to be searched. In *United States v. Rabinowitz, infra,* the court said,

> A rule of thumb requiring that a search warant always be procured whenever practicable may be appealing from the vantage point of easy administration. But we cannot agree that this requirement should be crystalized into a *sine qua non* to the reasonableness of a search. It is fallacious to judge events retrospectively and thus determine, considering the time element alone, that there was time to procure a search warrant. Whether there was time may well be dependent upon considerations other than the ticking off of minutes or hours. The judgment of the officers as to when to close the trap on a criminal committing a crime in their presence or who they have reasonable cause to believe is committing a felony is not determined solely upon whether there was time to procure a search warrant. Some flexibility will be accorded law officers engaged in daily battle with criminals for whose restraint criminal laws are essential (*U.S. v. Rabinowitz,* 339 U.S. 56 (1950)).

The Court, in *Johnson v. U.S.,* 333 U.S.10, stated three circumstances which may justify a warrantless search:

1. Where a suspect is fleeing or likely to flee.
2. Where the search is of a movable vehicle, rather than a permanent dwelling.
3. Where evidence or contraband is threatened with removal or destruction.

The *mere inconvenience* to the officers coupled with the slight delay necessary to prepare papers and present evidence to a magistrate will never justify the bypassing of the constitutional requirements of a warrant.

See **5.2.2.2.**

5.2.4. CONSENT. Searches and seizures made without a proper warrant are generally regarded as unreasonable and violative of the fourth amendment. However, there are several exceptions to the requirement of obtaining a warrant for the purpose of search, notably, consent (*Judd v. U.S.*, 190 F.2d 649 (1951)).

A number of motives may prompt an individual to consent to a search of his home, car, office, or other area. Among these may be the following:

1. The party is innocent of any wrongdoing and wishes to eliminate any suspicion immediately.
2. The party is guilty, knows that a warrant will be obtained, and sees no reason to delay the inevitable.
3. The suspect attempts to bluff the police into believing his innocence by proclaiming his noninvolvement in any criminal activity, with the invitation to search being given to strengthen his position.

Consent problems generally arise when evidence discovered as the result of a consented-to search is offered for admission against the consenting party. If the consent cannot be proven, the defendant will claim no consent, or consent under duress and the search will fail as being unreasonable.

This section will concentrate on who may give consent, when, and how. In addition, scope of waiver, and the foundational requirements necessary to evidence a valid consent will be discussed.

Waiver contemplates the relinquishment of a known right, given voluntarily, knowingly, and intelligently. Relating to searches and seizures, this means giving up one's constitutional right to be free from unreasonable searches and seizures, as required in the fourth amendment (*Johnson v. Zerbst*, 304 U.S.458 (1938) and *Zap v. U.S.*, 328 U.S.624 (1946)).

Once a valid consent is recognized, all claims by the defendant as to misconduct on the part of the officers conducting the search will be barred. For example, if officers obtain consent to search after arresting the defendant, assuming the consent was valid, the unlawful arrest may not be claimed by the accused as a bar to the introduction of evidence taken in the search.

A waiver may operate as a consent against the person affected by, and agreeing to, the search any time prior to its commencement. A consent given *after* the search has been conducted would appear to be per se unreasonable. In this situation, the prosecution would indeed have a heavy burden of showing a valid, voluntary waiver.

Consent to search may be given a) orally, b) by actions, c) by a written waiver, d) by law.

5.2.4.1. *Oral.* A person may give consent to search by appropriate words. In the following cases, consent was found.

An officer without a warrant makes a request to search and the accused replies, "all right," "all right, go ahead," "go ahead and search, you don't need a warrant." *Hernandez v. State,* 129 S.W. 2d 301 (1938).

"Go ahead and look." *Compton v. State,* 186 S.W.2d 74 (1945).

"They are mine, go ahead and take them." *Clark v. State,* 221 S.W.2d 602 (1949).

Contra, however, in *Stroud v. Commonwealth,* 175 S.W.2d 368 (1943), an officer, armed with a search warrant, came to the defendant's home. He read the warrant for the purpose of searching, and exacting compliance with the court order. In this situation, it was held that the citizen was compelled to submit to the search. By telling the officer "all right, just search," the homeowner was merely showing respect for and obedience to law. A consent was not found, regardless of the validity of the warrant.

If it is shown that mere submission to authority was intended, rather than an unequivocal consent, then consent *will not be inferred.* It should be noted in this regard that a search cannot be justified on the basis of consent where that consent has been given, as in *Stroud, supra,* only after the official conducting the search has asserted that he possesses a warrant (*Bumper v. North Carolina,* 391 U.S.543 (1968)).

5.2.4.2. *Actions.* If an individual, by a free and voluntary act, consents to a search, he will be held to have waived his immunity to an unreasonable search and seizure. For example, a motorist is stopped for erratic driving. He voluntarily opens his trunk to

Figure 4-1

. . . .

(Date)

. . . .

(Location)

I, ... , having been informed of my constitutional right not to have a search made of the premises hereinafter mentioned without a search warrant and of my right to refuse to consent to such a search, hereby authorize . . . .

. . . . , and . . . .

. . . . , Special Agents of the Federal Bureau of Investigation, United States Department of Justice, to conduct a complete search of my premises located at . . . .

. . . . These agents are authorized by me to take from my premises any letters, papers, materials or other property which they may desire.

This written permission is being given by me to the above-named Special Agents voluntarily and without threats or promises of any kind.

(Signed)

Witnesses:

show its contents to the officer. His actions may constitute a waiver (*Ford v. State,* 121 P.2d 320 (1942)). Likewise, where the defendant hands over the keys so the officer may look into the trunk or glove compartment. The giving of the keys will constitute a waiver (*Longo v. State,* 26 So.2d 818 (1946)).

To qualify, the actions of the defendant must be *clear and unequivocal,* and not merely submissions to authority.

5.2.4.3. *Written Waiver.* Figures 4-1, 4-2, and 4-3 present consent forms used by federal and state agencies. Note the simplicity in the form employed by the Federal Bureau of Investigation. The FBI form, after setting forth the date and location of search, makes it clear that the party consenting understands that he has the right to refuse. Permission is then given to specified agents to conduct a complete search of the premises in question, and to remove any articles desired. The waiver concludes with a statement of voluntariness. The state forms follow a similar format.

5.2.4.4. *Waiver by Law.* Consent to search may be implicit in licensing laws in certain instances. For example, an establishment serving alcoholic beverages is generally held to be open to in-

Figure 4-2

VOLUNTARY CONSENT TO SEARCH PROPERTY

I .... having been informed of my constitutional right not to have a search made of (the premises) hereinafter mentioned without a search warrant, and of my right to refuse to consent to such a search, hereby authorize ....

....

.... County of Adams, State of Colorado, acting for the People of the State of Colorado, to conduct a complete search of a building and adjacent premises or buildings located at ....

....

These officers are authorized by me to seize and take from this building and adjacent premises or buildings any letters, papers, materials, or other property which they may desire.

This written permission is being given by me to the above officers voluntarily and without threats or promise of any kind.

Signed ....

Date ....

Time ....

Witnesses:

....

....

....

....

Items Seized

....

Witness

spection for violation of statutes during the course of business. See *Amos v. U.S.,* 255 U.S.313 (1920) and *People v. White,* 65 CAL. RPTR. 923 (1968).

5.2.4.5. Scope of Consent. As can be seen in Figure 4-2, the scope of consent may be defined and limited as to area and purpose by the consenting party. In practice, this is rarely done. One may thus consent to have only a certain area searched, as for example, when one allows officers to search his garage and backyard, and nothing more. The officers must respect the limitations imposed, and may not go beyond the area allowed.

The consenting party may also agree to a search conducted for a limited purpose. An example would be where officers request

Figure 4-3

CONSENT TO SEARCH

I, _____ , know of my constitutional rights to refuse

to allow a police search of any part of my house and/or apartment No. _____

at _____ , Denver, Colorado, and/or

my _____ automobile. However, I have

decided to allow _____ , member(s) of the Denver

Police Department to search every part of my house and/or apartment No. _____

and/or my _____ automobile. They have my permission to take any letters,

papers, materials or other property they want. I have decided to make this consent carefully of

my own free will and without being subject to threats or promises. I know that anything they

discover can and may be used against me in a Court of Law.

Signed _____

Date _____

Witnesses: Time _____ (A.M.) (P. M.)

_____
Officer

_____
Officer

LIST PROPERTY TAKEN

Cross out words that do not apply.

Form 372 (2/71) DPD

I acknowledge that the above property
was taken by said Officers.

permission to look for a fugitive. This would preclude their opening drawers and file cabinets, or other areas which would be unreasonable in the light of their stated purpose.

5.2.4.6. *On Sight Observations.* Although officers may be limited as to areas and purpose, if, while searching pursuant to consent, they should observe contraband, instrumentalities, fruits, or mere evidence of criminal conduct, they may lawfully seize such items.

5.2.4.7. *Showing of Consent.* If consent is to be relied upon by the prosecution as justification for a search, then the prosecution must affirmatively show that such consent was given intelligently, knowingly, and voluntarily by a person who had the right to consent (*State of Montana v. Tomich,* 332 F.2d 987 (1964) and *Channel v. U.S.,* 285 F.2d 217 (1960)). The question of consent is one for the jury to consider, in light of all the facts presented (*Reed v. State,* 79 A.2d 852 (1951)).

In order for a consent to be valid, the prosecution must demonstrate that the waiver was given voluntarily, with no threats, express or implied, or coercion. Voluntariness must be determined by all of the attendant circumstances surrounding the consent. Voluntariness implies doing an act freely, with design or intention, and not by accident, compulsion, or under fear of force. See *Ray v. U.S.,* 84 F.2d 654 (1936) and *Kovach v. U.S.,* 53 F.2d 639 (1931).

> 5.2.4.7.1. Case Example. The defendent was arrested late at night without a warrant and booked on an open charge of investigation (of house-breaking). He was questioned for several hours by various officers, then taken to his home some distance away, handcuffed and in the custody of four officers. The officers claimed that the defendant had consented to a search because, at the jail, he told the officers, "I have nothing to hide, you can go there and see for yourself." Should the evidence found in the search be admitted?

No. The court found no express waiver of the defendant's constitutional rights, but merely a statement which could be interpreted to be false bravado of a small-time criminal. The court further found that under the circumstances, there was not much else the defendant could do but consent, as he had not been charged with a crime, he had been in jail for several hours, and had not been taken before a committing magistrate (*Judd v. U.S.,* 190 F.2d 649 (1951)).

The consent may not be the product of duress, coercion, persuasion, or fraud. Thus, invitation to enter one's home, when extended to armed officers who demand entrance, is usually considered as secured by force (*U.S. v. Marquette,* 271 F.120 (1920)). A similar result occurs if an officer displays his credentials and declares that he has come to make a search. Also considered as "secured by force" is *People v. Chatman,* 54 N.E.2d 631 (1944), where the defendant admitted an officer to his room, when the officer, without a warrant, threatened to break down the door. The ensuing search was held unlawful. See also *U.S. v. Lerner,* 100 F. Supp. 765 (1951).

In summary, if the consent to search is obtained by the use of force, coercion, or show of supreme authority, there is no consent (*Pekar v. U.S.,* 315 F.2d 319 (1963) and also *Weed v. U.S.,* 340 F.2d 827 (1965)).

The consent must be intelligently given. Factors to be considered in assessing this criteria would include the following:

1. Age of the party giving consent.
2. Experience with law enforcement procedures and the criminal justice system.
3. Intelligence.
4. Education.
5. Crimes under investigation.
6. Capacity to understand the meaning of a consent and the ramifications thereto.
7. Condition of the defendant (physical and mental) at the time of consent.
8. Place of consent.
9. Time of consent.
10. To whom given.

5.2.4.8. *Unequivocal Consent.* In order to be considered voluntary, a consent must be unequivocal, specific, and intelligently given (*Judd v. U.S., supra* and *Simmons v. Bomar,* 349 F.2d 365 (1965)).

Silence on the part of one aggrieved by a search may or may not constitute consent. Mere failure to object, in the absence of a clear indication of waiver, will not be held voluntary. Thus, where officers come to the door and advise that they would like to search, and the owner opens the door to admit them, consent may *not* be inferred.

One is not held to have consented to the search of his premises where it is accomplished pursuant to an apparently valid warrant. On the contrary, the legal effect is that consent is on the basis of such a warrant, and permission is construed as an intention to abide by the law and not resist the search under the warrant (*Bull v. Armstrong,* 48 So.2d 467 (1950)).

The statement by a defendant, after having been shown a warrant, "That is fine and dandy, go right ahead," was held merely to signify that he did not intend to resist the officer in the execution of the warrant (*Denton v. State,* 70 P.2d 135, 1937)).

One cannot complain of an unlawful search where he "misplaces his trust," and mistakenly believes that the person he is dealing with is *not* a law enforcement officer.

5.2.4.8.1. Case Example. A federal narcotics agent misrepresented his identity, and stated his willingness to buy narcotics from the defendant. He was subsequently invited into the defendant's home where a narcotics sale was consummated on two occasions. On none of the buys did the agent take, see, or hear anything not contemplated by the defendant as a necessary part of his illegal business. The narcotics were introduced in evidence at the defendant's trial. Should they have been?

Yes. The United States Supreme Court affirmed the conviction, saying that the defendant's business was entitled to no greater protection than if it had been conducted on the street or other public place. The officers' "search and seizure" did not go past the "authority" given by the defendant to enter his home (*Lewis v. U.S.,* 385 U.S.206 (1966)). See also *Hoffa v. U.S., supra.*

5.2.4.9. *Rights Advisement.* In *Gorman v. U.S.,* 380 F.2d 158 (1967), the court stated that it was not necessary to specifically advise an arrestee of his right not to consent to a search, providing the *Miranda* warnings were given with respect to self-incrimination and counsel. If a suspect, in custody, is given his rights, then he may not be heard to complain if he thereafter consents to a search. "It is only in the context of custody, with its inherently coercive effect, and its consequent deprivation of significant freedom of action, that *Miranda* warnings are required." *Government of Virgin Islands v. Berne,* 412 F.2d 1055 (1969).

In the context of rights advisement and waivers intelligently given, the court, in *U.S. v. Blalock,* 255 F. Supp. 268 (1966), stated:

> The requirement of an "intelligent" consent implies that the subject of the search must have been aware of his rights, for an intelligent consent can only embrace waiver of a known right. . . . Certainly one cannot intelligently surrender that which he does not know he has. The fourth amendment requires no less knowing a waiver then do the fifth and sixth amendments. The requirement of knowledge in each serves the same purpose, i.e. to prevent the possibility that the ignorant may surrender their rights more readily than the shrewd. . . . To require law enforcement officers to advise the subject under investigation of their right to insist on a search warrant would impose no great burden, nor would it unduly or unreasonably impede criminal investigations.

See also *People v. Paulin,* 305 N.Y.S.2d 607 (1968), where it was held that if the consent to seizure of items was an integral part of an illegally obtained statement from the defendant, then such seizure would not be justified on the grounds of consent.

5.2.4.10. *Countermand of Consent.* There is a split of authority as to whether a search, once consented to, may subsequently be countermanded and stopped. One view holds that it may not be, unless the search goes beyond that which was consented to. The other view holds that the search waiver may be withdrawn at any time. See *State v. Lett,* 178 N.E.2d 96 (1961) and *People v. Martinez,* 65 CAL. RPTR. 920 (1968).

5.2.4.11. *Who May Consent.* It is axiomatic that a party must have the ability to waive constitutional rights before a valid consent to search can be effected. What this means is that one cannot waive the rights of another. There is a limited class of persons who may waive rights as to searches without warrants. Generally it is held that an *owner* or *one in possession* may consent to a search. A person in possession can be a tenant, co-tenant, or one having immediate custody and control over the area, coupled with a real or apparent authority to consent.

5.2.4.12. *Waiver by Another.* Immunity from unreasonable

searches and seizures can be waived only by the person whose rights are affected. In certain instances, one may have the requisite authority or interest to waive another's rights. However, this authority may not be inferred or presumed in the absence of clear grounds to assume such authority.

For example, in a few cases, consent may be properly given by members of one's family, by lessors, managers, and superintendents, and even custodians. This also applies to store owners, common carriers, and employees.

5.2.4.13. Family. Only where an equal right of control and possession exists may one family member consent to the search of an area used by another member of the family.

5.2.4.14. *Wife Consenting for Husband.* A wife may not waive the right to be free from unreasonable searches for her husband. The right to demand a warrant is a personal one. *Simmons v. State,* 229 P.2d 615 (1951). However, a wife may, in the husband's absence, allow officers to search areas used jointly by husband and wife. This would merely be an assertion of the wife's *own rights* to authorize entry into the premises where she lives and has coequal control (*U.S. v. Thompson,* 421 F.2d 373 (1970)).

Said the court in *Commonwealth ex rel. Cabey v. Rundle,* 248 A.2d 197 (1968), the question "becomes one of invasion of one's expected privacy. In the case of husband-wife consent for the absent mate, did the absent parties maintain and expect exclusive or joint control of the area in question? What is the interest the consenting mate has in the premises? If the husband and wife have the same right of access and use to the premises, then either may consent to a search." See also *Stein v. U.S.* 166 F.2d 851 (1948).

"When the husband is absent from the home, it is the wife who controls the premises, the ordinary household property, the family automobile, and with her husband's tacit consent determines who shall and who shall not enter the house on business or pleasure and what property they may take away with them. . . . When the usual relation exists between a husband and wife . . . and the property seized is a kind over which the wife normally exercises as much control as the husband, it is reasonable to conclude that she is in a position to consent to a search and seizure of property in their home (*People v. Carter,* 312 P.2d 665 (1957)).

5.2.4.15. *Husband Consent for Wife.* A husband likewise may not waive the constitutional rights of his wife. It should be noted that if both husband and wife are present and one consents to a search, while the other refuses, a warrant must be obtained. The law of joint tenancy which applies to property interest is limited in the case of a protesting cotenant (spouse) in that one tenant may not do any act to prejudice the interest of the other.

5.2.4.16. *Parent for Child.* A parent may consent to a search of a child's room, provided that the parent is able to show a proprietary interest in the area searched. Where no landlord-tenant situation exists, and the child is merely living in the home, or storing articles there, the parents may validly consent to a search (*Rees v. Peyton,* 225 F. Supp. 507 (1964)).

However, in *Reeves v. Warden, Md. Penitentiary,* 346 F.2d 915 (1965), the court held that a mother's consent to the search of a room used by her son, the defendant, and a dresser therein was invalid. This for the reason that here the son had almost exclusive use of the room, and hence would expect a measure of privacy in its use. Thus, he would be afforded the protection afforded by the fourth amendment.

5.2.4.17. *Child for Parent.* A child generally may not consent to a search of his parents' home. Consent must be based on ownership or interest in the area to be searched. Unless the child is legally able to speak for the parents, he may not waive parental constitutional rights (*People v. Jennings,* 298 P.2d 56 (1956)).

5.2.4.18. *Child for Child.* One member of a family may not consent to a search for another member of the family. Thus, where one brother admitted police and firemen into the family home for the purpose of search to gather evidence against another brother, it was held that the defendant's rights were violated, because the defendant was not afforded his constitutional right to demand a search warrant (*People v. Boyle,* 242 N.Y.S.2d 90 (1963)).

5.2.4.19. *Roomer.* A roomer may not consent to a search of a house in which he lives, but may waive warrant requirements as to areas to which he has the right to use and control.

The reverse situation also applies—the owner of a home may not consent to the search of a room rented by a roomer.

5.2.4.20. *Cotenants.* As noted, cotenants may consent to a search of shared areas, as long as the other cotenant (s) do not object at the time of search. If the cotenant is present, he has the right to demand a warrant.

5.2.4.21. *Employees.* An employer may not consent to the search of an area reserved exclusively for an employee. Such was the case in *U.S. v. Blok, supra,* where a consented-to search of the defendant's desk (by employer) was held violative of the fourth amendment.

An employee may not consent to a search of an employer's premises unless he has the real or apparent authority to give such consent (*People v. Carswell,* 308 P.2d 852 (1957).

5.2.4.22. *Partners.* One partner may consent to a search of property or areas used in connection with the partnership, which each partner has a coequal right of control (*U.S. v. Seferas,* 210 F.2d 69 (1954).

5.2.4.23. *Lessor-Lessee.* A landlord may not consent to the search of areas used exclusively by the tenant or lessee. This, *even though* the lease may state that the premises may be inspected for damage, waste, nuisance, and to make repairs. See *Chapman v. U.S.,* 365 U.S.610 (1961).

So in *Stoner v. California, supra,* the court refused to permit an otherwise lawful search of a hotel room to rest upon the consent of the hotel proprietor. The guest had a right to assert fourth amendment interests in the room. See subsection **5.3.**

5.2.4.24. *Custodian of Building.* If a caretaker or custodian lives in a house or building, and further has unqualified access to certain parts of the property, it may be reasonable for him to consent to a search of those areas under his control. *State v. Cook,* 411 P.2d 78 (1966).

5.2.4.25. *Property in Possession of Another.* A person who is in lawful possession of property which has been entrusted to him by the owner, but which property has since been abandoned, may consent to its search and seizure. So also, a lessor may allow a search of a room or premises of which the tenant has left with no apparent intention of returning. See *Abel v. U.S., supra.*

If the owner of a car lends the vehicle to another person, and further (1) attaches no restrictions as to use, (2) does not claim exclusive use or control of certain parts of the car (i.e. trunk or glove compartment, evidenced by withholding the keys thereto), and (3) the borrower does not exceed his authority, the user may consent to a search of the car when in his control. This consent will be effective against the owner (*U.S. v. Eldridge,* 302 F.2d 463 (1962)).

If an individual leaves a briefcase or suitcase, with keys, to the care of another for safekeeping, the bailee may consent to its search, where the search is reasonable under the circumstances. Thus, in *Sartain v. U.S.,* 303 F.2d 859 (1962), a friend in whose custody a case was left, which contained heroin, was effectively able to consent to its search after the arrest of the bailor (owner). *Contra,* in *Holzhey v. U.S.,* 223 F.2d 823 (1955), the defendant's daughter and son-in-law consented to a search of their premises wherein was stored a locked cabinet belonging to and used by the defendant. The rationale for suppressing the evidence taken was that this cabinet was (1) locked, which showed an expectation of privacy by its user, (2) was for the exclusive use of the defendant, and (3) was in a separate part of the house, allegedly used and rented by the defendant.

5.2.5. HEALTH AND SAFETY INSPECTIONS. Limited inspections of dwellings and buildings may be conducted pursuant to health and safety inspections, when in the public interest.

The leading case on the validity of searches conducted under the guise of health and safety statutes is *Camara v. Municipal Court of San Francisco,* 387 U.S.523 (1967).

The fact situation, taken from *Camara* follows:

> On November 6, an inspector from the Division of Housing Inspection, San Francisco, entered an apartment building to make a routine annual inspection for possible violations of the city's housing code. The building manager informed the inspector that the defendant, lessee of the ground floor, was using the rear of his area as a personal residence. Claiming that the building occupancy permit did

not allow residential use of the ground floor, the inspector confronted the defendant and demanded that he permit an inspection of the premises. The defendant refused because the inspector lacked a search warrant.

The inspector returned twice without a warrant, the defendant refusing each time to allow an inspection. The defendant was informed that he was required by law to permit an inspection under section 501 of the housing code, which stated: "Right to enter building. Authorized employees of the City department or City agencies, so far as may be necessary for the performance of their duties, shall, upon presentation of proper credentials, have the right to enter, at reasonable times any building, structure, or premises in the City to perform any duty imposed upon them by the Municipal Code."

The defendant nevertheless refused the inspectors access to his apartment without a search warrant. Thereafter a complaint was filed charging him with refusal to permit a lawful inspection, in violation of Section 507 of the code. The defendant was subsequently arrested and released on bail. He sought a Writ of Prohibition (see Chap. 9) to enjoin criminal proceedings against him.

The question presented to the court was, may a warrantless search be justified because it is in the public interest to inspect buildings. Basically, when would the search be reasonable or unreasonable, pursuant to the fourth amendment?

The court stated that the fourth amendment's purpose was to safeguard privacy and security of the individual against arbitrary intrusions by the government. This safeguard applies to all government agents—police and health inspectors alike. If a health inspector, under the guise of public interest, is permitted to inspect any building without a warrant, what is to stop the abuse of that privilege?

In the case example cited, the occupant had no way of knowing if, in fact, (1) the code required the proposed action of the inspector, (2) the lawful limits of the inspection power, or, (3) whether the inspector was acting under proper authority. In effect, the ordinance allowed the inspector alone to determine reasonableness in the field. The question is not whether searches may be made in any case, but may they be made without a warrant, in the absence of exigent or emergency circumstances. The court held that, since no emergency circumstances were shown, there was no reason why a warrant could not have been obtained: "if a public interest justifies the intrusion contemplated, then there is probable cause to issue a suitably restricted search warrant." Hence, the proposed warrantless search was an intrusion, and violative of the fourth amendment rights of the defendant.

In considering reasonableness standards, necessary to procure a limited warrant, the court stated that the criteria would not be as stringent as for a general search warrant. Thus, the passage of time between inspections, the nature of the building, and the condition of the entire area could all be taken into account in showing cause for a warrant.

In the present case, there were no emergency circumstances shown, such as a communicable disease, or threat of fire. The inspector's repeated return over a span of weeks evinced this fact. The defendant rightfully refused them admittance, and the Writ of Prohibition was subsequently granted, thereby enjoining the City of San Francisco from prosecuting the defendant for violation of the city code in not permitting the inspectors to conduct their search.

In summary, then, limited inspections for health and safety purposes may be conducted without a warrant only when prompted by emergency conditions. If no overwhelming public necessity is shown, the occupant is protected under the fourth amendment against any search, in the absence of a warrant. If the agents attempt to obtain a warrant, they must show probable cause, evidencing a public interest in the search. It should be noted that *Camara* specifically overruled *Frank v. Maryland*, 359 U.S.360 (1959).

5.3. Constitutionally Protected Areas

Under the fourth amendment, persons are guaranteed freedom from unreasonable government intrusion into their houses, papers, persons, and effects, as specified in the amendment. What the fourth amendment seeks to protect is the security a man relies on when he places himself or his property in a constitutionally protected area, be they his home, office, hotel room, automobile or elsewhere. Within specified areas, he is protected from unwarranted governmental intrusion (*Hoffa v. U.S.*, 385 U.S.293 (1966)). The protection of the fourth amendment extends to all, whether they be innocent or guilty, accused of a crime, aliens, deportees, or visitors to this country.

The factors of paramount importance in considering fourth amendment claims are the following: a) the nature of the individual's interest in the premises and b) the extent of claim of privacy of the premises searched (*U.S. v. Minker,* 312 F.2d 632 (1962)). Hence, a public utility such as a motor carrier is not to be accorded the same constitutional guarantee to privacy as an ordinary citizen would be in his private business. Likewise, corridors and yards about a motel are shared or *public* property and therefore are not protected. Hence, before a party can complain that his constitutional rights have been violated by an unreasonable search or seizure, it must be shown that the area searched was one that is constitutionally protected (*U.S. ex rel. Fletcher v. Wainwright,* 269 F. Supp. 224, 276 (1967)).

The fourth amendment protects that which an individual seeks to preserve as private (*Coates v. U.S.,* 413 F.2d 371 (1969)). Thus, inspection of premises open to the general public are not illegal searches.

The question which must be determined is, what and who are the unreasonable places and persons which the fourth amendment protects from searches?

5.3.1. PERSONS. The protection of the amendment against unreasonable searches and seizures extends to all equally, including those justly suspected of or accused of a crime, as well as innocent persons. The constitutional protection is available to all citizens, at all times, in all places, civilian or military, within the jurisdiction of the United States. However, the protection of the amendment does not extend to United States citizens in foreign countries. The reasonable search and seizure clause protects people, not places; the right of persons to be secure is thus a personal right.

5.3.1.1. *Aliens.* Aliens within the United States are entitled to the protection of the Constitution (*Schenck ex rel. Chow Fook Hong v. Ward,* 24 F. Supp. 776 (1938)).

5.3.1.2. *Arrested Persons.* A person validly arrested may be searched as incident to the arrest. However, the search must be strictly limited to the area within the control of the arrested party. The search must meet the test of reasonableness. *U.S. v. Blassick,* 422 F.2d 652 (1970).

5.3.1.3. *Border Searches.* Border searches are outside of the protection of the fourth amendment, and a search which would be unreasonable if conducted by police in an ordinary case may be reasonable when conducted by customs officials in lawful pursuit of unlawful imports, but only when incident to a border search. *John Bacall Imports, Ltd. v. U.S.,* 287 F. Supp. 916 1968.

5.3.1.4. *Convicts.* The court has held that the search of one, after sentence and under plea of guilty, while in jail awaiting transportation to the penitentiary, was not illegal. *Cline v. U.S.,* 116 F.2d 275 (1940).

5.3.1.5. *Corporations.* A corporation is not protected by immunity against self-incrimination which is guaranteed by the fifth amendment, but is entitled to protection against unreasonable searches and seizures of its papers under the fourth amendment. With regard to records, a corporation has a right to invoke the fourth amendment to protect itself from a *subpoena duces tecum* which would constitute an unreasonable search. In the absence of a showing that a summons calling for the production of books and records is overly broad, indefinite, or without basis for probable cause, the summons does not per se violate the protection of the amendment.

5.3.1.6. *Guests.* As the protections of the amendment are said to be personal in right, a guest, lessee, roomer, etc. enjoys equal personal protection from unreasonable searches and seizures, as does the homeowner.

5.3.1.7. *Minors.* Minors should be accorded the same constitutional rights against unreasonable searches and seizures as adults. However, the problem usually presented is that either the property or area in question does not belong, or is not under the exclusive control of the minor. For example, a school locker. In *People v. Overton,* 229 N.E.2d 596 (1967), the court held that the principal of a school rightfully consented to let detectives search a student's locker, even with an invalid warrant. It was held that the school had a valid interest in the student and discipline.

Under the fourth amendment, searches involving intrusions beyond the body's surface, on the mere chance that desired evidence might be obtained, are forbidden (i.e. the officer saw the accused swallow capsules believed to contain heroin). In the absence of a *clear indication* that such evidence will be found, officers are required to suffer the risk that such evidence may disappear until a warrant may be obtained. The amendment prohibits compelled intrusions into the body for blood sample to be analyzed for alcoholic content, if the intrusions are not justified by the circumstances or are made in an improper manner (*Schmerber v. California,* 384 U.S.757 (1966)).

Intrusions into the body to retrieve evidence have been held valid in the following examples:

> A defendant was apprehended as he entered the United States at Juarez International Bridge, by customs agents, who were informed that it was the defendant's purpose to import heroin from Mexico to the United States. The defendant was seen swallowing an envelope. The agents, after subduing and arresting the defendant, administered to him an emetic, which resulted in the vomiting of the heroin contained in the envelope which was seized and held as evidence against him. The search was held not to be a violation of the defendant's rights under the fourth amendment (*Barrera v. U.S.,* 276 F.2d 654 (1960)).
>
> A defendant was subjected to a fluoroscopic examination, to which no objection was made on his part. The exam disclosed a foreign object in the defendant's stomach. The administering by narcotics agents of an emetic did not constitute an unreasonable search (*King v. U.S.,* 258 F.2d 754 (1958)).

The search of a person must be reasonable to survive; thus, a physical examination of the defendant ordered to report for induction into the armed forces, which results in the discovery that he had taken a drug to cause abnormal physical conditions designed to cause rejection for service duty, was not an "unlawful search and seizure." The use of the evidence so obtained was not violative of either the fourth or fifth amendment (*Bratcher v. U.S.,* 149 F.2d 742 (1945)).

Similarly, examination of the defendant's hands under ultraviolet light to determine if he had touched stolen bank bags which had been dusted with flourescent powder was not a "search" within the meaning of the fourth amendment. The examination and accompanying activities did not violate the defendant's rights (*U.S. v. Richardson*, 388 F.2d 842 (1968).

Penis scraping revealing menstrual blood acquired from the rape victim constituted a permissible search of the person incident to a lawful arrest. It involved no intrusion of the body surface nor did it violate the prisoner's rights, in view of the threat of imminent destruction of evidence (*Brent v. White*, 398 F.2d 503 (1968)).

5.3.1.8. *Parolees and Probationers.* Parolees and probationers are covered by the fourth amendment. Accordingly, the constitutional prohibition against unreasonable searches and seizures would apply to a probationer and to his garage located near his home. Note that his status as a probationer would be a fact to be considered in determining whether or not the search of the garage, person, or premises was reasonable (*Martin v. U.S.*, 183 F.2d 436 (1950)). Also, the personal effects of a parole violator that have been turned over to officers by a third person after the incarceration of the violator does not strike an illegality if such articles are checked, even when they result in discovery of crimes which the parole violator committed (*Mason v. Cranor*, 227 F.2d 557, 1955)). See *People v. Santos*, 298 N.Y.S.2d 526 (1969) on degree of reasonableness required for search.

5.3.2. PLACES OF HABITATION. Constitutional guarantees apply to places of habitation. Included under this heading would be dwellings, homes, houses, barns, residences, apartments, rooming houses, hotels, boarding houses, and tourist camps. Title to the premises in question is not relevant to application of the right where the party claiming the right has a superior property or possessory interest against all the world (except possibly the true owner). For example, when a person is trespassing, his right to be protected against unreasonable searches and seizures must not be violated, notwithstanding he is trespassing.

Also, if a man owns more than one residence, the amendment protects all of his property all the time. Basically, that which a man considers his home will be afforded the constitutional protection even though he may spend most of his time at another location. A garage is also within the protected class.

5.3.2.1. *Apartment.* Apartment dwellers are afforded the full protection of the amendment. However, the occupants, in order to assert their constitutional rights, must either show a possessory or proprietary interest, or be aggrieved to contest a search. Thus, an officer, unlocking a door to another's apartment, entering it, searching it, and seizing personal property found therein, without a search warrant or permission, violates the fourth amendment, unless his conduct is within some exception, for example, search and seizure incident to a lawful arrest *(Jeffers v. U.S.,* 187 F.2d 498 342 U.S.48 (1951)). However, in *U.S. v. St. Clair,* 240 F. Supp. 338 (1965), the court held that actions of federal agents in gaining entrance to a common hallway, on which the defendant's apartment opened, and knocking on the defendant's door, did not violate the defendant's constitutional right to security against unlawful search and seizure.

5.3.2.2. *Barns.* Barns are considered as part of the curtilage and as such are considered within the protection of the fourth amendment, even though the structure may be several hundred feet from the house, and separated from the living quarters by fences, driveways, etc.

5.3.2.3. *Barber Shop.* Officers may enter a barber shop open to the public, observe possible criminal activity, and make any necessary arrests upon observance of such activity, all without a warrant. The fact that the area is open to the public allows a search without a warrant *(Smith v. U.S.,* 105 F.2d 778 (1939)).

5.3.2.4. *Buildings Outside Curtilage.* The protections afforded by the fourth amendment do not extend to open fields, or to unoccupied buildings, not within the curtilage, unless the owner reasonably expects that they will be considered as private, and acts accordingly.

5.3.2.5. *Buildings Within Curtilage.* Empty buildings within the curtilage are entitled to the privacy of the house which is protected by the fourth amendment. The courts have extended the meaning of the word "house" to include the grounds and buildings immediately surrounding a dwelling, whether enclosed or not (curtilage) (*Rosencranz v. U.S.,* 356 F.2d 310 (1966)). Essentially, the protection extends to all structures used by the owner in connection with his home or place of business. Thus, structures such as smokehouses (*U.S. v. Mullin,* 329 F.2d 295 (1964), garages, barns, chicken houses, sheds, and similar areas are protected (*Care v. U.S.,* 351 U.S. 932 (1956)).

In determining if a particular building falls into the protected class, factors to consider are as follows: a) the nature and extent of the homeowner's interest, b) the privacy of the areas into which the officers intend to go, c) the proximity of the building to the dwelling, and d) if it is, in substance, a part of the business of the occupants.

5.3.2.6. *Businesses and Offices.* Freedom from unreasonable searches and seizures extends to one's place of business as well as to his home (*U.S. ex rel. DeForte v. Mancusi,* 379 F.2d 897 (1967)). The protection of the amendment extends generally to commercial premises when they are not open to the public. Businessmen, like occupants of residence, have the constitutional right to go about their business, free from governmental interference in the context of the amendment. The court has held that in the case of public ordinances relating to inspections, the right is placed in jeodardy if the decision to enter and inspect for violation of regulatory laws can be made and enforced by an inspector in the field without official authority, as evidenced by a warrant (*See v. City of Seattle,* 387 U.S.541 (1967)). See also *Camara, supra.* It has been held that the owner of a warehouse could not be prosecuted for his insistence that a fire inspector obtain a warrant before entering a locked area. Also, it was held that police officers, not responding to an emergency situation in searching an employee's desk, must, in the absence of a search warrant, have compelling reasons to justify the search (*U.S. v. Blok,* 188 F.2d 1019 (1951)).

5.3.2.7. *Bus Station Lockers.* Where the renter of a public locker places items in that locker with the expectation of privacy, it has been held that an intrusion and removal of contents during the rental period must be in compliance with the fourth amendment standards. The fact that a locker company employee's inspection of a rental locker was constitutionally unimpeachable, did not relieve the government agents of the necessity of complying with the requirements of the amendment (*U.S. v. Small,* 297 F. Supp. 582 (1969)).

5.3.2.8. *Commercial Property Open to Public.* Inspection of property generally open to the public has been held not violative of the fourth amendment (*Founding Church v. U.S.,* 409 F.2d 1146 (1969)). Also, the search of an open-air nursery was not held unreasonable in the absence of a warrant. However, the mere fact that the premises was located in a commercial building would not justify an otherwise unreasonable search (*U.S. v. Rosenberg,* 416 F.2d 680 (1969)).

5.3.2.9. *Common Areas.* Common corridors, public hallways, landings and stairwells, or apartment buildings are not part of the tenant's home for the purpose of applying fourth amendment standards, and hence no warrant is necessary for search.

5.3.2.10. *Curtilage.* The word "house" has been enlarged by the courts to include the "curtilage" or ground and buildings immediately surrounding a dwelling. Protection of the amendment thus extends to adjacent buildings such as garages, smokehouses, chicken houses, and similar property. See also **5.3.2.5.**

5.3.2.11. *Dry Cleaning Shop.* Officers may enter a dry cleaning shop, as any other public place, for the purpose of conducting a search of the area. In addition, they may, with a showing of reasonable necessity, obtain and inspect items left at the cleaners by patrons. The situations are analogous to the case where officers obtain evidence from a pawnbroker voluntarily. In both the above situations, the bailor of the property will not have a standing to object (*Clarke v. State,* 402 S.W.2d 863 (1966)).

5.3.2.12. *Dwellings.* The home is accorded the full range of fourth amendment protections. Any agent of the government, acting under color of law, must have some valid basis in law for the intrusion. A much stricter standard of reasonableness under the amendment is required when there is an intrusion of privacy into the home in the absence of a warrant. The term "house," as used in the amendment, is not restricted to homes only, but extends to any place where a man lives and calls "home," such as trailers and farms.

5.3.2.13. *Evidence Discovered in Plain View.* It has been held that once officers are lawfully on one's premises, the officers are not to be precluded from observing items in plain sight without a warrant. Such items, if found to be contraband, would be admissible without a search warrant. Under the "open-view doctrine," objects falling in plain view of an officer who has the right to be in a position to have plain view, regardless of whether day or night, are subject to seizure and may be introduced into evidence. In the following examples, the courts have held the doctrine to apply:

1. Credit cards, which were plainly visible in a car which was in the lawful custody of the police, were not obtained by illegal search, and were thus admissible in a prosecution for forgery of a credit card.

2. A policeman saw a car operated at an excessive speed. When the officer stopped the vehicle and the occupant of the automobile reached for the registration card, the officer saw a weapon.

3. Officers, lawfully on the premises for the purpose of serving a valid search warrant, listing cigarettes as the objects of the warrant, were not precluded from seizing, without a warrant, concrete particles and coins which they found on the ground near the house, which they reasonably believed to be connected with a burglary they were investigating.

4. Police officers observed a sawed-off shotgun partially hidden under the driver's seat of a truck after the driver was lawfully arrested, but before any search was made of the truck.

The open-view doctrine does not attach, however, where the officer obtains his view through illegal means, for example, by an unlawful entry. Hence, the government cannot be heard to say that the doctrine applies where the observing officer has physically invaded a constitutionally protected area in order to secure his view (*Stamps v. State,* 428 P.2d 187 (1967)).

5.3.2.14. *Fire Escape.* Fire escapes, which are shared by occupants of buildings, may be open to plain view, and hence, no warrant would be necessary for their inspection. The same would apply, if the officer ascended the fire escape for a better view of an apartment. However, if the fire escape would be in the sole control of one dwelling, then it is doubtful that the officer could lawfully ascend it in order to put himself in a position to view certain actions.

5.3.2.15. *Garage.* If the garage can be considered within the curtilage, then it is protected.

A garage which was on the premises but not physically connected with the defendant's dwelling house proper was considered a part of the defendant's house in which he was secure against unreasonable searches and seizures (*State v. Brochu,* 237 A.2d 418 (1967)).

A detached family garage on the same lot as the family residence is entitled to the same degree of constitutional protection of privacy of contents as the residence (*People v. Hobbs,* 79 CAL. RPTR., 281 (1969)).

A garage located close to the rear of a residence, fifty to seventy-five feet from the street and partially surrounded by a fence which enclosed both the garage and house on three sides, fell within the dwelling house concept (*Commw. v. Murphy,* 233 N.E.2d 5 (1968)).

5.3.2.16. *Garbage and Trash.* Garbage cans without lids, which were located to the rear of a back porch area in the defendant's open back yard in which marijuana was found, were not protected against search. Generally, garbage and trash cans located outside the home, within plain view of the officers, do not require warrants, for their inspection.

5.3.2.17. *Home as Business.* When a home is converted into a commercial center to which outsiders are invited, for the purpose of transacting unlawful business, that business is entitled to no greater sanctity than if it were carried on in a store, garage, automobile, or on the street. Thus, a government agent, in the same manner as a private person, may accept an invitation to do business and may enter upon the premises for the very purposes contemplated by the occupant. *Lewis v. U.S.,* 385 U.S.206, 1966.

5.3.2.18. *Hospitals.* A person in a hospital has a right to expect some degree of privacy in his room, and as such, is afforded the protection of the fourth amendment. Hence, clothes obtained by a deputy sheriff, with the permission of a nurse on duty, from a hospital room in which the defendant was under sedation, the day after reporting-in with a bullet wound, were the subject of an unreasonable search and seizure and were inadmissible against the defendant, where no warrant had been obtained. *Morris v. Commw.,* 157 S.E.2d 191, 1967.

5.3.2.19. *Hotel and Motel Rooms.* The occupant of a hotel or motel room is entitled to the full protection of the fourth amendment. Thus, the court held that the right to privacy must be accorded with equal vigor both to transient hotel guests and to occupants of private permanent dwellings, and the transiency of the defendant's stay in the hotel room will not justify a search thereof without a warrant (*Eng Fung Jem v. U.S.,* 281 F. 2d 803 (1960)).

5.3.2.20. *Leased and Rented Premises.* The occupier of a leased or rented premises has the same rights under the fourth amendment as does the homeowner. The rights extend to all areas under the lessee's immediate and exclusive control. Thus such areas as common hallways, corridors, fire escapes, and the like would not be subject to the protection.

5.3.2.21. *Lockers.* For rented lockers, see **5.3.2.7.** In the case of school lockers, there is a divergence of opinion as to the right of search. One view is that if a student places items within a locker, with a reasonable expectation of privacy, then protection should be afforded under the fourth amendment. The other view holds that, in the case of students, the school officials stand in the position of *in loco parentis,* and share in matters of school discipline, a parental right to search a student's locker, where the items suspected of being contained in such locker may prove harmful to the student or others. *In Re Donaldson,* 75 CAL. RPTR. 220 (1969)).

5.3.2.22. *Offices.* One has standing to object to an unreasonable search of his office as well as his home (*Mancusi v. De Forte,* 392 U.S. 364 (1968)). See **5.3.2.6.**

5.3.2.23. Open Areas Adjacent to House, Open Lands or Fields.
Searches of open lands or fields, whether part of the curtilage or
not, have been held not to be within the protection of the fourth
amendment. Even the trespassing of government agents upon
open lands will not invalidate the search of such lands (*Mc-
Donald v. U.S.,* 383 F.2d 105 (1967)). Thus, a search of the
grounds of a farm which resulted in finding a cardboard box
bearing the name and address of a burglarized paint store was
on "open-field" search and was not unreasonable (*Jones v. State,*
441 S.W.2d 458 (1969)).

5.3.2.24. Prisons. Searches of cells may be conducted by officials
without warrants, provided the searches are not conducted for
the purpose of harassing or humiliating the inmates, or conducted in a cruel and unusual manner. The amendment does not
prohibit a custodian from searching a cell, even in the absence
of probable cause (*Moore v. People,* 467 P.2d 50 (1970)). Furthermore, the court has held that guards may be searched to insure prison security (*State v. Paruszewski,* 466 P.2d 787 (1970)).

5.3.2.25. Private Office as Home. Both private offices and homes
are protected by the fourth amendment. Hence, a private office
which is located within one's home would fall within the pur-
view of the amendment.

5.3.2.26. Public Corridor. Inspection of premises open to the general public do not constitute illegal searches. Accordingly, police
officers, in the performance of their duties may, without a warrant, enter common hallways of an apartment building or other
such area, without express permission to do so.

5.3.2.27. Public Premises. Areas open to the public may be inspected without a warrant, as long as the inspection or search is
during normal business hours, or at a time when the public is
free to move in the particular area. If the area is a park, street,
playground, etc., there would be no restrictions with respect to
right of search at any time. The rationale is that no one has
standing to object to a search of a public area, as no one has the
requisite possessory or proprietary interest in the area.

5.3.2.28. Public Streets. As noted in subsection **5.3.2.27.** one need not obtain a warrant to search a public street. However, this is not to say that one walking on the street would not come within the constitutionally protected class.

5.3.2.29. *Public Toilets.* A person who enters an enclosed stall in a public toilet and closes the door behind him is entitled at least to the modicum of privacy that the stall is designed to afford—certainly to the extent that he will not be joined by uninvited guests or spied upon by probing eyes. He may rely upon the protection of the fourth amendment (*Brown v. State*, 238 A.2d 147 (1968)). However, this is not to say that the police are not entitled to institute surveillance of public toilet stalls, even though they lack probable cause to believe that the person they may catch is engaged in the commission of a crime. The usual case arises in the investigation of homosexual activities. If the police have reasonable cause to believe that the stalls are being used in the commission of a crime, then evidence so obtained by a clandestine operation, would not be inadmissible merely because the occupant was not known prior to arrest (*Mitchell v. State*, 170 S.E.2d 765 (1969)).

5.3.2.30. *Rest Rooms.* The search of a rest room which is public in its accessibility to persons, would not fall within the protected class of the fourth amendment. However, if the rest room is designated as private, for example, in a restricted employee area of a store, the amendment would apply.

5.3.2.31. *School Dormitory.* Students who live in dormitories on a campus for which the student pays rent to the school, may *waive* objection to any reasonable searches conducted pursuant to reasonable and necessary regulations (*Moore v. Student Affairs Committee of Troy State University*, 284 F. Supp. 725 (1968)). The validity of the regulation authorizing the search of the room is determined by the test of reasonableness in the exercise of a college's supervisory duties. The court, in *Moore* stated that the constitutional boundary line between the right of school authorities to search rooms and the right of students to privacy must be based on a reasonable belief on the part of college authorities that a student is using the dorm room for purposes which are illegal, or which would otherwise seriously interfere with campus discipline.

College students who reside in dorms have a special relationship with the college involved, and insofar as the fourth amendment affects that relationship, it does not depend on either general theory of rights of privacy or on traditional property concepts *(Moore, supra)*.

5.3.2.32. *Service Stations*. If a service station is open to the public, public areas thereon are subject to search without warrant. If, for example, a fugitive came upon service station property, and secreted contraband, police would have the right, without a warrant, to make a general search of the public areas. However, the fugitive would still retain fourth amendment rights as to his person (possibly abrogated by search-incident-to-arrest rule). In addition, the owner of the station would usually not have standing to object to articles seized in public areas, unless those articles were to be used against him for some purpose *(People v. Lerch,* 221 N.E.2d 664 (1966)).

5.3.2.33. *Social Club*. The fact that one is at a private social club will not deprive him of his constitutional right to be free of unreasonable searches and seizures. *(People v. Kramer,* 239 N.Y.S. 2d 303 (1963)).

5.3.2.34. *Storage Rooms*. When one places articles in a storage room, with the expectation of privacy, the fourth amendment will extend its protection to such areas, provided the expectation of privacy is reasonable, and further provided that the area he places items in is designated for his use and under his control.

5.3.2.35. *Telephone Booths*. A person in a telephone booth, who enters the booth expecting that his conversation will be private, and not broadcast to the world, or listened to, may rely on the protection of the fourth amendment. What is important is that the person's expectation of privacy is reasonably made *(Katz v. U.S.,* 389 U.S.347 (1967)). A *telephone conversation* is also within the protection of the amendment *(Fountain v. U.S.,* 384 F.2d 624 (1967)).

5.3.2.36. *Tenant of Building.* See subsection **5.3.2.20.**

5.3.2.37. *Trailer Home.* A trailer home would fall within the protection of the fourth amendment, as a dwelling. However, if the trailer was stopped on a highway, while mobile, one would have to consider the circumstances in light of our discussion relating to automobile searches, probable cause, and warrant requirements. If an officer stopped the trailer, and had reasonable cause to believe a crime was in progress, or that contraband was aboard, or other enumerated exceptions (found in subsection **5.2.3.1.**) then the necessity of obtaining a search warrant could be dispensed with, because of the transitory nature of the trailer.

5.3.2.38. *Urban and Rural Areas.* The protections of the fourth amendment apply equally to rural, urban, or metropolitan areas. The fact that a house may be located in the middle of a two hundred acre tract of land or within a crowded city does not tighten or relax constitutional standards.

5.3.2.39. *Vacant Buildings Within Curtilage.* Empty buildings within the curtilage are entitled to the privacy of main dwellings which are protected by the amendment (*Morrison v. U.S.*, 262 F.2d 449 (1958)). A dwelling does not lose its character merely because it may be temporarily unoccupied. The fact that a dwelling or building may be unoccupied at the time of search does not permit a search without a warrant (*Roberson v. U.S.*, 165 F.2d 752 (1948)).

5.3.2.40. *Vacant Wooded Areas.* Lands outside of the curtilage are not protected against unreasonable searches and seizures, even though entry upon such land may constitute trespass (*U.S. v. Romano*, 203 F. Supp. 27 (1962)). See subsection **5.3.2.23.**

5.3.3. PAPERS. Abandoned property does not fall within the protection of the fourth amendment. If property is abandoned, officers in making a search thereof, do not violate any rights or security of a citizen as guaranteed by the amendment. So it was held that a defendant did not have standing to object to seizure of corporate records which had been abandoned by corporate officers (*U.S. v. Knight*, 412 F.2d 292 (1969); *Abel v. U.S.*, supra; *Hester v. U.S.*, 265 U.S.57 (1924); *Williams v. U.S.*, 344 F.2d 264 (1965)).

5.3.3.1. *Attorney's Files.* A 1956 case held that an attorney who had placed his office files in storage with a corporation before two *subpoenas duces tecum* were issued to require the corporation to produce, before a grand jury, all or parts of the books and papers, the attorney had sufficient control and possession in those books, so that he had a basis for claiming an unreasonable search and seizure, and hence was entitled to a *motion to quash* on such grounds (*Schwimmer v. U.S.*, 232 F.2d 855 (1956)).

5.3.3.2. *Bank Records.* Communications between a bank and depositor are not privileged. The banks' records of their transactions are subject to subpoena, and the customer has no standing to object to such subpoena of the bank's records. An Act of Congress authorizing a supervisor of the Internal Revenue Service to compel banks to permit an inspection of their books and papers connected with a public business, in which the United States has an interest, in the collection of revenue, has been held constitutional (*Stanwood v. Green*, F. Cas. (No. 13,301)).

The court commented on the examining of bank records in *Mobile First Nat'l Bank v. U.S.*, 267 U.S. 576 (1924), saying,

> As I understand the fourth amendment, it protects the parties to criminal prosecution against unreasonable searches and seizures of their papers, and I do not understand this to authorize a third party, who has books and papers which may be relevant to the inquiry, to refuse to produce such books and papers because of this amendment. This is not a question of a search and seizure of a party's books and papers, but of whether a witness who has information as to a party's dealings may be required to testify to those facts, and produce book entries as to such entries in connection with and supporting such testimony.

5.3.3.3. *Bankruptcy Files.* The fact that a person may have filed for bankruptcy, or has been adjudged bankrupt will not furnish grounds for violation of his fourth amendment rights. However, the fact the person is going through bankruptcy and probable cause exists to believe that he is concealing records from the receiver in bankruptcy, may furnish reasonable grounds for a search of such records (*Matthews v. Correa*, 135 F.2d 534 (1943)).

5.3.3.4. *Books and Papers.* There is no special sanctity in papers or books, as distinguished from other forms of property, which would render them immune to search and seizure. Fourth amendment protections apply equally to papers and other forms of property. However, a search warrant may be issued for papers or books, or the party in possession of such papers may be served with a *subpoena duces tecum,* ordering him to produce said books, records, etc. When a *subpoena duces tecum* is employed, a good cause showing must be made, as to relevancy and materiality of the requested documents. The subpoena may not be used to evade the reasonableness requirements of the amendment.

5.3.3.5. *Corporate Books.* Corporate records, like personal papers, may enjoy constitutional protection from unreasonable searches and seizures (*Schultz v. Yeager,* 394 U.S. 961 (1967)). Thus, where there was evidence of theft of corporate documents on behalf of the government, for use in proceedings before the Federal Trade Commission against the corporation, the theft and subsequent use thereof by the government was the equivalent of an unreasonable search and seizure. The commission's knowing acceptance and use of the documents, violated the amendment (*Knoll Associates Inc. v. FTC,* 397 F.2d 530 (1968)).

5.3.3.6. *Federal Income Tax Records.* The fourth amendment does not protect the owner and keeper of records of a taxpayer's business transactions from having such records examined by the Internal Revenue Commissioner under a statute permitting Internal Revenue agents to examine books, papers, records, or memoranda bearing upon matters required to be included in the income tax return (*First Nat'l Bank of Mobile v. U.S., supra*). See also 26 U.S.C.A. 3614 (a).

5.3.3.7. *Public Mail.* First class mail is protected by the amendment in that it cannot be seized, retained, or opened and searched, without authority of a search warrant (*Lustiger v. U.S.,* 390 U.S.951 (1967)). However, this does not preclude postal inspectors from copying information contained on the outside of sealed envelopes in the mail, where no substantial delay in the delivery of the mail is involved (mail covers). It should also be noted that the amendment's protections apply to mail moving wholly within the U.S.; it does not apply to mail coming from another country, at least when it appears that a customs determination must be made (*U.S. v. Sohnen,* 298 F. Supp. 51 (1969)).

The protection afforded by the amendment encompasses a period up to and including delivery. An interesting case concerned a first class letter, a portion of which was read through the envelope, which showed a possible solicitation or offer to murder someone. It was held that a police officer's opening of the letter without a search warrant, after it had been delivered but before its actual physical receipt by the addressee was a violation of the *addressor's* constitutional rights, thus the fruits of the search were inadmissible as evidence against the addressor. *State v. Hubka,* 461 P.2d 103, 1969.

5.3.3.8. *Prison Mail.* It has been held that censorship by prison authorities of a prisoner's mail and subsequent punishment inflicted upon a prisoner for violation of prison rules was not violative either of the amendment or of 18 U.S.C.A. 1702, 1708.

Statute 18 U.S.C. 1802 (Obstruction of Correspondence) punishes by fine and/or imprisonment anyone who takes any letter, post card or package, which has been entreated to the post office prior to delivery to the addressee, with the intent to obstruct the correspondence, or to pry into the business or secrets of another, or who opens, secretes, or destroys mail matter.

5.3.3.9. *Private Papers.* See subsection **5.3.3.**

5.3.3.10. *Public Records.* Public records may not be withheld from inspection. This principle applies not only to public documents in public offices but also to records required by law, pertaining to information of transactions which are applicable subjects of governmental regulations (*Bowles v. Insel,* 148 F.2d 91 (1945)).

The power of Congress, to require those engaged in business affecting a public interest to keep records which are subject to inspection by an administrator securing enforcement of a law, is not open to constitutional objection. Books and records so kept are not private matters but assume characteristics of public or quasi-public documents; they are nonprivileged and their custodian is not afforded the traditional protection of the amendment. In assuming their custody, he accepts the incident obligations to permit inspection (*U.S. v. Pine Valley Poultry Distributors Corp.,* 187 F. Supp. 455 (1960)).

5.3.4. EFFECTS.

5.3.4.1. *Clothing of the Accused.* The clothing of an accused may be searched without a warrant contemporaneous with, or shortly after, a valid arrest, for example, a person arrested on a charge of suspicion of rape, shortly after the offense was committed. He may be taken down to headquarters where his clothing could be checked for semen stains. If there is reasonable grounds to arrest the individual, there is probable cause for the search—no warrant being required. Coupled with exigent circumstances (if the tests were not run within a short time, they would lose their value) the search would be reasonable and not violate the fourth amendment rights.

However, the court has held contra where the defendant was arrested and searched, though not thoroughly. He was taken to jail and given prison clothes, his clothing and personal effects were placed in a property bag for routine safekeeping. Three days later the defendant's clothing was searched without a search warrant, and heroin was found in a watch pocket. The search could not be held valid by analogy to laboratory testing, in the absence of a warrant. Here the time element of three days controlled (*Brett v. U.S.,* 412 F.2d 401 (1969)).

5.3.4.2. *Conversations.* Conversations are within the scope of the fourth amendment. Hence, one who intends a conversation or transaction to be private and taken reasonable steps to keep it private, is protected from governmental intrusion unauthorized by warrant or well-defined specific circumstances. He is not protected from consequences of error if he places trust in the silence, duplicity, or complicity of a government agent or informer, or if he places physical evidence in plain view of government agents (*U.S. v. Haden,* 397 F.2d 460, 1968)). See also *Katz v. U.S., supra.* If a conversation is overheard in a public place, presumably without the use of electronic aids, that conversation would be admissible without a search warrant.

5.3.4.3. *Contraband.* As one cannot have a superior property interest in contraband such as stolen articles and narcotics, government agents may seize such in the course of a lawful search or when in plain view, for example, in a motor vehicle stop where the officer notices a sawed-off shotgun in the back seat of the car. A search warrant may be issued which lists the type of contraband which is sought and believed to be in the possession of a suspect. Likewise, instrumentalities of a crime, "fruits of a crime," "mere evidence," and stolen property may also be seized, without a warrant, when in plain view. A distinction should be noted between contraband in one's lawful possession, and articles used for illegal purposes. A sufficient right may exist to support an objection to seizure. If a search is conducted, it must meet constitutional standards. It must be noted that it is a violation of the Constitution to conduct an *unreasonable* search for items which may be subject to seizure. Hence, if the search is illegal, the seizure is invalid. Thus, if the owner stored contraband articles in another's hotel room and the police subsequently entered the room illegally and seized the contraband, the owner's constitutional rights were violated (*U.S. v. Jeffers, supra*).

5.3.4.4. *Foot Lockers.* When one places items in a foot locker with a reasonable expectation that the contents will be private and secure and the person has exclusive possession or use of the locker, the fourth amendment will protect its contents from intrusion in the absence of a warrant or exigent circumstances. An analogous case held that the contents of a suitcase, which was left by a defendant in an apartment of a friend, would be constitutionally protected effects, the seizure of which was entitled to a determination as to whether or not the search and seizure itself was lawful (*U.S. v. Brown*, 300 F. Supp. 1285 (1969)).

5.3.4.5. *Forfeited Property.* Property which is forfeited by reason of the crime with which it is connected is not entitled to legal protection, and is always rightfully subject to seizure on behalf of the government (*Milam v. U.S.*, 296 F. 629 (1924)). Thus, an officer may seize, without a warrant, property which is in the possession of a defendant which has, under the law, been forfeited to the government. In narcotics offenses, for example, the government has the right to seize any instrument of transportation used in violation of the statute. As to the vehicles seized, the government holds a superior property interest. Once seized, any search of such items is lawful in the absence of a warrant, as no one has proper standing to object.

5.3.4.6. *Game.* Game which is illegally in the possession of a hunter is seizable as evidence. Thus, a search by a game warden who, after entering to inspect property, found a hunter in possession of an illegal number of birds was valid. The legal seizing of the birds was not unreasonable (*U.S. v. Greenhead, Inc.,* 256 F. Supp. 890 (1966)).

5.3.4.7. *Mail Matter.* See subsection **5.3.3.**

5.3.4.8. *Nonvisible Contents of Automobile.* Nonvisible areas of an automobile, most often the trunk, may only be searched under exigent circumstances in the absence of a warrant. Mere inconvenience to the officer cannot justify a search of such areas unless a real urgency exists. Even with a showing of exigent or exceptional circumstances, the requisite probable cause must be present. Where a vehicle is safely under the control and for all purposes in custody of police, a warrant or consent to search should be obtained.

5.3.4.9. *Papers.* See subsection **5.3.3.**

5.3.4.10. *Parcel or Packages.* First class mail, sealed packages and parcels, having the proper postage, are protected from unreasonable searches and seizures. However, the inspection by the post office department or other governmental agents of an unsealed package not having upon it stamps sufficient to qualify it as first class mail is not an invasion of the owner's immunity from unreasonable searches and seizures (*Webster v. U.S.,* 92 F.2d 462 (1937)). Parcels and packages securely bound or fastened may be entitled to protection from intrusion if this is the owner's or possessor's reasonable expectation. Also, the mere surrender of custody of a package to a carrier such as an airline does not forfeit the sender's rights to privacy. Hence, a search of such packages in the absence of a warrant or in the absence of emergency circumstances will be held invalid (*Corngold v. U.S.,* 367 F.2d 1 (1966)).

5.3.4.11. *Private Papers.* See subsection **5.3.3.**

5.3.4.12. *Records.* See subsection **5.3.3.2.**

5.3.4.13. *Safe Deposit Box.* A safe deposit box would be protected by the fourth amendment and could not be searched in the absence of a warrant or exigent circumstance.

5.3.4.14. *Telephone Booths.* When a person enters a telephone booth, whether in a public place or not, with a reasonable expectation of privacy, he is entitled to the protection afforded by the fourth amendment as to unreasonable searches and seizures. See subsection **5.3.4.2.** Also see *Katz v. U.S., supra.*

5.3.4.15. *Telegrams.* The sender of interstate telegraphic messages has no substantial or procedural rights against the demand of lawful authority for the disclosure of the contents of a telegram. Such a demand does not invade his privacy or subject him to a "search or seizure" of his person or property. One sending a telegram cannot expect that the communications will not be seen by others. However, it must be noted that employees of telegraph companies are precluded by federal law from divulging the contents of radio or wire communications.

5.3.4.16. *Transportation.* Generally, police may search goods in the course of transportation, not incident to an arrest, where they have probable cause to believe that contraband is present (*People v. McGrew,* 75 CAL. RPTR. 378 (1969)).

5.3.4.17. *Air Transportation.* In *McGrew, supra* the court held that if police officers were called by an airline employee, who recognized marijuana in a footlocker which had been placed with the airline for shipping, the police had probable cause to search the locker without a warrant, and also to subsequently search another foot locker left at another airline by the same party. The sending party was also searched, as was his suitcase, when he went to buy his ticket.

5.3.4.18. *Car in Pursuit.* A car which is pursued by officers may be stopped and searched without a warrant:
   1. To insure the safety of the officers, to the extent necessary (i.e. areas in the car under the immediate control of the driver or passengers).

2. If the officers have reasonable grounds to believe that there is contraband or other seizable items (evidence, fruits, instrumentalities) in the vehicle and circumstances do not permit the obtaining of a warrant.
3. As incident to a lawful arrest.
4. By consent.

5.3.4.19. *Visible Articles.* Objects falling within the *plain view* of an officer, who has the right to be in such position to have that view, are subject to seizure and may be introduced into evidence. Mere observation does not constitute a search, where items are freely exposed. No search warrant is required where objects are in plain view (*Creighton v. U.S.,* 406 F.2d 651 (1968)). An observation made by an officer through an open door of a trailer parked near a bank was not a "search." Thus, also, the viewing of license numbers of cars in plain view was not a search. Nor are officers who are making an inventory of property conducting a search. However, the eye appearing over the transom or the peeking through a crack in the garage door does not come within the open-view doctrine. Evidence seized through such a search without a warrant is not admissible without a showing by those who seek exemption that the conduct was imperative (*Ashby v. State,* 228 So.2d 400 (1969)). See also subsection **5.3.2.13.** *U.S. v. Lee,* 274 U.S.559 (1927); *McDonald v. U.S.,* 335 U.S.451 (1948), and *Lundberg v. Buckkoe,* 338 F.2d 62 (1964).

5.4. Items Subject to Search and Seizure

Historically, searches for *property* were prima facie unreasonable, and thus unconstitutional unless the government could show some *superior right of possession* in the item to be searched for and seized. Thus, the action known as *replevin* was the keynote to common law search and seizure law. If the citizen had the right of replevin, that is, to recover from the government the items taken, then those items could not be subject to a seizure by the government, even with a warrant. In other words, if the remedy of replevin, which was in effect a law suit against the government to recover possession of property, would lie, the government would be precluded from conducting the search, or suffer the consequence of having the seized evidence rejected as taken in an unreasonable search and seizure.

Under early common law, the government was said to have a superior property interest in stolen goods (or fruits), instrumentalities of crime, and contraband. In the instance of stolen property, the common law practice was to have the true owner swear that his goods had been taken prior to government action. Today, no such procedure prevails. The government may simply demonstrate probable cause and lawfully search for stolen property, even though the true owner is unknown or unavailable to request and authorize the government to assert the owner's interest.

Regarding the seizure of instrumentalities, the court, in *Gouled, supra,* stated that the government could seize such items because they could be used to perpetrate future crimes.

Contraband is indeed property to which the government holds a superior property right, but only because it has decided to vest such interest in itself.

The premise that property interest controls as to the right of search and seizure has been discredited. Thus, even though the government may have a superior interest in property, its search and seizure may be deemed unreasonable, and hence a bar to its use as evidence. In other words, at common law, if the sovereign could demonstrate its property interest, for example, in contraband, then it would be reasonable for that sovereign to seize the property. The shift in judicial thinking away from property rights has seen a similar move toward interests in privacy.

The notion that the government could not seize evidence merely for the purpose of proving crime *(Gouled)* has also been discredited. The case of *Schmerber v. California, supra,* stated that it was reasonable to conduct otherwise permissible searches for the purpose of obtaining evidence which would aid in apprehending and convicting criminals.

In *Warden v. Hayden, supra,* the court held that the search for and seizure of "mere evidence" of a crime (which had previously been thought to be a violation of fourth amendment rights) was now permissible. The court said, "The requirements of the fourth amendment can secure the same protection of privacy whether the search is for mere evidence or for fruits, instrumentalities, or contraband.

Thus, an officer, in conducting a search incident to a lawful arrest, within previously enumerated confines of reasonableness, may search for:

1. Contraband.
2. Instrumentalities of crime.
3. Fruits of crime.
4. Mere evidence of crime.

There must be a nexus or connection between the items seized and criminal behavior. Thus, in the case of mere evidence, the probable cause must be examined in terms of cause to believe that the evidence sought will aid in a particular apprehension or conviction.

The argument against the rule permitting seizure of "mere evidence" is that "limitations upon the fruit to be gathered tend to limit the quest itself" (*U.S. v. Poller*, 43 F.2d 911 (1930)). However, being that the same probable cause requirements must be met in order to admit the mere evidence, the court felt that there would be no extension or demeaning of the fourth amendment safeguards. Hence, there is no valid reason to distinguish between intrusions for mere evidence from fruits, instrumentalities, or contraband. See *Warden v. Hayden,* reprinted *infra*.

5.5 Admissibility of Evidence

The common law allowed the introduction of evidence against an accused regardless of how obtained. This rule has been greatly modified, so that today any evidence which is the result of illegal conduct on the part of government agents is inadmissible in any court.

Because questions of admissibility of evidence are determined at the time of trial, rather than in pre-trial activity, the rules governing such admissibility will only be briefly outlined for the reader.

5.5.1. THE EXCLUSIONARY RULE. The Federal *exclusionary rule* was established by the Supreme Court in *Weeks v. U.S.*, 232 U.S. 383 (1914). *Weeks* held that evidence illegally obtained by *federal* agents acting under color of law would not be admissible in federal prosecutions. Note that pursuant to *Boyd v. U.S., supra,* the court did not bar illegally obtained evidence for use in a state court, nor illegally obtained state evidence in a federal court. The states were still free to follow either the common law or the federal rule.

In 1949, the court affirmed its *Weeks* ruling in *Wolf v. Colorado,* 338 U.S.25 (1949) by holding that a state conviction obtained through the use of evidence illegally obtained does not violate the due process clause of the fourteenth amendment, and hence, would not extend the protections of the fourth amendment to state action.

In 1961, the case of *Mapp v. Ohio,* 367 U.S.643 (1961) overruled the long line of cases since *Boyd,* holding that the fourth amendment was "incorporated" by the fourteenth and thus the commands of the fourth amendment were *applicable to the states.* This meant that any evidence sought to be admitted in any criminal trial, which was the product of unlawful government action, whether state or federal, would be inadmissible. *Mapp* operated prospectively, that is, in cases arising after the decision, and not as to convictions already obtained.

The admission of illegally seized evidence will *void* a conviction only where it is reasonable to infer that the evidence was material to the conviction and in fact prejudiced the defendant.

5.5.1.1. *Governmental Conduct.* The fourth amendment applies only to government agents, that is, persons acting under the color of law or through their official position as a law enforcement officer of a federal, state, or local agency.

5.5.1.2. *Federal Officers.* Evidence obtained by federal officers in violation of the fourth amendment may not be admitted in federal or state courts.

5.5.1.3. *State Officer's Silver Platter Doctrine.* Prior to 1960, evidence obtained in violation of fourth amendment rights by state officers was admissible in *federal* courts, if (1) no federal agents took part in the search and (2) the search was not instigated by the United States government. The *Silver Platter Doctrine* was adopted by several states, allowing illegally obtained evidence from federal officers to be admitted in state proceedings.

Elkins v. U.S., 364 U.S.206 (1960) held that evidence seized in violation of a defendant's rights by state officers could not be admitted in a federal trial. As noted, *supra,* one year later, *Mapp* held *all* illegally seized evidence inadmissible in any criminal trial. Evidence illegally seized is also not to be admitted in a quasi-criminal hearing, as in the case of a forfeiture proceeding. See *One 1958 Plymouth Sedan v. Commonwealth of Pa.,* 380 U.S.693 (1965). It appears that evidence will also be excluded in strictly civil matters, which has been obtained in violation of fourth amendment rights (*Williams v. Williams,* 221 N.E.2d 622 (1966)).

5.5.2. ACTION BY PRIVATE INDIVIDUALS. Unless at the instigation of government agents, searches conducted by private individuals do not fall within the protections of the fourth amendment (*Burdeau v. McDowell,* 256 U.S.465 (1921)). Thus, evidence seized by airline employees, burglars, employees, and former employees, foreign officials, motel owners, and private investigators has been admitted, where there was not any governmental collusion. However, it should be noted that a private individual, although he may seize evidence and turn it over to law enforcement agents, may not *consent* to seizure. See *consent, supra* and *Stapleton v. People,* 447 P.2d 967 (1969).

Although the states may develop their own standards relating to searches and seizures, these standards must not violate the *constitutional proscriptions* against unreasonable searches. Federal guidelines will control (*Ker v. California,* 374 U.S.23 (1963)).

5.5.3. WHAT IS EXCLUDED. The exclusionary rule applies to any evidence which is the direct or immediate result of unlawful official conduct (fruit of the poisonous tree). Illegally obtained evidence resulting from an unlawful arrest and search may not be used on direct or cross-examination to prove the offense charged. Such evidence may be admitted, however, for the limited purpose of *impeaching the credibility* of the defendant, where the following occur:

1. The defendant takes the stand in his own defense.
2. He voluntarily gives conflicting testimony.
3. The issue is raised as to the defendant's credibility as to matters *other* than the crime charged (*Walder v. U.S.,* 347 U.S.62 (1954)). See also *Harris v. U.S.,* 401 U.S.222 (1971).

5.5.4. FRUIT OF THE POISONOUS TREE. Any direct or indirect "fruits," that is, information, evidence, or confessions, derived from unlawfully obtained evidence must be excluded. In *Wong Sun v. U.S.,* 371 U.S.471 (1963), party X was arrested unlawfully. He shortly thereafter confessed to narcotics offenses and implicated Y. Subject Y voluntarily disclosed narcotics he had in his possession. Evidence from both X and Y was held inadmissible, as being the "fruits" of illegal government activity. However, if there is a sufficient break between unlawful conduct and the fruits obtained, as in *Wong Sun* (another part of the decision), where one of the defendants voluntarily came in several days later to make a confession, *that* second confession was held admissible. It was not "tainted" by the unlawful conduct.

5.5.4.1. *Reversal of Conviction.* The "automatic reversal rule" will not be applied to convictions where illegally obtained evidence has been improperly admitted, unless the admission can be shown to have been prejudicial to a finding of innocence. Mere "harmless error" will not reverse (*Fahy v. Connecticut,* 375 U.S.85 (1963)). Harmless error must be measured by federal standards. This means that a showing "beyond a reasonable doubt" must be made that the evidence in question did not contribute to the verdict.

5.5.5. MOTION TO SUPPRESS. To prevent illegally obtained evidence from being admitted, a *motion to suppress* is entered, generally prior to trial. *Standing* to object to the introduction of such evidence is conferred upon the following:
1. Persons who show a possessory interest in the property seized.
2. Persons who show a proprietary interest in the area or premises searched.
3. Persons who are the victim of the search and seizure, or against whom such search was directed (*Jones v. U.S., supra*). Also see Rule 41 (e) in Part VI, *supra.*

The above criteria make no distinction between property owners, lessees, tenants, or guests. Anyone legitimately on the premises when searched may object to the introduction of evidence against him.

Where possession itself is a crime (i.e. in narcotics offenses), one admitting possession to show standing so as to object to admission will not be prejudiced by such admissions. That is, his admissions of possession may not be used to convict, whether the motion to suppress is successful or not. See Annot., 50 A.L.R.2d 531, 1956.

Section 6. WARRANTS

" . . . no warrant shall issue, but upon probable cause, supported by oath or affirmation, and particularly describing the place to be searched, and the persons or things to be seized."

In this section, we will consider both the search and arrest warrant. The applicable *Federal Rules of Criminal Procedure,* reprinted in 18 U.S. Code, will serve to illustrate federal procedure used in obtaining and executing warrants. The Federal rules have been employed in many states as models for legislation.

6.1. Historical Perspective

The framers of the United States Constitution wrote the fourth amendment to insure that the unpopular "general writs" employed by King George in England would not be adopted in America. General writs were blank warrants, which allowed representatives of the king to search anything, anywhere, and anytime, without a showing of what we now call "probable cause."

Citizens under the king were not secure in their houses, persons, papers, or effects, as they were subject to government intrusion under the guise of legality, known as writs. Furthermore, the citizen was personally subject to arrest on the whim of a sheriff or other official. Accordingly, the second portion of the fourth amendment, dealing with warrants, was made quite specific in requiring that warrants issue only on probable cause (discussed *supra*), supported by oath or affirmation (before a magistrate) and particularly describing the place to be searched (no blanket warrants, hence forbidding exploratory searches) and the persons or things to be seized.

In the absence of the exceptions of arrest for offenses committed in one's presence, stop and frisk, exigent circumstances, consent, and health and safety inspections, arrests and searches will generally be held unreasonable. Any evidence seized during an unreasonable search will be held inadmissible in any subsequent proceeding against the accused.

6.2. Arrest

The first step in obtaining a warrant of arrest is to demonstrate, through a complaint, that a crime has been committed. The complaint, set forth in Figure 4-4, is a written statement of the essential facts which make up the offense charged. Federal rule 3 requires that the complaint be made upon oath before a commissioner or other officer employed to commit persons charged with offenses against the United States. Under state law, usually a state supreme court or district court judge may hear the complaint and issue the warrant. Often, any court of general jurisdiction may issue a warrant, limited to their political area of jurisdiction.

Figure 4-5 is the text of an actual complaint for violation of interstate gambling activities. The reader should note the very specific outlining of probable cause which was the basis for the arrest and search warrants, presented *supra*.

6.2.1. WARRANT OR SUMMONS UPON COMPLAINT

6.2.1.1. *Issuance.* If it appears from the complaint, or from an affidavit or affidavits filed with the complaint, that there is probable cause to believe that an offense has been committed and that the defendant has committed it, a warrant for the arrest of the defendant shall issue to any officer authorized by law to execute it. Upon the request of the attorney for the government, a summons instead of a warrant shall issue. More than one warrant or summons may issue on the same complaint. If a defendant fails to appear in response to the summons, a warrant shall issue.

6.2.1.2. *Form.* The *warrant* shall be signed by the commissioner and shall contain the name of the defendant or, if his name is unknown, any name or description by which he can be identified with reasonable certainty. It shall describe the offense charged in the complaint. It shall command that the defendant be arrested and brought before the nearest available commissioner. See Figure 4-6.

Figure 4-4

United States District Court
FOR THE

UNITED STATES OF AMERICA

v

Commissioner's Docket No.

Case No.

COMPLAINT for VIOLATION of

U.S.C. Title

Section

BEFORE..,
Name of Commissioner

....,
Address of Commissioner

The undersigned complainant being duly sworn states:

That on or about   , 19   , at

in the

District of

(1)

did(2)

And the complainant states that this complaint is based on

And the complainant further states that he believes that

are material witnesses in relation to this charge.

....,
Signature of Complainant.

....,
Official Title.

Sworn to before me, and subscribed in my presence,.... .. .., 19........

--,
United States Commissioner.

(1) Insert name of accused.
(2) Insert statement of the essential facts constituting the offense charged.

127

Figure 4-5

IN THE UNITED STATES DISTRICT COURT FOR THE DISTRICT OF NEBRASKA

United States of America

Magistrate's Docket No. ....

Magistrate's Case No. ....

Complaint for Violation of

v.

Title 18, U.S.C., 1084, 1952, 371

Before: Richard C. Peck, United States Magistrate, District of Nebraska, Omaha, Nebraska

Affiant John B. McPhee, Jr. being first duly sworn confirms and alleges as follows:

Affiant is, and at all times material hereto, has been a Special Agent of the Federal Bureau of Investigation assigned to Omaha, Nebraska.

Affiant hereby by reference incorporates that certain affidavit sworn to by him on December 11, 1970, and filed contemporaneously herewith into this affidavit as though it had been completely restated in this affidavit, and affiant affirms that all of the allegations in said affidavit are true and correct.

The foregoing constitutes affiants probable cause to believe that:

COUNT I

Between the 2nd day of December, 1970, and the 12th day of December, 1970, in Omaha, Nebraska, (defendant) and (———) a/k/a Mrs. (———), did use a facility in interstate commerce in transmitting and receiving gambling information by telephone transmitted from without the State, to Omaha, Nebraska, in the District of Nebraska, with intent to promote, manage, establish, carry on and facilitate the promotion, management, establishment and carrying on of an unlawful activity, said unlawful activity being a business enterprise involving gambling, in violation of Section 947, Reissue Revised Statutes of 1943, Chapter 28, of the State of Nebraska, and thereafter (defendant) did perform and cause to be performed acts to promote, manage, establish, and carry on and facilitate the promotion, management, establishment, and carrying on of said unlawful activity, in violation of Title 18, United States Code, Section 1952.

COUNT II

Between the 2nd day of December, 1970, and the 12th day of December, 1970, (———), a/k/a (———) and (defendant) being engaged in the business of betting and wagering, did knowingly use a wire communication facility, that is, telephone lines and circuits, for the transmission from Las Vegas, State of Nevada, to Omaha, Nebraska, in the District of Nebraska, of information assisting in the placing of bets and wages on sporting events and contests, such information consisting of betting odds, point spreads, and "line" informations, in violation of Title 18, United States Code, Section 1084.

128

COUNT III

From on or about June, 1970, and continuously thereafter, up to and including the date of the filing of this Complaint, in the District of Nebraska and elsewhere, the defendants, wilfully and knowingly did combine, conspire, confederate and agree together and with each other and with diverse other persons whose names are to complainant unknown, to commit an offense against the United States, by knowingly using wire communication facilities, that is, telephone lines and circuits, for the transmission in interstate commerce from Las Vegas, State of Nevada, to Omaha, Nebraska, in the District of Nebraska, of information assisting in the placing of bets and wagers on sporting events and contests, such information consisting of betting odds, point spreads, and "line" information, in violation of Title 18, United States Code, Section 1084; and to use facilities in interstate commerce, being telephone lines and circuits extending from without the State into the State, with intent to promote, manage, establish, carry on and facilitate the promotion, management, establishment and carrying on of an unlawful activity. Said unlawful activity being a business enterprise involving gambling, in violation of Section 28-947, Reissue Revised Statutes of 1943 of the State of Nebraska, and, thereafter, one or more of the said conspirators did perform and cause to be performed acts to promote, manage, establish, and carry on and facilitate the promotion, management, establishment, and carrying on of said unlawful activities, in violation of Title 18, United States Code, Section 1952.

OVERT ACTS

At the times hereinafter mentioned the defendants committed the following overt acts in furtherance of said conspiracy and to effect the objects thereof:

(1) On or about the 6th day of December, 1970, in the District of Nebraska, defendant, (———) did make a telephone call from Las Vegas, Nevada, to (defendant) at Omaha, Nebraska, furnishing him gambling or wagering information consisting of the "line" or point spread on various college football games to be played subsequent to her call.

(2) That (defendant) and (———) on numerous occasions between December 3, 1970, and December 11, 1970, did receive gambling or wagering information regarding major sporting events and did accept bets and exchange gambling or wagering information in regards to major sporting events from and to numerous different individuals.

In violation of Title 18, United States Code, Section 371.

. . . .
John B. McPhee, Jr., Special Agent
Federal Bureau of Investigation

Sworn to before me and subscribed in my presence, this   day of December, 1970.

. . . .
Richard C. Peck
United States Magistrate

129

Figure 4-6

Form A. O. 90 (Rev. 7-26-50)

𝔘𝔫𝔦𝔱𝔢𝔡 𝔖𝔱𝔞𝔱𝔢𝔰 𝔇𝔦𝔰𝔱𝔯𝔦𝔠𝔱 ℭ𝔬𝔲𝔯𝔱

FOR THE

_____

Commissioner's Docket No................

Case No................

UNITED STATES OF AMERICA

v

WARRANT OF ARREST

To ....¹·

You are hereby commanded to arrest ...., and bring him
here insert name of defendant or description

forthwith before the nearest available United States Commissioner to answer to a complaint charging him

with
here describe offense charged in complaint

in violation of U.S.C. Title,   , Section

Date   , 19   ....,
                                                            United States Commissioner.

1. Here insert designation of officer to whom warrant is issued.

RETURN

Received   , 19   at   , and executed by arrest of

                        at   on   , 19   .

                                        ....,
                                                                              Name.
                                        ....,
                                                                              Title.
Date   .... District of ....

                        , 19   By.., Deputy

Figure 4-7

United States District Court

FOR THE

Commissioner's Docket No..............

Case No................

UNITED STATES OF AMERICA

v

SUMMONS

To

_{Name of Defendant}

You are hereby summoned to appear before the undersigned United States Commissioner

, at

_{place}

on , 19 , **at** _{time} o'clock M. to answer to a complaint charging you

with _{here describe offense charged in complaint}

in violation of U.S.C. Title Section

Date , 19

....
United States Commissioner.

This summons was received by me at **on**

19

....
Defendant.

RETURN*

This summons was served by me on , 19 **in the following manner:**

....
Name.

....
Title.

*As to who may serve the summons and the manner of its service see Rule 4 (c) of the Federal Rules of Criminal Procedure and Rule 4 (c) of the Rules of Civil Procedure.

Figure 4-8

DOCKET NO.

CRIMINAL SUMMONS AND COMPLAINT

IN THE COUNTY COURT IN AND FOR THE CITY AND COUNTY OF DENVER

STATE OF COLORADO

THE PEOPLE OF THE STATE OF COLORADO, PLAINTIFF, VERSUS

NAME_____DEFENDANT

ADDRESS_____

THE PEOPLE OF THE STATE OF COLORADO TO THE ABOVE NAMED DEFENDANT, GREETINGS:
YOU ARE HEREBY ORDERED TO APPEAR BEFORE THIS COURT AT THE TIME AND PLACE SPECIFIED TO ANSWER
TO CHARGES OF VIOLATING THE COLORADO REVISED STATUTES, 1963, AS AMENDED, AS INDICATED BELOW,
WHICH OCCURRED IN THE CITY AND COUNTY OF DENVER STATE OF COLORADO ON_____196____
AT THE APPROXIMATE LOCATION OF:_____

STATUTE ALLEGED TO
HAVE BEEN VIOLATED
(SECTION NUMBER):

CONTRARY TO THE FORM OF THE STATUTE IN SUCH CASE MADE AND PROVIDED AND
AGAINST THE PEACE AND DIGNITY OF THE PEOPLE OF THE STATE OF COLORADO.

WITNESSES   COMPLAINANT_____

SERIAL NO._____

*The above named complainant knows or believes, and so alleges, that
the above named defendant violated the herein described section(s) of
the Colorado revised statutes, 1963, as amended, and further certifies
that a copy of this summons was duly served upon the defendant in
the manner prescribed by law.*

☐ *Bond not required*

☐ *Bond set in the amount of $_____*

☐ *Personal recognizance bond authorized*

By: _____

Court appearance at 8:00 a.m., on the

_____day of_____196_____room 111,
City and County Building.

NOTICE TO JAILOR: IF THE DEFENDANT IS NOT RELEASED ON BOND, HE
MUST BE BROUGHT TO THE FIRST MORNING SESSION OF COURT, FOLLOWING,
FOR ARRAIGNMENT.

Served by_____Date_____Time_____

The *summons* shall be in the same form as the warrant except that it shall summon the defendant to appear before a commissioner at a stated time and place.

6.2.1.3. Execution or Service and Return. The warrant shall be *executed by a marshal* or by some other officer authorized by law. The summons may be served by any person authorized to serve a summons in a civil action.

The warrant may be executed or the summons *may be served at any place* within the jurisdiction of the United States.

The warrant shall be executed by the arrest of the defendant. The officer need not have the warrant in his possession at the time of arrest, but upon request he shall show the warrant to the defendant as soon as possible. If the officer does not have the warrant in his possession at the time of arrest, he shall then inform the defendant of the offense charged and of the fact that a warrant has been issued. The summons shall be served upon a defendant by delivering a copy to him personally, or by leaving it at his dwelling house or usual place of abode with some person of suitable age and discretion then residing therein or by mailing it to the defendant's last known address.

The officer executing a warrant shall make return thereof to the commissioner or other officer before whom the defendant is brought pursuant to Rule 5. At the request of the attorney for the government, any unexecuted warrant shall be returned to the commissioner by whom it was issued and shall be cancelled by him. On or before the return day, the person to whom a summons was delivered for service shall make return thereof to the commissioner before whom the summons is returnable. At the request of the attorney for the government made at any time while the complaint is pending, a warrant returned unexecuted and not cancelled, or a summons returned unanswered, or a duplicate thereof, may be delivered by the commissioner to the marshal or other authorized person for execution or service.

In summary, the party seeking a warrant of arrest must state known, specific facts which will allow a neutral and detached magistrate to determine that there is probable cause for believing that a crime has been committed, and that the named individual has committed it. In other words, the affidavit must contain more than mere hearsay. A complaint must provide a foundation for the judgment of probable cause. It must provide the affiant's answer to the magistrate's hypothetical question, "What makes you think that the defendant committed the offense charged?" Simply stated, there must be enough information presented to the commissioner to enable him to make the judgment that the charges are not capricious and are sufficiently supported to justify bringing into play the succeeding steps of the criminal process (*Jaben v. U.S.*, 381 U.S.214 (1965)).

> 6.2.1.3.1. Case Example. The defendant was convicted of the unlawful purchase of narcotics in violation of federal law. The arrest of the defendant occurred after a narcotics agent obtained a warant of arrest from a United States Commissioner. The warrant, issued under Rules 3 and 4, was based on a written complaint, sworn to by the agent, which read in part:
>
> "The undersigned complainant being duly sworn states: That on or about January 26, 1956, at Houston, Texas, in the Southern District of Texas, the defendant did receive, conceal, etc. narcotic drugs, to wit: heroin hydrochloride with knowledge of unlawful importation, in violation of. . . .
>
> And the complainant further states that he believes that ———— and ———— are material witnesses in relation to this charge."
>
> Does the affidavit supply sufficient "probable cause" to form the basis of a lawful arrest?

No. The complaint was defective in not providing a sufficient basis upon which a finding of probable cause could be made. "Criminal Rules 3 and 4 provide that an arrest warrant shall be issued only upon a written and sworn complaint (1) setting forth "the essential facts constituting the offense charged," and (2) showing "that there is probable cause to believe that (such) an offense has been committed and that the defendant has committed it. . . ." The provisions of these rules must be read in light of the constitutional requirements they implement. The language of the fourth amendment, ". . . no warrants shall issue, but upon probable cause, supported by oath or affirmation, and particularly describing . . . the persons or things to be seized," of course applies to arrest as well as search warrants. . . . The protection afforded by these rules, when they are viewed against their constitutional background, is that the inferences from the facts which lead to the complaint ". . . be drawn by a neutral and detached magistrate instead of being judged by the officer engaged in the often competitive enterprise of ferreting out crime." (*Johnson v. United States, 333* U.S.10 (1948).) The purpose of the complaint is to enable the appropriate magistrate, here a commissioner, to determine whether the probable cause required to support a warrant exists. The commissioner must judge for himself the persuasiveness of the facts relied on by a complaining officer to show probable cause. He should not accept without question the complainant's *mere conclusions* that the person whose arrest is sought has committed a crime *(Giordenello v. U.S., supra).*

The court found that the complaint contained no affirmative allegations that the affiant spoke with personal knowledge of the matters contained therein, nor does the complaint indicate any sources for the complainant's belief.

As provided by Rule 4 (e), the warrant must be issued by a commissioner or magistrate. This magistrate must be a judicial officer empowered by statute to issue warrants. In addition, he must be a neutral and detached magistrate, meaning that if he is in any way connected with the prosecutorial function, the warrant will be invalid. See *Coolidge v. New Hampshire,* 403 U.S. 443 (1971), where a conviction was overturned, in part because an arrest warrant had been issued by the Attorney General of the state, who was spearheading the investigation in which the defendant was suspect. The court noted that the Attorney General was certainly not the detached, neutral magistrate required under the fourth amendment.

6.2.2. FORM

The arrest warrant must (1) be signed by the commissioner, (2) list the offense charged, and (3) sufficiently identify the defendant. The arrest warrant will be valid until executed or cancelled. The summons simply commands the named defendant to appear at a specific place and time. A sworn complaint is still required for the summons.

If the warrant appears on its face to be valid, there is no liability on the arresting officer, if later, the warrant is in fact found defective. However, if the wrong person is arrested, the officer will be liable, since he has an absolute duty to arrest the named individual. Generally, the arrestee has no right to resist the arresting officer, even if it later turns out that the warrant was defective.

6.2.3. EXECUTION, SERVICE, AND RETURN

The warrant may be executed at any time until cancelled. Further, the warrant may be served any place in the jurisdiction, and need not be in the possession of the arresting officer at the time of arrest. Additionally, if the warrant is for a felony, the arrest may be made at any time. Arrest for a misdemeanor offense may be limited to daytime arrest only.

Once the arrest warrant is obtained, it should be served promptly. However, the court has said in *U.S. v. Joines*, 258 F.2d 471 (1958), that there is no right to be arrested promptly. It must be noted that an unnecessary delay may subject the police officer to the charge of holding the warrant in order to use the arrest most advantageously to justify an incidental search.

6.2.4. MANNER

Under the Federal rules, the officers making the arrest must announce their *purpose and authority* prior to breaking in. This allows voluntary compliance with the order and avoids violence. The court has proposed notable exceptions to the authority and purpose requirement, in that, if the arrestee (s) know of the authority and purpose of the arrest, the officers need not announce same. Furthermore, if the officer reasonably believes that there will be a real danger to life, or that evidence can and will be destroyed prior to entry, they may enter without announcing their authority and purpose. (The above is consistent with the "no-knock" provisions of federal legislation.)

A failure to announce, where an announcement must be made, will result in an unlawful arrest, and will invalidate any search that is conducted incidentally to the arrest (*Ker v. California*, *supra*, and *Sabbath v. U.S.*, 391 U.S.585 (1968)).

6.2.5. RETURN

Once the arrest is effected, the warrant must be endorsed and returned to the issuing magistrate. Rule 5 (a) sets forth the procedure whereby the accused is brought before the commissioner and advised of the charges against him.

6.2.6. PROCEEDINGS BEFORE COMMISSIONER

6.2.6.1 *Appearance Before Commissioner.* An officer making an arrest under a warrant issued upon a complaint or any person making an arrest without a warrant shall take the arrested person without unnecessary delay before the nearest available commissioner or before any other nearby officer empowered to commit persons charged with offense against the laws of the United States. When a person arrested without a warrant is brought before a commissioner or other officer, a complaint shall be filed forthwith.

6.2.6.2. *Statement by the Commissioner.* The commissioner shall inform the defendant of the complaint against him and of any affidavit filed therewith, of his right to retain counsel, of his right to request the assignment of counsel if he is unable to obtain counsel, and of his right to have a preliminary examination. He shall also inform the defendant that he is not required to make a statement and that any statement made by him may be used against him. The commissioner shall allow the defendant reasonable time and opportunity to consult counsel and shall admit the defendant to bail as provided in these rules.

The arrestee must be brought before the commissioner or magistrate without unnecessary delay. In *Mallory v. U.S.,* 354 U.S. 449 (1957), the court said,

> The scheme for initiating a federal prosecution is plainly defined. The police may not arrest upon mere suspicion but only probable cause. The next step in the proceedings is to arraign the arrested person before a judicial officer as quickly as possible so that he may be advised of his rights and so that the issues of probable cause may be promptly determined. The arrested person may, of course, be booked by the police. But he is not to be taken to police headquarters in order to carry out a process of inquiry that lends itself, even if not so designed, to eliciting damaging statements to support the arrest and ultimately guilt.
>
> The duty enjoined upon arresting officers to arraign "without unnecessary delay" indicates that the command does not call for mechanical or automatic obedience. Circumstances may justify a brief delay between arrest and arraignment, as for example, where the story volunteered by the accused is subject to quick verification through third parties. But the delay must not be of a nature to give opportunity for the extraction of a confession.

It should be noted that the *Mallory* decision was handed down some time prior to *Miranda* and *Escobedo, supra.* See also *Mc-Nabb v. U.S.,* 318 U.S.332 (1943), where the court stated that the gist of Rule 5 (a) is that "the person arrested under warrant shall be taken before a commissioner or magistrate without unnecessary delay."

6.2.6.3. State and Federal Arrest Standards. The states may require more stringent procedures in the instance of arrest and searches with or without warrants. However, they may not require less than the federal standards. It should also be noted that the laws of the state where the arrest occurs is determinative in federal cases. Thus, evidence illegally obtained according to state law will be inadmissable in a federal court, even if constitutional requirements are not violated *(U.S. v. Di Re, supra).*

6.2.7. UNLAWFUL ARREST

Several ramifications may flow from an unlawful arrest. These include the following:

1. Evidence gathered as the result of an unlawful arrest may not be used against the accused.
2. An action against the officers may lie for civil damages. In this connection the Supreme Court held in *Bivens v. Six Unknown Named Agents,* 403 U.S.388 (1971) that indeed law enforcement agents (here federal narcotics) may be civilly liable to a defendant where they have violated his constitutional rights. Governmental immunity from suit will not apply. This decision puts the government agent on the same footing as a private citizen with regard to the infringement of another's constitutional rights. The reader is also directed to the Civil Rights Act of 1964, with regard to the deprivation of one's *civil rights* under color of law.
3. It may be a crime to make an unlawful arrest.
4. Disciplinary action on the part of the law enforcement agency may result.

Usually, a court's jurisdiction will not be defeated merely because the arrestee was brought before it by unlawful means. Even a forcible abduction from another jurisdiction will not impair the court's ability to try the individual *(Ker v. Illinois,*

Figure 4-9

United States District Court

FOR THE

....

UNITED STATES OF AMERICA

vs.

Commissioner's Docket No.................

Case No.................

AFFIDAVIT FOR
SEARCH WARRANT

BEFORE

Name of Commissioner

Address of Commissioner

The undersigned being duly sworn deposes and says:

That he (has reason to believe) that (on the person of)
(is positive)[1] (on the premises known as)

* in the District of

there is now being concealed certain property, namely

here describe property

which are

here give alleged grounds for search and seizure

And that the facts tending to establish the foregoing grounds for issuance of a Search Warrant are as follows:

....,
Signature of Affiant.

....,
Official Title, if any.

Sworn to before me, and subscribed in my presence,   , 19

....,
United States Commissioner.

[1] The Federal Rules of Criminal Procedure provide: "The warrant shall direct that it be served in the daytime, but if the affidavits are positive that the property is on the person or in the place to be searched, the warrant may direct that it be served at any time." (Rule 41C)

139

Figure 4-10

𝕮𝖔𝖚𝖓𝖙𝖞 𝕮𝖔𝖚𝖗𝖙

In the County Court
City and County of Denver } **AFFIDAVIT FOR SEARCH WARRANT**
State of Colorado

BEFORE __The undersigned County Judge_____

The undersigned, an officer authorized by law to execute warrants within the City and County of Denver, State of Colorado, being duly sworn deposes and says: That he (has reason to believe) (is positive) that on (the premises) (on the person) known as_____ _____ in the City and County of Denver, State of Colorado, there is now located certain property, to-wit:

which _____
      (Here give alleged grounds for search and seizure — Colorado Rules of Criminal Procedure as set forth in Rule 41)

and the facts tending to establish the foregoing grounds for issuance of a search warrant are as follows:

_____
                                                      Signature of Affiant.

Sworn to before me and subscribed in my presence this_____ day of_____, 19____, in the City and County of Denver, State of Colorado.

_____
                                                      County Judge

Affidavit for Search Warrant
Form 370 (5/70) P/D

APPLICATION AND AFFIDAVIT FOR SEARCH WARRANT

State of Colorado
County of Adams

In the .... Court

Before ...., Judge

...., affiant, being first duly sworn, upon oath deposeth and says: That affiant has reason to believe that on the person of or on the premises at or in the motor vehicle described as

....

in the County of Adams, State of Colorado, is located certain property, to-wit:

....

for which a search warrant may be issued under the provisions of Rule 41, Colo. R. Crim. P., on grounds that said property is stolen; that said property is designed and intended for use as a means of committing a criminal offense; that said property is or has been used as a means of committing a criminal offense; that the possession of said property is illegal; and that said property would be material evidence in a subsequent criminal prosecution.

The facts which give rise to this belief and which establish probable cause to believe that grounds for the issuance of a search warrant exist are the following:

Application is hereby made for issuance of a search warrant, directed to any officer authorized by law to execute warrants in the county wherein said property is located, commanding said officer to search forthwith the person or place hereinabove named for said property, and the said property and every part thereof to take, remove and seize, using such force as may reasonably be required in the execution of the warrant, and directing that return thereof be made to the judge issuing the warrant.

Affiant has read the above and foregoing application and affidavit, and the statements therein contained are true to the best of his knowledge, information and belief.

....

Subscribed and sworn to before me this .... day of ...., 19.....

....

Judge

119 U.S.436 (1886)). It should be noted, however, that officers indulging in such practice could be subjected to prosecution under kidnapping laws (*Sewel v. U.S.*, 406 F.2d 1289 (1969)).

6.3. Search Warrant

To provide the necessary security against unreasonable intrusions upon the private lives of individuals, the framers of the

Figure 4-11

United States District Court

FOR THE

Commissioner's Docket No.

Case No.

UNITED STATES OF AMERICA

v.

SEARCH WARRANT

To

Affidavit having been made before me by

that he $\left\{\begin{array}{l}\text{has reason to believe}\\\text{is positive}^1\end{array}\right\}$ that $\left\{\begin{array}{l}\text{on the person of}\\\text{on the premises known as}\end{array}\right\}$

in the   District of

there is now being concealed certain property, namely ....

here describe property

which are ....

here give alleged grounds for search and seizure

and as I am satisfied that there is probable cause to believe that the property so described is being concealed on the $\left\{\begin{array}{l}\text{person}\\\text{premises}\end{array}\right\}$ above described and that the foregoing grounds for application for issuance of the search warrant exist.

You are hereby commanded to search forthwith the $\left\{\begin{array}{l}\text{person}\\\text{place}\end{array}\right\}$ named for the property specified, serving this warrant and making the search $\left\{\begin{array}{l}\text{in the daytime}\\\text{at any time in the day or night}^1\end{array}\right\}$ and if the property be found there to seize it, leaving a copy of this warrant and a receipt for the property taken, and prepare a written inventory of the property seized and return this warrant and bring the property before me within ten days of this date, as required by law.

Dated this   day of   , 19

....,

U. S. Commissioner.

1. The Federal Rules of Criminal Procedure provide: "The warrant shall direct that it be served in the daytime, but if the affidavits are positive that the property is on the person or in the place to be searched, the warrant may direct that it be served at any time." (Rule 41C)

Figure 4-12

RETURN

I received the attached search warrant _____ , 19 ____ , and have executed it as follows:

On _____ , 19 __ at _____ o'clock ___ M, I searched {the person / the premises} described in the warrant and

I left a copy of the warrant with ....
name of person searched or owner or "at the place of search"
together with a receipt for the items seized.

The following is an inventory of property taken pursuant to the warrant:

This inventory was made in the presence of

and

I swear that this Inventory is a true and detailed account of all the property taken by me on the warrant.

....

Subscribed and sworn to and returned before me this _____ day of _____ , 19 __

....
United States Commissioner.

fourth amendment required adherence to judicial processes whenever possible. Thus, a search warrant is required whenever a search is to be made, in the absence of certain recognized exceptions. The court, in speaking of obtaining warrants prior to conducting searches, stated in *McDonald v. U.S.*, 335 U.S.451 (1948), "We are not dealing with formalities. The presence of a search warrant serves a high function. Absent some grave emergency, the fourth amendment has interposed a magistrate between the citizen and the police. This was done not to shield the criminals nor to make the home a safe haven for illegal activities. It was done so that an objective mind might weigh the need to invade that privacy in order to enforce the law. The right of privacy was deemed too precious to entrust to the discretion of those whose job is the detection of crime and the arrest of criminals. . . . And so the Constitution requires a magistrate to pass on the desires of the police before they violate the privacy of the home."

6.4. Search and Seizure

6.4.1. AUTHORITY TO ISSUE WARRANT. A search warrant authorized by this rule may be issued by a judge of the United States or of a state, commonwealth, territorial court of record, or by a United States commissioner within the district wherein the property sought is located.

6.4.2. GROUNDS FOR ISSUANCE. A warrant may be issued under this rule to search for and seize any property.
  1. Stolen or embezzled in violation of the laws of the United States.
  2. Designed or intended for use or which is or has been used as the means of committing a criminal offense.
  3. Possessed, controlled, or designed or intended for use or which is or has been used in violation of Title 18, U.S.C., §957.*

6.4.3. ISSUANCE AND CONTENTS. A warrant shall issue only on affidavit sworn to before the judge or commissioner and establishing the grounds for issuing the warrant. If the judge or commissioner is satisfied that grounds for the application exist or that there is probable cause to believe that they exist, he shall issue a warrant identifying the property and naming or describing the person or place to be searched. The warrant shall be directed to a civil officer of the United States authorized to enforce or assist in enforcing any law thereof or to a person so authorized by the President of the United States. It shall state the grounds or prob-

---

* 18 U.S.C. 3103a. Additional grounds for issuing warrant. In addition to the grounds for issuing a warrant in section 3103 of this title (rule 41): a warrant may be issued to search for and seize any property that constitutes evidence of a criminal offense in violation of the law of the United States.

able cause for its issuance and the names of the persons whose affidavits have been taken in support thereof. It shall command the officer to search forthwith the person or place named for the property specified. The warrant shall direct that it be served in the daytime, but if the affiants are positive that the property is on the person or in the place to be searched, the warrant may direct that it be served at any time. It shall designate the district judge or the commissioner to whom it shall be returned.

6.4.4. EXECUTION AND RETURN WITH INVENTORY. The warrant may be executed and returned only within ten days after its date. The officer taking property under the warrant shall give to the person from whom or from whose premises the property was taken a copy of the warrant and a receipt for the property taken or shall leave the copy and receipt at the place from which the property was taken. The return shall be made promptly and shall be accompanied by a written inventory of any property taken. The inventory shall be made in the presence of the applicant for the warrant and the person from whose possession or premises the property was taken, if they are present, or in the presence of at least one credible person other than the applicant for the warrant or the person from whose possession or premises the property was taken, and shall be verified by the officer. The judge or commissioner shall upon request deliver a copy of the inventory to the person from whom or from whose premises the property was taken and to the applicant for the warrant.

6.4.5. MOTION FOR RETURN OF PROPERTY AND TO SUPPRESS EVIDENCE. A person aggrieved by an unlawful search and seizure may move the district court for the district in which the property was seized for the return of the property and to suppress for use as evidence anything so obtained on the ground that (1) the property was illegally seized without warrant, or (2) the warrant is insufficient on its face, or (3) the property seized is not that described in the warrant, or (4) there was not probable cause for believing the existence of the grounds on which the warrant was issued, or (5) the warrant was illegally executed. The judge shall receive evidence on any issue of fact necessary to the decision of the motion. If the motion is granted, the property shall be restored unless otherwise subject to lawful detention and it shall not be admissible in evidence at any hearing or trial.

The motion to suppress evidence may also be made in the district where the trial is to be held. The motion shall be made before the trial or hearing unless opportunity did not exist or the defendant was not aware of the grounds for the motion, but the court in its discretion may entertain the motion at the trial or hearing.

6.4.6. RETURN OF PAPERS TO CLERK. The judge or commissioner who has issued a search warrant shall attach to the warrant a copy of the return, inventory, and all other papers in connection therewith and shall file them with the clerk of the district court for the district in which the property was seized.

6.4.7. SCOPE AND DEFINITION. This rule does not modify any act, inconsistent with it, regulating search, seizure, and the issuance and execution of search warrants in circumstances for which special provision is made. The term "property" is used in this rule to include documents, books, papers, and any other tangible objects.

6.5. Summary, State and Federal Practice

6.5.1. AUTHORITY TO ISSUE WARRANT

As in Rule 4, a warrant may be issued by a United States judge or commissioner. In the case of nonfederal warrants, generally a judge presiding over a court of general jurisdiction, such as county or district court, may issue.

6.5.2. GROUNDS FOR ISSUANCE

Search warrants may issue only for contraband, fruits, instrumentalities, or evidence of criminal conduct. See *Warden v. Hayden, supra.*

6.5.3. ISSUANCE AND CONTENTS

Search warrants may issue only upon an affidavit, sworn before the magistrate, demonstrating that there is probable cause to believe grounds exist for its issuance. The magistrate may not serve merely as a rubber stamp for the police, but must make an informed, intelligent, and deliberate determination upon the facts or circumstances *presented in the affidavit under oath (Aguilar v. Texas*, 378 U.S.108 (1964); *Giordenello v. U.S., supra; U.S. v. Harris*, 403 U.S.573 (1971)).

The affidavits for search warrants must be tested and interpreted by courts in a common sense and realistic fashion. The magistrate's finding of probable cause may rest upon evidence which is not legally competent in a criminal trial. This would include heresay based upon information from an informant that the affiant believes to be reliable and credible. See *U.S. v. Ventresca*, 380 U.S.102 (1965); *Rugendorf v. U.S.*, 376 U.S.528 (1964); and *Jones v. U.S.*, 362 U.S.257 (1960).

It must be noted that if the affidavit is based on information obtained from someone other than the affiant (heresay), some of the underlying circumstances which would make it possible for the magistrate to judge the validity of the informants' conclusions must be set forth, such as evidence sought is where the informant said it was, and the facts must justify the magistrate's finding that the informant was reliable (*Spinelli v. U.S., supra* and *McCray v. Illinois*, 386 U.S.300 (1967)).

Aguilar v. Texas, supra, set out alternative tests in allowing heresay from an informant to form the basis of probable cause: The informant must declare either that (1) he has personally seen or perceived the fact or facts asserted, or (2) that his information is heresay, but there is good reason for believing it. See also *Costello v. U.S.*, 324 F.2d 260 (1963).

The warrant must specifically identify the property to be seized and name or describe the persons or place to be searched. The description must be particular enough so the executing officers may readily identify the subject of the warrant.

The requirement that the items to be seized be particularly described was inserted into the amendment to prevent general searches. Thus, the seizing of items not listed in the warrant, which do not fall within the exceptions noted, will be unlawful. There is nothing left to the discretion of the officer in executing the warrant. He may seize only those items listed.

The search warrant must be directed to a named or described law enforcement agent. It must state the grounds for its issuance, and the names of persons whose affidavits have been used in its support. See Annot., 49 A.L.R.2d (1209).

When the items to be seized are books, and the basis of the seizure is the ideas which they contain, there must be scrupulous exactitude in the warrants' description (*Stanford v. Texas,* 379 U.S.476 (1965)).

A warrant which directs the seizure of certain items does not authorize the seizure of items not described therein. However, if during a lawful execution of warrant, officers observe items not mentioned in the warrant, but which are contraband, instrumentalities, fruits, or evidence of specific criminal conduct, such items may be seized without obtaining another warrant. See *Maron v. U.S., supra; Johnson v. U.S.,* 293 F.2d 539 (1961); *Abel v. U.S.;* and *Harris v. U.S., supra.*

6.5.4. EXECUTION AND RETURN

The search warrant, unlike the arrest warrant, must be served in the daytime unless the magistrate is satisfied that the public interest requires that it should not be subject to such a restriction. A daytime warrant served after sunset or after dark is void. *Jones v. U.S., supra; U.S. v. Gosser,* 339 F.2d 102 (1964); and *Pugliese v. U.S.,* 343 F.2d 837 (1965).

The search warrant is valid for ten days from date of issue and before it is served, the officers must, as with warrants of arrest, announce their authority and purpose (in the absence of exceptions noted). See *Miller v. U.S.,* 357 U.S.301 (1958). Generally, a copy of the warrant will be given to the aggrieved party at the time of search, in addition to a copy of a property inventory of items taken. The warrant, after being executed, must be returned to the issuing magistrate with an inventory of the items taken.

6.5.5. MOTION TO SUPPRESS AND RETURN OF PROPERTY

A person aggrieved by an unlawful search and seizure may, upon the grounds specified in rule 41 (e), petition the district court wherein the property was seized to return the property, and suppress its use in evidence.

6.6. Warrant to Obtain Fingerprints and Other Identification Evidence Prior to Arrest

Frequently the police have a strong suspicion that a certain in-

Figure 4-13

County Court

<table>
<tr><td>

In the County Court
City and County of Denver
State of Colorado

The People of the State
of Colorado

</td><td>

Before The Denver County Court _____

SEARCH WARRANT

</td></tr>
</table>

To _____ an officer authorized by law to execute warrants within the City and County of Denver, State of Colorado, having this date filed an affidavit for a Search Warrant in conformity with the provisions of Colorado Rules of Criminal Procedure (Rule 141), for the following described property, to-wit:

believed to be situated (at the place) or (on the person) known as: _____
_____ , City and County of Denver, State of Colorado.
upon one or more grounds as set forth in Rule 141, Colorado Rules of criminal procedure, namely:

and as I am satisfied that there is probable cause to believe that the property so described is located on the (person) (premises) above described. YOU ARE THEREFORE COMMANDED to search forthwith the place or person above described for the property described (during the daytime) (at any time) and to make return of this Warrant to the undersigned County Judge within 10 days of the date thereof, and to deliver to the person from whom the property is taken or from whose premise the property is taken, a copy of this Warrant together with a receipt for the property taken, or, in lieu thereof, to leave the copy and receipt at the place from which the property is taken, and to deliver to the undersigned County Judge a written inventory of the property with the return of this warrant.

Dated on _____ , 19____ , in the City and County of Denver, State of Colorado.

_____
County Judge

Search Warrant
Form 371 (8/66) P/D

149

Figure 4-14

CITY AND COUNTY OF DENVER
STATE OF COLORADO   } **RETURN AND INVENTORY**

I, _____ , received the within Search Warrant

on _____ , 19 _____ , and duly executed it as follows:

On _____ , 19 _____ , at _____ o'clock ___ M., I searched

(the person) (the premises) described in the search warrant and left a copy of the search warrant

with: _____
                    (Name of person searched, or owner, or at the place of search)

together with an inventory of the property taken.

The following is an inventory of property taken pursuant to the search warrant:

This inventory was made by _____
                                        (Signature of officer who obtained warrant)

in the presence of _____
                                        (Signature of another officer or credible person)

and is a true and detailed account of all property taken pursuant to the search warrant.

dividual has committed a crime under investigation. However, the law enforcement agency may not have a prior record of the suspect, which would yield fingerprints, photographs, voice prints, or other identification material. In such cases, it is desirable to order the individual to submit to fingerprinting or other processes, without actually arresting the person. The court has held that where there is no probable cause for arrest, an individual may not be summarily picked up on a pretext charge simply for the purpose of being brought down to the station for printing, photographing, or other tests, in the absence of consent on the part of the suspect. Any evidence which is taken during such an illegal detention may not be used subsequently against the person (*Davis v. Mississippi*, 394 U.S.721 (1969)). What this means is that one or more suspects of a particular crime cannot be brought to the station and fingerprinted, unless they voluntarily come. The same would hold true with regard to handwriting exemplars, blood or urine specimens, hair samples, lineups, or other nontestimonial identification procedures. Again, it must be noted that the exclusion of this type of evidence will only result where there is no valid waiver, or if there is an unlawful arrest.

Section 7. PRIVACY

This section deals with the right to privacy under the fourth amendment. Specifically, the admissibility of evidence obtained by wiretapping, eavesdropping, and electronic surveillance are discussed.

Mapp v. Ohio, discussed *supra*, although not connected with the problem of wiretapping, established the principle that evidence secured in violation of certain fourth amendment rights is inadmissible. *Mapp* in fact overruled every state court decision admitting evidence secured by electronic eavesdropping when the police had committed any trespass.

Electronic eavesdropping has attained a great deal of popularity in recent years for prosecutions where there is little tangible evidence of the crime itself, such as with narcotics, gambling, bribery, and conspiracy offenses. Quaere, is electronic surveillance "unreasonable" within the terms of the fourth amendment?

Figure 4-15

SEARCH WARRANT

State of Colorado   In the .... Court

       ss.

County of Adams   Before ...., Judge

The People of the State of Colorado

TO: Any officer authorized by law to execute warrants within the County of Adams, State of Colorado, *Greetings:*

Whereas, application and affidavit for a search warrant for the following described property, to-wit:

has this date been subscribed, sworn to and filed with this Court under and pursuant to the provisions of Rule 41, Colo. R. Crim. P., by ....

.............................., affiant (s) ; and *Whereas* the undersigned judge is satisfied that there is probable cause to believe that there exists one or more of the grounds prescribed by said rule for issuance of a search warrant, namely:

That said property is stolen.

That said property is designed and intended for use as a means of committing a criminal offense.

That said property is or has been used as a means of committing a criminal offense.

That the possession of said property is illegal.

And that said property would be material evidence in a subsequent criminal prosecution.

And whereas said property is believed to be situate at the place, on the person, and/or in the motor vehicle described as:

....,

in the County of Adams, State of Colorado;

You are hereby commanded to search forthwith the place, person or vehicle above described for said property, and the said property and every part thereof to take, remove and seize, using such force as may reasonably be required in the performance of the acts and duties hereby commanded; to deliver to the person from whom or from whose premises the property is taken a copy of this warrant together with a receipt for the property taken, or, in lieu thereof, to leave the said copy and receipt at the place from which the property is taken; and

You are directed to make return of this warrant to Judge ....

.................................., whose office is located in the Hall of Justice of Adams County, 1931 East Bridge Street, Brighton, Colorado, accompanied by a written and verified inventory of the property taken, WITHIN TEN (10) DAYS OF THE DATE HEREOF.

Dated this .... day of ...., A.D. 19.....

Approved as to form:

Floyd Marks,

District Attorney

....

                               Judge

By ....

     Deputy District Attorney

Figure 4-16

RETURN OF SEARCH WARRANT

State of Colorado

ss.

County of Adams

On the .... day of ...., A.D., 19...., I duly executed the attached Search Warrant at .... in the County of ...., State of Colorado by searching the person, place, premises, or motor vehicle in said warrant described; and by taking into my possession therefrom the property described in the *inventory of property taken on search warrant* hereto attached, and by (strike one):

1. Giving to ...., the person from whom or from whose premises the property was taken, a copy of the warrant and a receipt for the property taken.

2. Leaving at the place from which the property was taken a copy of the warrant and a receipt for the property taken.

The undersigned is an officer authorized by law to execute warrants in the said county wherein the said property was located at the time of execution of the Search Warrant.

....

Officers

....

Official Title

The courts have allowed the admittance of information gained as the result of eavesdropping, on the theory that the *source* of the evidence was not a matter of judicial determination, providing that no trespass was committed in its interception. The principle of the *exclusionary rule,* which developed first in the Federal Courts in the *Weeks* decision, applied originally to federal officers only. The rule stated that information obtained by federal officers who trespassed was inadmissible, while the same information, if obtained in like manner by state officers, *was* admissible. It did not matter by what means the information was intercepted, i.e. wiretapping or bug, as long as no trespass was committed. The demise of the so-called "silver platter doctrine" which allowed the practice of permitting illegally gotten evidence from state officials to be admitted in federal or state prosecutions, came with *Elkins v. U.S.,* 364 U.S.206 (1960). After *Elkins,* any illegally obtained evidence was inadmissible in fed-

Figure 4-17

The following is the text of a federal application for a search warrant concerning gambling activities.

IN THE UNITED STATES DISTRICT COURT FOR THE DISTRICT OF NEBRASKA

United States of America,	Magistrate's Doc. No. 1
Plaintiff,	Case No. 8
v.	Application for Search Warrant
In re premises known as the	
Located Defendant.	

Comes now John B. McPhee, Jr., Special Agent, Federal Bureau of Investigation, and requests Richard C. Peck, United States Magistrate for the District of Nebraska, to forthwith issue a search warrant to the above-named applicant, and Special Agents of the Federal Bureau of Investigation, for the search of the premises described above and in the affidavit executed by John B. McPhee, Jr., Special Agent, Federal Bureau of Investigation, which is attached hereto and by this reference made a part hereof as if fully set forth herein, which affidavit is submitted as the grounds and probable cause for the issuance of said search warrant pursuant to the provisions of Rule 41 of the Federal Rules of Criminal Procedure.

AFFIDAVIT

United States of America

ss.

District of Nebraska

Before me the undersigned, Richard C. Peck, United States Magistrate for the District of Nebraska, personally appeared John B. McPhee, Jr., who being first duly sworn deposes and says:

1. That affiant is a Special Agent of the Federal Bureau of Investigation, at all times pertinent hereto stationed at Omaha, Nebraska.

2. I have supervised the conducting of the investigation of the offenses of Max Abramson and, as a result of my personal participation in that investigation and of reports made to me by Agents under my direction, I am familiar with all the circumstances of the offenses herein related.

3. From my experience in the investigation of over seventy-five interstate gambling investigations and from consultations with other Special Agents of the Omaha, Nebraska, office of the Federal Bureau of Investigation, I know that a bookmaker in the bookmaking business must receive and furnish "line" information. This is necessary to stimulate the betting activity and to enable him to operate his business with the greatest chance of profit. The "line" is the point spread or odds in an athletic contest used in placing or receiving bets.

When it is stated the "line" was given on football games by a bookmaker, what is meant is that the odds on a football game were given to someone by the bookmaker. The odds on a football game are quoted on the teams themselves. As an example, if the bookmaker quotes a "line" as Nebraska 10 over Oklahoma what is meant is that Nebraska is favored by 10 points to beat Oklahoma. "Line" information is also furnished for all sporting events, including, but not limited to, baseball, basketball, football, boxing matches, hockey games, and horse races.

"Line" information is usually given out on the first call of each day with each person. The bookmaker will receive his "line" from a handicapper who specializes in determining what the odds will be in an athletic contest. The bookmaker will then furnish the "line" to his customers, who will study it, compare it with other "lines" and/or "prices," and then make a wager at that time or later that day. The "line" or point spread on sporting contests tends to change from day to day as respective abilities of the teams are assessed; such factors as sickness or injury to key players will have a great effect on the sports "line."

A professional bookmaker will usually make or accept bets only after he has received his "line" information. Your affiant knows through his investigation of gambling matters that calls involving the making or accepting of a sports wager are usually short in duration, rarely lasting over thirty seconds.

Constant access to a telephone is necessary for the successful operation of a bookmaking business. In order for a bookmaker to carry on his illegal activities, it is generally necessary for him to periodically change the location of the telephone facility he utilizes in furtherance of his gambling activities. This is done to avoid detection by the authorities. It is also a commonplace practice for bookmakers to attempt to disguise the location of the telephone they utilize in furtherance of their gambling activities by using pay telephones or telephones listed to third parties or by having third parties act as intermediaries.

4. From information gleaned from investigations conducted by your affiant and other Special Agents of the Federal Bureau of Investigation, and physical surveillances, your affiant believes that (defendant) is a bookmaker engaged in the business of making illicit wages on major sports events and utilizes telephone number (———) in the operation of said bookmaking business.

(a) A confidential informant hereinafter referred to as Confidential Informant I has furnished reliable information to the Omaha Office of the Federal Bureau of Investigation continuously since April, 1968. Said information provided by Confidential Informant I has been repeatedly substantiated by independent investigation and has led to four arrests for gambling offenses and to one conviction for Interstate Transmission of Wagering Information, 18 USC 1084. On November 10, 1970, Confidential Informant I informed your affiant that he personally observed wages on major sports events being placed in the Rocket Recreation Center in the Securities Building basement in the presence of (defendant) as recently as the first week of November, 1970. The official listed location for the Securities Building is (——————). The (——————) is located in the basement of this building, with its entrance located at (——————). This is the address of the (——————) which will be referred to herein.

Confidential Informant I is a self-admitted habitual gambler. Confidential Informant I has admitted to your affiant that as a result of his gambling activities he knows and associates with recognized hoodlums and gamblers in the (——————) area. As a direct result of these associations he has known (defendant) as a major Omaha bookmaker for the last twenty years.

Confidential Informant I last furnished information to your affiant on November 10, 1970, at which time he stated that (defendant) was conducting a large bookmaking operation out of the (——————).

(b) A confidential informant hereinafter referred to as Confidential Informant II has been furnishing reliable information continuously to Agents of the Omaha Office of the Federal Bureau of Investigation since November 8, 1965. The information provided by Confidential Informant II has been repeatedly substantiated by independent investigation and has led to at least ten arrests involving gambling offenses. Confidential Informant II is a self-admitted bookmaker who has admitted to affiant that his sole source of income is derived from his bookmaking activities. Confidential Informant II has held conversations with (defendant) regarding gambling activities on at least five occasions during the last four months. In these conversations (defendant) has told Confidential Informant II that he receives "line" information from Las Vegas and this is the "line" information he uses in conducting his bookmaking business. As a result of those conversations Confidential Informant II has learned that the son-in-law of (defendant) is residing in Las Vegas, Nevada, and is facilitating (defendant's) receipt of "line" information. Confidential Informant II admits that as a result of his bookmaking activities in the last five years he associates with other bookmakers and known gamblers in the Omaha area. As a result of his dealings and conversations with other known bookmakers and gamblers he knows that (defendant) is one of the largest bookmakers in the Omaha, Nebraska area and that he receives his "line" information daily from a source in Las Vegas, Nevada. Confidential Informant II has last supplied information to your affiant with regard to (defendant's) gambling activities on November 10, 1970.

(c) John R. Anderson is a Special Agent of the Federal Bureau of Investigation assigned to the Omaha, Nebraska, Office. Special Agent Anderson has been working under the direction of your affiant in the scope of this investigation. Special Agent Anderson reported to your affiant that he has a confidential informant hereinafter referred to as Confidential Informant III who has reported to Special Agent Anderson that he is a self-admitted professional gambler. Confidential Informant III has informed Agent Anderson that he has conducted gambling transactions consisting of wagers on major sports events with (defendant) continuously for at least the last five years. On November 20, 1970, Confidential Informant III informed Agent Anderson that he has called (defendant) at the above-mentioned location, telephone number (———), at least ten times in the last six months, and on each of these occasions has received "line" information from (defendant) and that he personally has placed bets with (defendant). On November 22, 1970, Confidential Informant III advised that he had been in personal contact with (defendant) at the (———) on November 21, 1970, and had placed a bet with him on a sports event. He further advised Special Agent Anderson that he knows the son-in-law of (defendant), and that he further knows through conversations with defendant that (———) is presently in Las Vegas, and that (———) is aiding his father-in-law, (defendant) in receiving his "line" information from Las Vegas. Confidential Informant III last furnished information regarding (defendant's) gambling activities to Special Agent John R. Anderson on December 11, 1970.

(d) On October 14, 1970, Larry Thompson, Special Agent, Intelligence Division of the Internal Revenue Service, informed your affiant of the following facts:

He stated that approximately 12:20 PM on September 4, 1970, he was present in the (———) and overheard a conversation emanating from one of the two pay telephone booths located therein. Special Agent Thompson heard an unidentified man discuss what appeared to be a wager of 1,000.00 dollars on a baseball game between the New York Mets and the Chicago Cubs. Special Agent Thompson observed this unidentified individual approach (defendant) who was at that time engaged in a telephone conversation. While still on the phone, (defendant) had in his hand what appeared to be a football point sheet. When (defendant) hung up the telephone he engaged the unidentified man in a conversation which was overheard by Special Agent Thompson. (Defendant) stated, "What have you got for me?" and the unidentified man stated that he had 1,000.00 dollars for the Met-Cubs game and did he (the defendant) want it. (The defendant) asked the unidentified individual, "Is it O.K.?" Special Agent Thompson was not able to hear the unidentified man's reply but he did then hear (defendant) state, "You O.K. it, then I'll take it." Special Agent Larry Thompson has been an Internal Revenue Agent for four years, during which time he has spent more than 1,000 man hours analyzing gambling transactions. As a result of his experience in this field he stated to your affiant that it was his professional opinion that this conversation was in regard to an illicit wagering transaction on a major sporting event.

(e) The records of the Northwestern Bell Telephone Company indicate that telephone number (———) is listed to (———). Three extensions for this number are listed. Such extensions are identified as being located in the kitchen, card room, and the pool room of said establishment.

(f) Information furnished to your affiant resulting from confidential informants and periodic surveillances conducted by the Federal Bureau of Investigation and other law enforcement agencies indicates that (defendant) has been present and has been conducting his affairs at the (———) on a continuous basis for the last ten years.

(g) Under the direction of your affiant two-man surveillance teams were placed in the (———) referred to supra between 10:00 AM and 1:00 PM on the following days: November 12, November 13, November 17, November 18, November 21, and November 22, 1970. On November 19 and November 20, 1970, a one-man surveillance was conducted. A total of six agents participated in this surveillance. The agents informed your affiant that (defendant) was present within the (———) between the hours of 10:00 AM and 1:00 PM on each of these days.

(h) On Saturday, November 21, 1970, Special Agents Gerald F. Godfrey and Placide J. Jumonvillo of the Omaha Office of the Federal Bureau of Investigation were assigned by your affiant to conduct a surveillance at the premises known as the (———) referred to supra. Special Agent Godfrey informed your affiant that on Saturday, November 21, 1970, at 11:52 AM a call came into the (———) that (defendant) answered this call on the phone located immediately behind the main counter; that he spoke for a period of four and one-half minutes; that immediately after hanging up on this call he made a series of eight successive calls, no call lasting over thirty seconds. At 12:42 PM Special Agent Godfrey and Special Agent Jumonvillo were standing at the counter when they heard (defendant) say on the phone, "What are the odds on the Michigan game?" Agent Godfrey personally observed the phone on which (defendant) received the calls referred to herein and on which he was speaking when he referred to the Michigan State game and saw that the number listed on the phone was (———).

(i) The (defendant is located in the basement of (———) and is composed of a large lobby containing a counter, numerous pinball machines, and two public telephones; a pool room with pool and snooker tables; a card room with several card tables; and a cafe with kitchen. Also in the basement area is a cocktail lounge known as (———), which uses the same entrance as the (———).

(j) That on December 11, 1970, Confidential Informant III, hereinabove mentioned in subparagraph (c), advised Special Agent Anderson, who has advised affiant, that he has placed a bet with (defendant) within the past four days and (defendant) at that time was located at the (———).

(k) That on December 7, 1970, Confidential Informant III, hereinbefore mentioned in subparagraph (c), advised Special Agent John R. Anderson that through personal conversations with (defendant) that they are conducting a joint gambling business and accepting bets on various major sporting events.

6. Your affiant is familiar with the affidavit executed by Stanley R. Wheeler, Special Agent of the Intelligence Division of the Internal Revenue Service, executed in Clark County, Nevada, on November 24, 1970, and attached hereto. Your affiant believes as a result of the investigation referred to herein that the said (second party) referred to in the attached affidavit is in fact the son-in-law of (defendant) and that he is presently residing in Las Vegas. Your affiant knows of his own personal knowledge that (defendant) has access to and frequently uses telephone number (———) located in the (———) Securities Building, Omaha, Nebraska. As a result of the investigation referred to herein your affiant has reason to believe that (defendant) is receiving his "line" information from Las Vegas, Nevada, on this phone and utilizing this phone to conduct his bookmaking business.

7. As a result of my experience in investigating gambling offenses in the State of Nebraska, I know that Nebraska law prohibits the accepting and making of bets on sports events other than the parimutuel betting conducted at legally authorized race tracks pursuant to state law.

8. On December 2, 1970, Federal Judge Richard E. Robinson, Chief Judge, United States District Court for the District of Nebraska, signed an order authorizing electrical interception of telephone communications of (defendant) and others to and from telephone number (———). Pursuant to this order, Special Agents of the Federal Bureau of Investigation Intercepted telephone communications ordered by the Court. On December 3, 1970, at approximately 12:12 PM Central Standard Time, an incoming telephone call was intercepted by Special Agents Gerald F. Godfrey and John R. Anderson. During this conversation, (defendant) received football "line" information from an individual who affiant has reason to believe was (a fourth party), at that time located in Las Vegas, Nevada.

Special Agent M. B. Parker, Federal Bureau of Investigation, Las Vegas, Nevada, advised affiant on December 10, 1970, that F.B.I. Special Agent Bernard E. Haven, Las Vegas, Nevada, advised him that on December 3, 1970, he personally observed (the fourth party) make a telephone call from a phone booth located in Las Vegas, Nevada, and that he placed numerous coins in the telephone, indicating a long-distance call was being placed.

That Special Agent Anderson has advised affiant that he has interviewed or spoken with (the third party) and (defendant) and is familiar with their voices. That as a result of this familiarity he recognized (the defendant's) voice during the above telephone conversation.

9. That pursuant to the above-mentioned order issued by Judge Robinson Special Agent Anderson intercepted numerous telephone conversations wherein gambling information was exchanged and bets taken on major sports events by both (the third party) and (the defendant). That on December 6, 1970, at 1:01 PM, pursuant to the above-mentioned order, F.B.I.

Special Agents Gerald F. Godfrey and John B. McPhee, Jr., intercepted a call received at the (——) believed to be from (the fifth party) a/k/a (the second party) in Las Vegas, Nevada, wherein (the fifth party) furnished "line" information to (defendant) on various college football games.

10. That affiant has interviewed and had conversations with (defendant) on several occasions and is familiar with his voice. As a result of his familiarity with the voice of (defendant), he recognized his voice during the above telephone conversation.

11. That affiant knows of his personal knowledge that (the third party and defendant) both frequent the (——) described supra on a continuous daily basis and have done so for the last several years.

That in view of the above, affiant has probable cause to believe:

That (defendant) is using telephone number (——) in receiving gambling or wagering information from without the State of Nebraska and he and (the third party) are utilizing said information, and conspiring among themselves and with others to utilize this information, in their gambling business within the State of Nebraska, in violation of Nebraska State law, and all in violation of 18, United States Code, Sections 1084, 1952, and 371.

That (the fifth party) did on December 6, 1970, furnish by interstate communication from Las Vegas, Nevada, to (defendant), in Omaha, Nebraska, gambling information to be used by (defendant) and others in their gambling business, in violation of 18, United States Code, 1084.

That on December 3, 1970, (the fourth party) did furnish from Las Vegas, Nevada, to (defendant) in Omaha, Nebraska, by use of an interstate communication; to wit, by telephone, gambling or wagering information to be used by (defendant) and others in their gambling business, in violation of 18, United States Code, 1084.

That based on all of the above information affiant has probable cause to believe that a search of the premises of (——), as hereinabove described, will disclose gambling paraphernalia, including but not limited to betting slips, sport schedules with "line" or "point spread" information, records, and papers used by (the third party and defendant) in recording their gambling and betting information, and monies received in their gambling transactions, all being evidence of their conducting and conspiring to conduct gambling activities through the receipt of gambling or wagering information by telephone from without the State of Nebraska, in violation of 18, United States Code, Sections 1084, 1952, and 371.

. . . .
John B. McPhee, Jr.

Subscribed in my presence and sworn to before me this . . . . day of December, 1970.

. . . .
Richard C. Peck
United States Magistrate
District of Nebraska

Figure 4-18

IN THE UNITED STATES DISTRICT COURT FOR THE DISTRICT OF NEBRASKA

United States of America,	Magistrate's Doc. No. 1
Plaintiff,	Case No. 8
v.	SEARCH WARRANT
Defendant.	

To: John B. McPhee, Jr., Special Agent, Federal Bureau of Investigation, and other special agents of the Federal Bureau of Investigation.

Affidavit having been made before me by John B. McPhee, Jr., Special Agent, Federal Bureau of Investigation, that he has reason to believe and does believe that on the premises described above there are situated gambling paraphernalia, including but not limited to betting slips, sports schedules with "line" or "point spread" information, records, and papers used by (———) and (defendant) in recording their gambling and betting information, monies received in their gambling transactions, and telephone, which have been used or are being used in violations of 18, United States Code, 1084, 1952, and 371.

You are hereby commanded to search the premises hereinbefore named for the property specified, serving this warrant and making this search in the daytime, and if the property be found there, to seize it, prepare a written inventory of the property seized, and if any seized bring the property before me.

. . . .

Richard C. Peck
United States Magistrate
District of Nebraska

eral court, regardless of who procured it, whether federal or state officer. When *Mapp* was decided in 1961, the last obstacle forbidding the introduction of illegally seized evidence was removed. Subsequent to which, evidence secured in an unreasonable search and seizure could not be admitted in either state or federal court. See *Lopez v. U.S.,* 373 U.S.427 (1963).

Under the fourth amendment, the questions which must be answered are, what is unwarranted intrusion, and how far may law enforcement officers go before their "search" becomes unreasonable and the evidence obtained thereby inadmissible? *Katz v. U.S.,* reprinted *infra,* decided in 1967, determined that the right to privacy does not rest on considerations grounded in property rights (and trespassory invasions thereof), but rather on the *personal* right of privacy. The right may be claimed by an aggrieved party, subject to certain limitations set forth in the opinion. The personal right to be free from governmental intrusion follows the individual wherever he may be and when he reasonably expects such privacy.

7.1. *Katz v. United States*

Mr. Justice Stewart delivered the opinion of the Court.

The petitioner was convicted in the District Court for the Southern District of California under an eight-count indictment charging him with transmitting wagering information by telephone from Los Angeles to Miami and Boston, in violation of a federal statute. At trial the Government was permitted, over the petitioner's objection, to introduce evidence of the petitioner's end of telephone conversations, overheard by FBI agents who had attached an electronic listening and recording device to the outside of the public telephone booth from which he had placed his calls. In affirming his conviction, the Court of Appeals rejected the contention that the recordings had been obtained in violation of the fourth amendment, because "[t]here was no physical entrance into the area occupied by [the petitioner]." We granted certiorari in order to consider the constitutional questions thus presented.

The petitioner has phrased those questions as follows:

1. Whether a public telephone booth is a constitutionally protected area so that evidence obtained by attaching an electronic listening recording device to the top of such a booth is obtained in violation of the right to privacy of the user of the booth.
2. Whether physical penetration of a constitutionally protected area is necessary before a search and seizure can be said to be violative of the fourth amendment to the United States Constitution.

We decline to adopt this formulation of the issues. In the first place, the correct solution of fourth amendment problems is not necessarily promoted by incantation of the phrase "constitutionally protected area." Secondly, the fourth amendment cannot be translated into a general constitutional "right to privacy." That

Note: Katz v. U.S., 389 U.S. 347, 88 S.Ct. 507, 19 L.Ed.2d 576 (1967) .

amendment protects individual privacy against certain kinds of governmental intrusion, but its protections go further, and often have nothing to do with privacy at all. Other provisions of the Constitution protect personal privacy from other forms of governmental invasion. But the protection of a person's *general* right to privacy—his right to be let alone by other people—is, like the protection of his property and of his very life, left largely to the law of the individual states.

Because of the misleading way the issues have been formulated, the parties have attached great significance to the characterization of the telephone booth from which the petitioner placed his calls. The petitioner has strenuously argued that the booth was a "constitutionally protected area." The Government has maintained with equal vigor that it was not. But this effort to decide whether or not a given "area," viewed in the abstract, is "constitutionally protected" deflects attention from the problem presented by this case. The fourth amendment protects people, not places. What a person knowingly exposes to the public, even in his own home or office, is not a subject of fourth amendment protection. . . . But what he seeks to preserve as private, even in an area accessible to the public, may be constitutionally protected. . . .

The Government stresses the fact that the telephone booth from which the petitioner made his calls was constructed partly of glass, so that he was as visible after he entered it as he would have been if he had remained outside. But what he sought to exclude when he entered the booth was not the intruding eye—it was the uninvited ear. He did not shed his right to do so simply because he made his calls from a place where he might be seen. No less than an individual in a business office, in a friend's apartment, or in a taxicab, a person in a telephone booth may rely upon the protection of the fourth amendment. One who occupies it, shuts the door behind him, and pays the toll that permits him to place a call is surely entitled to assume that the words he utters into the mouthpiece will not be broadcast to the world. To read the Constitution more narrowly is to ignore the vital role that the public telephone has come to play in private communication.

The Government contends, however, that the activities of its agents in this case should not be tested by fourth amendment requirements, for the surveillance technique they employed involved no physical penetration of the telephone booth from which the petitioner placed his calls. It is true that the absence of such penetration was at one time thought to foreclose further fourth amendment inquiry, *Olmstead v. U.S.,* 277 U.S.438, 457, 464, 466; *Goldman v. U.S.,* 316 U.S.129, 134-136, for that amendment was thought to limit only searches and seizures of tangible property. But "[t]he premise that property interests control the right of the Government to search and seize has been discredited." *Warden v. Hayden,* 387 U.S.294, 304. Thus, although a closely divided court supposed in *Olmstead* that surveillance without any trespass and without the seizure of any material object fell outside the ambit of the Constitution, we have since departed from the narrow view on which that decision rested. Indeed, we have expressly held that the fourth amendment governs not only the seizure of tangible items, but extends as well to the recording of oral statements, overheard without any "technical trespass under . . . local property law." *Silverman v. U.S.,* 365 U.S.505, 511. Once this much is acknowledged, and once it is recognized that the fourth amendment protects people—and not simply "areas"—against unreasonable searches and seizures, it becomes clear that the reach of that amendment cannot turn upon the presence or absence of a physical intrusion into any given enclosure.

We conclude that the underpinnings of *Olmstead* and *Goldman* have been so eroded by our subsequent decisions that the "trespass" doctrine there enunciated can no longer be regarded as controlling. The government's activities in electronically listening to and recording the petitioner's words violated the privacy upon which he justifiably relied while using the telephone booth and thus constituted a "search and seizure" within the meaning of the fourth amendment. The fact that the electronic device employed to achieve that end did not happen to penetrate the walls of the booth can have no constitutional significance. The question remaining for decision, then, is whether the search and seizure conducted in this case complied with constitutional standards. In that regard, the government's position is that its agents acted in an entirely defensible manner: They did not begin their electronic surveillance until investigation of the petitioner's activities had established a strong probability that he was using the telephone in question to transmit gambling information to persons in other states, in violation of federal law. Moreover, the surveillance was limited, both in scope and in duration, to the specific purpose of establishing the contents of the petitioner's unlawful telephone communications. The agents confined their surveillance to the brief periods during which he used the telephone booth, and they took great care to overhear only the conversations of the petitioner himself.

Accepting this account of the government's actions as accurate, it is clear that this surveillance was so narrowly circumscribed that a duly authorized magistrate properly notified of the need for such investigation, specifically informed of the basis on which it was to proceed, and clearly apprised of the precise intrusion it would entail, could constitutionally have authorized, with appropriate safeguards, the very limited search and seizure that the government asserts in fact took place. Only last term we sustained the validity of such an authorization, holding that, under sufficiently "precise and discriminate circumstances," a federal court may empower government agents to employ a concealed electronic device "for the narrow and particularized purpose of ascertaining the truth of the . . . allegations" of a "detailed factual affidavit alleging the commission of a specific criminal offense." *Osborn v. U.S.,* 385 U.S.323, 329-330. Discussing that holding, the court in *Berger v. New York,* 388 U.S.41, said that "the order authorizing the use of the electronic device" in *Osborn* "afforded similar protections to those . . . of conventional warrants authorizing the seizure of tangible evidence." Through those protections, "no greater invasion of privacy was permitted than was necessary under the circumstances." *Id.,* at 57. Here, too, a similar judicial order could have accommodated "the legitimate needs of law enforcement"* by authorizing the carefully limited use of electronic surveillance.

The government urges that, because its agents relied upon the decisions in *Olmstead* and *Goldman,* and because they did no more here than they might properly have done with prior ju-

---

* *Lopez v. U.S.,* 373 U.S.427, 464 (dissenting opinion of Mr. Justice Brennan).

dicial sanction, we should retroactively validate their conduct. That we cannot do. It is apparent that the agents in this case acted with restraint. Yet the inescapable fact is that this restraint was imposed by the agents themselves, not by a judicial officer. They were not required, before commencing the search, to present their estimate of probable cause for detached scrutiny by a neutral magistrate. They were not compelled, during the conduct of the search itself, to observe precise limits established in advance by a specific court order. Nor were they directed, after the search had been completed, to notify the authorizing magistrate in detail of all that had been seized. In the absence of such safeguards, this court has never sustained a search upon the sole ground that officers reasonably expected to find evidence of a particular crime and voluntarily confined their activities to the least intrusive means consistent with that end. *Searches conducted without warrants have been held unlawful "notwithstanding facts unquestionably showing probable cause," Agnello v. U.S.,* 269 U.S.20, 33, for the Constitution requires "that the deliberate, impartial judgment of a judicial officer . . . be interposed between the citizen and the police. . . ." *Wong Sun v. U.S.,* 371 U.S.471, 481-482. "Over and again this court has emphasized that the mandate of the [fourth] amendment requires adherence to judicial processes," *U.S. v. Jeffers,* 342 U.S. 48, 51, and *that searches conducted outside the judicial process, without prior approval by judge or magistrate, are per se unreasonable under the fourth amendment*—subject only to a few specifically established and well-delineated exceptions.

It is difficult to imagine how any of those exceptions could ever apply to the sort of search and seizure involved in this case. Even electronic surveillance substantially contemporaneous with an individual's arrest could hardly be deemed an incident of that arrest. Nor could the use of electronic surveillance without prior authorization be justified on grounds of hot pursuit. And, of course, the very nature of electronic surveillance precludes its use pursuant to the suspect's consent.

The government does not question these basic principles. Rather, it urges the creation of a new exception to cover this case. It argues that surveillance of a telephone booth should be exempted from the usual requirement of advance authorization by a magistrate upon a showing of probable cause. Omission of such authorization

> "bypasses the safeguards provided by an objective predetermination of probable cause, and substitutes instead the far less reliable procedure of an after-the-event justification for the . . . search, too likely to be subtly influenced by the familiar shortcomings of hindsight judgment." *Beck v. Ohio,* 379 U.S. 89, 96.

And bypassing a neutral predetermination of the scope of a search leaves individuals secure from fourth amendment violations "only in the discretion of the police." *Id.* at 97.

These considerations do not vanish when the search in question is transferred from the setting of a home, an office, or a hotel room to that of a telephone booth. Wherever a man may be, he is entitled to know that he will remain free from unreasonable searches and seizures. The government agents here ignored *"the procedure of antecedent justification . . . that is central to the Fourth Amendment,"* a procedure that the authors hold to be a constitutional precondition of the kind of electronic surveillance involved in this case. Because the surveillance here failed to meet that condition, and because it led to the petitioner's conviction, the judgment must be reversed.

It is so ordered.

The reader should have extracted several points from the *Katz* ruling:

1. The fourth amendment protects people, not places. Thus, where one reasonably anticipates that his uttered words will not be monitored by government officials, the words will receive the protection of the amendment.
2. What is open to the public view does not fall within the protected class. (See subsection 5.3.)
3. The previous distinction between trespassory invasion, and nonphysical intrusion in conducting a surveillance is no longer determinative of whether fourth amendment rights have been violated.
4. Given the requisite probable cause which would be sufficient for the procurement of a search warrant, government agents may not initiate or conduct a search by electronic means, without prior judicial approval from a neutral, detached magistrate.

5. A search warrant may be obtained upon suitable application, for the limited purpose of conducting an electronic surveillance.

Katz should be distinguished from cases where the defendant misplaces his "trust" and divulges information to a second party, who later is found to be a government agent. The distinction rests on the reasonableness of the defendant in expecting privacy in his dealings with others regarding criminal purposes.

In *Lopez v. U.S., infra,* the defendant attempted to bribe an Internal Revenue agent. The agent had a concealed wire recorder on his person, during the transaction. At trial, the recording was admitted into evidence over objection. The court stated that the agent would have been able to testify to the defendant's actions, and hence the recording served as corroboration of the agent's testimony. The case was distinguished from those where electronic devices were actually planted by agents to effect an unlawful intrusion into an area where privacy would be expected. Here, once it was established that the agent could testify to the transaction, there was no constitutional intrusion. "We think the risk the petitioner took in offering a bribe to the agent fairly included the risk that the offer would be accurately reproduced in court, whether by faultless memory, or mechanical recording."

So also in *On Lee,* where an undercover agent entered a laundry to talk with the defendant, who was wired for sound (with transmitter), the statements overheard by other agents were admissible against the defendant (*On Lee v. U.S.,* 343 U.S.747 (1952)). See *U.S. v. White,* 405 F.2d 838, 394 U.S.957 (1969).

7.1.1. STANDING. Who has "standing" to object to introduction of evidence obtained by unlawful eavesdropping? In *Alderman v. U.S.,* 394 U.S.165 (1969), the court said,

> . . . Any petitioner would be entitled to the supression of government evidence originating in electronic surveillance violative of his own fourth amendment rights to be free from unreasonable searches and seizures. Such violation would occur if the United States unlawfully overheard conversations of a petitioner himself or conversations occurring on his premises, whether or not he was present or participated in those conversations.

Standing should be granted to every person who participates in a conversation he legitimately expects will remain private, for it is such persons that *Katz* protects.

In 1968, as part of the Omnibus Crime Control and Safe Streets Act, Congress enacted broad legislation dealing with electronic eavesdropping. The prohibitions encompass interception, disclosure, or other use of wire or oral communications. In addition, the statutes cover manufacturing, distribution, possession, and advertising of devices intended to be used for the unlawful interception of communications. Unlawfully intercepted communications and their fruits were declared inadmissible in all governmental proceedings. Furthermore, a civil cause of action was provided for persons whose communications were unlawfully intercepted, disclosed, or used.

The aforementioned prohibitions are subject to equally broad exceptions, which allow government agencies to engage in wiretapping and electronic surveillance for the purpose of ferreting out certain types of crime. Statutes dealing with wiretapping and electronic surveillance may be found in 18 U.S.C. 2510 *et seq*.

7.1.2. §2516. AUTHORIZATION FOR INTERCEPTION OF WIRE OR ORAL COMMUNICATIONS. The Attorney General, or any Assistant Attorney General specially designated by the Attorney General, may authorize an application to a Federal judge of competent jurisdiction for, and such judge may grant in conformity with section 2518 of this chapter an order authorizing or approving the interception of wire or oral communications by the Federal Bureau of Investigation, or a Federal agency having responsibility for the investigation of the offense as to which the application is made, when such interception may provide or has provided evidence of the following:

1. Any offense punishable by death or by imprisonment for more than one year under sections 2274 through 2277 of title 42 of the United States Code (relating to the enforcement of the Atomic Energy Act of 1954), or under the following chapters of this title: chapter 37 (relating to espionage), chapter 105 (relating to sabotage), chapter 115 (relating to treason), or chapter 102 (relating to riots).

2. A violation of section 186 or section 501 (c) of title 29, United States Code (dealing with restrictions on payments and loans to labor organizations), or any offense which involves murder, kidnapping, robbery, or extortion, and which is punishable under this title.

3. Any offense which is punishable under the following sections of this title: section 201 (bribery of public officials and witnesses), section 224 (bribery in sporting contests), section 1084 (transmission of wagering information), section 1503 (influencing or injuring an officer, juror, or witness generally), section 1510 (obstruction of criminal investigations), section 1751 (Presidential assassinations, kidnapping, and assault), section 1951 (interference with commerce by threats or violence), section 1952 (interstate and foreign travel or transportation in aid of racketeering enterprises), section 1954 (offer, acceptance, or solicitation to influence operations of employee benefit plan), section 659 (theft from interstate shipment), section 664 (embezzlement from pension and welfare funds), or sections 2314 and 2315 (interstate transportation of stolen property).

4. Any offense involving counterfeiting punishable under section 471, 472, or 473 of this title.

5. Any offense involving bankruptcy fraud or the manufacture, importation, receiving, concealment, buying, selling, or otherwise dealing in narcotic drugs, marihuana, or other dangerous drugs, punishable under any law of the United States.

6. Any offense including extortion in credit transactions under sections 892, 893, or 894 of this title.

7. Any conspiracy to commit any of the foregoing offenses.

The principal prosecuting attorney of any state, or the principal prosecuting attorney of any political subdivision thereof, if such attorney is authorized by a statute of that state to make application to a state court judge of competent jurisdiction for an order authorizing or approving the interception of wire or oral communications, may apply to such judge for, and such judge may grant in conformity with section 2518 of this chapter and with the applicable state statute, an order authorizing or approving the interception of wire or oral communications by investigative or law enforcement officers having responsibility for the investigation of the offense as to which the application is made, when such interception may provide or has provided evidence of the commission of the offense of murder, kidnapping, gambling, robbery, bribery, extortion, or dealing in narcotic drugs, marihuana or other dangerous drugs, or other crime dangerous to life, limb, or property, and punishable by imprisonment for more than one year, designated in any applicable state statute authorizing such interception, or any conspiracy to commit any of the foregoing offenses.

7.1.3. §2517. AUTHORIZATION FOR DISCLOSURE AND USE OF INTERCEPTED WIRE OR ORAL COMMUNICATIONS. Any investigative or law enforcement officer who, by any means authorized by this chapter, has obtained knowledge of the contents of any wire or oral communication, or evidence derived therefrom, may disclose such contents to another investigative or law enforcement officer to the extent that such disclosure is appropriate to the proper performance of the official duties of the officer making or receiving the disclosure.

Any investigative or law enforcement officer who, by any means authorized by this chapter, has obtained knowledge of the contents of any wire or oral communication or evidence derived therefrom may use such contents to the extent such use is appropriate to the proper performance of his official duties.

Any person who has received, by any means authorized by this chapter, any information concerning a wire or oral communication, or evidence derived therefrom intercepted in accordance with the provisions of this chapter may disclose the contents of that communication or such derivative evidence while giving testimony under oath or affirmation in any criminal proceeding in any court of the United States or of any state or in any federal or state grand jury proceeding.

No otherwise privileged wire or oral communication intercepted in accordance with, or in violation of, the provisions of this chapter shall lose its privileged character.

When an investigative or law enforcement officer, while engaged in intercepting wire or oral communications in the manner authorized herein, intercepts wire or oral communications relating to offenses other than those specified in the order of authorization or approval, the contents thereof, and evidence derived therefrom, may be disclosed or used as provided in paragraphs 1 and 2 of this subsection. Such contents and any evidence derived therefrom may be used under paragraph 3 of this subsection when authorized or approved by a judge of competent jurisdiction where such judge finds on subsequent application that the contents were otherwise intercepted in accordance with the provisions of this chapter. Such application shall be made as soon as practicable.

7.1.4. §2518. Procedure for Interception of Wire or Oral Communications. Each application for an order authorizing or approving the interception of a wire or oral communication shall be made in writing upon oath or affirmation to a judge of competent jurisdiction and shall state the applicant's authority to make such application. Each application shall include the following information:

1. The identity of the investigative or law enforcement officer making the application, and the officer authorizing the application.

2. A full and complete statement of the facts and circumstances relied upon by the applicant, to justify his belief that an order should be issued, including a) details as to the particular offense that has been, is being, or is about to be committed, b) a particular description of the nature and location of the facilities from which or the place where the communication is to be intercepted, c) a particular description of the type of communications sought to be intercepted, d) the identity of the person, if known, committing the offense and whose communications are to be intercepted.

3. A full and complete statement as to whether or not other investigative procedures have been tried and failed or why they reasonably appear to be unlikely to succeed if tried or to be too dangerous.

4. A statement of the period of time for which the interception is required to be maintained. If the nature of the investigation is such that the authorization for interception

should not automatically terminate when the described type of communication has been first obtained, a particular description of facts establishing probable cause to believe that additional communications of the same type will occur thereafter.

5. A full and complete statement of the facts concerning all previous applications known to the individual authorizing and making the application, made to any judge for authorization to intercept, or for approval of interceptions of, wire or oral communications involving any of the same persons, facilities or places specified in the application, and the action taken by the judge on each such application.

6. Where the application is for the extension of an order, a statement setting forth the results thus far obtained from the interception, or a reasonable explanation of the failure to obtain such results.

The judge may require the applicant to furnish additional testimony or documentary evidence in support of the application.

Upon such application the judge may enter an ex parte order, as requested or as modified, authorizing or approving interception of wire or oral communications within the territorial jurisdiction of the court in which the judge is sitting, if the judge determines on the basis of the facts submitted by the applicant that the following apply:

1. There is probable cause for belief that an individual is committing, has committed, or is about to commit a particular offense enumerated in §2516 of this chapter.

2. There is probable cause for belief that particular communications concerning that offense will be obtained through such interception.

3. Normal investigative procedures have been tried and have failed or reasonably appear to be unlikely to succeed if tried or to be too dangerous.

4. There is probable cause for belief that the facilities from which, or the place where, the wire or oral communications are to be intercepted are being used, or are about to be used, in connection with the commission of such offense, or are leased to, listed in the name of, or commonly used by such person.

Each order authorizing or approving the interception of any wire or oral communication shall specify the following:

1. The identity of the person, if known, whose communications are to be intercepted.
2. The nature and location of the communications facilities as to which, or the place where, authority to intercept is granted.
3. A particular description of the type of communication sought to be intercepted, and a statement of the particular offense to which it relates.
4. The identity of the agency authorized to intercept the communications and of the person authorizing the application.
5. The period of time during which such interception is authorized, including a statement as to whether or not the interception shall automatically terminate when the described communication has been first obtained.

No order entered under this section may authorize or approve the interception of any wire or oral communication for any period longer than is necessary to achieve the objective of the authorization, nor in any event longer than thirty days. Extensions of an order may be granted, but only upon application for an extension made in accordance with paragraph 1 of this subsection and the court making the findings required by paragraph 3 of this subsection. The period of extension shall be no longer than the authorizing judge deems necessary to achieve the purposes for which it was granted and in no event for longer than thirty days. Every order and extension thereof shall contain a provision that the authorization to intercept shall be executed as soon as practicable, shall be conducted in such a way as to minimize the interception of communications not otherwise subject to interception under this chapter, and must terminate upon attainment of the authorized objective, or in any event in thirty days.

Whenever an order authorizing interception is entered pursuant to this chapter, the order may require reports to be made to the judge who issued the order showing what progress has been made toward achievement of the authorized objective and the need for continued interception. Such reports shall be made at such intervals as the judge may require.

Notwithstanding any other provision of this chapter, any investigative or law enforcement officer, specially designated by the Attorney General or by the principal prosecuting attorney of any state or subdivision thereof acting pursuant to a statute of that state, who reasonably determines:

1. An emergency situation exists with respect to conspiratorial activities threatening the national security interest or to conspiratorial activities characteristic of organized crime that requires a wire or oral communication to be intercepted before an order authorizing such interception can with due diligence be obtained.

2. There are grounds upon which an order could be entered under this chapter to authorize such interception.

Any law enforcement officer, specially designated, may intercept such wire or oral communication if an application for an order approving the interception is made in accordance with this section within forty-eight hours after the interception has occurred, or begins to occur. In the absence of an order, such interception shall immediately terminate when the communication sought is obtained or when the application for the order is denied, whichever is earlier. In the event such application for approval is denied, or in any other case where the interception is terminated without an order having been issued, the contents of any wire or oral communication intercepted shall be treated as having been obtained in violation of this chapter, and an inventory shall be served as provided for in the listing (4) of this section on the person named in the application.

The contents of any wire or oral communication intercepted by any means authorized by this chapter shall, if possible, be recorded on tape or wire or other comparable device. The recording of the contents of any wire or oral communication under this subsection shall be done in such a way as will protect the recording from editing or other alterations. Immediately upon the expiration of the period of the order, or extensions thereof, such recordings shall be made available to the judge issuing such order and sealed under his directions. Custody of the recordings shall be wherever the judge orders. They shall not be destroyed except upon an order of the issuing or denying judge and in any event shall be kept for ten years. Duplicate recordings may be made for use or disclosure pursuant to the provisions of paragraph 1 and 2 of §2517 of this chapter for investigations. The presence of the seal provided for by this subsection, or a satisfactory explanation for the absence thereof, shall be a prerequisite for the use or disclosure of the contents of any wire or oral communication or evidence derived therefrom under paragraph 3 of §2517.

Applications made and orders granted under this chapter shall be sealed by the judge. Custody of the applications and orders shall be wherever the judge directs. Such applications and orders shall be disclosed only upon a showing of good cause before a judge of competent jurisdiction and shall not be destroyed except on order of the issuing or denying judge, and in any event shall be kept for ten years.

Any violation of the provisions of this subsection may be punished as contempt of the issuing or denying judge.

Within a reasonable time but not later than ninety days after the filing of an application for an order of approval under section 2518 which is denied or the termination of the period of an order or extensions thereof, the issuing or denying judge shall cause to be served, on the persons named in the order or the application, and such other parties to intercepted communications as the judge may determine in his discretion that is in the interest of justice, an inventory which shall include notice of the following:

1. The fact of the entry of the order or the application.
2. The date of the entry and the period of authorized, approved or disapproved interception, or the denial of the application.
3. The fact that during the period wire or oral communications were or were not intercepted.

The judge, upon the filing of a motion, may in his discretion make available to such person or his counsel for inspection such portions of the intercepted communications, applications, and orders as the judge determines to be in the interest of justice. Or an ex parte showing of good cause to a judge of competent jurisdiction, the serving of the inventory required by this subsection may be postponed.

The contents of any intercepted wire or oral communication or evidence derived therefrom shall not be received in evidence or otherwise disclosed in any trial, hearing, or other proceeding in a federal or state court unless each party, not less than ten days before the trial, hearing, or proceeding, has been furnished with a copy of the court order, and accompanying application, under which the interception was authorized or approved. This ten-day period may be waived by the judge if he finds that it was not possible to furnish the party with the above information ten days before the trial, hearing, or proceeding and that the party will not be prejudiced by the delay in receiving such information.

Any aggrieved person in any trial, hearing, or proceeding in or before any court, department, officer, agency, regulatory body, or other authority of the United States, a state, or a political subdivision thereof, may move to suppress the contents of any intercepted wire or oral communication, or evidence derived therefrom, on the following grounds:

1. The communication was unlawfully intercepted.
2. The order of authorization or approval under which it was intercepted is insufficient on its face.
3. The interception was not made in conformity with the order of authorization or approval.

Such motion shall be made before the trial, hearing, or proceeding unless there was no opportunity to make such motion or the person was not aware of the grounds of the motion. If the motion is granted, the contents of the intercepted wire or oral communication, or evidence derived therefrom, shall be treated as having been obtained in violation of this chapter. The judge, upon the filing of such motion by the aggrieved person, may in his discretion make available to the aggrieved person or his counsel for inspection such portions of the intercepted communication or evidence derived therefrom as the judge determines to be in the interests of justice.

In addition to any other right to appeal, the United States shall have the right to appeal from an order granting a motion to suppress or the denial of an application for an order of approval, if the United States attorney shall certify to the judge or other official granting such motion or denying such application that the appeal is not taken for purposes of delay. Such appeal shall be taken within thirty days after the date the order was entered and shall be diligently prosecuted.

7.1.5. §2519. REPORTS CONCERNING INTERCEPTED WIRE OR ORAL COMMUNICATIONS. Within thirty days after the expiration of an order (or each extension thereof) entered under subsection **7.1.4.** or the denial of an order approving an interception, the issuing or denying judge shall report the following to the administrative office of the United States court:

1. The fact that an order or extension was applied for.
2. The kind of order or extension applied for.
3. The fact that the order or extension was granted as applied for, was modified, or was denied.
4. The period of interceptions authorized by the order, and the number and duration of any extensions of the order.
5. The offense specified in the order or application, or extension of an order.
6. The identity of the applying investigative or law enforcement officer and agency making the application and the person authorizing the application.
7. The nature of the facilities from which or the place where communications were to be intercepted.

In January of each year the Attorney General, an Assistant Attorney General specially designated by the Attorney General, or the principal prosecuting attorney of a state, or the principal prosecuting attorney for any political subdivision of a state, shall report to the administrative office of the United States Courts the following:

1. The information required by the above listing with respect to each application for an order or extension made during the preceding calendar year.
2. A general description of the interceptions made under such order or extension, including a) the approximate nature and frequency of incriminating communications intercepted, b) the approximate nature and frequency of other communications intercepted, c) the approximate number of persons whose communications were inter-

cepted, and d) the approximate nature, amount, and cost of the manpower and other resources used in the interceptions.

3. The number of arrests resulting from interceptions made under such order or extension, and the offenses for which arrests were made.

4. The number of trials resulting from such interceptions.

5. The number of motions to suppress made with respect to such interceptions, and the number granted or denied.

6. The number of convictions resulting from such interceptions and the offenses for which the convictions were obtained and a general assessment of the importance of the interceptions.

7. The information with respect to orders or extensions obtained in a preceding calendar year.

In April of each year the director of the administrative office of the United States courts shall transmit to the Congress a full and complete report concerning the number of applications for orders authorizing or approving the interception of wire or oral communications and the number of orders and extensions granted or denied during the preceding calendar year. Such reports shall include a summary and analysis of the data required to be filed with the administrative office. The director of the administrative office of the United States courts is authorized to issue binding regulations dealing with the content and form of the reports required to be filed.

Section 8. CITED CASES

8.1. *Chimel v. California*

Mr. Justice Stewart delivered the opinion of the Court.

This case raises basic questions concerning the permissible scope under the fourth amendment of a search incident to a lawful arrest.

The relevant facts are essentially undisputed. Late in the afternoon of September 13, 1965, three police officers arrived at the Santa Ana, California, home of the petitioner with a warrant au-

Note: Chimel v. California, 395 U.S.752, 89 S.Ct. 2034, 23 L.Ed.2d 685 (1969).

thorizing his arrest for the burglary of a coin shop. The officers knocked on the door, identified themselves to the petitioner's wife, and asked if they might come inside. She ushered them into the house, where they waited ten or fifteen minutes until the petitioner returned home from work. When the petitioner entered the house, one of the officers handed him the arrest warrant and asked for permission to "look around." The petitioner objected, but was advised that "on the basis of the lawful arrest," the officers would nonetheless conduct a search. No search warrant had been issued.

Accompanied by the petitioner's wife, the officers then looked through the entire three-bedroom house, including the attic, the garage, and a small workshop. In some rooms the search was relatively cursory. In the master bedroom and sewing room, however, the officers directed the petitioner's wife to open drawers and "to physically move contents of the drawers from side to side so that [they] might view any items that would have come from [the] burglary." After completing the search, they seized numerous items—primarily coins, but also several medals, tokens, and a few other objects. The entire search took between forty-five minutes and an hour.

At the petitioner's subsequent state trial on two charges of burglary, the items taken from his house were admitted into evidence against him, over his objection that they had been unconstitutionally seized. He was convicted, and the judgments of conviction were affirmed by both the California District Court of Appeal, 61 CAL. RPTR. 714, and the California Supreme Court, 68 Cal.2d 436, 439 P.2d 333, 67 CAL.RPTR. 421. Both courts accepted the petitioner's contention that the arrest warrant was invalid because the supporting affidavit was set out in conclusory terms, but held that since the arresting officers had procured the warrant "in good faith," and since in any event they had had sufficient information to constitute probable cause for the petitioner's arrest, that arrest had been lawful. From this conclusion the appellate courts went on to hold that the search of the petitioner's home had been justified, despite the absence of a search warrant, on the ground that it had been incident to a valid arrest. We granted certiorari in order to consider the petitioner's substantial constitutional claims (393 U.S.958).

Without deciding the question, we proceed on the hypothesis that the California courts were correct in holding that the arrest of the petitioner was valid under the Constitution. This brings us directly to whether the warrantless search of the petitioner's entire house can be constitutionally justified as incident to that arrest. The decisions of this Court bearing upon that question have been far from consistent, as even the most cursory review makes evident.

[The Court's discussion of early cases is omitted.]

. . . [I]n *Harris v. U.S.*, 331 U.S.145, decided in 1947 . . . officers had obtained a warrant for Harris' arrest on the basis of his alleged involvement with the cashing and interstate transportation of a forged check. He was arrested in the living room of his four-room apartment, and in an attempt to recover two canceled checks thought to have been used in effecting the forgery, the officers undertook a thorough search of the entire apartment. Inside a desk drawer they found a sealed envelope marked "George Harris, personal papers." The envelope, which was then torn open, was found to contain altered selective service documents, and those documents were used to secure Harris' conviction for violating the Selective Training and Service Act of 1940. The Court rejected Harris' fourth amendment claim, sustaining the search as "incident to arrest." *Id.*, at 151.

Only a year after Harris, however, the pendulum swung again. In *Trupiano v. U.S.*, 334 U.S.699, agents raided the site of an illicit distillery, saw one of several conspirators operating the still, and arrested him, contemporaneously "seiz[ing]" the illicit distillery." *Id.*, at 702. The Court held that the arrest and others made subsequently had been valid, but that the unexplained failure of the agents to procure a search warrant—in spite of the fact that they had had more than enough time before the raid to do so—rendered the search unlawful. The opinion stated:

> It is a cardinal rule that, in seizing goods and articles, law enforcement agents must secure and use search warrants wherever reasonably practicable. . . . This rule rests upon the desirability of having magistrates rather than police officers determine when searches and seizures are permissible and what limitations should be placed upon such activities. . . . To provide the necessary security against unreasonable intrusions upon the private lives of individuals, the framers of the

fourth amendment required adherence to judicial processes wherever possible. And subsequent history has confirmed the wisdom of that requirement.

A search or seizure without a warrant as an incident to a lawful arrest has always been considered to be a strictly limited right. It grows out of the inherent necessities of the situation at the time of the arrest. But there must be something more in the way of necessity than merely a lawful arrest. *Id.,* at 705, 708.

In 1950, two years after *Trupiano,* came *U.S. v. Rabinowitz,* 339 U.S.56, the decision upon which California primarily relies in the case now before us. In *Rabinowitz,* federal authorities had been informed that the defendant was dealing in stamps bearing forged overprints. On the basis of that information they secured a warrant for his arrest, which they executed at his one-room business office. At the time of the arrest, the officers "searched the desk, safe, and file cabinets in the office for about an hour and a half," *id.,* at 59, and seized 573 stamps with forged overprints. The stamps were admitted into evidence at the defendant's trial, and this Court affirmed his conviction, rejecting the contention that the warrantless search had been unlawful. The Court held that the search in its entirety fell within the principle giving law enforcement authorities "[t]he right 'to search the place where the arrest is made in order to find and seize things connected with the crime. . . .' " *Id.,* at 61. Harris was regarded as "ample authority" for that conclusion. *Id.,* at 63. The opinion rejected the rule of *Trupiano* that "in seizing goods and articles, law enforcement agents must secure and use search warrants wherever reasonably practicable." The test, said the Court, "is not whether it is reasonable to procure a search warrant, but whether the search was reasonable." *Id.,* at 66.

Rabinowitz has come to stand for the proposition, *inter alia,* that a warrantless search "incident to a lawful arrest" may generally extend to the area that is considered to be in the "possession" or under the "control" of the person arrested. And it was on the basis of that proposition that the California courts upheld the search of the petitioner's entire house in this case. That doctrine, however, at least in the broad sense in which it was applied by the California courts in this case, can withstand neither historical nor rational analysis.

Even limited to its own facts, the *Rabinowitz* decision was, as we have seen, hardly founded on an unimpeachable line of authority. . . .

Nor is the rationale by which the state seeks here to sustain the search of the petitioner's house supported by a reasoned view of the background and purpose of the fourth amendment. Mr. Justice Frankfurter wisely pointed out in his *Rabinowitz* dissent that the amendment's proscription of "unreasonable searches and seizures" must be read in light of "the history that gave rise to the words"—a history of "abuses so deeply felt by the colonies as to be one of the potent causes of the Revolution. . . ." 339 U.S., at 69. The amendment was in large part a reaction to the general warrants and warrantless searches that had so alienated the colonists and had helped speed the movement for independence. In the scheme of the amendment, therefore, the requirement that "no warrants shall issue, but upon probable cause," plays a crucial part. As the court put it in *McDonald v. U.S.*, 335 U.S. 451:

> We are not dealing with formalities. The presence of a search warrant serves a high function. Absent some grave emergency, the fourth amendment has interposed a magistrate between the citizen and the police. This was not done to shield criminals or to make the home a safe haven for illegal activities. It was done so that an objective mind might weigh the need to invade that privacy in order to enforce the law. The right of privacy was deemed too precious to entrust to the discretion of those whose job is the detection of crime and the arrest of criminals. . . . And so the Constitution requires a magistrate to pass on the desires of the police before they violate the privacy of the home. We cannot be true to that constitutional requirement and excuse the absence of a search warrant without a showing by those who seek exemption from the constitutional mandate that the exigencies of the situation made that course imperative. *Id.*, at 455–456.

. . . Clearly, the general requirement that a search warrant be obtained is not lightly to be dispensed with, and "the burden is on those seeking [an] exemption [from the requirement] to show the need for it. . . ." *U.S. v. Jeffers*, 342 U.S. 48, 51.

Only last term in *Terry v. Ohio*, 392 U.S. 1, we emphasized that "the police must, whenever practicable, obtain advance judicial approval of searches and seizures through the warrant procedure," *Id.,* at 20, and that "[t]he scope of [a] search must be 'strictly tied to and justified by' the circumstances which rendered its initiation permissible." *Id.,* at 19. The search undertaken by the officer in that "stop and frisk" case was sustained under that test, because it was no more than a "protective . . . search for weapons." *Id.,* at 29. But in a companion case, *Sibron v. New York,* 392 U.S.40, we applied the same standard to another set of facts and reached a contrary result, holding that a policeman's action in thrusting his hand into a suspect's pocket had been neither motivated by nor limited to the objective of protection. Rather, the search had been made in order to find narcotics, which were in fact found.

A similar analysis underlies the "search incident to arrest" principle, and marks its proper extent. When an arrest is made, it is reasonable for the arresting officer to search the person arrested in order to remove any weapons that the latter might seek to use in order to resist arrest or effect his escape. Otherwise, the officer's safety might well be endangered, and the arrest itself frustrated. In addition, it is entirely reasonable for the arresting officer to search for and seize any evidence on the arrestee's person in order to prevent its concealment or destruction. And the area into which an arrestee might reach in order to grab a weapon or evidentiary items must, of course, be governed by a like rule. A gun on a table or in a drawer in front of one who is arrested can be as dangerous to the arresting officer as one concealed in the clothing of the person arrested. There is ample justification, therefore, for a search of the arrestee's person and the area "within his immediate control"—construing that phrase to mean the area from within which he might gain possession of a weapon or destructible evidence.

There is no comparable justification, however, for routinely searching rooms other than that in which an arrest occurs—or, for that matter, for searching through all the desk drawers or other closed or concealed areas in that room itself. Such searches, in the absence of well-recognized exceptions, may be made only under the authority of a search warrant. The "adherence to judicial processes" mandated by the fourth amendment requires no less.

It is argued in the present case that it is "reasonable" to search a man's house when he is arrested in it. But that argument is founded on little more than a subjective view regarding the acceptability of certain sorts of police conduct, and not on considerations relevant to fourth amendment interests. Under such an unconfined analysis, fourth amendment protection in this area would approach the evaporation point. It is not easy to explain why, for instance, it is less subjectively "reasonable" to search a man's house when he is arrested on his front lawn—or just down the street—than it is when he happens to be in the house at the time of arrest. As Mr. Justice Frankfurter put it:

> To say that the search must be reasonable is to require some criterion of reason. It is no guide at all either for a jury or for district judges or the police to say that an "unreasonable search" is forbidden—that the search must be reasonable. What is the test of reason which makes a search reasonable? The test is the reason underlying and expressed by the fourth amendment: the history and the experience which it embodies and the safeguards afforded by it against the evils to which it was a response. *U.S. v. Rabinowitz, 339 U.S.,* at 83 (dissenting opinion).

Thus, although "[t]he recurring questions of the reasonableness of searches" depend upon "the facts and circumstances—the total atmosphere of the case," *Id.,* at 63, 66 (opinion of the court), those facts and circumstances must be viewed in the light of established fourth amendment principles.

It would be possible, of course, to draw a line between *Rabinowitz* and *Harris* on the one hand, and this case on the other. For *Rabinowitz* involved a single room, and *Harris* a four-room apartment, while in the case before us an entire house was searched. But such a distinction would be highly artificial. The rationale that allowed the searches and seizures in *Rabinowitz* and *Harris* would allow the searches and seizures in this case. No consideration relevant to the fourth amendment suggests any point of rational limitation, once the search is allowed to go beyond the area from which the person arrested might obtain weapons or evidentiary items. The only reasoned distinction is one between a search of the person arrested and the area within his reach on the one hand, and more extensive searches on the other.

The petitioner correctly points out that one result of decisions such as *Rabinowitz* and *Harris* is to give law enforcement officials the opportunity to engage in searches not justified by probable cause, by the simple expedient of arranging to arrest suspects at home rather than elsewhere. We do not suggest that the petitioner is necessarily correct in his assertion that such a strategy was utilized here, but the fact remains that had he been arrested earlier in the day, at his place of employment rather than at home, no search of his house could have been made without a search warrant. In any event, even apart from the possibility of such police tactics, the general point so forcefully made by Judge Learned Hand in *U.S. v. Kirschenblatt,* 16 F.2d 202, remains:

> After arresting a man in his house, to rummage at will among his papers in search of whatever will convict him, appears to us to be indistinguishable from what might be done under a general warrant; indeed, the warrant would give more protection, for presumably it must be issued by a magistrate. True, by hypothesis the power would not exist, if the supposed offender were not found on the premises; but it is small consolation to know that one's papers are safe only so long as one is not at home. *Id.,* at 203.

Rabinowitz and *Harris* have been the subject of critical commentary for many years, and have been relied upon less and less in our own decisions. It is time, for the reasons we have stated, to hold that on their own facts, and insofar as the principles they stand for are inconsistent with those that we have endorsed today, they are no longer to be followed.

Application of sound fourth amendment principles to the facts of this case produces a clear result. The search here went far beyond the petitioner's person and the area from within which he might have obtained either a weapon or something that could have been used as evidence against him. There was no constitutional justification, in the absence of a search warrant, for extending the search beyond that area. The scope of the search was, therefore, "unreasonable" under the fourth and fourteenth amendments, and the petitioner's conviction cannot stand.

Reversed.

8.2. *Mapp v. Ohio*

Mr. Justice Clark delivered the opinion of the Court.

Appellant stands convicted of knowingly having had in her possession and under her control certain lewd and lascivious books, pictures, and photographs in violation of §2905.34 of Ohio's Revised Code. As officially stated in the syllabus to its opinion, the Supreme Court of Ohio found that her conviction was valid though "based primarily upon the introduction in evidence of lewd and lascivious books and pictures unlawfully seized during an unlawful search of defendant's home." (170 Ohio St. 427-428, 166 N.E.2d 387, 388.)

On May 23, 1957, three Cleveland police officers arrived at appellant's residence in that city pursuant to information that "a person [was] hiding out in the home, who was wanted for questioning in connection with a recent bombing, and that there was a large amount of policy paraphernalia being hidden in the home." Miss Mapp and her daughter by a former marriage lived on the top floor of the two-family dwelling. Upon their arrival at that house, the officers knocked on the door and demanded entrance but appellant, after telephoning her attorney, refused to admit them without a search warrant. They advised their headquarters of the situation and undertook a surveillance of the house.

The officers again sought entrance some three hours later when four or more additional officers arrived on the scene. When Miss Mapp did not come to the door immediately, at least one of the several doors to the house was forcibly opened and the policemen gained admittance. Meanwhile Miss Mapp's attorney arrived, but the officers, having secured their own entry and continuing in their defiance of the law, would permit him neither to see Miss Mapp nor to enter the house. . . .

The state says that even if the search were made without authority, or otherwise unreasonably, it is not prevented from using the unconstitutionally seized evidence at trial, citing *Wolf v. People of State of Colorado,* 1949, 338 U.S.25, at page 33, 69 S.Ct.

Note: 367 U.S.643, 1961, 81 S.Ct. 1684, 6 L.Ed.2d 1081. Rehearing denied 82 S.Ct. 23.

1359, at page 1364, 93 L.Ed. 1782, in which this court did indeed hold "that in a prosecution in a state court for a state crime the fourteenth amendment does not forbid the admission of evidence obtained by an unreasonable search and seizure." On this appeal, of which we have noted probable jurisdiction, 364 U.S. 868, 81 S.Ct. 111, 5 L.Ed.2d 90, it is urged once again that we review that holding.

Seventy-five years ago, in *Boyd v. U.S.*, 1886, 116 U.S.616, 630, 6 S.Ct. 524, 532, 29 L.Ed. 746, considering the fourth and fifth amendments as running "almost into each other" on the facts before it, this court held that the doctrines of those amendments

> apply to all invasions on the part of the government and its employees of the sanctity of a man's home and the privacies of life. It is not the breaking of his doors, and the rummaging of his drawers, that constitutes the essence of the offence; but it is the invasion of this indefeasible right of personal security, personal liberty, and private property. Breaking into a house and opening boxes and drawers are circumstances of aggravation; but any forcible and compulsory extortion of a man's own testimony or of his private papers to be used as evidence to convict him of crime or to forfeit his goods, is within the condemnation [of those amendments].

. . . Less than 30 years after *Boyd,* this court, in *Weeks v. U.S.,* 1914, 232 U.S.383, at pages 391-392, 34 S.Ct. 341, at page 344, 58 L.Ed. 652, stated that

> the fourth amendment put the courts of the United States and federal officials, in the exercise of their power and authority, under limitations and restraints [and] forever secure[d] the people, their persons, houses, papers, and effects, against all unreasonable searches and seizures under the guise of law and the duty of giving to it force and effect is obligatory upon all entrusted under our Federal system with the enforcements of the laws.

Specifically dealing with the use of the evidence unconstitutionally seized, the Court concluded:

> If letters and private documents can thus be seized and held and used in evidence against a citizen accused of an offense, the protection of the fourth amendment declaring his right to be secure against such searches and seizures is of no value, and, so far as those thus placed are concerned, might as well be stricken from the Constitution. The efforts of the courts and their officials to bring the guilty to punish-

ment, praiseworthy as they are, are not to be aided by the sacrifice of those great principles established by years of endeavor and suffering which have resulted in their embodiment in the fundamental law of the land. At page 393 of 232 U.S., at page 344 of 34 S.Ct.

Finally, the Court in that case clearly stated that use of the seized evidence involved "a denial of the constitutional rights of the accused." At page 398 of 232 U.S., at page 346 of 34 S.Ct. Thus, in the year 1914, in the *Weeks* case, this court "for the first time" held that "in a federal prosecution the fourth amendment barred the use of evidence secured through an illegal search and seizure." *Wolf v. People of State of Colorado, supra,* 338 U.S. at page 28, 69 S.Ct. at page 1361....

In 1949, thirty-five years after *Weeks* was announced, this court, in *Wolf v. People of State of Colorado, supra,* again for the first time, discussed the effect of the fourth amendment upon the states through the operation of the Due Process Clause of the fourteenth amendment. It said:

"[W]e have no hesitation in saying that were a state affirmatively to sanction such police incursion into privacy it would run counter to the guaranty of the fourteenth amendment." At page 28 of 338 U.S., at page 1361 of 69 S.Ct.

Nevertheless, after declaring that the "security of one's privacy against arbitrary intrusion by the police" is "implicit in 'the concept of ordered liberty' and as such enforceable against the states through the Due Process Clause," cf. *Palko v. State of Connecticut,* 1937, 302 U.S.319, 58 S.Ct. 149, 82 L.Ed. 288, and announcing that it "stoutly adhere[d]" to the *Weeks* decision, the court decided that the *Weeks* exclusionary rule would not then be imposed upon the states as "an essential ingredient of the right." 338 U.S. at pages 27-29, 69 S.Ct. at page 1362. The court's reasons for not considering essential to the right to privacy, as a curb imposed upon the states by the Due Process Clause, that which decades before had been posited as part and parcel of the fourth amendment's limitation upon federal encroachment of individual privacy, were bottomed on factual considerations.

While they are not basically relevant to a decision that the exclusionary rule is an essential ingredient of the fourth amendment as the right it embodies is vouchsafed against the states by the Due Process Clause, we will consider the current validity of the factual grounds upon which *Wolf* was based.

The court in *Wolf* first stated that "[t]he contrariety of views of the states" on the adoption of the exclusionary rule of *Weeks* was "particularly impressive" (338 U.S. at page 29, 69 S.Ct. at page 1362); and, in this connection, that it could not "brush aside the experience of states which deem the incidence of such conduct by the police too slight to call for a deterrent remedy by overriding the [states'] relevant rules of evidence." At pages 31-32 of 338 U.S., at page 1363 of 69 S.Ct. While in 1949, prior to the *Wolf* case, almost two-thirds of the states were opposed to the use of the exclusionary rule, now, despite the *Wolf* case, more than half of those since passing upon it, by their own legislative or judicial decision, have wholly or partly adopted or adhered to the *Weeks* rule. See *Elkins v. U.S.*, 1960, 364 U.S.206; Appendix, at pages 224-232, 80 S.Ct. 1437, at pages 1448-1453, 4 L.Ed.2d (1669). Significantly, among those now following the rule is California, which, according to its highest court, was "compelled to reach that conclusion because other remedies have completely failed to secure compliance with the constitutional provisions." *People v. Cahan,* 1955, 44 Cal.2d 434, 445, 282 P.2d 905, 911, 50 A.L.R.2d 513. In connection with this California case, we note that the second basis elaborated in *Wolf* in support of its failure to enforce the exclusionary doctrine against the states was that "other means of protection" have been afforded "the right to privacy." 338 U.S. at page 30, 69 S.Ct. at page 1362. The experience of California that such other remedies have been worthless and futile is buttressed by the experience of other states. The obvious futility of relegating the fourth amendment to the protection of other remedies has, moreover, been recognized by this Court since *Wolf.* See *Irvine v. People of State of California,* 1954, 347 U.S. 128, 137, 74 S.Ct. 381, 385, 98 L.Ed. 561.

Likewise, time has set its face against what *Wolf* called the "weighty testimony" of *People v. Defore,* 1926, 242 N.Y. 13, 150 N.E. 585. There Justice (then Judge) Cardozo, rejecting adoption of the *Weeks* exclusionary rule in New York, had said that "[t]he Federal rule as it stands is either too strict or too lax." 242 N.Y. at page 22, 150 N.E. at page 588. However, the force of that reasoning has been largely vitiated by later decisions of this Court. These include the recent discarding of the "silver platter" doctrine which allowed federal judicial use of evidence seized in violation of the Constitution by state agents, *Elkins v. United States, supra,* the relaxation of the formerly strict requirements as to standing to challenge the use of evidence thus seized, so that now the procedure of exclusion, "ultimately referable to constitutional safeguards," is available to anyone even "legitimately on [the] premises" unlawfully searched, *Jones v. U.S.,* 1960, 362 U.S.257, 266-267, 80 S.Ct. 725, 734, 4 L.Ed.2d 697; and finally, the formulation of a method to prevent state use of evidence unconstitutionally seized by federal agents, *Rea v. U.S.,* 1956, 350 U.S.214, 76 S.Ct. 292, 100 L.Ed. 233. Because there can be no fixed formula, we are admittedly met with "recurring questions of the reasonableness of searches," but less is not to be expected when dealing with a Constitution, and, at any rate, "[r]easonableness is in the first instance for the [trial court] to determine." *U.S. v. Rabinowitz,* 1950, 339 U.S.56, 63, 70 S.Ct. 430, 434, 94 L.Ed. 653.

It, therefore, plainly appears that the factual considerations supporting the failure of the *Wolf* Court to include the *Weeks* exclusionary rule when it recognized the enforceability of the right to privacy against the states in 1949, while not basically relevant to the constitutional consideration, could not, in any analysis, now be deemed controlling.

Some five years after *Wolf,* in answer to a plea made here term after term that we overturn its doctrine on applicability of the *Weeks* exclusionary rule, this court indicated that such should not be done until the states had "adequate opportunity to adopt or reject the [*Weeks*] rule." *Irvine v. People of State of California, supra,* 347 U.S. at page 134, 74 S.Ct. at page 384. There again it was said:

> Never until June of 1949 did this court hold the basic search-and-seizure prohibition in any way applicable to the states under the fourteenth amendment. *Ibid.*

And only last term, after again carefully reexamining the *Wolf* doctrine in *Elkins v. U.S., supra,* the court pointed out that "the controlling principles" as to search and seizure and the problem of admissibility "seemed clear" (364 U.S. at page 212, 1441 of 80 S.Ct.) until the announcement in *Wolf* "that the Due Process Clause of the fourteenth amendment does not itself require state courts to adopt the exclusionary rule" of the *Weeks* case. At page 213 of 364 U.S., at page 1442 of 80 S.Ct. At the same time, the court pointed out, "the underlying constitutional doctrine which Wolf established . . . that the Federal Constitution prohibits unreasonable searches and seizures by state officers" had undermined the "foundation upon which the admissibility of state-seized evidence in a federal trial originally rested." *Ibid.* The court concluded that it was therefore obliged to hold, although it chose the narrower ground on which to do so, that all evidence obtained by an unconstitutional search and seizure was inadmissible in a federal court regardless of its source. Today we once again examine *Wolf's* constitutional documentation of the right to privacy free from unreasonable state intrusion, and after its dozen years on our books, are led by it to close the only courtroom door remaining open to evidence secured by official lawlessness in flagrant abuse of that basic right, reserved to all persons as a specific guarantee against that very same unlawful conduct. We hold that all evidence obtained by searches and seizures in violation of the Constitution is, by that same authority, inadmissible in a state court.

Since the fourth amendment's right of privacy has been declared enforceable against the states through the Due Process Clause of the fourteenth, it is enforceable against them by the same sanction of exclusion as is used against the Federal Government. Were it otherwise, then just as without the *Weeks* rule the assurance against unreasonable federal searches and seizures would be "a form of words," valueless and undeserving of mention in a perpetual charter of inestimable human liberties, so too, without that rule the freedom from state invasions of privacy would be so ephemeral and so neatly severed from its conceptual nexus with the freedom from all brutish means of coercing evidence as not to merit this Court's high regard as a freedom "implicit in 'the concept of ordered liberty.' " At the time that the Court held in *Wolf* that the amendment was applicable to the states through the Due Process Clause, the cases of this court, as we have seen, had steadfastly held that as to federal officers the fourth amendment included the exclusion of the evidence seized in violation of its provisions. Even *Wolf* "stoutly adhered" to that proposition. The right to privacy, when conceded operatively enforceable against the states, was not susceptible of destruction by avulsion of the sanction upon which its protection and enjoyment had always been deemed dependent under the *Boyd, Weeks* and *Silverthorne* cases. Therefore, in extending the substantive protections of due process to all constitutionally unreasonable searches—state or federal—it was logically and constitutionally necessary that the exclusion doctrine, an essential part of the right to privacy, be also insisted upon as an essential ingredient of the right newly recognized by the *Wolf* case. In short, the admission of the new constitutional right by *Wolf* could not consistently tolerate denial of its most important constitutional privilege, namely, the exclusion of the evidence which an accused had been forced to give by reason of the unlawful seizure. To hold otherwise is to grant the right but in reality to withhold its privilege and enjoyment. Only last year the court itself recognized that the purpose of the exclusionary rule "is to deter—to compel respect for the constitutional guaranty in the only effectively available way—by removing the incentive to disregard it." *Elkins v. U.S., supra,* 364 U.S. at page 217, 80 S.Ct. at page 144. . . .

There are those who say, as did Justice (then Judge) Cardozo, that under our constitutional exclusionary doctrine "[t]he criminal is to go free because the constable has blundered." *People v. Defore,* 242 N.Y. at page 21, 150 N.E. at page 587. In some cases this will undoubtedly be the result. But, as was said in *Elkins,* "there is another consideration—the imperative of judicial integrity." 364 U.S. at page 222, 80 S.Ct at page 1447. The criminal goes free, if he must, but it is the law that sets him free. Nothing can destroy a government more quickly than its failure to observe its own laws, or worse, its disregard of the charter of its own existence. As Mr. Justice Brandeis, dissenting, said in *Olmstead v. U.S.,* 1928, 277 U.S. 438, 485, 48 S.Ct. 564, 575, 72 L.Ed. 944: "Our government is the potent, the omnipresent teacher. For good or for ill, it teaches the whole people by its example. If the government becomes a lawbreaker, it breeds contempt for law; it invites every man to become a law unto himself; it invites anarchy." Nor can it lightly be assumed that, as a practical matter, adoption of the exclusionary rule fetters law enforcement. Only last year this court expressly considered that contention and found that "pragmatic evidence of a sort" to the contrary was not wanting. *Elkins v. U.S., supra,* 364 U.S. at page 218, 80 S.Ct. at page 1444. The Court noted that

> The federal courts themselves have operated under the exclusionary rule of *Weeks* for almost half a century; yet it has not been suggested either that the Federal Bureau of Investigation has thereby been rendered ineffective, or that the administration of criminal justice in the federal courts has thereby been disrupted. Moreover, the experience of the states is impressive. The movement towards the rule of exclusion has been halting but seemingly inexorable. *Id.,* 364 U.S. at pages 218–219, 80 S.Ct. at pages 1444–1445.

The ignoble shortcut to conviction left open to the state tends to destroy the entire system of constitutional restraints on which the liberties of the people rest. Having once recognized that the right to privacy embodied in the fourth amendment is enforceable against the states, and that the right to be secure against rude invasions of privacy by state officers is, therefore, constitutional in origin, we can no longer permit that right to remain an empty promise. Because it is enforceable in the same manner and to like effect as other basic rights secured by the Due Process Clause, we can no longer permit it to be revocable at the whim of any police officer who, in the name of law enforcement itself, chooses to suspend its enjoyment. Our decision, founded on reason and truth, gives to the individual no more than that which the Constitution guarantees him, to the police officer no less than that to which honest law enforcement is entitled, and to the courts, that judicial integrity so necessary in the true administration of justice.

The judgment of the Supreme Court of Ohio is reversed and the cause remanded for further proceedings not inconsistent with this opinion.

Reversed and remanded.

8.3. *Stoner v. California*

Mr. Justice Stewart delivered the opinion of the Court.

The petitioner was convicted of armed robbery after a jury trial in the Superior Court of Los Angeles County, California. At the trial several articles which had been found by police officers in a search of the petitioner's hotel room during his absence were admitted into evidence over his objection. A District Court of Appeal of California affirmed the conviction, and the Supreme Court of California denied further review. We granted certiorari, limiting review "to the question of whether evidence was admitted which had been obtained by an unlawful search and seizure." 374 U.S.826. For the reasons which follow, we conclude that the petitioner's conviction must be set aside.

The essential facts are not in dispute. On the night of October 25, 1960, the Budget Town Food Market in Monrovia, California, was robbed by two men, one of whom was described by eyewitnesses as carrying a gun and wearing horn-rimmed glasses and a grey jacket. Soon after the robbery a checkbook belonging to the petitioner was found in an adjacent parking lot and turned over to the police. Two of the stubs in the checkbook indicated that checks had been drawn to the order of the Mayfair Hotel in Pomona, California. Pursuing this lead, the officers learned from the Police Department of Pomona that the petitioner had a previous criminal record, and they obtained from the Pomona police a photograph of the petitioner. They showed the photograph to the two eyewitnesses to the robbery, who both stated that the picture looked like the man who had carried the gun. On the basis of this information the officers went to the Mayfair Hotel in Pomona at about 10 o'clock on the night of October 27. They had neither search nor arrest warrants. There then transpired the following events, as later recounted by one of the officers:

> We approached the desk and asked the night clerk if there was a party by the name of Joey L. Stoner living at the hotel. He checked his records and stated "Yes, there is." And we asked him what room

---

Note: 376 U.S.483, 84 S.Ct. 889, 11 L.Ed.2d 856 (1964).

he was in. He stated he was in Room 404 but he was out at this time.

We asked him how he knew that he was out. He stated that the hotel regulations required that the key to the room would be placed in the mail box each time they left the hotel. The key was in the mail box, and he therefore knew he was out of the room.

We asked him if he would give us permission to enter the room, explaining our reasons for this.

Q. What reasons did you explain to the clerk?

A. We explained that we were there to make an arrest of a man who had possibly committed a robbery in the City of Monrovia, and that we were concerned about the fact that he had a weapon. He stated, "In this case, I will be more than happy to give you permission and I will take you directly to the room."

Q. Is that what the clerk told you?

A. Yes, sir.

Q. What else happened?

A. We left one detective in the lobby, and Detective Oliver, Officer Collins, and myself, along with the night clerk, got on the elevator and proceeded to the fourth floor, and went to Room 404. The night clerk placed a key in the lock, unlocked the door, and says, "Be my guest."

The officers entered and made a thorough search of the room and its contents. They found a pair of horn-rimmed glasses and a grey jacket in the room, and a .45-caliber automatic pistol with a clip and several cartridges in the bottom of a bureau drawer. The petitioner was arrested two days later in Las Vegas, Nevada. He waived extradition and was returned to California for trial on the charge of armed robbery. The gun, the cartridges and clip, the horn-rimmed glasses, and the grey jacket were all used as evidence against him at his trial.

The search of the petitioner's room by the police officers was conducted without a warrant of any kind, and it therefore "can survive constitutional inhibition only upon a showing that the surrounding facts brought it within one of the exceptions to the rule that a search must rest upon a search warrant" (*Jones v. U.S.,* 357 U.S.493, 499; *U.S. v. Jeffers,* 342 U.S.48, 51) *Rios v. U.S.,* 364 U.S.253, 261. . . .

. . . [T]he respondent has made no argument that the search can be justified as an incident to the petitioner's arrest. Instead, the argument is made that the search of the hotel room, although conducted without the petitioner's consent, was lawful because it was conducted with the consent of the hotel clerk. We find this argument unpersuasive.

Even if it be assumed that a state law which gave a hotel proprietor blanket authority to authorize the police to search the rooms of the hotel's guests could survive constitutional challenge, there is no intimation in the California cases cited by the respondent that California has any such law. Nor is there any substance to the claim that the search was reasonable because the police, relying upon the night clerk's expressions of consent, had a reasonable basis for the belief that the clerk had authority to consent to the search. Our decisions make clear that the rights protected by the fourth amendment are not to be eroded by strained applications of the law of agency or by unrealistic doctrines of "apparent authority."

It is important to bear in mind that it was the petitioner's constitutional right which was at stake here, and not the night clerk's nor the hotel's. It was a right, therefore, which only the petitioner could waive by word or deed, either directly or through an agent. It is true that the night clerk clearly and unambiguously consented to the search. But there is nothing in the record to indicate that the police had any basis whatsoever to believe that the night clerk had been authorized by the petitioner to permit the police to search the petitioner's room.

At least twice this Court has explicitly refused to permit an otherwise unlawful police search of a hotel room to rest upon consent of the hotel proprietor (*Lustig v. U.S.*, 338 U.S.74; *U.S. v. Jeffers*, 342 U.S.48). In *Lustig* the manager of a hotel allowed police to enter and search a room without a warrant in the occupant's absence, and the search was held unconstitutional. In *Jeffers* the assistant manager allowed a similar search, and that search was likewise held unconstitutional.

It is true, as was said in *Jeffers,* that when a person engages a hotel room he undoubtedly gives "implied or express permission" to "such persons as maids, janitors or repairmen" to enter his room "in the performance of their duties." 342 U.S., at 51. But the conduct of the night clerk and the police in the present case was of an entirely different order. In a closely analogous situation the Court has held that a search by police officers of a house occupied by a tenant invaded the tenant's constitutional right, even though the search was authorized by the owner of the house, who presumably had not only apparent but actual authority to enter the house for some purposes, such as to "view waste." *Chapman v. U.S.*, 365 U.S.610. The Court pointed out that the officers' purpose in entering was not to view waste but to search for distilling equipment, and concluded that to uphold such a search without a warrant would leave tenants' homes secure only in the discretion of their landlords.

No less than a tenant of a house, or the occupant of a room in a boarding house, *McDonald v. U.S.*, 335 U.S.451, a guest in a hotel room is entitled to constitutional protection against unreasonable searches and seizures. *Johnson v. U.S.*, 333 U.S.10. That protection would disappear if it were left to depend upon the unfettered discretion of an employee of the hotel. It follows that this search without a warrant was unlawful. Since evidence obtained through the search was admitted at the trial, the judgment must be reversed. *Mapp v. Ohio*, 367 U.S.643.

It is so ordered.

8.4. *Warden, Maryland Penitentiary v. Hayden*

Mr. Justice Brennan delivered the opinion of the Court.

We review in this case the validity of the proposition that there is under the fourth amendment a "distinction between merely evidentiary materials on the one hand, which may not be seized either under the authority of a search warrant or during the course of a search incident to arrest, and on the other hand, those objects which may validly be seized including the instrumentalities and means by which a crime is committed, the fruits of crime such as stolen property, weapons by which escape of the person arrested might be effected, and property the possession of which is a crime."

A Maryland court sitting without a jury convicted respondent of armed robbery. Items of his clothing, a cap, jacket, and trousers, among other things, were seized during a search of his home, and were admitted in evidence without objection. After unsuccessful state court proceedings, he sought and was denied federal habeas corpus relief in the District Court for Maryland. A divided

---

Note: 387 U.S.294, 87 S.Ct. 1642, 18 L.Ed.2d 782 (1967).

panel of the Court of Appeals for the Fourth Circuit reversed. 363 F.2d 647. The Court of Appeals believed that *Harris v. U.S.,* 331 U.S.145, 154, sustained the validity of the search, but held that respondent was correct in his contention that the clothing seized was improperly admitted in evidence because the items had "evidential value only" and therefore were not lawfully subject to seizure. We granted certiorari. 385 U.S.926. We reverse.

[The facts and the first part of the Court's opinion, in which the Court concluded that the search of the defendant's home was lawful, are printed above.]

We come, then, to the question whether, even though the search was lawful, the Court of Appeals was correct in holding that the seizure and introduction of the items of clothing violated the fourth amendment because they are "mere evidence." The distinction made by some of our cases between seizure of items of evidential value only and seizure of instrumentalities, fruits, or contraband has been criticized by courts and commentators. The Court of Appeals, however, felt "obligated to adhere to it." 363 F.2d, at 655. We today reject the distinction as based on premises no longer accepted as rules governing the application of the fourth amendment.

Nothing in the language of the fourth amendment supports the distinction between "mere evidence" and instrumentalities, fruits of crime, or contraband. On its face, the provision assures the "right of the people to be secure in their persons, houses, papers, and effects . . . ," without regard to the use to which any of these things are applied. This "right of the people" is certainly unrelated to the "mere evidence" limitation. Privacy is disturbed no more by a search directed to a purely evidentiary object than it is by a search directed to an instrumentality, fruit, or contraband. A magistrate can intervene in both situations, and the requirements of probable cause and specificity can be preserved intact. Moreover, nothing in the nature of property seized as evidence renders it more private than property seized, for example, as an instrumentality; quite the opposite may be true. Indeed, the distinction is wholly irrational, since, depending on the circumstances, the same "papers and effects" may be "mere evidence" in one case and "instrumentality" in another. See comment, 20 U.Chi.L.Rev. 319, 320-322 (1953).

In *Gouled v. U.S.,* 255 U.S.298, 309, the Court said that search warrants "may not be used as a means of gaining access to a man's house or office and papers solely for the purpose of making search to secure evidence to be used against him in a criminal or penal proceeding. . . ." The Court derived from *Boyd v. U.S.,* [116 U.S.616 (1886)] the proposition that warrants "may be resorted to only when a primary right to such search and seizure may be found in the interest which the public or the complainant may have in the property to be seized, or in the right to the possession of it, or when a valid exercise of the police power renders possession of the property by the accused unlawful and provides that it may be taken," 255 U.S., at 309; that is, when the property is an instrumentality or fruit of crime, or contraband. Since it was "impossible to say, on the record . . . that the government had any interest" in the papers involved "other than as evidence against the accused . . . ," "to permit them to be used in evidence would be, in effect, as ruled in the *Boyd case,* to compel the defendant to become a witness against himself." *Id.,* at 311.

The items of clothing involved in this case are not "testimonial" or "communicative" in nature, and their introduction therefore did not compel the respondent to become a witness against himself in violation of the fifth amendment. *Schmerber v. California,* 384 U.S.757. This case thus does not require that we consider whether there are items of evidential value whose very nature precludes them from being the object of a reasonable search and seizure.

The fourth amendment ruling in *Gouled* was based upon the dual, related premises that historically the right to search for and seize property depended upon the assertion by the Government of a valid claim of superior interest, and that it was not enough that the purpose of the search and seizure was to obtain evidence to use in apprehending and convicting criminals. The common law of search and seizure after *Entick v. Carrington,* 19 How.St.Tr. 1029, reflected Lord Camden's view, derived no doubt from the political thought of his time, that the "great end, for which men entered into society, was to secure their property." *Id.,* at 1066. Warrants were "allowed only where the primary right to such a search and seizure is in the interest which the public or complainant may have in the property seized." Lasson, *The History and Development of the Fourth Amendment to the United States Constitution* 133-134. Thus stolen property—the fruits of crime—was always subject to seizure. And the power to search for stolen property was gradually extended to cover "any property which the private citizen was not permitted to possess," which included instrumentalities of crime (because of the early notion that items used in crime were forfeited to the state) and contraband. Kaplan, *Search and Seizure: A No-Man's Land in the Criminal Law,* 49 CALIF.L.REV. 474, 475, 1961. No separate governmental interest in seizing evidence to apprehend and convict criminals was recognized; it was required that some property interest be asserted. The remedial structure also reflected these dual premises. Trespass, replevin, and the other means of redress for persons aggrieved by searches and seizures, depended upon proof of a superior property interest. And since a lawful seizure presupposed a superior claim, it was inconceivable that a person could recover property lawfully seized. As Lord Camden pointed out in *Entick v. Carrington, supra,* at 1066, a general warrant enabled "the party's own property [to be] seized before and without conviction, and he has no power to reclaim his goods, even after his innocence is cleared by acquittal."

The premise that property interests control the right of the Government to search and seize has been discredited. Searches and seizures may be "unreasonable" within the fourth amendment even though the Government asserts a superior property interest at common law. We have recognized that the principal object of the fourth amendment is the protection of privacy rather than property, and have increasingly discarded fictional and procedural barriers rested on property concepts. . . .

The development of search and seizure law . . . is replete with examples of the transformation in substantive law brought about through the interaction of the felt need to protect privacy from unreasonable invasions and the flexibility in rulemaking made possible by the remedy of exclusion. We have held, for example, that intangible as well as tangible evidence may be suppressed . . . and that an actual trespass under local property law is unnecessary to support a remediable violation of the fourth amendment. . . . In determining whether someone is a "person aggrieved by an unlawful search and seizure" we have refused "to import into the law . . . subtle distinctions, developed and refined by the common law in evolving the body of private property law which, more than almost any other branch of law, has been shaped by distinctions whose validity is largely historical." *Jones v. U.S.,* 362 U.S., at 266. And with particular relevance here, we have given recognition to the interest in privacy despite the complete absence of a property claim by suppressing the very items which at common law could be seized with impunity: stolen goods . . . instrumentalities . . . and contraband. . . .

The premise in *Gouled* that government may not seize evidence simply for the purpose of proving crime has likewise been discredited. The requirement that the government assert in addition some property interest in material it seizes has long been a fiction, obscuring the reality that government has an interest in solving crime. *Schmerber* settles the proposition that it is reasonable, within the terms of the fourth amendment, to conduct otherwise permissible searches for the purpose of obtaining evidence which would aid in apprehending and convicting criminals. The requirements of the fourth amendment can secure the same protection of privacy whether the search is for "mere evidence" or for fruits, instrumentalities or contraband. There must, of course, be a nexus—automatically provided in the case of fruits, instrumentalities or contraband—between the item to be seized and criminal behavior. Thus in the case of "mere evidence," probable cause must be examined in terms of cause to believe that the evidence sought will aid in a particular apprehension or conviction. In so doing, consideration of police purposes will be required. . . . But no such problem is presented in this case. The clothes found in the washing machine matched the description of those worn by the robber and the police therefore could reasonably believe that the items would aid in the identification of the culprit.

The remedy of suppression, moreover, which made possible protection of privacy from unreasonable searches without regard to proof of a superior property interest, likewise provides the procedural device necessary for allowing otherwise permissible searches and seizures conducted solely to obtain evidence of crime. For just as the suppression of evidence does not entail a declaration of superior property interest in the person aggrieved, thereby enabling him to suppress evidence unlawfully seized despite his inability to demonstrate such an interest (as with fruits, instrumentalities, contraband), the refusal to suppress evidence carries no declaration of superior property interest in the state, and should thereby enable the state to introduce evidence lawfully seized despite its inability to demonstrate such an interest. And, unlike the situation at common law, the owner of property would not be rendered remediless if "mere evidence" could lawfully be seized to prove crime. For just as the suppression of evidence does not in itself necessarily entitle the aggrieved person to its return (as, for example, contraband), the introduction of "mere evidence" does not in itself entitle the state to its retention. Where public officials "unlawfully seize or *hold* a citizen's realty or chattels, recoverable by appropriate action at law or in equity . . . ," the true owner may "bring his possessory action to reclaim that which is wrongfully withheld." *Land v. Dollar,* 330 U.S.731, 738. (Emphasis added.)

The survival of the *Gouled* distinction is attributable more to chance than considered judgment. Legislation has helped perpetuate it. Thus, Congress has never authorized the issuance of search warrants for the seizure of mere evidence of crime. . . . *Gouled* concluded, needlessly it appears, that the Constitution virtually limited searches and seizures to these categories. After *Gouled,* pressure to test this conclusion was slow to mount. Rule 41 (b) of the Federal Rules of Criminal Procedure incorporated the *Gouled* categories as limitations on federal authorities to issue warrants and *Mapp v. Ohio,* 367 U.S.643, only recently made the "mere evidence" rule a problem in the state courts. Pressure against the rule in the federal courts has taken the form rather of broadening the categories of evidence subject to seizure, thereby creating considerable confusion in the law.

The rationale most frequently suggested for the rule preventing the seizure of evidence is that "limitations upon the fruit to be gathered tend to limit the quest itself." *U.S. v. Poller,* 43 F.2d 911, 914 (C.A.2d Cir. 1930). But privacy "would be just as well served by a restriction on search to the even-numbered days of the month. . . . And it would have the extra advantage of avoiding hair-splitting questions. . . ." Kaplan, at 479. The "mere evidence" limitation has spawned exceptions so numerous and confusion so great, in fact, that it is questionable whether it affords meaningful protection. But if its rejection does enlarge the area of permissible searches, the intrusions are nevertheless made after fulfilling the probable cause and particularity requirements of the fourth amendment and after the intervention of "a neutral and detached magistrate. . . ." *Johnson v. U.S., 333* U.S. 10, 14. The fourth amendment allows intrusions upon privacy under these circumstances, and there is no viable reason to distinguish intrusions to secure "mere evidence" from intrusions to secure fruits, instrumentalities, or contraband.

The judgment of the Court of Appeals is reversed.

CHAPTER 5

THE FIFTH AMENDMENT

No person shall be held to answer for a capital or otherwise infamous crime unless on a presentment or indictment of a grand jury, except in cases arising in land or naval forces, or in the militia, when in actual service in the time of war or public danger; nor shall any person be subject for the same offense to be twice put in jeopardy of life or limb; nor shall be compelled in any criminal case to be a witness against himself, nor be deprived of life, liberty, or property, without due process of law; nor shall private property be taken for public use without just compensation.

FIFTH AMENDMENT

THREE prohibitions contained in the fifth amendment are applicable to criminal procedure: a) compelling a person to be a witness against himself in a criminal case; b) subjecting any person to double jeopardy for the same offense, and c) charging a person with a capital or infamous crime except by indictment of a grand jury.

Section I. CUSTODIAL INTERROGATION AND CONFESSION

1.1. Introduction

No person . . . shall be compelled in any criminal case to be a witness against himself. . . .

This guarantee not only applies to federal procedure, but also to the states through the due process clause of the fourteenth amendment (*Brown v. Miss.*, 297 U.S.278, 1936; *Malloy v. Hogan*, 378 U.S.1). Generally, for an admission or confession made outside of court by one suspected of a crime, to be admissible at trial, the confession made outside of court must be voluntary and free from coercion.

1.1.1. DEVELOPMENT OF THE FEDERAL STANDARD. Within the federal court system, the Supreme Court has developed the rule that any statements, even if shown to have been voluntarily made, may not be used against the defendant if it was obtained while the accused was unduly detained while waiting to be taken before a magistrate, as is required by the *Federal Rules of Criminal Procedure,* Rule 5a. Since prompt arraignment after arrest was federal procedure, rather than constitutional law, the state courts were free to reject it. This rule of federal policy became known as the McNabb-Mallory Rule. *McNabb v. U.S.,* 318 U.S.332 (1942); *Mallory v. U.S.,* 354 U.S.449 (1957).

Subsequently, the Supreme Court ruled in *Massiah v. U.S.,* 377 U.S.201 (1964), that the defendant had been denied the protections of the sixth amendment when his own incriminating words, elicited without benefit of counsel, between indictment and trial, were admitted against him at the trial. In *Escobedo* and *Miranda* (see subsection **1.1.2.**) the defendants were denied certain constitutionally-based procedural safeguards after being taken into custody, and consequently their convictions were reversed due to the inadmissibility of the confessions so obtained.

Four years after the *Escobedo* decision, Congress essentially overturned *Miranda* and *Escobedo* in the federal courts by enacting the *Omnibus Crime Control and Safe Streets Act of 1968* (18 USC 3501), which requires, in part, that a confession be "voluntarily" given, before it is admissible in court. Confession is defined as, "Any confession of guilt of any criminal offense, or any self-incriminating statement made or given orally or in writing." 18 USC 3501 (e).

Under the existing federal standard, "voluntariness" is determined by considering: a) the elapsed time between arrest and arraignment, if the confession was made during that interval, b) whether the defendant knew the nature of the offense he was being charged with (or suspected of) when he made the confession, c) whether the defendant was advised that he need not say anything and any statement that he might make could be used against him, d) had he been advised of his right to counsel, prior to questioning, and e) was the defendant without counsel when he confessed? In addition, statements must be given within six hours following arrest or other detention; however, the trial judge may determine that because of the distance travelled and the type of transportation used that six hours is not a *reasonable* time period and revoke the requirement.

The aforementioned Omnibus Crime Control bill is applicable

Figure 5-1

CONFESSIONS

Federal Standard	State Standard
McNabb v. U.S. (1943)	Brown v. Miss. (1936)
Mallory v. U.S. (1957)	Spano v. N.Y. (1959)
↓	(fourteenth amendment)
Massiah v. U.S. (1964)	↓
(sixth amendment)	Malloy v. Hogan (1964)
	(fifth amendment)

Escobedo v. Ill. (1964)
Miranda v. Arizona (1966)
(5th and sixth amendments)

Omnibus Crime Control	Miranda Standard
and Safe Streets Act of	Mathis v. U.S. (1968)
1968 (18 USC 3501)	Orzoco v. Texas (1969)

in any criminal prosecution by the United States or by the District of Columbia.

1.1.1.1. *Admissibility of Confessions.* (18USC3501) In any criminal prosecution brought by the United States or by the District of Columbia, a confession shall be admissible in evidence if it is voluntarily given. Before such confession is received in evidence, the trial judge shall, out of the presence of the jury, determine any issue as to voluntariness. If the trial judge determines that the confession was voluntarily made, it shall be admitted in evidence and the trial judge shall permit the jury to hear relevant evidence on the issue of voluntariness and shall instruct the jury to give such weight to the confession as the jury feels it deserves under all the circumstances.

The trial judge in determining the issue of voluntariness shall take into consideration all the circumstances surrounding the giving of the confession, including: a) the time elapsing between arrest and arraignment of the defendant making the confession, if it was made after arrest and before arraignment, b) whether such defendant knew the nature of the offense with which he was charged or of which he was suspected at the time of making the confession, c) whether or not such defendant was advised or knew that he was not required to make any statement and that any such statement could be used against him, d) whether or not such defendant had been advised prior to questioning of his right to the assistance of counsel; and e) whether or not such defendant was without the assistance of counsel when questioned and when giving such confession.

The presence or absence of any of the above-mentioned factors to be taken into consideration by the judge need not be conclusive on the issue of voluntariness of the confession.

In any criminal prosecution by the United States or by the District of Columbia, a confession made or given by a person who is a defendant therein, while such person was under arrest or other detention in the custody of any law-enforcement officer or law-enforcement agency, shall not be inadmissible solely because of delay in bringing such person before a magistrate or other officer empowered to commit persons charged with offenses against the laws of the United States or of the District of Columbia if such confession is found by the trial judge to have been made voluntarily and if the weight to be given the confession is left to the jury and if such confession was made or given by such person within six hours immediately following his arrest or other detention: *provided,* that the time limitation contained in this subsection shall not apply in any case in which the delay in bringing such person before such magistrate or other officer beyond such six-hour period is found by the trial judge to be reasonable considering the means of transportation and the distance to be travelled to the nearest available such magistrate or other officer.

Nothing contained in this section shall bar the admission in evidence of any confession made or given voluntarily by any person to any other person without interrogation by anyone, or at any time at which the person who made or gave such confession was not under arrest or other detention.

As used in this section, the term "confession" means any confession of guilt of any criminal offense or any self-incriminating statement made or given orally or in writing.

1.1.2. DEVELOPMENT OF THE STATE STANDARD. In the days before the *Miranda* decision, the United States Supreme Court based a rule on the fourteenth amendment which governed the admissibility of confessions in state criminal trials. The rule excluded involuntary, coerced confessions from admission in state court proceedings on the basis that such was a violation of due process of law as protected by the fourteenth amendment. At first, confessions were excluded when they were the result of coercion by brutal beatings and physical abuse of the defendant (*Brown v. Miss.,* 297 U.S.278 (1936)). Then the coercion concept was extended to include torture of the mind as well as the body; for example, where the defendant's will was overwhelmed by official pressure, fatigue and sympathy falsely aroused during an eight-hour interrogation (*Spano v. N.Y.,* 360 U.S.315 (1959)). Finally, the privilege against self-incrimination in the fifth amendment was made binding on the state courts through the Due Process Clause of the fourteenth amendment, by *Malloy v. Hogan,* 378 U.S.1 (1964).

In *Escobedo* (see Chap. 6), the defendant was not warned of his constitutional right to remain silent and was denied the assistance of counsel, a sixth amendment right, and hence, no statement elicited by the police during the questioning could be used against him at his trial (*Escobedo v. Ill.,* 378 U.S.478 (1964)).

1.1.3. THE MIRANDA STANDARD AS THE STATE STANDARD. Simply stated, the *Miranda Standard* requires that a suspect be informed of his constitutional rights before being subjected to custodial interrogation. (*Miranda* requirements, strictly speaking, are now required on the state level only, since the passage of the Omnibus Crime Bill of 1968. However, as a matter of procedure, the specific *Miranda warnings* are still given to persons suspected of committing federal crime, prior to interrogation.)

1.1.3.1. *Miranda Case Example.* Ten days after an eighteen-year-old girl was kidnapped and forcibly raped, Miranda was arrested and taken into the police station. He was held incommunicado and questioned in a special interrogation room for two hours in a police-dominated atmosphere without being advised of his constitutional right to remain silent, or to consult with or have his attorney present during the interrogation. Miranda made self-incriminating statements which resulted in a written confession of the kidnapping and the rape. Was the court correct in admitting the written confession into evidence at the trial?

No, said the United States Supreme Court. In reversing the conviction, the court said that the failure to inform Miranda of his constitutional rights made the statements *inadmissible* because the fifth amendment provides that one cannot compel an individual to be a witness against himself. Further, a knowing and intelligent waiver *could not be presumed* from a typed statement that appeared on the confession which stated that the confession was "voluntary" and made with full knowledge by the defendant of his rights. *When an individual is taken into custody or otherwise deprived of his freedom in any significant way by authorities and subjected to questioning, the following proce-*

dural safeguards must be made known to him before any questioning can take place:
1. That he has the right to remain silent.
2. That anything he might say can be used against him in a
   court of law.
3. That he has the right to the presence of an attorney before and during interrogation.
4. That if he cannot afford an attorney, one will be appointed for him, if he so desires.

These rights must be made known to the individual throughout
the interrogation and if at any time the suspect requests the
presence or advice of an attorney, questioning must stop until
the request is met or waived. The individual may voluntarily, knowingly and intelligently waive these rights and agree
to make a statement or answer questions. However, the prosecution, at trial, before evidence can be admitted, must demonstrate
that the warnings and the waiver were given the accused, with
the opportunity afforded to exercise the rights. If waived, it must
be demonstrated, that a *knowing* and *intelligent* waiver was made
before questioning of the accused began.

The *Miranda* warnings must be given only when custodial interrogation is about to begin. Custodial interrogation is defined
by the court as questioning by law enforcement officers after an
individual has been taken into custody or deprived of his freedom in any significant way, for example, arrest and custody.
Some courts have broadened the definition of custodial interrogation to include questioning of an individual who merely
thinks he is being deprived of his freedom in a significant way.

Contrastingly, *Miranda* does not restrict the law enforcement
officer in the initial phase of a criminal investigation. Thus, on-
the-scene questioning of witnesses is not governed by the Miranda
requirement, nor is the individual that voluntarily walks into a
police station to confess to a crime. The courts have repeatedly
held that spontaneous statements which are made in the absence of interrogation do not require the giving of the *Miranda*
warnings, *regardless* of where the statement is given, be it in jail,
on the street, in a police cruiser, or in the individual's home or
car.

Two factors which carry a great amount of weight in determining whether the interrogation is custodial or not are as follows: a) who conducted the interrogation, and b) where was it conducted.

Generally, if the questioning is conducted by law enforcement officers, chances are that the interrogation is custodial. However, when an interrogation is conducted by a police officer, a) on the street, b) in a hospital, c) at the suspect's home, car, or place of business, or d) at the residence or business of a third person, it is most likely to be a noncustodial interrogation. The distinction between custodial versus noncustodial settings is based on the inherent coerciveness of the surroundings to the accused. Thus, one would not feel the same compulsion to "talk" while in one's own home or car, as would one in a police cruiser or jail. This is one of the key reasons that warnings are required in any custodial setting, for custodial situations, either physically or psychologically, are often, correctly or not, equated with coercion and duress. *Miranda* warnings are usually required when the interrogation takes place in jail, in a police station or vehicle, and at the sheriff's office.

In addition to the above mentioned factors (the person who conducts the interrogation and the place of interrogation) four other factors are recognized in determining whether an interrogation is custodial or not: a) the time of day the interrogation takes place, b) who the suspect is, c) how far along the investigation is at the time of interrogation, and d) the nature of the interrogation.

The later the hour of the interrogation, the more likely the suspect will be intimidated and the more likely the interrogation will be held custodial. Also, the proximity of time and place of the interrogation with respect to the time and the scene of the crime is important.

The age, knowledge, intelligence, experience, mental condition and physical condition of the accused are also important factors to be considered.

An *investigation* can be broken down into seven steps for ascertaining its import for *Miranda* purposes: a) suspicion, b) knowledge that a crime has been committed, c) probable cause for arrest, d) obtaining an arrest warrant, e) arrest, f) pre-trial incarceration, and g) indictment.

The nature of the *interrogation* is determined by a number of factors, some of which are the following: the manner in which the questions are asked (i.e. formal, accusatory, or casual), the number of questions asked, the isolation of the suspect from friends, handcuffing, searching, use of threat, use of force, and if any of the *Miranda* warnings were given.

If a *confession is to be used* in evidence against the defendant and the *Miranda* warnings were not given, the prosecution must prove that confession was not the result of custodial interrogation as discussed above.

1.1.3.2. *Volunteered Statements.* Statements that are not the product of custodial interrogation do not require the *Miranda* warning. If the police merely listen and do not question the volunteer, the statements made do not fall under *Miranda*. However, if the police initiate the questioning and do not assume a passive role, the interrogation may be found to be custodial (*People v. Leon,* 288 N.Y.S.2d 746 (1968); *People v. Matthews,* 70 CAL.RPTR. 756 (1968)). The prosecution must prove, at trial, by at least a *preponderance* of evidence that this confession was voluntary. Of course, the states may adopt a higher standard (*Lego v. Twomey,* 404 U.S. 477, 1972).

1.1.3.3. *On-the-Scene Questioning.* Usually, on-the-scene questioning is not considered custodial interrogation (*State v. Corrigan,* 228 A.2d 568 (1967)). Similarly, a number of courts have held that questioning during the commission of a crime is not custodial interrogation. For example, undercover officers asked questions of the defendants while defendants were in the process of selling marijuana to the officers who were riding in an unmarked police car with them. Subsequently, the defendants were arrested. The court said that the officers had no requirement to inform the defendants of their constitutional rights prior to the time of arrest (*People v. Stenchever,* 57 CAL. RPTR. 14 (1967)).

1.1.3.4. *Reasonable Belief of Custody Test.* This concept is an expansion by certain courts, of the *Miranda* definition of custodial interrogation. It not only applies *custodial interrogation* to situations where the suspect is questioned while actually deprived of his freedom in any significant way, but to situations where the person questioned, reasonably *believes* that he is being deprived of his freedom in a significant way (*People v. Hazel*, 60 Cal.Rptr. 437 (1967); (*People v. Rodney P. (Anonymous)*, 233 N.E.2d 255 (1967)).

1.2. Interrogation by Law Enforcement Officers Under Miranda

1.2.1. On the Street

A plainclothes inspector in an unmarked vehicle observed two men get into a cab, one carrying a phonograph and the other a television set. The one carrying the television had run quickly to the cab. The inspector followed the cab and when it stopped, the two emerged. He enlisted the help of two uniformed police officers, encircled the defendants and asked them questions. The defendants made incriminating statements. Also, a tin box, which was on top of the phonograph, was found to contain marijuana. The defendants were then arrested. Should the *Miranda* warnings have been given?

Yes. The defendants, although on the street, had been deprived of their freedom of action in a significant way before the questioning began, and thus they should have been given the *Miranda* warnings (*People v. Reason*, 276 N.Y.S.2d 196 (1966)).

Ten minutes after an attempted robbery, an officer saw two men that fit the description of the wanted pair. He called them over to his car and questioned them at gunpoint. After the defendants made incriminating statements, they were arrested. The suspects were not permitted to leave during the interrogation. Should the *Miranda* warnings have been given?

Yes. The defendants questioned by an officer with a drawn gun were clearly deprived of their freedom in a significant way. The officer had no intention of letting the defendants escape and the defendants themselves could have reached no other conclusion. Once the officer draws his gun and freedom of the defendant is restricted, he may not be questioned further until the *Miranda* warnings are given (*People v. Shivers*, 233 N.E.2d 836 (1967)).

A police officer saw a suspect in a homicide case and told him to stop. The officer grabbed the suspect's arm and asked him if he had been on a certain street and the defendant said yes. While still holding the defendant, other officers frisked and handcuffed him. He made a second incriminating statement. Was the interrogation custodial?

Yes. The defendant was physically detained and such detention constituted a deprivation of freedom in a significant way and was likely to affect the defendant's will to resist, and compel him to speak where he would not otherwise do so freely, thus making necessary the giving of the *Miranda* warnings (*People v. McKay,* 287 N.Y.S.2d 795 (1968)).

> An officer saw a man twice enter a car and remove property which he handed to his companion. The officer asked if the car belong to them. He then asked the license number. They said Ohio plates instead of Iowa plates. The men were arrested for petit larceny. Should the pair have been advised of the *Miranda* rights?

No. The pair had been detained because the officer felt that their conduct required investigation and they were only questioned briefly. Furthermore, the answers had not been the product of coercion and were voluntary. Custodial interrogation, or arrest, does not necessarily take place when a citizen is stopped and questioned in the course of a routine police investigation (*Green v. U.S.,* 234 A.2d 177 (1967)).

> About midnight an officer spoted a car heavily loaded with barbed wire. Upon stopping the car the officer asked the driver his name, who the car belonged to and where he got the wire. The defendant said he stole the car and the wire. Should the *Miranda* warnings have been given before questioning?

No. The confession was volunteered and spontaneously given without any compelling influences. Basically, it was within the *Miranda* exception, general on-the-scene investigation and questioning as to facts surrounding a crime. (*Miranda* recognizes at least two exceptions: a) general on-the-scene questioning as to facts surrounding a crime, and b) statements freely volunteered without compelling influences) (*Nevels v. State,* 216 So.2d 529 (1968)).

> After receiving an anonymous tip that a certain person was driving a stolen vehicle, the officer found the vehicle by a tavern and asked the defendant to step outside. The officer asked the defendant where he worked and lived, and if the car was his. The officer did not know for sure that the car was stolen, nor did he have an intent to arrest

the defendant. Was this custodial interrogation requiring the *Miranda* warnings?

No, for three reasons: (1) the questioning only lasted for a few minutes, (2) the questioning was casual and routine, and (3) there was no purpose or intent into tricking the defendant to confessing (*U.S. v. Gibson*, 392 F.2d 373 (1968)).

> An officer saw the defendant in the back seat of a taxi with some identification cards on the floor, between his feet. The officer merely asked the man his name. The defendant replied, incriminating himself. Should he have been informed of his constitutional rights before being asked his name?

.No. The police officer has made no arrest and was not interrogating the defendant. *Miranda* does not go so far as to hold that a police officer cannot ask a suspicious individual his name before informing him of his constitutional rights (*Sharbor v. Gathright*, 295 F. Supp. 386 (1969)).

> Unaware that a burglary was being committed, an officer observed two men carrying a number of items, including a stereo, out of an apartment house. The officer asked the men where they were taking the stereo. Should the defendants have been warned of their constitutional rights?

No. The defendants were only under investigation, not arrest. The on-the-scene questioning was merely the investigation of suspicious circumstances and freedom of the defendants had not been impaired (*People v. Singleton*, 63 CAL.RPTR. 324 (1967)).

> An officer saw a man walking in the rain, without a raincoat, carrying a new typewriter case in a neighborhood where many typewriters had been stolen. The suspect was found to be carrying radios. The officer asked where he was going and if he had a receipt for the radios. The suspect admitted that he had stolen the radios. The officer arrested the man and advised him of his rights. Should he have been given the *Miranda* warnings earlier?

No. When persons are (1) temporarily detained by police, (2) questioned briefly, and (3) the police do not have probable cause to arrest, the *Miranda* warnings need not be given. There is a distinction between one briefly detained when suspected of a crime and one in custody, accused of a crime (*People v. Manis*, 74 CAL.RPTR. 423 (1969)).

1.2.2. IN THE POLICE VEHICLE

A police officer asked the defendant to step out of his house and into the police car. During questioning, the defendant admitted entering another's house. The defendant returned to his house and the officer left. The next day the defendant was arrested and charged with burglary. Was the interrogation custodial?

No. The defendant was in fact free of restraint at all times and left the scene of the interrogation a free man, he was not in custody when he was being interviewed. It is unlikely that an officer will produce involuntary self-incriminations on the part of a guilty person if that person is not under arrest or under any other form of restraint (*State v. Travis,* 441 P.2d 597 (1968)).

An officer found a car matching the description of one used in a rape and asked the driver of the car to step into the police car. The defendant and the officer talked about things of general interest until the defendant made an incriminating statement. Should the *Miranda* warnings have been given?

No. The defendant was interviewed in the cruiser car as a matter of convenience. He was not under any restraint. The officer had no basis for an arrest until the defendant made his statement. When asked about the girl he had in the car the night before, he volunteered a complete statement. The court quoted from *Miranda v. Arizona* (384 U.S.436), (1966).

In dealing with statements obtained through interrogation, we do not purport to find all confessions inadmissible. Confessions remain a proper element in law enforcement. Any statement given freely and voluntarily without any compelling influences is, of course, admissible in evidence. The fundamental import of the privilege while an individual is in custody is not whether he is allowed to talk to the police without the benefit of warnings and counsel, but whether he can be interrogated. There is no requirement that police stop a person who enters a police station and states that he wishes to confess to a crime, or a person who calls the police to offer a confession or any other statement he desires to make. Volunteered statements of any kind are not barred by the fifth amendment and their admissibility is not affected by our holding today. (*State v. Caha,* 165 N.W.2d 362 (1969)).

* * *

Police stopped the defendant in the street after being directed to apprehend him in a homicide case. The defendant was held by the arms, handcuffed, and taken to the police station where he was questioned. The defendant made incriminating statements and at no time were the *Miranda* warnings given. Should the defendant have been warned of his rights?

Yes. The defendant was denied his freedom in a significant way and such detention was likely to affect his will to resist and compel him to speak where he would not otherwise do so freely. "Being held by a police officer by manual force is as effective a taking into custody as is restraint by means of a drawn gun." (*People v. McKay,* 287 N.Y.S.2d 795, 1968).

> Officers went to investigate a possible assault or homicide and found the defendant and the apartment covered with blood. The body of a woman lying in a pool of blood was also found. The officer took the defendant by the arm to the patrol car where he questioned him. The defendant made incriminating statements. At no time were the *Miranda* warnings given. Should the warnings have been given?

Yes. The officer's action in placing his hand on the defendant's arm and leading him outside to the patrol car was an infringement of the defendant's freedom of action that required the officer to fully advise the defendant of his constitutional rights under *Miranda* before he could ask any questions (*State v. Saunders,* 435 P.2d 39, 1967).

1.2.3. AT THE POLICE STATION

> The defendant read in the paper that fingerprint evidence had been found in a murder case and subsequently called the police and said that he had been at the murder scene to do repair work. The defendant went to the police station after being asked to do so and upon being questioned made an incriminating statement. The *Miranda* warnings were then given. Should the warning have been given earlier?

No. The initial statements made by the defendant prior to receiving the required warnings of his constitutional rights were not in response to in-custody interrogation designed to elicit incriminating information. The defendant had volunteered to give a statement as to his activities in the home of the decedent, and the police merely afforded him the opportunity of accounting for his presence there. It was only after the defendant indicated that he had a criminal record that the police, as a precaution to preserve the admissibility of any statements they might obtain, warned the defendant of his constitutional rights (*People v. Hill,* 452 P.2d 329 (1969)).

> The defendant voluntarily went to the police station to review events of a party that a murder victim had attended. The officer noticed scratch marks on the defendant's neck and asked him to take his shirt off. More scratches were found on his back. The officer then stopped the questioning and said the defendant was now a suspect and informed him of his constitutional rights. Should the defendant have been informed earlier of his rights?

No. The interrogation of the defendant became an in-custody interrogation when the officer observed the scratches and the investigation "focussed" on the defendant. At this point the warnings were given. Until this time there was nothing to suggest that the defendant, who voluntarily came to the police station, was in custody or deprived of his freedom (*Commonwealth v. Fisher,* 238 N.E.2d 525 (1968)).

> The sixteen-year-old defendant was kept at the police station for eight hours, although his house was only two blocks away. He was (1) fingerprinted, (2) required to remove his pants and one shoe for analysis, and (3) questioned for five hours. He subsequently confessed and was given the *Miranda* warnings. Were the warnings timely?

No. Although the defendant had not been arrested, he was physically deprived of his freedom in a significant way, or in such a way that a reasonable person would believe he was so deprived. It was improper for the police to wait until he confessed to give the *Miranda* warnings, in this case they should have been given when the youth was first brought in (*People v. Ellingsen,* 65 CAL.RPTR. 744 (1968)).

> The sheriff, after a brief investigation at the scene of a burglary, took a sixteen-year-old boy to his office and questioned him for one-half hour. The boy was requested to remove his shoes since footprints were found near the scene of the crime. The boy was returned home but later, after footprints were compared, he was asked to go back to the sheriff's office. The boy made a full confession. He was arrested. Should the *Miranda* warnings have been given?

Yes. Notwithstanding that the defendant's confession was voluntary, in the sense that it was made without coercion or enticement, the circumstances were such to show that at the time the defendant was questioned about and confessed to the commission of the crime, he had been deprived of his freedom in a significant way and was subject to custodial interrogation. Before questioning commenced, the warnings should have been given. (*Johnson v. Commonwealth*, 160 S.E.2d 793 (1968)).

1.2.4. IN JAIL

> A fifteen-year-old girl was held in *protective custody* at a juvenile detention center for several days. During such time the girl answered questions asked by detectives who were conducting an investigation regarding livestock theft. A *counselor* was present during such questioning. The defendant's testimony was not used in evidence against her, but was used merely for impeachment purposes. Should the *Miranda* warnings have been given?

No. The court said that there was no need here for the detectives to advise the girl of her constitutional rights as the investigation for conspiracy to steal livestock was generalized and had not focussed on this particular girl (*State v. Cole*, 448 P.2d 523, 1968)).

> After arrest for parole violation, the defendant was questioned during a twenty-day period while in a maximum security cell. He was the prime suspect in a homicide case and at no time was he given the *Miranda* warnings. Should the warnings have been given?

Yes. The defendant should have been warned of his constitutional rights at the time of his arrest and incarceration and before questioning. Here, he had been arrested on a pretext of parole violation when, in reality, he was the principal suspect in a homicide case (*Commonwealth v. Leaming*, 247 A.2d 590 (1968)).

> A police officer questioned an inmate at the State prison about an offense unrelated to that for which he was in custody, to determine if he had committed it. The *Miranda* warnings were not given. Should they have been?

Yes. The court said that since the inmate had been questioned while in custody, even though the questions were unrelated to the offense he was imprisoned for, it was *custodial interrogation* and the *Miranda* warnings should have been given (*People v. Woodberry*, 71 CAL.RPTR. 165 (1968)).

The defendant, while in custody and subsequent to arrest, made a statement to the sheriff in response to a question, that he owned a wallet found by a jail trustee in the patrol car that brought the defendant to jail. The defendant was not warned that he had a right to remain silent. Should he have been informed of his rights?

Yes. Before the prosecutor may use statements uttered by an accused in custodial interrogation, it must be shown that he was warned of his rights under the United States Constitution (*U.S. v. Kucinich*, 404 F.2d 262 (1968)).

1.2.5. AT SUSPECT'S HOME

The defendant was charged with having committed an act of juvenile delinquency. F.B.I. agents went to her home to question her and to determine if she had had sexual intercourse with five jurors during a trial, as she claimed she had. Were *Miranda* warnings required pending the investigation of alleged obstruction of justice?

No. The rule of *Miranda* was not applicable where at the time of the interview the defendant a) was not in any way restrained of her freedom, b) was not under arrest, c) was not in custody, d) the interview was in her own home, e) no warrant for her arrest was outstanding, and f) no charge had been made against her. The interview was entirely *investigatory* (*U.S. v. Essex*, 275 F. Supp. 393 (1967)).

A police officer went to the defendant's house because a witness said that he had seen the defendant run from the scene of a burglary. Before the officer questioned the defendant, he advised him of his rights, subsequent to which, an incriminating statement was made. Did the officer need to give the *Miranda* warnings in this situation?

No. The court said that the requirements of *Miranda* have no application where a) the defendant is not in custody or detained and b) the questioning takes place in a relaxed situation such as the defendant's home where his family is present. *Miranda* deals with the individual that is subject to custodial police interrogation (*State v. Noriega*, 433 P.2d 281 (1967)).

A sheriff's deputy interrogated a woman in her home about the shooting death of her husband. The defendant was not free to leave during the questioning and she was an obvious suspect in the homicide. *Miranda* warnings were not given. Should she have been advised of her rights?

Yes. Since she (1) was not free to leave and (2) was the obvious suspect, it was imperative for the law enforcement officers involved to inform the defendant of her constitutional rights pursuant to the privilege against self-incrimination (*State v. Anderson*, 428 P.2d 672 (1967)).

> Officers with a search warrant entered a girl's dwelling and found her in a bedroom with a male companion. Furthermore, the officers found cigarette paper of the type used to roll marijuana cigarettes. They asked the girl if the paper belonged to her, she said yes. Upon finding a plastic container and asking what was in it, she replied, "Grass I guess." Should the *Miranda* warnings have been given?

Yes. From the time the officers entered, the defendant was deprived of her freedom of action in a significant way. This is all that is required with respect to the custody issue in *Miranda*. It is not necessary for the defendant to be in *actual* custody (*People v. Wilson*, 74 CAL.RPTR. 131 (1968)).

1.2.6. AT SUSPECT'S BUSINESS

> Officers with a search warrant, providing for the arrest of the defendant in the event narcotics were found, entered his drugstore and found a brown paper bag. In the presence of a clean-up boy and two clerks, the officers asked "What is this?" The defendant answered, "It is heroin, you have got me this time." Did the question presented constitute custodial interrogation?

No. The defendant was not under arrest and the officers stated that they had no reason to arrest him until they found the contraband. The court held that the answer was admissible in court as it was made while the defendant was not in custody (*Brown v. State*, 437 S.W.2d 828 (1968)).

> A custodian at a university was interviewed by a police officer in a room at the school about a theft from a campus safe. He admitted committing the crime. Should the *Miranda* warnings have been given?

No. The defendant had not been arrested at the time of his admission of the crime. Until he made the admission he was only part of a general investigation. He had not been requested to go to police headquarters or a precinct station, and he was on the premises of his employer. In no way was the defendant deprived of his freedom as he was free to go, up to the time of the admission. There is no need for *Miranda* warnings to be given to all who choose to cooperate with law enforcement officers in the furtherance of a general investigation (*U.S. v. Delamarra,* 275 F. Supp. 1 (1967)).

> An F.B.I. agent questioned the defendant in the familiar surroundings of her own place of business while her husband was present. Subsequent to making a statement, she was convicted for the interstate transportation of a stolen automobile. Was she under custodial interrogation?

No. She was not in custody nor was she otherwise deprived of her freedom of action in any significant way. Since *Miranda* is specifically limited to custodial interrogation, the warnings did not have to be given (*Archer v. U.S.,* 393 F2d 124 (1968)).

1.2.7. IN SUSPECT'S VEHICLE

> A police officer stopped a car at 3:30 AM which was being driven at a slow speed with its headlights off. Upon approaching the car, the officer saw a passenger, bleeding profusely, whose face was beaten beyond recognition. The officer asked who owned the car and the driver said that he did not know. The officer then asked the passenger who beat him, and the passenger pointed to the driver. The officer asked the driver if he had beaten the passenger. He then noticed that the driver's knuckles were skinned. The officer radioed the dispatcher and found that the car was stolen. The men were arrested. Should the *Miranda* warnings have been given?

No. *Miranda* permits general, on-the-street investigation of citizens not under restraint. The material indication that the police are still in a state of investigation is the routineness of the inquiry. Some inquiry can be made as part of an investigation notwithstanding limited and brief restraints by the police in their efforts to screen crimes from relatively routine mishaps. For example, it is not uncommon for citizens to forget their permits and registration cards. Although this type of mishap produces incidental detention and restraint while the possibility of a stolen car is checked out, it does not produce the kind of custodial situation contemplated by the *Miranda* doctrine (*Allen v. U.S.,* 390 F.2d 476 (1968)).

> Officers stopped a car that had been weaving back and forth across the center line of the street. The driver was told to get out of the car and was questioned in the presence of two female companions. During questioning, the officer told the driver to roll up his sleeves, and upon

doing so, fresh puncture marks were discovered in each arm. The driver was arrested for driving while under the influence of narcotics. Should the *Miranda* warnings have been given before the questioning took place?

No. The formal arrest is not an adequate dividing line to use as a rule to determine when the constitutional rights must be given, after a suspect has been stopped. When the police have both reasonable grounds to believe that a crime has been committed and that the defendant is the one who committed it, the warnings must be given. Here, the questioning before the defendant's arrest was general on-the-scene questioning which is permissible under *Miranda*. The officers smelled the driver's breath and looked at his arms. This was part of the process of investigation or determining if a crime had been committed. Questions asked at this time are investigative (*State v. Tellez,* 431 P.2d 691 (1967)).

Officers stopped a car that failed to stop for a red light. The driver was unable to produce a driver's license or registration. He was further questioned as to the ownership of certain narcotics found in the car. Should the *Miranda* warnings have been given?

Yes. The fact that the driver was unable to produce a driver's license or registration or explain ownership of the car gave the officers probable cause to believe that the car had been stolen. Furthermore, the observation of the defendant by the officers gave them probable cause to believe the defendant was guilty of possession of narcotics, before he was asked about the contents of the car. Once an officer has probable cause to believe that the person being detained for interrogation has committed an offense, the interrogation becomes custodial, because the defendant would not be permitted to leave, and accordingly, the suspect must be warned of his constitutional rights before further questions can be asked (*People v. Ceccone,* 67 Cal.Rptr. 499 (1968)).

1.2.8. At Third Person's Residence

A police officer arrived at the victim's home outside the city limits and found the deceased lying on the kitchen floor and the defendant lying beside the body, wounded. The officer asked what had happened, to which the defendant replied, "Baby, I told you I loved you. I told you I would hurt you if you didn't go with me." Should the officer have warned the defendant of his rights before asking the question?

No. The officer involved had been summoned to the home of decedent. He was a city officer and the jurisdiction was that of the sheriff of the county. The officer made no effort to take the defendant into custody and did not question him beyond the initial query of "What happened?" He simply waited until the sheriff arrived (*Truex v. State,* 210 So.2d 424 (1968)).

> In a triple murder case, a statement was obtained from the defendant during an interview by an investigating officer at the home of the defendant's neighbor. The defendant was not under arrest nor was he in custody. Should the *Miranda* warnings have been given?

No. The defendant was not then under arrest, in custody, or deprived of his freedom of action in any significant way; the investigation had not yet reached the accusatory stage (*Steigler v. Superior Court of New Castle County,* 252 A.2d 300 (1969)).

> A forty-four-year-old plumber was working in a house when a 3½-year-old girl, living there, told her mother that a man had "peed in her panties." Two officers came to the home and found the defendant still working in the basement. One officer asked the defendant if he had done anything to the girl, to which the defendant made an incriminating statement. Should the defendant have been given the *Miranda* warnings?

No. The defendant was asked one simple question in the basement of the home. He was not in custody, he was there as a workman by his own choice and hence the *Miranda* rule did not apply (*State v. Lipker,* 241 N.E.2d 171 (1968)).

1.2.9. At Third Person's Business

> A plainclothes officer stationed inside a restaurant posed as a killer seeking a job for "big money." The officer conversed with a suspect, as a friend would, and did not take him into physical custody until the conversation was over. Should the *Miranda* warnings have been given?

No. There was nothing which indicated that the suspect believed he was denied his freedom of action. The conversation was friendly and was free from coercive influences. The *Miranda* requirement, according to the court, does not depend on the intent of the law enforcement officer, but on whether the suspect was, or thought he was, deprived of his freedom in any significant way (*People v. Ward,* 72 CAL.RPTR. 46 (1968)).

> Officers, responding to a complaint about suspicious activities at a car wash at 3:30 AM, saw three men running from the building. Upon catching up with one of the men, the defendant told the officer that he had never done anything like this before. The officer, unaware that a crime had been committed, asked the defendant what he had done. After being told that they had planned to break into the car wash, the officer asked how they planned to do it. Should the *Miranda* warnings have been given?

No. The defendant's answers were not the product of custodial interrogation initiated by the law enforcement officer. The officer had merely sought to clarify the defendant's original admission and was not required to prevent the defendant from explaining (*State v. Perry,* 237 N.E.2d 891 (1968)).

> The defendant was arrested for shoplifting and was taken to a room in the basement of the store, where he was interrogated at length by the arresting officer and the store detective. The defendant made some incriminating statements to the effect that the car he was driving was stolen. Neither the law enforcement officer nor the store detective was aware at the time of the interrogation that the defendant's car was stolen. Should the *Miranda* warnings have been given?

Yes. The defendant was under arrest at the time of the interrogation and it did not matter that the arrest was for an offense unrelated to the one he revealed during the questioning (*People v. Ryff,* 284 N.Y.S.2d 953 (1967)).

1.2.10. AT THE HOSPITAL

> Within an hour after an automobile accident, the defendant was questioned by a police officer at the hospital. The officer asked the defendant if he had been driving at the time of the accident. The defendant was uncertain of the correct answer. The officer asked why he did not know if he had been driving, or not, the defendant replied that he was drunk. During the brief questioning about the motor vehicle homicide, the defendant walked freely about the hospital. Should the *Miranda* warnings have been given?

No. The atmosphere was not compulsive and the defendant had not been isolated or limited in his freedom of action in any significant way during the short period of interrogation (*People v. Gilbert*, 154 N.W.2d 800 (1967)).

> A wounded patient at the hospital was questioned by a police officer trying to determine who had shot him. At the time of the questioning the officer was unaware that the patient had been shot while attempting a robbery. Were the *Miranda* warnings required?

No. The officer did not warn the patient of his constitutional rights because he was not in custody and the investigation of the robbery had not focussed on him. The patient was merely questioned as a victim of a shooting and the officer was not aware of any connection between the patient and the robbery. The warnings are not required under these circumstances (*Tillery v. State*, 238 A.2d 125 (1968)).

> The defendant accidentally shot himself after escaping from the scene of a robbery. When police officers arrived at the hospital, the defendant was undergoing intravenous feeding and was not capable of movement. The officers interrogated the defendant for well over an hour, before he admitted participation in the crime. The defendant was arrested the following morning. Should *Miranda* warnings have been given?

Yes. Formal arrest does not necessarily mark the point when an interrogation becomes custodial. It was unnecessary in this case for the police to restrict the defendant's freedom of movement. Official custody could have been imposed in substitution for the restraint of the circumstances at any time by the police since the methods of custodial restraint were the equivalent of the actual restraint (*People v. Tanner*, 295 N.Y.S.2d 709 (1968)).

> While the wounded defendant was in a hospital operating room being prepared for surgery, he was given *some* warnings and then questioned by police officers as to his hitting of another man. The defendant was under a sedative and in considerable pain. Should the complete *Miranda* warnings have been given?

Yes. The defendant was told that he had the right to an attorney and that he did not have to answer questions. He was *not* told that anything he said could be used against him in a court of law and that if he could not afford an attorney, one would be appointed for him prior to any questioning (*State v. Ross*, 157 N.W.2d 860 (1968)).

1.3. Volunteered Statements Under *Miranda*

1.3.1. ON THE STREET. In the following cases the question of the custodial nature of volunteered or spontaneous statements made on the street is explored.

> In the early morning hours, police officers observed two men outside the front door of a liquor store. Pruning shears were protruding from the front door. Two other individuals were sitting in a station wagon parked in front. After all four were arrested the defendant said that his companions should be let go because he was the only one breaking into the liquor store. Was the statement a product of custodial interrogation requiring the *Miranda* warnings?

No. The defendant was not protected by *Miranda* for two reasons. a) He was never interrogated by the officers. What he said was without denial, gratuitous and spontaneous. b) The statements were not produced by custodial interrogation but were an effort to exculpate his companions (*Cameron v. State,* 214 So.2d 370 (1968)).

> The defendant asked a police officer on the street if he could talk to him and the officer said go ahead. "I just shot a man," the defendant remarked. Was the officer required to give the *Miranda* warnings before he told the defendant he could talk?

No. The admission was not the product of custodial interrogation and thus the requirements of *Miranda* were not necessary (*People v. Smith,* 74 CAL.RPTR. 379 (1969)).

1.3.2. IN THE POLICE VEHICLE. In the following cases volunteered or spontaneous statements made in or near a police vehicle were held *not* to require the *Miranda* warnings as they were not the product of custodial interrogation.

> Two officers investigating a breaking and entering found the defendant hiding in the basement of the building. They handcuffed him and drove him to the police station in the squad car. After being advised that he could remain silent, the defendant volunteered a number of incriminating statements. Did the *Miranda* rule apply?

No. The statements made by the defendant were voluntarily made and not the product of custodial interrogation (*Strait v. State,* 164 N.W.2d 505 (1969)).

The defendant was arrested by police officers at the scene of a robbery. While getting into the police vehicle he asked, "How much time can I get for this?" "For what?" the police officer replied. "For robbing that lady in the store," admitted the defendant. Did the *Miranda* rule apply?

No. Even though the defendant had been in custody, the officer's question was asked merely in response to the defendant's question, and the admission by the defendant cannot be considered to be the product of custodial interrogation (*Campbell v. State,* 243 A.2d 642 (1968)).

1.3.3. AT THE POLICE STATION. In the following cases volunteered or spontaneous statements made in the police station or sheriff's office were held *not* to require the *Miranda* warnings as they were not the product of custodial interrogation.

The defendant entered the police station voluntarily and confessed to having committed a burglary. Should he have been advised of his constitutional rights before being allowed to confess?

No. Under *Miranda* there is no requirement that police stop a person from confessing when he voluntarily enters a police station. The *Miranda* decision was not intended to hamper the traditional investigatory function of the law enforcement officer (*Taylor v. Page,* 381 F.2d 717 (1967)).

The defendant entered a police station to turn himself in for a homicide. While he was being booked, the officer remarked that the deceased must have given the defendant a bad time. The defendant made an incriminating statement. Was the statement a product of custodial confession requiring the *Miranda* warnings?

No. The remark of the officer was not put as a question and furthermore did not suggest that the officer expected an incriminating statement in response (*State v. Smith,* 452 P.2d 195 (1969)).

The defendant stabbed his girl friend and went to the police station to see an officer that he regarded as a friend. After the defendant made a statement, the officer asked about the extent of the stab wounds and if she was still alive. The defendant replied that he had stabbed her seven or eight times. After confirming the stabbing by radio, the defendant was placed under arrest. Was the interrogation custodial?

No. When the defendant entered the police station the officer did not know anything about the killing. The statements made by the defendant were voluntary and made before arrest, and as such cannot be considered the product of custodial interrogation (*Newhouse v. State,* 420 S.W.2d 729 (1967)).

1.3.4. In Jail. In the following cases volunteered or spontaneous statements made in the jail or prison were held *not* to require the *Miranda* warnings as they were not the product of custodial interrogation.

> A police officer brought a suspect's lunch to his jail cell and while engaged in a general conversation the suspect confessed. Was this custodial interrogation?

No. The conversation was unrelated to the crime and the confession was not induced by interrogation, but freely given by the suspect (*Bazzell v. State,* 250 A.2d 674 (1969)).

> The defendant sawed through the bars of the jail window and was caught by a police officer while still on the prison grounds. Before the officer could say anything, the defendant said "I did it." "Did what?" the officer questioned. The defendant answered that he sawed the window. Should the officer have given the *Miranda* warnings?

No. The officer's question was an inquiry invited by the defendant's own remark. Law enforcement officers are not required to quiet a suspect that wishes to confess to an unsolved crime (*People v. Mercer,* 64 Cal.Rptr. 861 (1967)).

1.3.5. At Volunteer's Home. In the following cases volunteered or spontaneous statements made at the volunteer's residence were held *not* to require the *Miranda* warnings as they were not the product of custodial interrogation.

> A deputy sheriff arrived at the scene of a homicide in the defendant's home and asked a third person what happened. The defendant made a voluntary and spontaneous confession. Should the deputy sheriff have advised everyone present of their constitutional rights before asking what happened?

No. Statements made at an on-the-scene investigation where nobody has been arrested, detained, or charged are not under the *Miranda* rule. The voluntary confession was not a product of custodial interrogation (*State v. Oxentine,* 154 S.E.2d 529 (1967)).

> Police officers were investigating an unregistered distillery located some distance behind the defendant's home. While standing a few feet from their own front porch, both defendants made incriminating statements. Should the *Miranda* warnings have been given?

No. The statements made by the defendants were not the result of questioning but were voluntary. At the time they were made, the defendants were not under arrest, nor were they deprived of their freedom of action in a significant way (*McMillian v. U.S.,* 399 F.2d 478 (1968)).

1.3.6. IN VOLUNTEER'S VEHICLE. In the following cases volunteered or spontaneous statements made in or near the volunteer's vehicle were held *not* to require the *Miranda* warnings as they were not the product of custodial interrogation.

> On the afternoon of a bank robbery two officers stopped a vehicle and asked the driver (defendant) for his operator's license. He was placed under arrest when it was learned that he did not have one. Incriminating evidence fell to the ground and the officers began to interrogate the defendant's female companion, whereupon the defendant made an incriminating remark. Should the *Miranda* warnings have been given?

No. The statement by the defendant was independent of police questions and was volunteered at the time of arrest (*Anderson v. U.S.,* 399 F.2d 753 (1968)).

> A deputy sheriff was directed to the defendant's car at the scene of a bank robbery. The deputy sheriff told the defendant to put his hands up and get out of the car. Before any questions were asked the defendant confessed to robbing the bank. Should defendant have been warned of his rights?

No. The defendant confessed spontaneously. His statements were not the product of interrogation but were entirely voluntary (*Pitman v. U.S.,* 380 F.2d 368 (1967)).

1.4. Interrogation by Those Other Than Law Enforcement Officers Under *Miranda*

When private detectives, private security guards, private police, or store detectives interrogate a suspect, it is usually held that such is *not* custodial interrogation requiring the *Miranda* warnings.

> Private detectives suspected the branch manager of a furnace supply company of being responsible for a money shortage in the company. Private investigators confronted the defendant in his office and requested that he write a letter to his employer admitting his wrongdoing. Should the private detectives have given the defendant the constitutional warnings before obtaining the statement of guilt?

No. The court quoted from *Schaumberg v. State,* 432 P.2d 500 (1967):

> . . . the purport of *Escobedo* and *Miranda* is to prevent oppressive police tactics which violate individual rights and produce involuntary confessions. Though *Miranda* said there can be no doubt that the fifth amendment privilege is available to protect persons from being compelled to incriminate themselves in all settings in which their freedom of action is curtailed, it is clear that the thrust of the decision was aimed against the "potentiality for compulsion" . . . found in custodial interrogation initiated by police officers. . . .

A private investigator is not an officer of the law, and in such capacity he is not required to render a constitutional warning prior to the taking of a statement in the nature of a confession (*People v. Omell,* 166 N.W.2d 279 (1968)).

> Security guards at the county hospital discovered that the defendant had apparently burglarized an automobile parked at the hospital. While waiting for the police, the security guards detained and questioned the defendant. Should the security guards have given the *Miranda* warnings prior to questioning?

No. There can be custodial interrogation by law enforcement officers *only.* The determining factor is whether or not the security guard is employed by an agency of Federal, state or local Government whose primary duty is to enforce the law (*People v. Wright,* 57 CAL.RPTR. 781 (1967)).

1.5. Notes

1.5.1. WAIVER. Some courts conclude that the finding of an express statement by the accused that he wishes to *waive* one or more of his rights is not necessary before there can be an effective waiver of his rights to remain silent and to have counsel present during interrogation. The circumstances under which a statement is made, of course, must clearly show that it was made voluntarily, knowingly, and intelligently with full awareness by the accused of his rights. In *State v. Adams,* the defendant understood his rights and was not prevented by threats, promises, cajoling, or other means, from exercising his rights. He freely answered many questions, refrained from answering others, and selectively suggested he desired his counsel to be present, as to some, whereupon interrogation on such issues terminated. Under such circumstances the defendant waived his right to have counsel present during interrogation and his right to remain silent (*State v. Adams,* 458 P.2d 558 (1969)).

Other courts require that the defendant state that he wishes to waive his rights.

Voluntary waiver will not be accepted if it follows actual physical force, threats, promises and/or psychological coercion.

Three additional factors which militate against valid waiver of rights during interrogation and prior to confession are the following: a) incommunicado incarcerations, b) lengthy interrogation, and c) the giving of warnings that are not followed closely, in time, by confession.

Under *Miranda,* the defendant may withdraw his waiver of the privilege against self-incrimination any time before the questioning or during the questioning, and if the suspect expresses a desire to speak with his counsel, or wants an attorney, at any time during the questioning, the interrogation must stop until an attorney is present.

Some courts hold that once the suspect has invoked the right to remain silent, questioning cannot be resumed unless the right has again been waived expressly by the suspect (*People v. Fioritto,* 441 P.2d 625 (1968)).

If the defendant has retained counsel, and during the interrogation he clearly and knowingly has waived his right to have his attorney present, the police need not inform the attorney that an interrogation is taking place (*Coughlan v. U.S.,* 391 F.2d 371 (1968)).

Miranda warnings should be given when the suspect is questioned by a person appointed by the state, such as a physician or psychiatrist. This is also true if the police *send* a cellmate in to get information out of the suspect.

A number of jurisdictions use "rights cards" (see Fig. 5-2) which are read to the suspect, read back by the suspect to the officer, and the suspect is asked if he wishes to waive his rights. Video tapes and motion picture film may be used to record and prove the knowing, intelligent, and voluntary waiver of rights.

1.5.2. STANDING—JUS TERTII RULE. As discussed in Chapter four, in *Alderman v. U.S.,* one does not have standing to assert the constitutional rights of another. Does this rule of constitutional law apply to *Miranda* rights? Yes, said the court in *People v. Varnum,* where it was explained that no one other than the person questioned has standing to object to the admission of evidence obtained in violation of the *Miranda* rights (*People v. Varnum,* 427 P.2d 772 (1967)). Similarly, the court stated that the safeguards set forth in *Miranda* pertaining to self-incrimination are personal in nature (*People v. Denham,* 241 N.E.2d 415 (1968)).

1.5.3. IMMUNITY FROM PROSECUTION

> Certain police officers were charged with fixing traffic tickets. Before being questioned, each officer was warned: a) that anything he might say could be used against him in a court of law, b) that he had the privilege not to answer the questions if they would incriminate him, and c) if he refused to answer questions he would be subject to removal from office. No immunity was granted and the officers answered the questions. They were convicted for conspiracy to obstruct the administration of the traffic laws. Was the choice given to the officers, either to forfeit their jobs or to incriminate themselves, correct?

No. The officers were not allowed to make a free and rational choice. This was a form of duress and coercion. Under the fourteenth amendment, a state cannot use the threat of discharge to secure incriminating evidence against an employee. The protection of the individual under the fourteenth amendment protects the individual against the use of coerced statements in subsequent criminal proceedings against him (*Garity v. New Jersey,* 385 U.S.493 (1967)).

> A lawyer refused to produce certain personal financial records on demand and refused to testify at a judicial inquiry where he was being investigated for professional misconduct. The lawyer said that the records and testimony would incriminate him. The court ordered him disbarred and held that the constitutional privilege against self-incrimination was not available to him. Was the court correct in

Figure 5-2

ADVISEMENT FORM

Name _____ Birthdate _____

Date _____ Time _____ Location _____

You have a right to remain silent.

Anything you say can be used as evidence against you in court.

You have a right to talk to a lawyer before questioning and have him present during questioning.

If you cannot afford a lawyer, one will be appointed for you before questioning.

Do you understand each of these rights I have read to you?

Answer _____

Signature of the Person Advised _____

Knowing my rights and knowing what I am doing, I now wish to voluntarily talk to you.

Signature of the Person Advised _____

Witnessed by _____

Signature of the Advising Officer _____

DPD 369 (6/67)

holding that the fifth amendment right against self-incrimination did
not apply to lawyers?

No. The United States Supreme Court said that the Self-Incrimination Clause of the fifth amendment has been absorbed into
the fourteenth amendment and its protection extends to lawyers, as well as other persons. One should not have to pay the
price of disbarment and loss of livelihood for asserting the privilege against self-incrimination; lawyers, as well as policemen,
should enjoy first-class citizenship *(Spevack v. Klein,* 385 U.S.
511 (1967)).

> In 1968, a New York City patrolman was called to testify before a
> grand jury concerning the performance of his official duties. The New
> York court discharged him from his job for refusing to waive his
> right against self-incrimination before testifying. Was the court cor-
> rect?

No. The privilege against self-incrimination will not be a bar
to dismissal from the force if the policeman refuses to answer
questions specifically, directly, and narrowly related to the performance of his official duties. In this case, however, the patrolman was discharged from office, not for failure to answer questions about his official duty, but for refusal to waive a constitutional right. In other words, the patrolman was discharged for
refusing to relinquish the protections of the privilege against
self-incrimination, and such was error *(Gardner v. Broderick,*
392 U.S.273 (1968)).

> . . . we hold the constitutional rule to be that a state witness may
> not be compelled to give testimony which may be incriminating under
> federal law unless the compelled testimony and its fruits cannot be
> used in any manner by federal officials in connection with a criminal
> prosecution against him. We conclude, moreover, that in order to
> implement this constitutional rule and accommodate the interests of
> the State and Federal governments in investigating and prosecuting
> crime, the Federal Government must be prohibited from making any
> such use of compelled testimony and its fruits *(Murphy v. Water-
> front Com'n of N.Y. Harbor,* 378 U.S.52 (1964)).

Since 1857 there have been *federal immunity statutes* of one
form or another, which protect the individual testifying in a federal proceeding from prosecution as a result of the testimony.
Congress has regularly authorized administrative agencies to

give a witness immunity and compel testimony. Since 1968, the Department of Justice has had the statutory power to compel testimony in court by granting immunity to the individual testifying, in a great number of federal crimes (18 U.S.C. 2514). The federal statutes not only give immunity from prosecution, but also from forfeiture or penalty arising from a compelled testimony. If a key witness is given immunity from prosecution, the jury must be informed (*Giglio v. United States,* 405 U.S. 150, 1972).

1.5.4. CONFESSION OF JUVENILES. A number of states have statutes that require the probation officer to be notified as soon as possible after the arrest of a child under the age of eighteen years. In such states the police may not subject a juvenile to formal interrogation without permission of the person appointed by law whose job it is to see that the interrogation procedure is conducted in a manner consistent with the purposes and policies of juvenile rehabilitation (*State of Arizona v. Shaw,* 378 P.2d 487 (1963)).

Generally the court will require more detail in the account leading up to the confession of a juvenile than it will for the confession of an adult.

1.5.5. REMEDIES IF MIRANDA RULE VIOLATED. The most practical remedy available to the defendant when his rights have been violated is to have the confession excluded from the admissible evidence. Some jurisdictions automatically reverse conviction on appeal, when the *Miranda* rights have been violated in obtaining the confession. Other remedies are civil action against the police and complaint to the police department. (*Bivens v. Six Unknown Named Agents of Federal Bureau of Narcotics,* 403 U.S.388, 1971).

Section 2. SELF-INCRIMINATION

No person . . . shall be compelled in any criminal case to be a witness against himself;

Fifth Amendment

2.1. Pre-trial Identification

2.1.1. BLOOD SAMPLES

The defendant was arrested at a hospital where he was being treated for injuries sustained in an automobile accident. At the direction of a police officer, a physician withdrew a blood sample from the defendant's body. Chemical analysis of the sample revealed that the defendant was intoxicated. Did the taking of such a sample violate the defendant's rights against self-incrimination under the fifth amendment?

No. The privilege only protects the accused from being compelled to testify against himself, or otherwise provide the State with communicative or testimonial evidence, and the withdrawal of blood and the use of the analysis in evidence was neither the defendant's testimony nor evidence relating to some communicative act or writing by the defendant (*Schmerber v. California*, 384 U.S.757 (1966)).

2.1.2. Voice and Lineup

A man with a small strip of tape on each side of his face entered a federally insured bank and robbed it. Subsequently, at a post-indictment lineup conducted at the courthouse, the defendant and five or six other prisoners were observed by two bank employees. Each person in the line wore a small strip of tape on each side of his face and each said, "put the money in the bag." Both bank employees identified the defendant as the bank robber. Did the the lineup, or anything that the defendant was required to do in the lineup, violate his privilege against self-incrimination?

No. Compelling the defendant to exhibit his person for observation by a prosecution witness prior to trial involved no compulsion of the defendant to give evidence having *testimonial* significance. It was simply compulsion to exhibit his person, not compulsion to disclose any knowledge that he might have. Compelling the defendant to speak the words uttered by the robber was not compulsion to utter statements of a testimonial nature; the defendant was required to use his voice to identify a physical characteristic, not to admit or speak his guilt (*United States v. Wade*, 388 U.S.218 (1967)).

2.1.3. One-Man Lineup

A single suspect was brought to a hospital room for identification by a stabbing victim. Did this pretrial confrontation for the purposes of identification result in such unfairness that it infringed on the accused's right to due process of law?

No. The delay in assembling a full lineup may have been fatal, an immediate hospital confrontation was imperative. No one knew how long the victim might live. As the victim could not visit the jail, the police followed the only feasible procedure and took the defendant to the hospital room. The usual police station lineup was out of the question. Furthermore, the victim was the only person in the world that could exonerate the defendant (*Stovall v. Denno*, 388 U.S.293 (1967)).

2.1.4. ON-THE-SCENE IDENTIFICATION

A witness heard the breaking of glass and the sounds of a blaring radio. Upon investigation, he found the radio on the sidewalk in front of a broken shop window. He stationed himself in a gas station across the street and saw a man emerge from the shop. He reported the incident to the police. The police arrested a suspect, meeting the description given by the witness shortly thereafter, and drove the witness to a shoe shine shop for identification. The witness identified the suspect as the man he had seen coming out of the shop. Was on-the-scene identification proper?

Yes. It was 5:00 AM and a long delay would have ensued in summoning the suspect's counsel or in observing a formal lineup. Such delay might not only detain an innocent suspect, but diminish the reliability of any identification obtained. Prompt confrontations in similar circumstances will, if anything, promote fairness by assuring reliability of identification, and speedy release of an innocent suspect (*Russel v. U.S.*, 408 F.2d 1280 (1969)).

2.1.5. HANDWRITING. The United State Supreme Court holds that the taking of handwriting exemplars from a defendant after his arrest and their subsequent use against him, over his objection, does not violate the privilege against self-incrimination. The court said that a mere handwriting sample, like the voice or the body itself, is an identifying characteristic, and as such is outside of the protection of the fifth amendment right against self-incrimination. This is to be distinguished from that which is contained in the writing itself, which may be incriminating (*Gilbert v. Calif.*, 388 U.S.263 (1967)).

2.1.6. FINGERPRINTS. The taking of fingerprints over the objection of the suspect does not violate the privilege against self-incrimination (*U.S. v. Laub Baking Co.,* 283 F. Supp. 217 (1968)). Similarly, in *Schmerber,* the court said,

> . . . both federal and state courts have usually held that it (the privilege against self-incrimination) offers no protection against compulsion to submit to fingerprinting, photographing, or measurements, to write or speak for identification, to appear in court, to stand, to assume a stance, to walk, or to make a particular gesture. The distinction which has emerged, often expressed in different ways, is that the privilege is a bar against compelling communications or testimony, but that compulsion which makes a suspect or accused the source of real or physical evidence does not violate it. (*Schmerber v. California,* 384 U.S.757 (1966)).

2.1.7. PHOTOGRAPHS

> One day after a bank robbery, F.B.I. agents showed group photographs, which contained two suspects, to eyewitnesses. One of the suspects was identified. At the trial the eyewitnesses identified the suspect that they had identified in the photograph. Did the photographic identification procedure unduly prejudice the defendants?

No. It must be recognized that improper employment of photographs by police may sometimes cause witnesses to err in identifying criminals. A witness may have obtained only a brief glimpse of a criminal, or may have seen him under poor conditions. Even if the police subsequently follow the most correct photographic identification procedures and show him the pictures of a number of individuals without indicating whom they suspect, there is some danger that the witness may make an incorrect identification. This danger will be increased if the following occur: a) the police display to the witness only the picture of a single individual who generally resembles the person he saw, b) they show him the pictures of several persons among which the photograph of a single such individual recurs or is in some way emphasized, or c) the police indicate to the witness that they have other evidence that one of the persons pictured committed the crime. Regardless of how the initial misidentification comes about, the witness thereafter is apt to retain in his memory the image of the photograph rather than of the person actually seen, reducing the trustworthiness of subsequent lineup or courtroom identification. However, in the present case the court said that the following guidelines were met, thus avoiding incorrect identification in employment of photographs: a) prompt police action; b) at least six photographs were used; c) mostly group photographs were employed; d) the witnesses were alone when they observed the photographs; e) there was subsequent confirmation of the identification; f) the witnesses had good opportunity to observe the defendant during the robbery; and g) the witnesses' memory was fresh one day after the robbery (it should be noted that the above mentioned guidelines are not absolute, but that each case must be decided on its own facts and circumstances). (*Simmon v. U.S.,* 390 U.S.377 (1968).)

2.1.8. LIE DETECTORS (POLYGRAPHS). The results of a lie detector test are generally inadmissible as evidence whether offered by prosecution or defense. Likewise, testimony that the defendant refused to take a lie detector test is inadmissible and such admission results in reversible error.

Although the results of, and reference to, a lie detector test are presently inadmissible, the data obtained from a test may lead to admissible evidence. Thus, the privilege against self-incrimination may come into play.

Whether or not a defendant may be compelled to submit to a lie detector test has been the subject of intense debate, with the arguments directed towards the question of whether or not the results are "testimonial" in nature. The *Bowen v. Eyman* court, after considering the data in *Schmerber v. California,* is of the opinion that a compulsory lie detector examination would infringe upon the privilege against self-incrimination.

It follows then that a testimony concerning the defendant's refusal to take the test is constitutionally impermissible (*Bowen v. Eyman,* 324 F. Supp. 339 (1970)).

> Some tests seemingly directed to obtain "physical evidence," for example, lie detector tests measuring changes in body function during interrogation, may actually be directed to eliciting responses which are essentially testimonial. To compel a person to submit to testing in which an effort will be made to determine his guilt or innocence on the basis of physiological responses, whether willed or not, is to evoke the spirit and history of the fifth amendment. Such situations call to mind the principle that the protection of the privilege "is as broad

as the mischief against which it seeks to guard" *(Schmerber v. California*, 384 U.S.757 (1966)) .

Compare the reasons for inadmissibility in the passage quoted from *Schmerber, supra,* with the court in *State v. Perry* which follows.

> It is well settled that the results of a lie detector test are inadmissible in evidence against an accused because, up to the present at least, such tests have not proved completely reliable, and in the extension of this rule, that evidence that such a test was taken or refused by a defendant cannot be brought to the jury's attention either directly or indirectly *(State v. Perry,* 142 N.W.2d 573 (1966)) .

2.2. The Accused as Witness on the Stand

The privilege against self-incrimination protects an individual from being compelled to be a witness against himself. Accordingly, the accused *in a criminal trial* may refuse to testify. The fifth amendment has direct application to the Federal Government and application on the states by reason of the fourteenth amendment, and as such, forbids comment (in state and federal proceedings) by the prosecution on the silence of the accused and forbids instructions by the court that such silence is evidence of guilt *(Griffin v. California,* 380 U.S.609 (1965)). However, if the accused *does* take the stand in his own defense, he waives his privilege of refusal to testify and must answer inquiries relevant to the charge (s) against him on *cross-examination (Johnson v. U.S.,* 318 U.S.189 (1942)). In a recent case, *Harris v. New York,* 401 U.S.222 (1971), the court upheld the use of statements that did not meet the *Miranda* standards when they were used to impeach the credibility of the accused when he took the stand in his own defense (see *Walder v. U.S.,* Chap. 4).

Section 3. DOUBLE JEOPARDY

> . . . nor shall any person be subject for the same offense to be twice put in jeopardy of life or limb.
>
> *Fifth Amendment*

When a defendant is acquitted, the double jeopardy clause precludes a second trial. (The government cannot appeal an acquittal.) The government may not retry and resentence an individual that has already been found guilty and served his sentence. These are two of the three constitutional protections that are said to be found in the Double Jeopardy Clause. By "government," one means either state or federal, as the double jeopardy prohibition represents a fundamental right that applies to the states through the fourteenth amendment, as well as directly to the Federal Government (*Benton v. Maryland,* 395 U.S.784 (1969)).

The constitutional protections found in the fifth amendment which guarantee against double jeopardy are as follows: a) protection against a second prosecution for the same offense after acquittal, b) protection against a second prosecution for the same offense after conviction, and c) protection against *multiple punishment* for the same offense (*North Carolina v. Pearce,* 395 U.S. 711 (1969)).

Jeopardy attaches when a) the defendant pleads "not guilty," b) when a competent jury is impaneled, sworn, and charged with the case, or c) if a jury is waived, when the trial begins before the court.

One is *not* put in jeopardy when the information or indictment is so incomplete that it will not support a conviction or the court does not have jurisdiction over the offense and the accused.

Jeopardy may attach and not be a bar to further jeopardy: a) when the defendant *waives* the first jeopardy by asking that the conviction be set aside and/or asking for a new trial, b) when the defendant waives the first jeopardy by appealing to a higher court (*U.S. v. Tateo,* 377 U.S.463 (1964)) or c) when there is a valid reason for the trial court to discharge the jury, such as the illesss of a juror. Once the jury has been discharged in such a case, the accused may be tried a second time for the same offense.

Note that without waiver, once jeopardy has *attached,* the defendant cannot be prosecuted a second time for the offense of the first trial or any offense *included* in the first offense. When a trial judge, on his own motion, declared a mistrial to enable the governments witnesses to consult with their own attorneys, he abused his discretion in discharging the jury and reprosecution of the defendant would have engaged this double jeopardy provision (*United States v. Jorn,* 400 U.S. 470, 1971).

The defendant was charged with setting fire to a house and consequently causing the death of a woman. The jury found the defendant guilty of arson and second degree murder. The defendant appealed the murder conviction and at the new trial he was found guilty of first degree murder and was given the death sentence. His defense at the second trial, of double jeopardy, was rejected by the court. Was the defendant placed in double jeopardy for the same offense?

Yes. Under the established principles of former jeopardy, the defendant's jeopardy for *first* degree murder came to an end when the jury was discharged so that he could not be retried for that particular offense. When a defendant is placed in jeopardy before a jury, and that jury is discharged without his consent, he cannot be tried again for the particular offense. Here the first jury had a choice of finding the defendant guilty of either first degree murder *or* second degree murder. The jury found him guilty of second degree murder and it was from that conviction that the defendant appealed. The jury had not made a finding with respect to his guilt on the first degree murder charge, however, he was in jeopardy to that offense. Upon being tried a second time for first degree murder, the defendant was placed in jeopardy a second time. At no time did he waive the defense of double jeopardy just because his appeal was from the conviction of second degree murder. When a man has been convicted of second degree murder, he cannot be said to give up or waive his constitutional defense of former jeopardy on a charge of first degree murder in order to secure a reversal of an erroneous conviction of the lesser offense (*Green v. U.S.,* 355 U.S. 184 (1957)).

When one is tried for an offense which includes a lesser offense, the jury is permitted to find the defendant guilty of either the greater or the lesser offense. If the jury convicts the defendant of the lesser offense, such verdict acquits the defendant of the greater offense and he cannot be tried again for the greater offense.

A number of tests have been developed to enable one to determine if the offense charged in the second indictment is the same offense that the defendant was placed in jeopardy for in the first indictment: a) Could the defendant have been convicted under the first indictment for the offense charged in the second indictment; if so, double jeopardy is an available defense to the second indictment; b) If the law and facts in the second indictment would not be supported under the first indictment, the offenses are not the same and former jeopardy is not available as a defense; c) If the government has an election to prosecute the defendant for a greater or lesser offense and convicts on the lesser offense, the lesser offense is included within the greater offense, and is jeopardy barring a charge on the greater offense; or d) If all the facts do not exist when the defendant is convicted of a lesser offense, then conviction of the lesser offense is no bar to conviction of the greater offense, as where the defendant is convicted of assault and battery and subsequently the victim dies, the assault and battery conviction will not bar indictment for homicide.

3.1. Dual Sovereignty Theory

When an individual robs a federally insured savings bank, he violates the laws of both the state and the Federal Government. The Federal Government can try the defendant for the federal crime even if the state has found him "not guilty" of breaking the state law (*Bartkus v. Illinois,* 359 U.S.121 (1959)). Conversely, a state may prosecute and even impose an additional sentence on an individual found guilty in federal court. *Abbate v. U.S.,* 359 U.S.187 (1959). Such results are possible as both the federal and state sovereignties may protect identical interests. This is known as the Theory of Dual Sovereignty.

3.2. Multiple Punishment

The Double Jeopardy Clause requires that time already served must be fully credited in sentencing a second time for the same offense. In other words, the second sentence must be reduced by the amount of time served under the first sentence. If the second sentence was not reduced by the time served under the first sentence, the defendant would receive multiple punishment for the same offense (*North Carolina v. Pearce,* 395 U.S.711 (1969)).

Note that the double jeopardy provision does not prevent a trial judge from imposing a more severe sentence upon reconviction (*Stroud v. U.S.,* 251 U.S.15 (1919)). However, when a judge does impose a more severe sentence on the defendant upon reconviction, the reasons for his doing so must affirmatively appear. For example, new facts may develop between the first and second trial which might be considered in aggravation of sentence.

In *Gavieres v. U.S.*, 220 U.S.338 (1911), the court in quoting a previous case said that a conviction or acquittal on one indictment is not a bar to a subsequent conviction and sentence upon another, unless the evidence which supported conviction on one of them would have been sufficient to support a conviction on the other. If a single act is an offense against two or more statutes, and each statute requires proof of a fact which the other does not, an acquittal or conviction under either statute does not exempt the defendant from prosecution and punishment under the other statute.

Petite v. U.S., 361 U.S.529 (1960) indicates that several offenses arising out of a single transaction should be alleged and tried together and not be the basis for multiple prosecutions of the defendant for the single transaction.

Section 4. THE GRAND JURY

No person shall be held to answer to a capital, or otherwise infamous crime, unless on a presentment or indictment of a grand jury, except in cases arising in the land or naval forces, or in the militia, when in actual service in time of war or public danger. . . .

Fifth Amendment

The selection and drawing of the grand jurors is generally performed according to local statutes, which designate the proper person to make the selection. If there is substantial deviation from the statutory requirements in the method of selecting the jurors, the grand jury is rendered illegal.

A grand jury is composed of sixteen to twenty-three jurors. Regardless of the number, however, twelve must concur in an accusation. Generally, a grand jury sits for the purpose of investigating a history of lawbreaking in a particular area, or a named person suspected of committing a crime. When the grand jury is satisfied that probable cause exists to find a person guilty, an indictment or charge is handed down. If the grand jury fails to return an indictment against a named suspect in custody, he must be set free. The United States Supreme Court has held that the grand jury clause of the fifth amendment is not absorbed into the due process clause of the fourteenth amendment and thus, the grand jury is not constitutionally required in state proceedings. Nevertheless, many states have grand juries by virtue of their state constitution (*Hurtado v. Calif.*, 110 U.S.516 (1884)). Members of the military are not entitled to a civil grand jury, instead they are tried by court-martial; similarly for members of the militia during time of war.

The grand jury inquiries into crimes by a) reviewing evidence and returning an indictment, b) investigating hospitals, jails, and other public institutions, and c) investigation of grievances and scandals of public officials.

In larger cities, it is not unusual for grand juries to sit continuously throughout the year, although no grand jury may serve more than eighteen months. Rule 6 of the Federal Rules of Criminal Procedure governs federal grand juries.

In the interest of justice the investigations, deliberations, and proceedings of a grand jury are conducted in secret. Specific reasons frequently given for the policy of secrecy are the following: a) to prevent escape of a person who has been indicted but not yet arrested, b) to protect the jurors, c) to protect the reputation of persons investigated who are not subsequently indicted, d) to promote freedom of disclosure by prosecutors and e) to prevent the subornation of perjury in an attempt to discredit facts presented. The modern trend is to divulge the proceedings of the grand jury once the indictment has been found and the accused arrested.

An offense which may be punished by death is prosecuted by indictment. An offense which may be punished by a prison term or hard labor of more than one year is prosecuted by indictment, unless the indictment is waived, it is prosecuted by information. Any offense, with the exception of those just mentioned, may be prosecuted by either indictment or information. Usually, an indictment is presented by a grand jury, and an information is filed by a prosecuting officer. (Rule 7 of the Federal Rules of Criminal Procedure deals with the *indictment* and the *information*.)

A court cannot permit a defendant to be tried on *charges* that do not appear in the indictment against him (*Stirone v. U.S.,* 361 U.S.212 (1960)).

A *witness* before a grand jury cannot insist on a constitutional right to be represented by counsel (*In Re Goban,* 352 U.S. 330 (1957)). Rule 6 (d) of the Federal Rules of Criminal Procedure maintains the practice that a witness called before a grand jury may not be accompanied by counsel, since a grand jury proceeding is an investigation rather than a prosecution against the witness (*People v. Ianniello,* 235 N.E.2d 439 (1968)). However, he may be allowed to consult with counsel before answering questions, at the discretion of the grand jury.

In a grand jury proceeding the privilege against self-incrimination may be invoked: a) when the evidence may form a nexus in the logical flow of reasoning which might lead to the witness' conviction of a crime, *and* b) if the court decides the question calls for an incriminating statement.

A defendant could be required to stand trial and a conviction may be sustained where only *hearsay* evidence (not personal or first-hand to the witness) is presented to the grand jury (*Costello v. U.S.,* 350 U.S.359 (1956)). Also, an indictment will not be dismissed because the grand jury was not told that it was hearing hearsay evidence (*U.S. v. Payton,* 363 F.2d 996 (1966)).

> The defendant was charged with murder by the district attorney. There was no grand jury indictment. He was convicted and sentenced to death. The defendant, on appeal, contended that the fourteenth amendment due process clause made the grand jury an essential element in a criminal proceeding. Was he correct?

No. To have grand juries in state proceedings is a matter of state constitutional law only and it is not unfair to dispense with the grand jury where state law does not require such (*Hurtado v. California,* 110 U.S.516 (1884)). (Federal Rules of Criminal Procedure, Rule 6, the grand jury.)

4.1. Summoning Grand Juries

The court shall order one or more grand juries to be summoned at such times as the public interest requires. The grand jury shall consist of not less than sixteen nor more than twenty-three members. The court shall direct that a sufficient number of legally qualified persons be summoned to meet this requirement.

4.2. Objections to Grand Jury and to Grand Jurors

4.2.1. CHALLENGES. The attorney for the government or a defendant who has been held to answer in the district court may challenge the array of jurors on the ground that the grand jury was not selected, drawn or summoned in accordance with law, and may challenge an individual juror on the ground that the juror is not legally qualified. Challenges shall be made before the administration of the oath to the jurors and shall be tried by the court.

4.2.2. MOTION TO DISMISS. A motion to dismiss the indictment may be based on objections to the array or on the lack of legal qualification of an individual juror, if not previously determined upon challenge. An indictment shall not be dismissed on the ground that one or more members of the grand jury were not legally qualified if it appears from the record kept pursuant subsection **4.3.** of this rule that twelve or more jurors, after deducting the number not legally qualified, concurred in finding the indictment.

4.3. Foreman and Deputy Foreman

The court shall appoint one of the jurors to be foreman and another to be deputy foreman. The foreman shall have power to administer oaths and affirmations and shall sign all indictments. He or another juror designated by him shall keep a record of the number of jurors concurring in the finding of every indictment and shall file the record with the clerk of the court, but the record shall not be made public except on order of the court. During the absence of the foreman, the deputy foreman shall act as foreman.

4.4. Who May Be Present

Attorneys for the government, the witness under examination, interpreters when needed and, for the purpose of taking the evidence, a stenographer or operator of a recording device may be present while the grand jury is in session, but no person other than the jurors may be present while the grand jury is deliberating or voting.

4.5. Secrecy of Proceedings and Disclosure

Disclosure of matters occurring before the grand jury other than its deliberations and the vote of any juror may be made to the attorneys for the government for use in the performance of their duties. Otherwise a juror, attorney, interpreter, stenographer, operator of a recording device, or any typist who transcribes recorded testimony may disclose matters occurring before the grand jury only when so directed by the court preliminarily to or in connection with a judicial proceeding or when permitted by the court at the request of the defendant upon a showing that grounds may exist for a motion to dismiss the indictment because of matters occurring before the grand jury. No obligation of secrecy may be imposed upon any person except in accordance with this rule. The court may direct that an indictment shall be kept secret until the defendant is in custody or has given bail, and in that event the clerk shall seal the indictment and no person shall disclose the finding of the indictment except when necessary for the issuance and execution of a warrant or summons.

4.6. Finding and Return of Indictment

An indictment may be found only upon the concurrence of twelve or more jurors. The indictment shall be returned by the grand jury to a judge in open court. If the defendant is in custody or has given bail and twelve jurors do not concur in finding an indictment, the foreman shall so report to the court in writing forthwith.

4.7. Discharge and Excuse

A grand jury shall serve until discharged by the court but no grand jury may serve more than eighteen months. The tenure and powers of a grand jury are not affected by the beginning or expiration of a term of court. At any time for cause shown the court may excuse a juror either temporarily or permanently, and in the latter event the court may impanel another person in place of the juror excused.*

---

* Sections 4.1 to 4.7 are from F.R.C.P., Rule 6.

Section 5. QUOTED CASES

5.1. *Miranda v. Arizona*

Mr. Chief Justice Warren delivered the opinion of the Court.

The cases before us raise questions which go to the roots of our concepts of American criminal jurisprudence: the restraints society must observe consistent with the Federal Constitution in prosecuting individuals for crime. More specifically, we deal with the admissibility of statements obtained from an individual who is subjected to custodial police interrogation and the necessity for procedures which assure that the individual is accorded his privilege under the fifth amendment to the Constitution not to be compelled to incriminate himself. . . .

Our holding will be spelled out with some specificity in the pages which follow but briefly stated it is this: the prosecution may not use statements, whether exculpatory or inculpatory, stemming from custodial interrogation of the defendant unless it demonstrates the use of procedural safeguards effective to secure the privilege against self-incrimination. By custodial interrogation, we mean questioning initiated by law enforcement officers after a person has been taken into custody or otherwise deprived of his freedom of action in any significant way. As for the procedural safeguards to be employed, unless other fully effective means are devised to inform accused persons of their right of silence and to assure a continuous opportunity to exercise it, the following measures are required. Prior to any questioning, the person must be warned that he has a right to remain silent, that any statement he does make may be used as evidence against him, and that he has a right to the presence of an attorney, either retained or appointed. The defendant may waive effectuation of these rights, provided the waiver is made voluntarily, knowingly, and intelligently. If, however, he indicates in any manner and at any stage of the process that he wishes to consult with an attorney before speaking, there can be no questioning. Likewise, if the individual is alone and indicates in any manner that he does not wish to be interrogated, the police may not question him. The mere fact that he may have an-

---

Note: Miranda v. Arizona, 384 U.S.436 (1966).

swered some questions or volunteered some statements on his own does not deprive him of the right to refrain from answering any further inquiries until he has consulted with an attorney and therefore consents to be questioned.

The constitutional issue we decide in each of these cases is the admissibility of statements obtained from a defendant questioned while in custody and deprived of his freedom of action. In each, the defendant was questioned by police officers, detectives, or a prosecuting attorney in a room in which he was cut off from the outside world. In none of these cases was the defendant given a full and effective warning of his rights at the outset of the interrogation process. In all the cases, the questioning elicited oral admissions, and in three of them, signed statements as well which were admitted at their trials. They all thus share salient features —incommunicado interrogation of individuals in a police-dominated atmosphere, resulting in self-incriminating statements without full warnings of constitutional rights.

An understanding of the nature and setting of this in-custody interrogation is essential to our decisions today. The difficulty in depicting what transpires at such interrogations stems from the fact that in this country they have largely taken place incommunicado. From extensive factual studies undertaken in the early 1930's, including the famous Wickersham Report to Congress by a Presidential Commission, it is clear that police violence and the "third degree" flourished at that time. In a series of cases decided by this Court long after these studies, the police resorted to physical brutality—beatings, hanging, whipping—and to sustained and protracted questioning incommunicado in order to extort confessions. The 1961 Commission on Civil Rights found much evidence to indicate that "some policemen still resort to physical force to obtain confessions," 1961 Comm'n on Civil Rights Rep, Justice, pt 5, 17. The use of physical brutality and violence is not, unfortunately, relegated to the past or to any part of the country. Only recently in Kings County, New York, the police brutally beat, kicked, and placed lighted cigarette butts on the back of a potential witness under interrogation for the purpose of securing a statement incriminating a third party (*People v. Portelli,* 15 N.Y.2d 235, 205 N.E.2d 857, 257 N.Y.S.2d 931 (1965)).

The examples given above are undoubtedly the exception now, but they are sufficiently widespread to be the object of concern. Unless a proper limitation upon custodial interrogation is achieved—such as these decisions will advance—there can be no assurance that practices of this nature will be eradicated in the foreseeable future.

Again we stress that the modern practice of in-custody interrogation is psychologically rather than physically oriented. As we have stated before, "Since *Chambers v. Florida,* 309 U.S.227, this Court has recognized that coercion can be mental as well as physical, and that the blood of the accused is not the only hallmark of an unconstitutional inquisition." *Blackburn v. Alabama,* 361 U.S.199, 206 (1960). Interrogation still takes place in privacy. Privacy results in secrecy and this in turn results in a gap in our knowledge as to what in fact goes on in the interrogation rooms. A valuable source of information about present police practices, however, may be found in various police manuals and texts which document procedures employed with success in the past, and which recommend various other effective tactics. These texts are used by law enforcement agencies themselves as guides. It should be noted that these texts professedly present the most enlightened and effective means presently used to obtain statements through custodial interrogation. By considering these texts and other data, it is possible to describe procedures observed and noted around the country.

The officers are told by the manuals that the "principal psychological factor contributing to a successful interrogation is *privacy*—being alone with the person under interrogation."*

To highlight the isolation and unfamiliar surroundings, the manuals instruct the police to display an air of confidence in the suspect's guilt and from outward appearance to maintain only an interest in confirming certain details. The guilt of the subject is to be posited as a fact. The interrogator should direct his comments toward the reasons why the subject committed the act, rather than to court failure by asking the subject whether he did it. Like other men, perhaps the subject has had a bad family life, had an unhappy childhood, had too much to drink,

---

* Inbau and Reid, Criminal Interrogation and Confessions (1962).

had an unrequited attraction to women. The officers are instructed to minimize the moral seriousness of the offense, to cast blame on the victim or on society. These tactics are designed to put the subject in a psychological state where his story is but an elaboration of what the police purport to know already—that he is guilty. Explanations to the contrary are dismissed and discouraged.

The texts thus stress that the major qualities an interrogator should possess are patience and perseverance. . . .

The manuals suggest that the suspect be offered legal excuses for his actions in order to obtain an initial admission of guilt. . . .

When the techniques described above prove unavailing, the texts recommend they be alternated with a show of some hostility. One ploy often used has been termed the "friendly-unfriendly" or the "Mutt and Jeff" act. . . .

The interrogators sometimes are instructed to induce a confession by trickery. . . .

The manuals also contain instructions for police on how to handle the individual who refuses to discuss the matter entirely, or who asks for an attorney or relatives. . . .

From these representative samples of interrogation techniques, the setting prescribed by the manuals and observed in practice becomes clear. In essence, it is this: To be alone with the subject is essential to prevent distraction and to deprive him of any outside support. The aura of confidence in his guilt undermines his will to resist. He merely confirms the preconceived story the police seek to have him describe. Patience and persistence, at times relentless questioning, are employed. To obtain a confession, the interrogator must "patiently maneuver himself or his quarry into a position from which the desired object may be obtained."* When normal procedures fail to produce the needed result, the police may resort to deceptive strategems such as giving false legal advice. It is important to keep the subject off-balance, for example, by trading on his insecurity about himself or his surroundings. The police then persuade, trick, or cajole him out of exercising his constitutional rights.

Even without employing brutality, the "third degree" or the

---

* Inbau and Reid, Lie Detection and Criminal Interrogation (3d ed. 1953), 185.

specific stratagems described above, the very fact of custodial interrogation exacts a heavy toll on individual liberty and trades on the weakness of individuals. . . .

In the cases before us today, given this background, we concern ourselves primarily with this interrogation atmosphere and the evils it can bring. In No. 759, *Miranda v. Arizona,* the police arrested the defendant and took him to a special interrogation room where they secured a confession. In No. 760, *Vignera v. New York,* the defendant made oral admissions to the police after interrogation in the afternoon, and then signed an inculpatory statement upon being questioned by an assistant district attorney later the same evening. In No. 761, *Westover v. U.S.,* the defendant was handed over to the Federal Bureau of Investigation by local authorities after they had detained and interrogated him for a lengthy period, both at night and the following morning. After some two hours of questioning, the federal officers had obtained signed statements from the defendant. Lastly, in No. 584, *California v. Stewart,* the local police held the defendant five days in the station and interrogated him on nine separate occasions before they secured his inculpatory statement.

In these cases, we might not find the defendants' statements to have been involuntary in traditional terms. Our concern for adequate safeguards to protect precious fifth amendment rights is, of course, not lessened in the slightest. In each of the cases, the defendant was thrust into an unfamiliar atmosphere and run through menacing police interrogation procedures. The potentiality for compulsion is forcefully apparent, for example, in *Miranda,* where the indigent Mexican defendant was a seriously disturbed individual with pronounced sexual fantasies, and in *Stewart,* in which the defendant was an indigent Los Angeles Negro who had dropped out of school in the sixth grade. To be sure, the records do not evince overt physical coercion or patented psychological ploys. The fact remains that in none of these cases did the officers undertake to afford appropriate safeguards at the outset of the interrogation to insure that the statements were truly the product of free choice.

It is obvious that such an interrogation environment is created for no purpose other than to subjugate the individual to the will of his examiner. This atmosphere carries its own badge of intimidation. To be sure, this is not physical intimidation, but it is equally destructive of human dignity. The current practice of incommunicado interrogation is at odds with one of our nation's most cherished principles—the individual may not be compelled to incriminate himself. Unless adequate protective devices are employed to dispel the compulsion inherent in custodial surroundings, no statement obtained from the defendant can truly be the product of his free choice.

From the foregoing, we can readily perceive an intimate connection between the privilege against self-incrimination and police custodial questioning. It is fitting to turn to history and precedent underlying the Self-Incrimination Clause to determine its applicability in this situation.

We sometimes forget how long it has taken to establish the privilege against self-incrimination, the sources from which it came and the fervor with which it was defended. Its roots go back into ancient times. . . . We may view the historical development of the privilege as one which groped for the proper scope of governmental power over the citizen. As a "noble principle often transcends its origins," the privilege has come rightfully to be recognized in part as an individual's substantive right, a "right to a private enclave where he may lead a private life. That right is the hallmark of our democracy." *U.S. v. Grunewald*, 233 F.2d 556, 579, 581-582 (Frank, J., dissenting), revd, 353 U.S.391 (1957). We have recently noted that the privilege against self-incrimination—the essential mainstay of our adversary system—is founded on a complex of values, *Murphy v. Waterfront Comm'n,* 378 U.S.52, 55-57, note 5 (1964); *Tehan v. Shott*, 382 U.S.406, 414-415, note 12 (1966). All these policies point to one overriding thought: the constitutional foundation underlying the privilege is the respect a government—state or federal—must accord to the dignity and integrity of its citizens. To maintain a "fair state-individual balance," to require the government "to shoulder the entire load," 8 Wigmore, Evidence (McNaughton, rev, 1961), 317, to respect the inviolability of the human personality, our accusatory system of criminal justice demands that the government seeking to punish an individual produce the evidence against him by its own independent labors, rather than by the cruel, simple expedient of compelling it from his own mouth

(*Chambers v. Florida,* 309 U.S.227, 235-238 (1940)). In sum, the privilege is fulfilled only when the person is guaranteed the right "to remain silent unless he chooses to speak in the unfettered exercise of his own will." *Malloy v. Hogan,* 378 U.S.1, 8 (1964).

The question in these cases is whether the privilege is fully applicable during a period of custodial interrogation. In this Court, the privilege has consistently been accorded a liberal construction. We are satisfied that all the principles embodied in the privilege apply to informal compulsion exerted by law-enforcement officers during in-custody questioning. An individual swept from familiar surroundings into police custody, surrounded by antagonistic forces, and subjected to the techniques of persuasion described above cannot be otherwise than under compulsion to speak. As a practical matter, the compulsion to speak in the isolated setting of the police station may well be greater than in courts or other official investigations, where there are often impartial observers to guard against intimidation or trickery.

Our holding [in *Escobedo v. Illinois*] stressed the fact that the police had not advised the defendant of his constitutional privilege to remain silent at the outset of the interrogation, and we drew attention to that fact at several points in the decision, 378 U.S., at 483, 485, 491. This was no isolated factor, but an essential ingredient in our decision. The entire thrust of police interrogation there, as in all the cases today, was to put the defendant in such an emotional state as to impair his capacity for rational judgment. The abdication of the constitutional privilege —the choice on his part to speak to the police—was not made knowingly or competently because of the failure to apprise him of his rights; the compelling atmosphere of the in-custody interrogation, and not an independent decision on his part, caused the defendant to speak.

A different phase of the *Escobedo* decision was significant in its attention to the absence of counsel during the questioning. There, as in the cases today, we sought a protective device to dispel the compelling atmosphere of the interrogation. In *Escobedo,* however, the police did not relieve the defendant of the anxieties which they had created in the interrogation rooms. Rather, they denied his request for the assistance of counsel, 378

U.S., at 481, 488, 491. This heightened his dilemma, and made his later statements the product of this compulsion. Cf. *Haynes v. Washington*, 373 U.S.503, 514 (1963). The denial of the defendant's request for his attorney thus undermined his ability to exercise the privilege—to remain silent if he chose or to speak without any intimidation, blatant or subtle. The presence of counsel, in all the cases before us today, would be the adequate protective device necessary to make the process of police interrogation conform to the dictates of the privilege. His presence would insure that statements made in the government-established atmosphere are not the product of compulsion.

It was in this manner that *Escobedo* explicated another facet of the pre-trial privilege, noted in many of the court's prior decisions: the protection of rights at trial. That counsel is present when statements are taken from an individual during interrogation obviously enhances the integrity of the fact-finding processes in court. The presence of an attorney, and the warnings delivered to the individual, enable the defendant under otherwise compelling circumstances to tell his story without fear, effectively, and in a way that eliminates the evils in the interrogation process. Without the protections flowing from adequate warnings and the rights of counsel, "all the careful safeguards erected around the giving of testimony, whether by an accused or any other witness, would become empty formalities in a procedure where the most compelling possible evidence of guilt, a confession, would have already been obtained at the unsupervised pleasure of the police." *Mapp v. Ohio*, 367 U.S.643, 685 (1961) (Harlan, J., dissenting).

Today, then, there can be no doubt that the fifth amendment privilege is available outside of criminal court proceedings and serves to protect persons in all settings in which their freedom of action is curtailed from being compelled to incriminate themselves. We have concluded that without proper safeguards the process of in-custody interrogation of persons suspected or accused of crime contains inherently compelling pressures which work to undermine the individual's will to resist and to compel him to speak where he would not otherwise do so freely. In order to combat these pressures and to permit a full opportunity to exercise the privilege against self-incrimination, the accused must be adequately and effectively apprised of his rights and the exercise of those rights must be fully honored.

It is impossible for us to foresee the potential alternatives for protecting the privilege which might be devised by Congress or the states in the exercise of their creative rule-making capacities. Therefore we cannot say that the Constitution necessarily requires adherence to any particular solution for the inherent compulsions of the interrogation process as it is presently conducted. Our decision in no way creates a constitutional straitjacket which will handicap sound efforts at reform, nor is it intended to have this effect. We encourage Congress and the states to continue their laudable search for increasingly effective ways of protecting the rights of the individual while promoting efficient enforcement of our criminal laws. However, unless we are shown other procedures which are at least as effective in apprising accused persons of their right of silence and in assuring a continuous opportunity to exercise it, the following safeguards must be observed.

At the outset, if a person in custody is to be subjected to interrogation, he must first be informed in clear and unequivocal terms that he has the right to remain silent. For those unaware of the privilege, the warning is needed simply to make them aware of it—the threshold requirement for an intelligent decision as to its exercise. More important, such a warning is an absolute prerequisite in overcoming the inherent pressures of the interrogation atmosphere. It is not just the subnormal or woefully ignorant who succumb to an interrogator's imprecations, whether implied or expressly stated, that the interrogation will continue until a confession is obtained or that silence in the face of accusation is itself damning and will bode ill when presented to a jury. Further, the warning will show the individual that his interrogators are prepared to recognize his privilege should he choose to exercise it.

The fifth amendment privilege is so fundamental to our system of constitutional rule and the expedient of giving an adequate warning as to the availability of the privilege so simple, we will not pause to inquire in individual cases whether the defendant was aware of his rights without a warning being given. Assessments of the knowledge the defendant possessed, based on information as to his age, education, intelligence, or prior contact with authorities, can never be more than speculation; a warning is a clear-cut fact. More important, whatever the background of the person interrogated, a warning at the time of the interrogation is indispensable to overcome its pressures and to insure that the individual knows he is free to exercise the privilege at that point in time.

The warning of the right to remain silent must be accompanied by the explanation that anything said can and will be used against the individual in court. This warning is needed in order to make him aware not only of the privilege, but also of the consequences of foregoing it. It is only through an awareness of these consequences that there can be any assurance of real understanding and intelligent exercise of the privilege. Moreover, this warning may serve to make the individual more acutely aware that he is faced with a phase of the adversary system—that he is not in the presence of persons acting solely in his interest.

The circumstances surrounding in-custody interrogation can operate very quickly to overbear the will of one merely made aware of his privilege by his interrogators. Therefore, the right to have counsel present at the interrogation is indispensable to the protection of the fifth amendment privilege under the system we delineate today. Our aim is to assure that the individual's right to choose between silence and speech remains unfettered throughout the interrogation process. A once-stated warning, delivered by those who will conduct the interrogation, cannot itself suffice to that end among those who most require knowledge of their rights. A mere warning given by the interrogators is not alone sufficient to accomplish that end. Prosecutors themselves claim that the admonishment of the right to remain silent without more "will benefit only the recidivist and the professional." Brief for the National District Attorneys Association as amicus curiae, p. 14. Even preliminary advice given to the accused by his own attorney can be swiftly overcome by the secret interrogation process. Cf. *Escobedo v. Illinois,* 378 U.S.478, 485, note 5. Thus, the need for counsel to protect the fifth amendment privilege comprehends not merely a right to consult with counsel prior to questioning, but also to have counsel present during any questioning if the defendant so desires.

The presence of counsel at the interrogation may serve several significant subsidiary functions as well. If the accused decides to talk to his interrogators, the assistance of counsel can mitigate the dangers of untrustworthiness. With a lawyer present the likelihood that the police will practice coercion is reduced, and if coercion is nevertheless exercised the lawyer can testify to it in court. The presence of a lawyer can also help to guarantee that the accused gives a fully accurate statement to the police and that the statement is rightly reported by the prosecution at trial . . . .

An individual need not make a pre-interrogation request for a lawyer. While such request affirmatively secures his right to have one, his failure to ask for a lawyer does not constitute a waiver. No effective waiver of the right to counsel during interrogation can be recognized unless specifically made after the warnings we here delineate have been given. The accused who does not know his rights and therefore does not make a request may be the person who most needs counsel. . . .

Accordingly we hold that an individual held for interrogation must be clearly informed that he has the right to consult with a lawyer and to have the lawyer with him during interrogation under the system for protecting the privilege we delineate today. As with the warnings of the right to remain silent and that anything stated can be used in evidence against him, this warning is an absolute prerequisite to interrogation. No amount of circumstantial evidence that the person may have been aware of this right will suffice to stand in its stead. Only through such a warning is there ascertainable assurance that the accused was aware of this right.

If an individual indicates that he wishes the assistance of counsel before any interrogation occurs, the authorities cannot rationally ignore or deny his request on the basis that the individual does not have or cannot afford a retained attorney. The financial ability of the individual has no relationship to the scope of the rights involved here. The privilege against self-incrimination secured by the Constitution applies to all individuals. The need for counsel in order to protect the privilege exists for the indigent as well as the affluent. In fact, were we to limit these constitutional rights to those who can retain an attorney, our decisions today would be of little significance. The cases before us as well as the vast majority of confession cases with which we have dealt in the past involve those unable to retain counsel. While authorities are not required to relieve the accused of his poverty, they have the obligation not to take advantage of indigence in the administration of justice. Denial of counsel to the indigent at the time of interrogation while allowing an attorney to those who can afford one would be no more supportable by reason or logic than the similar situation at trial and on appeal struck down in *Gideon v. Wainwright,* 372 U.S.335 (1963), and *Douglas v. California,* 372 U.S.353 (1963).

In order to fully apprise a person interrogated of the extent of his rights under this system, it is necessary to warn him not only that he has the right to consult with an attorney, but also that if he is indigent a lawyer will be appointed to represent him. Without this additional warning, the admonition of the right to consult with counsel would often be understood as meaning only that he can consult with a lawyer if he has one or has the funds to obtain one. The warning of a right to counsel would be hollow if not couched in terms that would convey to the indigent—the person most often subjected to interrogation—the knowledge that he too has a right to have counsel present. As with the warnings of the right to remain silent and of the general right to counsel, only by effective and express explanation to the indigent of this right can there be assurance that he was truly in a position to exercise it.

Once warnings have been given, the subsequent procedure is clear. If the individual indicates in any manner, at any time prior to or during questioning, that he wishes to remain silent, the interrogation must cease. At this point he has shown that he intends to exercise his fifth amendment privilege; any statement taken after the person invokes his privilege cannot be other than the product of compulsion, subtle or otherwise. Without the right to cut off questioning, the setting of in-custody interrogation operates on the individual to overcome free choice in producing a statement after the privilege has been once invoked. If the individual states that he wants an attorney, the interrogation must cease until an attorney is present. At that time, the individual must have an opportunity to confer with the attorney and to have him present during any subsequent questioning. If the individual cannot obtain an attorney and he indicates that he wants one before speaking to police, they must respect his decision to remain silent.

This does not mean, as some have suggested, that each police station must have a "station house lawyer" present at all times to advise prisoners. It does mean, however, that if police propose to interrogate a person they must make known to him that he is entitled to a lawyer and that if he cannot afford one, a lawyer will be provided for him prior to any interrogation. If authorities conclude that they will not provide counsel during a reasonable period of time in which investigation in the field is carried out, they may do so without violating the person's fifth amendment privilege so long as they do not question him during that time.

If the interrogation continues without the presence of an attorney and a statement is taken, a heavy burden rests on the government to demonstrate that the defendant knowingly and intelligently waived his privilege against self-incrimination and his right to retained or appointed counsel. *Escobedo v. Illinois,* 378 U.S.478, 490, note 14.

This Court has always set high standards of proof for the waiver of constitutional rights (*Johnson v. Zerbst,* 304 U.S.458 (1938)), and we reassert these standards as applied to in-custody interrogation. Since the state is responsible for establishing the isolated circumstances under which the interrogation takes place and has the only means of making available corroborated evidence of warnings given during incommunicado interrogation, the burden is rightly on its shoulders.

An express statement that the individual is willing to make a statement and does not want an attorney followed closely by a statement could constitute a waiver. But a valid waiver will not be presumed simply from the silence of the accused after warnings are given or simply from the fact that a confession was in fact eventually obtained. . . .

Moreover, where in-custody interrogation is involved, there is no room for the contention that the privilege is waived if the individual answers some questions or gives some information on his own prior to invoking his right to remain silent when interrogated.

Whatever the testimony of the authorities as to waiver of rights by an accused, the fact of lengthy interrogation or incommunicado incarceration before a statement is made is strong evidence that the accused did not validly waive his rights. In these circumstances the fact that the individual eventually made a statement is consistent with the conclusion that the compelling influence of the interrogation finally forced him to do so. It is inconsistent with any notion of a voluntary relinquishment of the privilege. Moreover, any evidence that the accused was threatened, tricked, or cajoled into a waiver will, of course, show that the defendant did not voluntarily waive his privilege. The requirement of warnings and waiver of rights is a fundamental with respect to the fifth amendment privilege and not simply a preliminary ritual to existing methods of interrogation.

The warnings required and the waiver necessary in accordance with our opinion today are, in the absence of a fully effective equivalent, prerequisites to the admissibility of any statement made by a defendant. No distinction can be drawn between statements which are direct confessions and statements which amount to "admissions" of part or all of an offense. The privilege against self-incrimination protects the individual from being compelled to incriminate himself in any manner; it does not distinguish degrees of incrimination. Similarly, for precisely the same reason, no distinction may be drawn between inculpatory statements and statements alleged to be merely "exculpatory." If a statement made were in fact truly exculpatory it would, of course, never be used by the prosecution. In fact, statements merely intended to be exculpatory by the defendant are often used to impeach his testimony at trial or to demonstrate untruths in the statement given under interrogation and thus to prove guilt by implication. These statements are incriminating in any meaningful sense of the word and may not be used without the full warnings and effective waiver required for any other statement. In *Escobedo* itself, the defendant fully intended his accusation of another as the slayer to be exculpatory as to himself.

The principles announced today deal with the protection which must be given to the privilege against self-incrimination when the individual is first subjected to police interrogation while in custody at the station or otherwise deprived of his freedom of action in any way. It is at this point that our adversary system of criminal proceedings commences, distinguishing itself at the outset from the inquisitorial system recognized in some countries. Under the system of warnings we delineate today or under any other system which may be devised and found effective, the safeguards to be erected about the privilege must come into play at this point.

Our decision is not intended to hamper the traditional function of police officers in investigating crime. See *Escobedo v. Illinois*, 378 U.S. 478, 492. When an individual is in custody on probable cause, the police may, of course, seek out evidence in the field to be used at trial against him. Such investigation may include inquiry of persons not under restraint. General on-the-scene questioning as to facts surrounding a crime or other general questioning of citizens in the fact-finding process is not affected by our holding. It is an act of responsible citizenship for individuals to give whatever information they may have to aid in law enforcement. In such situations the compelling atmosphere inherent in the process of in-custody interrogation is not necessarily present.

In dealing with statements obtained through interrogation, we do not purport to find all confessions inadmissible. Confessions remain a proper element in law enforcement. Any statement given freely and voluntarily without any compelling influences is, of course, admissible in evidence. The fundamental import of the privilege while an individual is in custody is not whether he is allowed to talk to the police without the benefit of warnings and counsel, but whether he can be interrogated. There is no requirement that police stop a person who enters a police station and states that he wishes to confess to a crime, or a person who calls the police to offer a confession or any other statement he desires to make. Volunteered statements of any kind are not barred by the fifth amendment and their admissibility is not affected by our holding today.

To summarize, we hold that when an individual is taken into custody or otherwise deprived of his freedom by the authorities and is subjected to questioning, the privilege against self-incrimination is jeopardized. Procedural safeguards must be employed to protect the privilege, and unless other fully effective means are adopted to notify the person of his right of silence and to assure that the exercise of the right will be scrupulously honored, the following measures are required. He must be warned prior to any questioning that he has the right to remain silent, that anything he says can be used against him in a court of law, that he has the right to the presence of an attorney, and that if he cannot afford an attorney one will be appointed for him prior to any questioning if he so desires. Opportunity to exercise these rights must be afforded to him throughout the interrogation. After such warnings have been given, and such opportunity afforded him, the individual may knowingly and intelligently waive these rights and agree to answer questions or make a statement. But unless and until such warnings and waiver are demonstrated by the prosecution at trial, no evidence obtained as a result of interrogation can be used against him.

A recurrent argument made in these cases is that society's need for interrogation outweighs the privilege. This argument is not unfamiliar to this Court. The whole thrust of our foregoing discussion demonstrates that the Constitution has prescribed the rights of the individual when confronted with the power of government when it provided in the fifth amendment that an individual cannot be compelled to be a witness against himself. That right cannot be abridged. . . .

If the individual desires to exercise his privilege, he has the right to do so. This is not for the authorities to decide. An attorney may advise his client not to talk to police until he has had an opportunity to investigate the case, or he may wish to be present with his client during any police questioning. In doing so an attorney is merely exercising the good professional judgment he has been taught. This is not cause for considering the attorney a menace to law enforcement. He is merely carrying out what he is sworn to do under his oath—to protect to the extent of his ability the rights of his client. In fulfilling this responsibility the attorney plays a vital role in the administration of criminal justice under our Constitution.

In announcing these principles, we are not unmindful of the burdens which law enforcement officials must bear, often under trying circumstances. We also fully recognize the obligation of all citizens to aid in enforcing the criminal laws. This Court, while protecting individual rights, has always given ample latitude to law enforcement agencies in the legitimate exercise of their duties. The limits we have placed on the interrogation process should not constitute an undue interference with a proper system of law enforcement. As we have noted, our decision does not in any way preclude police from carrying out their traditional investigatory functions. Although confessions may play an important role in some convictions, the cases before us present graphic examples of the overstatement of the "need" for confessions. In each case authorities conducted interrogations ranging up to five days in duration despite the presence, through standard investigating practices, of considerable evidence against each defendant. Further examples are chronicled in our prior cases. . . .

It is also urged that an unfettered right to detention for interrogation should be allowed because it will often redound to the benefit of the person questioned. When police inquiry determines that there is no reason to believe that the person has committed any crime, it is said, he will be released without need for further formal procedures. The person who has committed no offense, however, will be better able to clear himself after warnings, with counsel present than without. It can be assumed that in such circumstances a lawyer would advise his client to talk freely to police in order to clear himself.

Custodial interrogation, by contrast, does not necessarily afford the innocent an opportunity to clear themselves. A serious consequence of the present practice of the interrogation alleged to be beneficial for the innocent is that many arrests "for investigation" subject large numbers of innocent persons to detention and interrogation. In one of the cases before us, No. 584, *California v. Stewart,* police held four persons, who were in the defendant's house at the time of the arrest, in jail for five days until defendant confessed. At that time they were finally released. Police stated that there was "no evidence to connect them with any crime." Available statistics on the extent of this practice where it is condoned indicate that these four are far from alone in being subjected to arrest, prolonged detention, and interrogation without the requisite probable cause. . . .

Because of the nature of the problem and because of its recurrent significance in numerous cases, we have to this point discussed the relationship of the fifth amendment privilege to police interrogation without specific concentration on the facts of the cases before us. We turn now to these facts to consider the application to these cases of the constitutional principles discussed above. In each instance, we have concluded that statements were obtained from the defendant under circumstances that did not meet constitutional standards for protection of the privilege.

On March 13, 1963, petitioner, Ernesto Miranda, was arrested at his home and taken in custody to a Phoenix police station. He was there identified by the complaining witness. The police then took him to "interrogation room No. 2" of the detective bureau. There he was questioned by two police officers. The officers admitted at trial that Miranda was not advised that he had a right to have an attorney present. Two hours later, the officers emerged from the interrogation room with a written confession signed by Miranda. At the top of the statement was a typed paragraph stating that the confession was made voluntarily, without threats or promises of immunity and "with full knowledge of my legal rights, understanding any statement I make may be used against me."

At his trial before a jury, the written confession was admitted into evidence over the objection of defense counsel, and the officers testified to the prior oral confession made by Miranda during the interrogation. Miranda was found guilty of kidnapping and rape. He was sentenced to twenty to thirty years' imprisonment on each count, the sentences to run concurrently. On appeal, the Supreme Court of Arizona held that Miranda's constitutional rights were not violated in obtaining the confession and affirmed the conviction (98 Ariz.18, 401 P.2d 721). In reaching its decision, the court emphasized heavily the fact that Miranda did not specifically request counsel.

We reverse. From the testimony of the officers and by the admission of respondent, it is clear that Miranda was not in any way apprised of his right to consult with an attorney and to have one present during the interrogation, now was his right not to be compelled to incriminate himself effectively protected in any other manner. Without these warnings the statements were inadmissible. The mere fact that he signed a statement which contained a typed-in clause stating that he had "full knowledge" of his "legal rights" does not approach the knowing and intelligent waiver required to relinquish constitutional rights. . . .

5.2. Schmerber v. California

Mr. Justice Brennan delivered the opinion of the Court.

The petitioner was convicted in Los Angeles Municipal Court of the criminal offense of driving an automobile while under the influence of intoxicating liquor. He had been arrested at a hospital while receiving treatment for injuries suffered in an accident involving the automobile that he had apparently been driving. At the direction of a police officer, a blood sample was then withdrawn from petitioner's body by a physician at the hospital.

The chemical analysis of this sample revealed a percent by weight of alcohol in his blood at the time of the offense which indicated intoxication, and the report of this analysis was admitted in evidence at the trial.

The petitioner objected to receipt of this evidence of the analysis on the ground that the blood had been withdrawn despite his refusal, on the advise of his counsel, to consent to the test. He contended that in that circumstance the withdrawal of the blood and the admission of the analysis in evidence denied him due process of law under the fourteenth amendment, as well as specific guarantees of the Bill of Rights secured against the states by that amendment: his privilege against self-incrimination under the fifth amendment; his right to counsel under the sixth amendment; and his right not to be subjected to unreasonable searches and seizures in violation of the fourth amendment. The Appellate Department of the California Superior Court rejected these contentions and affirmed the conviction.

We affirm.

THE DUE PROCESS CLAUSE CLAIM. *Breithaupt* was also a case in which police officers caused blood to be withdrawn from the driver of an automobile involved in an accident, and in which there was ample justification for the officer's conclusion that the driver was under the influence of alcohol. There, as here, the extraction was made by a physician in a simple, medically acceptable manner in a hospital environment.

There, however, the driver was unconscious at the time the blood was withdrawn and hence had no opportunity to object to

---

Note: Schmerber v. California, 384 U.S. 757 (1966).

the procedure. We affirmed the conviction there resulting from the use of the test in evidence, holding that under such circumstances the withdrawal did not offend "that 'sense of justice' of which we spoke in *Rochin v.* [People of] *California,* 1952, 342 U.S.165"; 352 U.S., at 435. *Breithaupt* thus requires the rejection of petitioner's due process argument, and nothing in the circumstances of this case* or in supervening events persuades us that this aspect of *Breithaupt* should be overruled.

THE PRIVILEGE AGAINST SELF-INCRIMINATION CLAIM. *Breithaupt* summarily rejected an argument that the withdrawal of blood and the admission of the analysis report involved in that state case violated the fifth amendment privilege of any person not to "be compelled in any criminal case to be a witness against himself," citing *Twining v. State of New Jersey,* 211 U.S.78. But that case, holding that the protections of the fourteenth amendment do not embrace this fifth amendment privilege, has been succeeded by *Malloy v. Hogan,* 378 U.S.1, 8. We there held that "[t]he fourteenth amendment secures against state invasion the same privilege that the fifth amendment guarantees against federal infringement—the right of a person to remain silent unless he chooses to speak in the unfettered exercise of his own will, and to suffer no penalty . . . for such silence." We therefore must now decide whether the withdrawal of the blood and admission in evidence of the analysis involved in this case violated petitioner's privilege. We hold that the privilege protects an accused only from being compelled to testify against himself, or otherwise provide the state with evidence of a testimonial or communicative nature, and that the withdrawal of blood and use of the analysis in question in this case did not involve compulsion to these ends.

It could not be denied that in requiring the petitioner to submit to the withdrawal and chemical analysis of his blood the state compelled him to submit to an attempt to discover evi-

---

* We "cannot see that it should make any difference whether one states unequivocally that he objects or resorts to physical violence in protest or is in such condition that he is unable to protest." *Breithaupt v. Abram,* 352 U.S., at 441 (WARREN, C. J., dissenting). It would be a different case if the police initiated the violence, refused to respect a reasonable request to undergo a different form of testing, or responded to resistance with inappropriate force.

dence that might be used to prosecute him for a criminal offense. He submitted only after the police officer rejected his objection and directed the physician to proceed. The officer's direction to the physician to administer the test over the petitioner's objection constituted compulsion for the purposes of the privilege. The critical question, then, is whether the petitioner was thus compelled "to be a witness against himself."

If the scope of the privilege coincided with the complex of values it helps to protect, we might be obliged to conclude that the privilege was violated. In *Miranda v. Arizona*, 384 U.S.436, at 460, the Court said of the interests protected by the privilege:

> All these policies point to one overriding thought: the constitutional foundation underlying the privilege is the respect a government—state or federal—must accord to the dignity and integrity of its citizens. To maintain a "fair state-individual balance," to require the government "to shoulder the entire load," to respect the inviolability of the human personality, our accusatory system of criminal justice demands that the government seeking to punish an individual produce the evidence against him by its own independent labors, rather than by the cruel, simple expedient of compelling it from his own mouth.

The withdrawal of blood necessarily involves puncturing the skin for extraction, and the percent by weight of alcohol in that blood, as established by chemical analysis, is evidence of criminal guilt. Compelled submission fails on one view to respect the "inviolability of the human personality." Moreover, since it enables the State to rely on evidence forced from the accused, the compulsion violates at least one meaning of the requirement that the State procure the evidence against an accused "by its own independent labors."

As the passage in *Miranda* implicitly recognizes, however, the privilege has never been given the full scope which the values it helps to protect suggest. History and a long line of authorities in lower courts have consistently limited its protection to situations in which the State seeks to submerge those values by obtaining the evidence against an accused through "the cruel, simple expedient of compelling it from his own mouth. In sum, the privilege is fulfilled only when the person is guaranteed the right 'to remain silent unless he chooses to speak in the unfettered exercise of his own will.'" *Ibid.* The leading case in this

Court is *Holt v. U.S.*, 218 U.S.245. There the question was whether evidence was admissible that the accused, prior to trial and over his protest, put on a blouse that fitted him. It was contended that compelling the accused to submit to the demand that he model the blouse violated the privilege. Mr. Justice Holmes, speaking for the Court, rejected the argument as "based upon an extravagant extension of the fifth amendment," and went on to say: "[T]he prohibition of compelling a man in a criminal court to be witness against himself is a prohibition of the use of physical or moral compulsion to extort communications from him, not an exclusion of his body as evidence when it may be material. The objection in principle would forbid a jury to look at a prisoner and compare his features with a photograph in proof." 218 U.S., at 252-253.

It is clear that the protection of the privilege reaches an accused's communications, whatever form they might take, and the compulsion of responses which are also communications, for example, compliance with a subpoena to produce one's papers (*Boyd v. U.S.*, 116 U.S.616). On the other hand, both federal and state courts have usually held that it offers no protection against compulsion to submit to fingerprinting, photographing, or measurements, to write or speak for identification, to appear in court, to stand, to assume a stance, to walk, or to make a particular gesture. The distinction which has emerged, often expressed in different ways, is that the privilege is a bar against compelling "communications" or "testimony," but that compulsion which makes a suspect or accused the source of "real or physical evidence" does not violate it.

Although we agree that this distinction is a helpful framework for analysis, we are not to be understood to agree with past applications in all instances. There will be many cases in which such a distinction is not readily drawn. Some tests seemingly directed to obtain "physical evidence," for example, lie detector tests measuring changes in body function during interrogation, may actually be directed to eliciting responses which are essentially testimonial. To compel a person to submit to testing in which an effort will be made to determine his guilt or innocence on the basis of physiological responses, whether willed or not, is to evoke the spirit and history of the fifth amendment. Such situations call to mind the principle that the protection of the privilege "is as broad as the mischief against which it seeks to guard." *Counselman v. Hitchcock,* 142 U.S.547, 562, 1892.

In the present case, however, no such problem of application is presented. Not even a shadow of testimonial compulsion upon or enforced communication by the accused was involved either in the extraction or in the chemical analysis. Petitioner's testimonial capacities were in no way implicated; indeed, his participation, except as a donor, was irrelevant to the results of the test, which depend on chemical analysis and on that alone. Since the blood test evidence, although an incriminating product of compulsion, was neither petitioner's testimony nor evidence relating to some communicative act or writing by the petitioner, it was not inadmissible on privilege grounds.

THE RIGHT TO COUNSEL CLAIM. This conclusion also answers petitioner's claim that, in compelling him to submit to the test in face of the fact that his objection was made on the advice of counsel, he was denied his sixth amendment right to the assistance of counsel. Since the petitioner was not entitled to assert the privilege, he has no greater right because counsel erroneously advised him that he could assert it. His claim is strictly limited to the failure of the police to respect his wish, reinforced by counsel's advice, to be left inviolate. No issue of counsel's ability to assist petitioner in respect of any rights he did possess is presented. The limited claim thus made must be rejected.

THE SEARCH AND SEIZURE CLAIM. In *Breithaupt,* as here, it was also contended that the chemical analysis should be excluded from evidence as the product of an unlawful search and seizure in violation of the fourth and fourteenth amendments. The Court did not decide whether the extraction of blood in that case was unlawful, but rejected the claim on the basis of *Wolf v. People of the State of Colorado,* 338 U.S.25, 1949. That case had held that the Constitution did not require, in state prosecutions for state crimes, the exclusion of evidence obtained in violation of the fourth amendment's provisions. We have since overruled *Wolf* in that respect, holding in *Mapp v. Ohio,* 367 U.S.643, that the exclusionary rule adopted for federal prosecutions in

Weeks v. U.S., 232 U.S.383, must also be applied in criminal prosecutions in state courts. The question is squarely presented therefore, whether the chemical analysis introduced in evidence in this case should have been excluded as the product of an unconstitutional search and seizure.

The overriding function of the fourth amendment is to protect personal privacy and dignity against unwarranted intrusion by the State. In *Wolf* we recognized "[t]he security of one's privacy against arbitrary intrusion by the police" as being "at the core of the fourth amendment" and "basic to a free society." 338 U.S., at 27. We reaffirmed that broad view of the amendment's purpose in applying the federal exclusionary rule to the states in *Mapp*.

The values protected by the fourth amendment thus substantially overlap those the fifth amendment helps to protect. History and precedent have required that we today reject the claim that the Self-Incrimination Clause of the fifth amendment requires the human body in all circumstances to be held inviolate against state expeditions seeking evidence of crime. But if compulsory administration of a blood test does not implicate the fifth amendment, it plainly involves the broadly conceived reach of a search and seizure under the fourth amendment. That amendment expressly provides that "[t]he right of the people to be secure in their *persons,* houses, papers, and effects, against unreasonable searches and seizures, shall not be violated." It could not reasonably be argued, and indeed respondent does not argue, that the administration of the blood test in this case was free of the constraints of the fourth amendment. Such testing procedures plainly constitute searches of "persons," and depend antecedently upon seizures of "persons," within the meaning of that amendment.

Because we are dealing with intrusions into the human body rather than with state interferences with property relationships or private papers—"houses, papers, and effects," we write on a clean slate. Limitations on the kinds of property which may be seized under warrant, as distinct from the procedures for search and the permissible scope of search, are not instructive in this context. We begin with the assumption that once the privilege against self-incrimination has been found not to bar compelled intrusions into the body for blood to be analyzed for alcohol content, the fourth amendment's proper function is to constrain, not against all intrusions as such, but against intrusions which are not justified in the circumstances, or which are made in an improper manner. In other words, the questions we must decide in this case are whether the police were justified in requiring petitioner to submit to the blood test, and whether the means and procedures employed in taking his blood respected relevant fourth amendment standards of reasonableness.

In this case, as will often be true when charges of driving under the influence of alcohol are pressed, these questions arise in the context of an arrest made by an officer without a warrant. Here, there was plainly probable cause for the officer to arrest petitioner and charge him with driving an automobile while under the influence of intoxicating liquor. The police officer who arrived at the scene shortly after the accident smelled liquor on the petitioner's breath, and testified that the petitioner's eyes were "bloodshot, watery, sort of a glassy appearance." The officer saw the petitioner again at the hospital within two hours of the accident. There he noticed similar symptoms of drunkenness. He thereupon informed the petitioner "that he was under arrest and he was entitled to the services of an attorney, and that he could remain silent, and anything he told me would be used against him in evidence."

While early cases suggest that there is an unrestricted "right on the part of the government always recognized under English and American law, to search the person of the accused when legally arrested, to discover and seize the fruits or evidences of crime," *Weeks v. U.S.*, 232 U.S.383, 392; *People v. Chiagles*, 237 N.Y. 193, 142 N.E. 583 (1923) (Cardozo, J.), the mere fact of a lawful arrest does not end our inquiry. The suggestion of these cases apparently rests on two factors—first, there may be more immediate danger of concealed weapons or of destruction of evidence under the direct control of the accused, *U.S. v. Rabinowitz*, 339 U.S.56, 72-73 (Frankfurter, J., dissenting); second, once a search of the arrested person for weapons is permitted, it would be both impractical and unnecessary to enforcement of the fourth amendment's purpose to attempt to confine the search to those objects alone. *People v. Chiagles,* 237 N.Y., at 197-198, 142 N.E., at 584. Whatever the validity of these considerations in general, they have little applicability with respect to searches involving intrusions beyond the body's surface. The interests in human dignity and privacy which the fourth amendment protects forbid any such intrusions on the mere chance that desired evidence might be obtained. In the absence of a clear indication that in fact such evidence will be found, these fundamental human interests require law officers to suffer the risk that such evidence may disappear unless there is an immediate search.

Although the facts which established probable cause to arrest in this case also suggested the required relevance and likely success of a test of petitioner's blood for alcohol, the question remains whether the arresting officer was permitted to draw these inferences himself, or was required instead to procure a warrant before proceeding with the test. Search warrants are ordinarily required for searches of dwellings, and absent an emergency, no less could be required where intrusions into the human body are concerned. The requirement that a warrant be obtained is a requirement that inferences to support the search "be drawn by a neutral and detached magistrate instead of being judged by the officer engaged in the often competitive enterprise of ferreting out crime." *Johnson v. U.S.,* 333 U.S.10, 13-14; see also *Aguilar v. State of Texas,* 378 U.S.108, 110-111. The importance of informed, detached, and deliberate determinations of the issue whether or not to invade another's body in search of evidence of guilt is indisputable and great.

The officer in the present case, however, might reasonably have believed that he was confronted with an emergency, in which the delay necessary to obtain a warrant, under the circumstances, threatened "the destruction of evidence," *Preston v. U.S.,* 376 U.S.364, 367. We are told that the percentage of alcohol in the blood begins to diminish shortly after drinking stops, as the body functions to eliminate it from the system. Particularly in a case such as this, where time had to be taken to bring the accused to a hospital and to investigate the scene of the accident, there was no time to seek out a magistrate and secure a warrant.

Given these special facts, we conclude that the attempt to secure evidence of blood-alcohol content in this case was an appropriate incident to the petitioner's arrest.

Similarly, we are satisfied that the test chosen to measure the petitioner's blood-alcohol level was a reasonable one. Extraction of blood samples for testing is a highly effective means of determining the degree to which a person is under the influence of alcohol. See *Breithaupt v. Abram,* 352 U.S., at 436, n. 3. Such tests are commonplace in these days of periodic physical examinations and experience with them teaches that the quantity of blood extracted is minimal, and that for most people the procedure involves virtually no risk, trauma, or pain. The petitioner is not one of the few who on grounds of fear, concern for health, or religious scruple might prefer some other means of testing, such as the "breathalyzer" test the petitioner refused. . . . We need not decide whether such wishes would have to be respected.

Finally, the record shows that the test was performed in a reasonable manner. The petitioner's blood was taken by a physician in a hospital environment according to accepted medical practices. We are thus not presented with the serious questions which would arise if a search involving use of a medical technique, even of the most rudimentary sort, were made by other than medical personnel or in other than a medical environment, for example, if it were administered by police in the privacy of the stationhouse. To tolerate searches under these conditions might be to invite an unjustified element of personal risk of infection and pain.

We thus conclude that the present record shows no violation of petitioner's right under the fourth and fourteenth amendments to be free of unreasonable searches and seizures. It bears repeating, however, that we reach this judgment only on the facts of the present record. The integrity of an individual's person is a cherished value of our society. That we today hold that the Constitution does not forbid the States minor intrusions into an individual's body under stringently limited conditions in no way indicates that it permits more substantial intrusions, or intrusions under other conditions.

Affirmed.

CHAPTER 6

THE SIXTH AMENDMENT

In all criminal prosecutions, the accused shall enjoy the right to a speedy and public trial, by an impartial jury of the state and district wherein the crime shall have been committed, which district shall have been previously ascertained by law, and to be informed of the nature and cause of the accusation; to be confronted with the witnesses against him; to have compulsory process for obtaining witnesses in his favor, and to have the assistance of counsel for his defense.

Sixth Amendment

Section I. SPEEDY AND PUBLIC TRIAL

In all criminal prosecutions, the accused shall enjoy the right to a speedy and public trial. . .

Sixth Amendment

COURT calendars are quite crowded in the larger cities and hence, if indictments were to be dismissed because a trial had not begun within a few months, or even a year (thus meeting the "speedy trial" requirement) many people now awaiting trial would be allowed to go free. This is not to be interpreted, however, that a person must wait indefinitely for trial.

U.S. v. Provoo, 350 U.S.857 (1955), was a prosecution for treason in which the trial was delayed from 1949 to 1955, during which time the defendant remained in jail. A habeas corpus petition was granted by reason of the delay, which was said to be a denial of the sixth amendment right to a speedy trial. It should be noted that the right to a speedy trial is guaranteed to an accused in a state court, as well as a federal court (*Klopfer v. State of North Carolina,* 386 U.S.213 (1967)).

The court in *U.S. v. Ewell,* 383 U.S.116 (1966), held that the passage of seventeen months between the arrest and later hearings on indictments did not violate the sixth amendment, since the delay was not *purposeful or oppressive,* nor did the defendant complain of the delay at the time.

In *Marion,* a three year delay between the commission of the offense and the filing of an indictment was not a violation of the speedy-trial provision. The provision has no application until the putative defendant becomes an "accused" (*United States v. Marion,* 404 U.S.307, 1971).

An accused may waive his right to a speedy trial a) by delaying the trial for strategic reasons, b) by asking for a continuance, c) by failing to object to delays, or d) by requesting a change in venue.

The defendant has the right to have the public attend the trial except in those cases where the national security might be involved. The right to a public trial does not prevent the court from excluding spectators when it is felt that the ends of justice will be met in so doing. Persons may be removed from the court, for example, a) when facilities are overcrowded, b) to prevent disturbances, c) in cases involving sex crimes where lurid or gruesome details may be disclosed, or d) for protection of the witnesses.

Section 2. TRIAL BY IMPARTIAL JURY

> . . . the right to . . . trial, by an impartial jury of the state and district wherein the crime shall have been committed, which district shall have been previously ascertained by law. . . .
>
> *Sixth Amendment*

Under the sixth amendment there are two types of offenses against the Federal Government, petty offenses and serious offenses (crimes). An individual charged with a petty offense is not entitled to a trial by jury, while an individual charged with a serious offense, that is to say a crime, is entitled to a trial by jury, in federal courts only, unless the particular state constitution so provides (*Palko v. Conn.,* 302 U.S.319 (1937)). A serious offense is one which carries a potential sentence of more than six months, even though the *actual* sentence imposed may be less than six months (*Baldwin v. New York,* 399 U.S.66 (1970)).

A trial by jury must consist of a) a judge with the power to instruct the jury, b) a jury of twelve persons, c) a jury whose verdict must be unanimous. Only the defendant may choose to have less than twelve jurors or less than a unanimous verdict.

Whether a jury sits in a federal court or a state court, it must be *impartial* (*Parker v. Gladden,* 385 U.S.363 (1966)). Thus, persons that are prejudiced against the defendant are not allowed to sit on the jury. For a jury to be impartial, it must not be drawn in a manner which is discriminatory with respect to race, color, or creed (*Patton v. Mississippi,* 332 U.S.463 (1947)).

Some verdicts have been reversed by the United States Supreme Court where newspapers have aroused the public to such a degree about the accused, the crime, or the trial, that a fair trial would be impossible in the area of circulation of the newspaper. In *Sheppard v. Maxwell,* 384 U.S.333 (1966), the defendant was convicted of second-degree murder. Five months prior to the trial, the citizenry of the community in which the trial was held was flooded with newspaper articles clearly accusing the defendant of the crime. Many, if not all of the members of the jury, had read the prejudicial comments about the defendant and hence the United States Supreme Court reversed the conviction by reason of the defendant's being denied his right to an impartial jury under the sixth amendment, made applicable to the states through the fourteenth amendment.

Note the complex problem that arises, namely, a fair trial versus the free press. Under the first amendment the courts cannot silence the newspaper, radio, or television commentary on trials.

Some remedies available to secure a fair trial include the following: a) change of venue, b) continuance, c) sequestration of jurors and witnesses, d) control of counsel, e) control of the police, f) control of the prosecution, and g) control of the press.

2.1. Venue

Changing the venue may allow the defendant to have a fairer trial in that the jurors may not have been exposed to the same amount of publicity about the crime prior to trial and may thus be able to more objectively judge the guilt or innocence of the defendant. Although not available to the government, an individual charged with a crime who feels that his trial may be prejudiced because of television or newspaper publicity can ask for a *change* of venue to another district (usually counties) in the state.

2.2. Continuance

A continuance is a delay in the proceeding which may allow passions to cool in the community, so that a fair trial may be had.

2.3. Sequestration

Sequestration or separating jurors and witnesses from all outside influences, including the news media and relatives, may help control public sentiment influencing their opinions.

The court can control counsel, prosecution, press, and police with respect to conduct both in and out of the courtroom, mainly through its contempt power.

Section 3. NATURE AND CAUSE OF ACCUSATION

> ... the accused shall enjoy the right ... to be informed of the nature and cause of the accusation. ...
>
> *Sixth Amendment*

The defendant must be told of the charges against him by clear and unambiguous language, and the statute, if any, that defines the offense must be clear in its definition.

It is essential that the defendant be told the charges against him so that he can prepare a defense and protect himself against possible double jeopardy. (In the federal court system, an act is a crime only if it is made so by statute, however, in some states the common law may exist and hence the judge can decide whether or not the act committed is a crime.)

If the defendant is indicted by a grand jury, his conviction can only be based on the charge specified in the indictment. An exception to the above rule is where the defendant is convicted of a lesser crime than that charged, which is included in the crime charged. In illustration, an individual may be convicted of second-degree murder stemming from a charge of first-degree murder, but he *cannot* be convicted of first-degree murder from a charge of second-degree murder. In other words, the greater crime of murder in the first-degree incompasses the lesser crime of murder in the second-degree and manslaughter. The defendant could have been charged instead with any of the *lesser* crimes. Conversely, a greater crime cannot flow from a crime of lesser degree. See discussion of ex post facto law in Chapter 9.

Section 4. RIGHT TO CONFRONTATION WITH THE WITNESS

... the accused shall enjoy the right . . . to be confronted with the witness against him. . . .

Sixth Amendment

The defendant has the right to challenge and cross-examine the witnesses that testify against him. This right is made binding on the states through the due process clause of the fourteenth amendment (*Pointer v. Texas,* 380 U.S.400 (1965)). Whether in federal or state court, the defendant has the right to be physically present when testimony is given against him, unless he waives the right by escape or disruptive conduct in the courtroom (*Illinois v. Allen,* 397 U.S.337 (1970)).

Exceptions to the right to cross-examine the witnesses exist: a) when a statement is introduced at the trial which was made by a dying person, b) when the witness testified at a grand jury, c) when a report made by an undercover agent or informant is used (*McCray v. Illinois,* 386 U.S.300 (1967)), or d) when a state rule permits the use of out-of-court statements of a co-conspirator, made after the commission of the crime. *Dutton v. Evans,* 400 U.S.74, 1970.

Section 5. COMPULSORY PROCESS CLAUSE

... the accused shall enjoy the right . . . to have compulsory process for obtaining witnesses in his favor. . . .

Sixth Amendment

It is the obligation of the government to subpoena people to appear in court who the defendant believes would be useful witnesses for him. This right is available in both state and federal criminal proceedings. *Washington v. Texas,* 388 U.S.14 (1967).

Section 6. RIGHT TO COUNSEL

In all criminal prosecutions, the accused shall enjoy the right . . . to have the Assistance of Counsel for his defense.

Sixth Amendment

It is a constitutional right of the accused in a criminal prosecution to have the assistance of counsel; however, the question as to what stage in the criminal proceeding the guarantee applies is not an easy one to answer. At what stage, between arrest and arraignment, is the accused entitled to the assistance of counsel? An important factor in the consideration of this question, is the "criticalness" of the particular proceeding. If the stage in question is determined to be "critical," the accused has the right to employ counsel and be represented by counsel; if he is financially unable to employ counsel, an attorney will be appointed for him by the court.

6.1. Federal Standard

Rule 44 of the Federal Rules of Criminal Procedure codified the practice of the federal courts to inquire if the accused was represented by counsel and, if not, was he advised that he could be.

> Rule 44.
>
> (a) *Right to Assigned Counsel.* Every defendant who is unable to obtain counsel shall be entitled to have counsel assigned to represent him at every stage of the proceedings from his initial appearance before the commissioner or the court through appeal, unless he waives such appointment.
>
> (b) *Assignment Procedure.* The procedures for implementing the right set out in subdivision (a) shall be those provided by law and by local rules of court established pursuant thereto. As amended Feb. 28, 1966, eff. July 1, 1966.

6.2. State Standard

The incorporation of the sixth amendment right to counsel into the Due Process Clause of the fourteenth amendment, which made it applicable to the states, took place in four phases.

1. *Powell v. Alabama* (1932)
   (counsel in death penalty cases).
2. *Betts v. Brady* (1942)
   (counsel in cases with "special circumstances").
3. *Gideon v. Wainwright* (1963)
   (counsel for all indigent criminal defendants).
4. *Escobedo v. Illinois* (1964)
   (counsel for all during custodial interrogation).

The defendant and eight other negroes were convicted of raping two white girls. They were too poor to afford counsel and none was appointed. The United States Supreme Court reversed the death sentence and held that in all capital cases, the state must appoint counsel if the defendant has none, as the defendant cannot properly defend himself (*Powell v. Alabama,* 287 U.S.45 (1932)).

* * *

The defendant requested counsel at his trial for robbery and the state refused to provide an attorney at state expense. Although he was too poor to afford an attorney the United States Supreme Court affirmed his conviction and held that the fourteenth amendment does not incorporate the sixth amendment right to counsel in criminal trials unless there are special circumstances (*Betts v. Brady,* 316 U.S. 455 (1942)).

* * *

The defendant, an indigent, was convicted of petty larceny after the court refused to appoint an attorney for him. The United States Supreme Court reversed the conviction and overruled *Betts v. Brady* and held that the sixth amendment right to counsel was incorporated in the fourteenth amendment and that all criminal defendants have the right to counsel and the state must appoint an attorney if the defendant cannot afford one (*Gideon v. Wainwright,* 372 U.S.335 (1963)).

* * *

The defendant was found guilty of driving on a suspended operator's license and was sentenced to one year imprisonment and 1,000 dollar fine. On *appeal* a jury found him guilty and he was sentenced to twelve months in jail and a 100 dollar fine. The defendant was indigent, and his request for assistance of counsel was denied. Was the defendant entitled to counsel?

Yes. When a layman faces possible imprisonment for twelve months, whatever the label of his offense, due process requires that he have the opportunity to defend himself by counsel. The distinction between felonies and misdemeanors is only a matter of designations applied by state law and federal constitutional rights do not hinge on such superficialities. The consequences of a *misdemeanor* conviction may well be more serious than those flowing from many felony convictions. Any incarceration of over thirty days, more or less, will usually result in loss of employment, with a consequent substantial detriment to the defendant and his family (*Marston v. Oliver,* 324 F. Supp. 691 (1971)).

Every court, state or federal, must allow an accused in a criminal proceeding to have his own defense attorney, and if he is too poor to afford an attorney, the government must supply one. If the defendant is denied benefit of counsel at the trial, any conviction obtained is *automatically reversed.*

At an *arraignment* the accused is entitled to the assistance of counsel before he enters a plea of guilty, if the arraignment is a critical stage in the criminal proceeding. In *Hamilton v. Alabama* the United States Supreme Court said, "Whatever may be the function and importance of arraignment in other jurisdictions, we have said enough to show that in Alabama it is a critical stage in the criminal proceeding. What happens there may affect the whole trial. Available defenses may be as irretrievably lost, if not then and there asserted, as they are when accused represented by counsel waives a right for strategic purposes . . . the presence of counsel could have anabled the accused to know all the defenses available to him and to plead intelligently." (*Hamilton v. Alabama,* 368 U.S.52 (1961).)

At stages prior to arraignment, the United States Supreme Court has said that the right to have the assistance of counsel accrues at the police investigation stage whenever a) the investigation is no longer an inquiry into an unsolved crime but has begun to focus on a particular suspect, b) the suspect has been taken into custody, c) the police use a process of interrogation that tends to elicit incriminating statements, d) the suspect has requested counsel and been denied such, or denied communication with retained counsel, and e) the suspect has not been warned of his right against self-incrimination (*Escobedo v. Illinois,* 378 U.S.478 (1964)).

Once it has been determined, under the federal or the state standard, that the accused has a right to counsel, to what extent may this right be exercised? Constitutional and statutory guarantees of right to counsel give the accused the right to communicate and consult freely with counsel prior to and during the trial. This right is subject to restrictions which would be necessary in the interest of maintaining order and security. For example, prison officials often post guards at interviews between an accused and his attorney, to prevent escape by the accused.

Prior to *Escobedo,* there was no right to counsel at the *inves-*

tigatory stages of a criminal case. Now, however, one may generally say that if the suspect requests to see an attorney upon being picked up, the police must allow him to secure an attorney before they can interrogate him. The right to counsel is contained in the *Miranda* warnings (discussed in Chap. 5) and must be given before any interrogation can begin. Recall the *Miranda* warnings: a) the suspect has the right to remain silent, b) anything he says can be used against him in a court of law, c) he has the right to the presence of an attorney before and during interrogation, and d) if he cannot afford an attorney, one will be appointed for him, before the start of the questioning, if he so desires.

6.3. Test of "Criticalness"

The accused is entitled to the assistance of counsel when the state's criminal proceeding is at a "critical stage." This factor is the most important in the determination of when the right to counsel arises.

A critical stage in a criminal proceeding is a point where prejudice to the accused may appear and later be introduced at the trial. One court held that the arraignment and preliminary hearing were not a critical stage of a criminal proceeding and that counsel need not be appointed (*State v. Richardson,* 399 P.2d 799 (1965)). Contrariwise, where the United States Supreme Court said that the arraignment is a critical stage of the criminal proceeding under Alabama state law (*Hamilton v. Alabama,* 368 U.S.52 (1961)). Similarly for preliminary hearing *Coleman v. Alabama,* 399 U.S.1, 1970; *Adams v. Illinois,* 405 U.S.278, 1972.

The name given to a particular stage in a criminal proceeding is not determinative of the criticalness of that stage. Rather, the court looks to the substance, not mere form. In general, then, *any* stage of a criminal proceeding which has the potential of later being detrimental to the accused at trial, is a critical stage (*State v. Jackson,* 400 P.2d 774 (1965)).

6.4. Accusatory Stage of Investigation

A suspect may have the right to counsel as early as the investigatory stage when the investigation has become *accusatory.*

The defendant was arrested for the possession of marijuana, which the police found in his car. He was questioned, and later that evening, while in custody, he confessed to the possession of marijuana. Prior to the confession, the defendant had not been advised of his rights to counsel and to remain silent, nor had there been a knowingly and intelligent waiver of such rights. Had the accusatory stage been reached when the defendant confessed?

Yes. The accusatory stage, that is to say the stage at which the right to counsel accrues, matures when two conditions are met: a) when the officers have arrested the subject, and b) when the officers have undertaken a process of interrogation that levels itself to eliciting imcriminating statements (*People v. Bilderbach,* 401 P.2d 921 (1965)).

The defendant was arrested as a robbery and murder suspect. He was held in custody for five days and interrogated daily, during which time he confessed to the robbery and murder. When the defendant confessed had the investigation reached the accusatory or critical stage?

Yes. The accusatory stage had been reached and the defendant was entitled to counsel. The accusatory stage occurs when the officers arrest the suspect and they interrogate in a manner likely to elicit incriminating statements. Furthermore, the arrest of the suspect is composed of two additional elements, which contribute to the accusatory state, that is, the investigation is no longer a general inquiry, and the suspect is in custody. With respect to the requirement that the interrogation lend itself to eliciting incriminating statements, the court said that it must analyze the situation which surrounds the questioning, including the length of interrogation, the nature of the interrogation, the time and place of the interrogation, and the conduct of the police during the interrogation (*People v. Stewart,* 400 P.2d 97 (1965)).

The defendant was seriously wounded in a gun battle inside a bank. He had been interrogated for about eight minutes at the hospital when he admitted that he fired the gun which killed the police officer. Was the accusatory stage reached?

No. The case was still investigatory in nature. The circumstances required that the defendant be questioned and his identity learned as soon as possible. The defendant was interviewed briefly, with consideration and awareness of his physical condition, and no violation of his right to counsel was shown. The fact that the defendant made the statements while in a wounded state did not require their exclusion (*Commonwealth v. Tracy,* 207 N.E.2d 16 (1965)).

> On a proper search warrant, stolen items were found in the defendants' apartment. The defendants were subsequently questioned and arrested. Were the statements made to the police officers, after the search, the result of questions asked which were accusatory in nature?

No. The inquiries were threshold in character and as such were investigatory, not accusatory. The questions gave the defendants opportunity to explain the circumstances they were in and as such, assisted the officers in determining whether the defendants were connected with the stolen items. The preliminary inquiries by the police did not suggest that they were carrying out an interrogation for the purpose of eliciting incriminating statements, notwithstanding the fact the statements were incriminating (*Commonwealth v. Lepore,* 207 N.E.2d 26 (1965)).

6.5. Police Duty During Investigation

6.5.1. RIGHT TO COUNSEL. Generally, before an arresting officer may begin interrogation of a person who is the focal suspect of a crime, the suspect must be advised of his right against self-incrimination, right to counsel, and right to be given counsel if indigent. One court held that in the absence of being given such information and assistance, the accused *could not intelligently waive his rights,* and a confession obtained in such a situation would be inadmissible. Moreover, the court said that a suspect who has never had any prior experience with the criminal process would not be expected to know of the help counsel could offer and would not demand such assistance and, as such be denied the constitutional right to counsel (*State v. Neely,* 398 P.2d 482 (1965)).

> The defendant was arrested for the murder of his brother-in-law. While he was being interrogated he repeatedly asked to speak to his lawyer, to which the police replied that his lawyer did not want to see him. Also during the interrogation his lawyer asked to see him and was told, "not until we are through interrogating him." Accord-

ingly, the defendant was not allowed to consult with his attorney during the entire interrogation. At no time was the defendant advised of his constitutional rights. Was the defendant denied his constitutional right to the assistance of counsel?

Yes. Although the interrogation took place before the defendant was formally indicted, the court said that where, as in this case, a) the investigation is no longer a general inquiry into an unsolved crime but has begun to *focus* on a particular suspect, b) the suspect has been taken into police custody, c) the police carry out a process of interrogation that lends itself to eliciting incriminating statements, d) the suspect has requested and been denied an opportunity to consult with his lawyer, and e) the police have not effectively warned him of his absolute constitutional right to remain silent, the accused has been denied the assistance of counsel in violation of the sixth amendment and as a result no statement elicited by the police during the interrogation may be used against him at a criminal trial (*Escobedo v. Illinios*, 378 U.S.478 (1964)).

> Defendant's conviction for malicious assault with a deadly weapon, resulting in death, was based on incriminating statements made to jail officers by defendant, who did not have counsel and was not advised of his right to counsel or to remain silent. Was defendant's confession properly admitted into evidence?

No. The defendant's constitutional rights were violated. At the time the statements were made, the police investigation had matured into the accusatory stage. In determining if the accusatory stage has been reached, one must be careful not to interfere with police investigation of an unsolved crime. Here, however, the investigation had focussed on the defendant as a suspect. The court said a confession would be inadmissible into evidence if a) the investigation was no longer an inquiry into an unsolved crime but began to focus on a suspect, b) the suspect in question was in custody, c) the suspect was not informed of his right to counsel or to remain silent and there was no waiver of these rights and d) the interrogation process lent itself to the eliciting of incriminating statements (*People v. Dorado*, 398 P.2d 361 (1965)).

> The defendant gave oral and written confessions to sheriff's depu-

ties while in custody as a suspect. He subsequently was prosecuted for grand theft. Should the defendant have been warned of his constitutional rights before interrogation?

Yes. When there is the possibility of denial of the right to counsel and where there is a threat of the right against self-incrimination, the suspect should be warned of his rights. When one is in custody at the accusatory stage, the officer must choose between advising the defendant of his rights or not being allowed to introduce the statements into evidence, for police authorities may not use any statement, voluntary or not, made by the accused in custody when the accusatory stage is reached, unless a) the accused has waived his right to counsel and his right to remain silent *and* b) the statements then made are voluntary and made with full knowledge of the constitutional rights involved (*People v. White,* 43 CAL.RPTR. 905 (1965)).

> The defendant was indicted by the grand jury for raping a four-year-old girl. While awaiting trial, a police investigator took him out of the jail cell and interrogated him. When the investigator asked why he did it, the defendant replied, "I don't know why." Was defendant denied his right to counsel when he made the incriminating statement?

Yes. Although the defendant had not requested counsel, the facts showed that, a) he was not experienced in criminal procedure, b) his intellectual abilities were at the low end of the normal range, c) he did not have much ability to function under stress, and d) he was subjected to a lengthy interrogation by a skillful law enforcement officer trying to obtain a confession. The interrogation was at the accusatory stage and the defendant was denied his constitutional right to counsel. Moreover, the court said that not all cases involving admission or confession require the assistance of counsel but that each case must be judged on its own facts (*Cooper v. Commonwealth,* 140 S.E.2d 688 (1965)).

> The defendant allegedly requested counsel but was turned down. Six days later he was interrogated by the prosecutor without being advised of his right to remain silent and without the assistance of counsel. During the interrogation the defendant made incriminating statements about a burglary. Was the defendant denied his constitutional right to the assistance of counsel?

Yes. If the investigation was no longer a general inquiry into an unsolved crime but had begun to focus on the defendant as a suspect, and if he had requested and was denied counsel, the incriminating statements made by him, during an interrogation where he was denied his constitutional right to counsel, could not be used against him (*Wright v. Dickson*, 336 F.2d 878 (1964)).

> The defendant was arrested by police officers in connection with a robbery. He was interrogated by a police officer who did not advise him of his right to remain silent. He did not have or request counsel, nor was he offered such assistance. The defendant not only admitted the robbery, but also admitted the killing of a policeman. Was the defendant denied his right to counsel when he admitted killing the police officer?

No. When the defendant admitted killing the policeman, he was under investigation for another crime (robbery); the killing was not the main focal point of the interrogation. Later, when the defendant was interrogated with respect to the killing, he was offered the assistance of counsel which he rejected, and such constituted an intelligent waiver (*Commonwealth v. Coyle*, 203 A.2d 782 (1964)).

6.5.2. COMMUNICATION WITH COUNSEL. The following three case examples deal with the right of a suspect to communicate with his counsel during police interrogation. In a number of cases the refusal by the police to honor the suspect's request for communication with his counsel has been held to violate his constitutional right to the assistance of counsel and as such, renders any statement made during the interrogation inadmissible in evidence.

> The defendant was arrested at 1:00 AM and gave a voluntary confession from 2:58 to 4:45 AM. Counsel for the defendant arrived at 3:00 AM while the police were taking the statement. He requested to see the defendant several times but was denied access to him. Was the statement taken properly admitted into evidence?

No. Even though the confession taken by the police was voluntary it should not have been admitted because the defendant was denied access to his counsel until the statement was completed. Police should permit counsel to have access to the defendant when counsel so requests. (*People v. Failla,* 199 N.E.2d 366 (1964).)

The defendant was arrested for operating a motor vehicle while under the influence of liquor and for failure to keep to the right. The police refused to allow him to telephone his counsel while he was being interrogated. Was defendant denied his constitutional right to counsel?

No. Before the accused's right to counsel can be recognized here, the following conditions must have been met:

1. A request must have been made by either the defendant or his attorney to communicate with the other and such was refused.
2. At the time of request, the defendant's mental faculties, in view of his sobriety or lack of sobriety, were such that he was able to communicate that he could understand and make himself understood in relation to the matter at hand (in determining such, one *might* employ the "totality of the circumstances" test, which includes: the age of the defendant, the character of the defendant, the situation, and whether free choice to refuse to talk was exercised by the defendant (*Duncan v. State,* 176 So.2d 840 (1965)).
3. The police at the time in question had completed their interrogation and medical examination. The court said that if all three conditions were found to have existed, the constitutional rights of the defendant had been violated and he should not be found guilty (*State v. Morrocco,* 203 A.2d 161 (1964)).

The defendant was charged with breach of the peace and resisting arrest after she caused a crowd to gather in a parking lot where she had been screaming and threatening to commit suicide. At the police station the defendant was denied the use of the telephone to call her lawyer and doctor. Were defendant's constitutional rights violated in this case?

No. The denial of the use of the telephone to call a doctor, relatives, and friends does not infringe on any right guaranteed by the constitution. Because of the defendant's physical and mental condition, she was unable to properly communicate and use a telephone. Furthermore, there was nothing in the record to show that the police had interrogated her. (This is *not* to say that the police could not have called counsel or relatives for her.) (*State v. Lillis*, 203 A.2d 313 (1964).)

6.6. Request for Counsel

The majority of the courts in the past, through somewhat circular reasoning, have held that the defendant must request the assistance of counsel before the constitutional right accrues; however, since *Miranda* (see Chap. 5, the *Miranda* Standard), it is a matter of constitutional law that the accused be informed of his right to counsel and supplied with counsel if he is unable to afford such when the accusatory stage of the proceedings have been reached.

6.7. Waiver

A person accused of a crime may waive his right to assistance of counsel if the waiver is given voluntarily, knowingly and intelligently, and the person is sufficiently informed as to the extent of the rights he is waiving.

> After arrest the defendant was told of his right to consult with an attorney and that anything he said would be held against him. He said that he did not want an attorney. Should the court have appointed an attorney for the defendant?

No. The defendant did not request counsel of his own, or any counsel, in fact, he stated that he did not want a lawyer. His confession later was voluntarily made and was not made inadmissible because he did not have counsel at the time he made it. If at any later state in the proceeding he had asked for the assistance of counsel, his right would "reattach." If he was *then* denied counsel, anything he would subsequently say would be inadmissible in evidence (*Powers v. State*, 402 P.2d 328 (1965)).

> The defendant confessed to a crime without the benefit of counsel. Later, with the advice of competent counsel, he voluntarily entered his plea of guilty to the charge of murder. Was he denied his constitutional right to counsel at any time during the proceeding?

No. The constitutional protections are primarily concerned with those who profess their innocence. They protect the innocent against the possibility of conviction of a crime he did not commit. The court held that where one accused of murder voluntarily pleads guilty upon arraignment, in open court, with the advice of competent counsel, the federal constitutional right to counsel is not violated. Notwithstanding the fact that the accused, before entering the guilty plea and at the preliminary hearing, was without counsel when he confessed to the crime (*Rainsberger v. State,* 399 P.2d 129 (1965)).

> A 17-year-old defendant of limited education and mental capacity said that he did not want to have the assistance of counsel and subsequently plead guilty to a charge of murder. Was the defendant denied the constitutional right to counsel?

Yes. When a person convicted in a state court has not intelligently and understandingly waived the benefit of counsel and where the circumstances show that his rights could not have been fairly protected without counsel, the Due Process Clause invalidates his conviction (*Moore v. Michigan,* 355 U.S.155 (1957)).

> An eighteen-year-old defendant pleaded guilty to being an accessory. He showed evidence of illiteracy and waived the right to counsel. Was the waiver valid?

No. The combination of circumstances of the youth of the accused, the complexity of the offense charged and the defectiveness of the information made the waiver of right to counsel by the defendant invalid. (*People v. Hardin,* 24 Cal.Rptr. 563 (1962)).

6.8. Guards, Jailers, and Privacy

The placement of prison guards in a room designated for consultation between the accused and his counsel may violate the right of the accused to the assistance of counsel.

> The defendants were denied the privilege of consulting with their attorneys, in that the sheriff refused to permit any conversation between them except in his presence. Was the constitutional right to the assistance of counsel of the defendants denied?

Yes. The demand of the constitution that one accused of a crime shall be accorded the benefit of counsel is not satisfied when the officer having the prisoner in custody requires that he be present at the interview. The law contemplates a private and confidential communication between the attorney and client. It seals the mouth of this attorney. His client may freely disclose to him all pertinent matters, but if they are heard by the sheriff, his mouth is not sealed. A communication ceases to be privileged when uttered in the presence of a third party. The insistence that the sheriff be present amounts to a denial of the privilege guaranteed by the constitution. (*Turner v. State,* 241 S.W.162 (1922); *Coplon v. U.S.,* 191 F.2d 749 (1951)).

> The defendants were indicted for murder and could not consult with counsel without an interpreter. When counsel requested permission to consult with defendants through an interpreter of his choosing, the sheriff and prosecuting attorney said he could on condition that another interpreter, selected by the prosecuting attorney and sheriff, be present. Were defendants denied their constitutional right to counsel?

Yes. As due process of law means a course of legal proceedings which must proceed according to established procedure and the aid of legal advise, and means of investigating the charge against the accused, it would be a denial of the constitutional rights of one who is held in prison and accused of a crime, to refuse counsel an opportunity to talk with him, unless someone else is present who may listen to what is said by the accused to his counsel. The accused in custody should be granted an opportunity to be alone with his attorney at reasonable hours, but within the sight of the officer or in a place where an escape could not occur (*Louie Yung v. Coleman,* 5 F. Supp. 702 (1934)).

> The defendant sat at counsel's table, located two feet away from and facing the trial jury, which enabled some of the jury to overhear certain defense conferences between the defendant and his counsel. Was the right to counsel infringed upon?

No. In the courtroom, both client and attorney are conscious of the presence of the jury and necessarily must know from the location of the jury box whether or not their conversations will be overheard. The necessity for conferring at the counsel table in a dim voice may have been an inconvenience, but it did not infringe upon any federal constitutional right (*U.S. v. Fay,* 230 F. Supp. 942 (1964)).

The defendant was forced to consult with his attorney in low tones as a federal correction officer refused to leave the room, which was twelve feet wide and twenty feet long. Was the defendant's right to counsel infringed upon?

No. The right of an accused to consult with his attorney in private is not one without some limitations, here counsel asked the client all of the questions he would have asked had there been no one in the room with them. Furthermore, whatever the officer may have overheard was not communicated to the government prosecutor and it did not appear that the defense of the defendant was prejudiced. The need for conferring in a low voice was an inconvenience but not an infringement on constitutional rights. Counsel had adequate time (four days) to make arrangements for another conference without the guard present (*Krull v. U.S.*, 240 F.2d 122 (1957)).

6.9. Lineups

The identification of the accused in a police lineup is a "critical" stage in a criminal proceeding, and as such, the accused has a right to the assistance of counsel.

After the defendant had been indicted and arrested for the robbery of a federally insured bank, an F.B.I. agent arranged to have bank employees observe a lineup of the defendant and six other men. Each man in the lineup was required to wear strips of tape on his face and repeat certain words as the robber had done. Counsel appointed for the defendant was not notified of the lineup. Subsequently, at the trial, the bank employees identified the defendant in direct examination as the robber. Was the defendant denied his constitutional right to counsel during the lineup?

Yes. Today's law enforcement machinery involves critical confrontations of the accused by the prosecutors at pretrial proceedings where the results might settle the fate of the accused and reduce the trial to a mere formality. The sixth amendment guarantee encompasses the assistance of counsel whenever necessary to assume a meaningful defense. The court said, "Since it appears that there is grave potential for prejudice, intentional or not, in the pre-trial lineup, which may not be capable of reconstruction at trial, and since presence of counsel itself can often avert prejudice and assure a meaningful confrontation at trial, there can be little doubt that for Wade the post-indictment line-up was a critical stage of the prosecution at which he was 'as much entitled to such aid . . . as at the trial itself.' Thus both Wade and his counsel should have been notified of the impending lineup, and counsel's presence should have been a requisite to conduct of the lineup, absent an 'intelligent waiver.' " (*U.S. v. Wade,* 388 U.S.218 (1967).)

6.10. Juvenile Court Proceedings

The United States Supreme Court has upheld the right to the assistance of counsel in juvenile court proceedings.

> A fifteen-year-old boy was committed as a juvenile delinquent. No notice was given to the boy's parents that he was being taken into custody. No petition alleging the delinquency was ever served. Furthermore, the court did not advise the boy or his parents of the right to counsel, that he did not have to testify or that any statement he might make could result in commitment as a delinquent. Were the constitutional guarantees of the boy violated?

Yes. The Due Process Clause of the fourteenth amendment requires that in respect of proceedings to determine delinquency which may result in commitment to an institution in which the juvenile's freedom is curtailed, the child and his parents must be notified of the child's right to be represented by counsel, that counsel will be appointed to represent the child.

The court held that the juvenile had been denied due process of law which for juveniles includes the following: a) written notice of the specific charges given to the family in adequate time for preparation for hearing, b) notification of the child's right to counsel and the availability of court-appointed counsel if they are unable to afford such, c) warning of privilege against self-incrimination, and d) absence of a valid confession, a commitment to delinquency must be preluded by sworn testimony and opportunity to cross-examination by the counsel for the child at the hearing (*In Re Gault,* 387 U.S.1 (1967)).

Certain constitutional requirements attendant upon state criminal proceedings have equal application to a state juvenile proceeding which is adjudicative in nature. Some of the rights available to juveniles are the following: a) right to appropriate notice, b) right to counsel, c) right to confrontation and cross-examination, d) privilege against self-incrimination, and e) a standard of proof beyond a reasonable doubt.

In a recent case, *McKeiver v. Pennsylvania,* the court said that trial by jury is not available as a matter of constitutional right in *juvenile* court's adjudicative stage.

> The imposition of the jury would not strengthen greatly, if at all, the fact-finding function, and would, contrarily, provide an attrition of the juvenile court's assumed ability to function in a unique manner. . . . If the jury trial were to be injected into the juvenile court system as a matter of right, it would bring with it into that system the traditional delay, the formality and the clamor of the adversary system and, possibly, the public trial. . . . If the formalities of the criminal adjudicative process are to be superimposed upon the juvenile court system, there is little need for its separate existence. Perhaps that ultimate dissolutionment will come one day, but for the moment we are disinclined to give impetus to it. (*McKeiver v. Pennsylvania,* 403 U.S.528 (1971).)

6.11. Remedies

Some of the remedies available when the defendant's right to communicate with his attorney has been abridged are habeas corpus, mandamus or mandatory injunction requiring the authorities to allow the defendant to have a private conference with his attorney, motion for continuance, new trial, dismissal, or contempt or criminal proceedings against the officer or jailer who infringed upon the constitutional right.

Section 7. QUOTED CASES

7.1. Escobedo v. Illinois

Mr. Justice Goldberg delivered the opinion of the Court.

The critical question in this case is whether, under the circumstances, the refusal by the police to honor petitioner's request to consult with his lawyer during the course of an interrogation constitutes a denial of "the Assistance of Counsel" in violation of the sixth amendment to the Constitution as "made obligatory upon the states by the fourteenth amendment," *Gideon*

Note: *Escobedo v. Illinois,* 378 U.S.478 (1964).

v. Wainwright, 372 U.S.335, 342, and thereby renders inadmissible in a state criminal trial any incriminating statement elicited by the police during the interrogation.

On the night of January 19, 1960, petitioner's brother-in-law was fatally shot. In the early hours of the next morning, at 2:30 AM, petitioner was arrested without a warrant and interrogated. Petitioner made no statement to the police and was released at 5:00 that afternoon pursuant to a state court writ of habeas corpus obtained by Mr. Warren Wolfson, a lawyer who had been retained by petitioner.

On January 30, Benedict DiGerlando, who was then in police custody and who was later indicted for the murder along with petitioner, told the police that petitioner had fired the fatal shots. Between 8:00 and 9:00 that evening, petitioner and his sister, the widow of the deceased, were arrested and taken to police headquarters. En route to the police station, the police "had handcuffed the defendant behind his back," and "one of the arresting officers told defendant that DiGerlando had named him as the one who shot" the deceased. Petitioner testified, without contradiction, that the "detectives said they had us pretty well, up pretty tight, and we might as well admit to this crime," and that he replied, "I am sorry but I would like to have advice from my lawyer." A police officer testified that although petitioner was not formally charged "he was in custody" and "couldn't walk out the door."

Shortly after pelitioner reached police headquarters, his retained lawyer arrived. The lawyer described the ensuing events in the following terms:

> On that day I received a phone call [from "the mother of another defendant"] and pursuant to that phone call I went to the Detective Bureau at 11th and State. The first person I talked to was the Sergeant on duty at the Bureau Desk, Sergeant Pidgeon. I asked Sergeant Pidgeon for permission to speak to my client, Danny Escobedo. Sergeant Pidgeon made a call to the Bureau lockup and informed me that the boy had been taken from the lockup to the Homicide Bureau. This was between 9:30 and 10:00 in the evening. Before I went anywhere, he called the Homicide Bureau and told them there as an attorney waiting to see Escobedo. He told me I could not see him. Then I went upstairs to the Homicide Bureau. There were several Homicide De-

tectives around and I talked to them. I identified myself as Escobedo's attorney and asked permission to see him. They said I could not. The police officer told me to see Chief Flynn who was on duty. I identified myself to Chief Flynn and asked permission to see my client. He said I could not. I think it was approximately 11:00. He said I couldn't see him because they hadn't completed questioning. [F]or a second or two I spotted him in an office in the Homicide Bureau. The door was open and I could see through the office. I waved to him and he waved back and then the door was closed, by one of the officers at Homicide.* There were four or five officers milling around the Homicide Detail that night. As to whether I talked to Captain Flynn any later that day, I waited around for another hour or two and went back again and renewed by [*sic*] request to see my client. He again told me I could not. I filed an official complaint with Commissioner Phelan of the Chicago Police Department. I had a conversation with every police officer I could find. I was told at Homicide that I couldn't see him and I would have to get a writ of habeas corpus. I left the Homicide Bureau and from the Detective Bureau at 11th and State at approximately 1:00 AM [Sunday morning] I had no opportunity to talk to my client that night. I quoted to Captain Flynn the Section of the Criminal Code which allows an attorney the right to see his client.

Petitioner testified that during the course of the interrogation he repeatedly asked to speak to his lawyer and that the police said that his lawyer "didn't want to see" him. The testimony of the police officers confirmed these accounts in substantial detail.

Notwithstanding repeated requests by each, petitioner and his retained lawyer were afforded no opportunity to consult during the course of the entire interrogation. At one point, as previously noted, petitioner and his attorney came into each other's view for a few moments but the attorney was quickly ushered away. Petitioner testified "that he heard a detective telling the attorney the latter would not be allowed to talk to [him] 'until they were done' " and that he heard the attorney being refused permission to remain in the adjoining room. A police officer testified that he had told the lawyer that he could not see petitioner until "we were through interrogating" him.

There is testimony by the police that during the interroga-

---

* Petitioner testified that this ambiguous gesture "could have meant most anything," but that he "took it upon [his] own to think that [the lawyer was telling him] not to say anything," and that the lawyer "wanted to talk" to him.

tion, petitioner, a twenty-two-year-old of Mexican extraction with no record of previous experience with the police, "was handcuffed" in a standing position and that he "was nervous, he had circles under his eyes and he was upset" and was "agitated" because "he had not slept well in over a week."

It is undisputed that during the course of the interrogation Officer Montejano, who "grew up" in petitioner's neighborhood, who knew his family, and who uses "Spanish language in [his] police work," conferred alone with petitioner "for about a quarter of an hour." Petitioner testified that the officer said to him "in Spanish that my sister and I could go home if I pinned it on Benedict DiGerlando," that "he would see to it that we would go home and be held only as witnesses, if anything, if we had made a statement against DiGerlando, that we would be able to go home that night." Petitioner testified that he made the statement in issue because of this assurance. Officer Montejano denied offering any such assurance.

A police officer testified that during the interrogation the following occurred:

> I informed him of what DiGerlando told me and when I did, he told me that DiGerlando was [lying] and I said, "Would you care to tell DiGerlando that?" and he said, "Yes, I will." So, I brought Escobedo in and he confronted DiGerlando and he told him that he was lying and said, "I didn't shoot Manuel, you did it."

In this way, petitioner, for the first time admitted to some knowledge of the crime. After that he made additional statements further implicating himself in the murder plot. At this point an Assistant State's Attorney, Theodore J. Cooper, was summoned "to take" a statement. Mr. Cooper, an experienced lawyer who was assigned to the Homicide Division to take "statements from some defendants and some prisoners that they had in custody," "took" petitioner's statement by asking carefully framed questions apparently designed to assure the admissibility into evidence of the resulting answers. Mr. Cooper testified that he did not advise petitioner of his constitutional rights, and it is undisputed that no one during the course of the interrogation so advised him.

Petitioner moved both before and during trial to suppress

the incriminating statement, but the motions were denied. Petitioner was convicted of murder and he appealed the conviction. . . . that "a Constitution which guarantees a defendant the aid of counsel at trial could surely vouchsafe no less to an indicted defendant under interrogation by the police in a completely extrajudicial proceeding. Anything less might deny a defendant 'effective representation by counsel at the only stage when legal aid and advice would help him.' " *Id.,* 377 U.S., at 204, 84 S.Ct., at 1202, quoting Douglas, J., concurring in *Spano v. New York,* 360 U.S.315, 326.

The interrogation here was conducted before petitioner was formally indicted. But in the context of this case, that fact should make no difference. When petitioner requested, and was denied, an opportunity to consult with his lawyer, the investigation had ceased to be a general investigation of "an unsolved crime." *Spano v. New York,* 360 U.S.315, 327 (Stewart, J., concurring). Petitioner had become the accused, and the purpose of the interrogation was to "get him" to confess his guilt despite his constitutional right not to do so. At the time of his arrest and throughout the course of the interrogation, the police told petitioner that they had convincing evidence that he had fired the fatal shots. Without informing him of his absolute right to remain silent in the face of this accusation, the police urged him to make a statement. As this Court observed many years ago:

> It cannot be doubted that, placed in the position in which the accused was when the statement was made to him that the other suspected person had charged him with crime, the result was to produce upon his mind the fear that, if he remained silent, it would be considered an admission of guilt, and therefore render certain his being committed for trial as the guilty person, and it cannot be conceived that the converse impression would not also have naturally arisen that, by denying, there was hope of removing the suspicion from himself (*Bram v. U.S.,* 168 U.S.532, 562).

Petitioner, a layman, was undoubtedly unaware that under Illinois law an admission of "mere" complicity in the murder plot was legally as damaging as an admission of firing of the fatal shots. *Illinois v. Escobedo,* 28 Ill.2d 41, 190 N.E.2d 825. The "guiding hand of counsel" was essential to advise petitioner of his rights in this delicate situation. *Powell v. Alabama*, 287 U.S.45, 69. This was the "stage when legal aid and advice" were most critical to petitioner (*Massiah v. U.S., supra*, 377 U.S., at 204). It was a stage surely as critical as was the arraignment in *Hamilton v. Alabama*, 368 U.S.52 and the preliminary hearing in *White v. Maryland*, 373 U.S.59. What happened at this interrogation could certainly "affect the whole trial," *Hamilton v. Alabama, supra*, 368 U.S. at 54, since rights "may be as irretrievably lost, if not then and there asserted, as they are when an accused represented by counsel waives a right for strategic purposes." *Ibid.* It would exalt form over substance to make the right to counsel, under these circumstances, depend on whether at the time of the interrogation, the authorities had secured a formal indictment. Petitioner had, for all practical purposes, already been charged with murder.

The New York Court of Appeals, whose decisions this Court cited with approval in *Massiah*, 377 U.S.201, at 205, has recently recognized that, under circumstances such as those here, no meaningful distinction can be drawn between interrogation of an accused before and after formal indictment. In *People v. Donovan*, 193 N.E.2d 628, that court, in an opinion by Judge Fuld, held that a "confession taken from a defendant, during a period of detention [prior to indictment], after his attorney had requested and been denied access to him" could not be used against him in a criminal trial (*Id.*, 193 N.E.2d at 629). The court observed that it "would be highly incongruous if our system of justice permitted the district attorney, the lawyer representing the state, to extract a confession from the accused while his own lawyer, seeking to speak with him was kept from him by the police." *Id.*, 193 N.E.2d at 629.

In *Gideon v. Wainwright*, 372 U.S.335, we held that every person accused of a crime, whether state or federal, is entitled to a lawyer at trial. The rule sought by the state here, however, would make the trial no more than an appeal from the interrogation; and the "right to use counsel at the formal trial [would be] a very hollow thing [if], for all practical purposes, the conviction is already assured by pre-trial examination." In re *Groban*, 352 U.S.330, 344 (Black, J., dissenting). "One can imagine a cynical prosecutor saying: 'Let them have the most illustrious counsel, now. They can't escape the noose. There is nothing that counsel can do for them at the trial.' " Ex parte Sullivan, D.C., 107 F. Supp. 514, 517-518.

It is argued that if the right to counsel is afforded prior to indictment, the number of confessions obtained by the police will diminish significantly, because most confessions are obtained during the period between arrest and indictment, and "any lawyer worth his salt will tell the suspect in no uncertain terms to make no statement to police under any circumstances" (*Watts v. Indiana,* 338 U.S.49, 59). (Jackson, J., concurring in part and dissenting in part.) This argument, of course, cuts two ways. The fact that many confessions are obtained during this period points up its critical nature as a "stage when legal aid and advice" are surely needed (*Massiah v. U.S., supra,* 377 U.S. at 204, 84 S.Ct. at 1202; *Hamilton v. Alabama, supra; White v. Maryland, supra*). The right to counsel would indeed be hollow if it began at a period when few confessions were obtained. There is necessarily a direct relationship between the importance of a stage to the police in their quest for a confession and the criticalness of that stage to the accused in his need for legal advice. Our Constitution, unlike some others, strikes the balance in favor of the right of the accused to be advised by his lawyer of his privilege against self-incrimination.

We have learned the lesson of history, ancient and modern, that a system of criminal law enforcement which comes to depend on the "confession" will, in the long run, be less reliable and more subject to abuses than a system which depends on extrinsic evidence independently secured through skillful investigation. As Dean Wigmore so wisely said:

> [A]*ny system of administration which permits the prosecution to trust habitually to compulsory self-disclosure as a source of proof must itself suffer morally thereby.* The inclination develops to rely mainly upon such evidence, and to be satisfied with an incomplete investigation of the other sources. The exercise of the power to extract answers begets a forgetfulness of the just limitations of that power. The simple and peaceful process of questioning breeds a readiness to resort to bullying and to physical force and torture. If there is a right to an answer, there soon seems to be a right to the expected answer, that is, to a

confession of guilt. Thus the legitimate use grows into the unjust abuse; ultimately, the innocent are jeopardized by the encroachments of a bad system. Such seems to have been the course of experience in those legal systems where the privilege was not recognized. 8 Wigmore, Evidence (3d ed. 1940), 309. (Emphasis in original.)

This Court also has recognized that "history amply shows that confessions have often been extorted to save law enforcement officials the trouble and effort of obtaining valid and independent evidence." *Haynes v. Washington,* 373 U.S.503, 519.

We have also learned the companion lesson of history that no system of criminal justice can, or should, survive if it comes to depend for its continued effectiveness on the citizens' abdication through unawareness of their constitutional rights. No system worth preserving should have to *fear* that if an accused is permitted to consult with a lawyer, he will become aware of, and exercise, these rights. If the exercise of constitutional rights will thwart the effectiveness of a system of law enforcement, then there is something very wrong with that system.

We hold, therefore, that where, as here, the investigation is no longer a general inquiry into an unsolved crime but has begun to focus on a particular suspect, the suspect has been taken into police custody, the police carry out a process of interrogations that lends itself to eliciting incriminating statements, the suspect has requested and been denied an opportunity to consult with his lawyer, and the police have not effectively warned him of his absolute constitutional right to remain silent, the accused has been denied "the assistance of counsel" in violation of the sixth amendment to the Constitution as "made obligatory upon the states by the fourteenth amendment," *Gideon v. Wainwright,* 372 U.S., at 342, and that no statement elicited by the police during the interrogation may be used against him at a criminal trial. . . .

Reversed and remanded.

7.2. U. S. v. Wade

Mr. Justice Brennan delivered the opinion of the Court.

The question here is whether courtroom identifications of an

Note: U.S. v. Wade, 388 U.S.218 (1967).

accused at trial are to be excluded from evidence because the accused was exhibited to the witnesses before trial at a post-indictment lineup conducted for identification purposes without notice to and in the absence of the accused's appointed counsel.

The federally insured bank in Eustace, Texas, was robbed on September 21, 1964. A man with a small strip of tape on each side of his face entered the bank, pointed a pistol at the female cashier and the vice president, the only persons in the bank at the time, and forced them to fill a pillowcase with the bank's money. The man then drove away with an accomplice who had been waiting in a stolen car outside the bank. On March 23, 1965, an indictment was returned against respondent, Wade, and two others for conspiring to rob the bank, and against Wade and the accomplice for the robbery itself. Wade was arrested on April 2, and counsel was appointed to represent him on April 26. Fifteen days later an F.B.I. agent, without notice to Wade's lawyer, arranged to have the two bank employees observe a lineup made up of Wade and five or six other prisoners and conducted in a courtroom of the local county courthouse. Each person in the line wore strips of tape such as allegedly worn by the robber and upon direction each said something like "put the money in the bag," the words allegedly uttered by the robber. Both bank employees identified Wade in the lineup as the bank robber.

At trial, the two employees, when asked on direct examination if the robber was in the courtroom, pointed to Wade. The prior lineup identification was then elicited from both employees on cross-examination. At the close of testimony, Wade's counsel moved for a judgment of acquittal or, alternatively, to strike the bank officials' courtroom identifications on the ground that conduct of the lineup, without notice to and in the absence of his appointed counsel, violated his fifth amendment privilege against self-incrimination and his sixth amendment right to the assistance of counsel. The motion was denied, and Wade was convicted. The Court of Appeals for the Fifth Circuit reversed the conviction and ordered a new trial at which the in-court identification evidence was to be excluded, holding that, though the lineup did not violate Wade's fifth amendment rights, "the lineup, held as it was, in the absence of counsel, already chosen to represent appellant, was a violation of his sixth amendment rights. . . ." 358 F.2d 557, 560. . . .

We reverse the judgment of the Court of Appeals. . . .

Neither the lineup itself nor anything shown by this record that Wade was required to do in the lineup violated his privilege against self-incrimination. We have only recently reaffirmed that the privilege "protects an accused only from being compelled to testify against himself, or otherwise provide the state with evidence of a testimonial or communicative nature. . . ." *Schmerber v. California*, 384 U.S.757, 761. We there held that compelling a suspect to submit to a withdrawal of a sample of his blood for analysis for alcohol content and the admission in evidence of the analysis report were not compulsion to those ends. That holding was supported by the opinion in *Holt v. U.S.*, 218 U.S.245, in which case a question arose as to whether a blouse belonged to the defendant. A witness testified at trial that the defendant put on the blouse and it had fit him. The defendant argued that the admission of the testimony was error because compelling him to put on the blouse was a violation of his privilege. The court rejected the claim as "an extravagant extension of the fifth amendment." Mr. Justice Holmes saying for the Court:

> [T]he prohibition of compelling a man in a criminal court to be witness against himself is a prohibition of the use of physical or moral compulsion to extort communications from him, not an exclusion of his body as evidence when it may be material (218 U.S., at 252-253) .

The court in *Holt*, however, put aside any constitutional questions which might be involved in compelling an accused, as here, to exhibit himself before victims of or witnesses to an alleged crime; the court stated, "we need not consider how far a court would go in compelling a man to exhibit himself." *Id.*, at 253.

We have no doubt that compelling the accused merely to exhibit his person for observation by a prosecution witness prior to trial involves no compulsion of the accused to give evidence having testimonial significance. It is compulsion of the accused to exhibit his physical characteristics, not compulsion to disclose any knowledge he might have. It is no different from compelling Schmerber to provide a blood sample or Holt to wear the blouse, and, as in those instances, is not within the cover of the privilege. Similarly, compelling Wade to speak within hearing distance of the witnesses, even to utter words purportedly uttered by the robber, was not compulsion to utter statements of a "testimonial" nature; he was required to use his voice as an identifying physical characteristic, not to speak his guilt. We held in *Schmerber, supra,* 384 U.S. at 761, that the distinction to be drawn under the fifth amendment privilege against self-incrimination is one between an accused's "communications" in whatever form, vocal or physical, and "compulsion which makes a suspect or accused the source of 'real or physical evidence,' " *Schmerber, supra,* 384 U.S. at 764. We recognized that "both federal and state courts have usually held that . . . [the privilege] offers no protection against compulsion to submit to fingerprinting, photography, or measurements, to write or speak for identification, to appear in court, to stand, to assume a stance, to walk, or to make a particular gesture." *Id.,* at 764. None of these activities becomes testimonial within the scope of the privilege because required of the accused in a pretrial lineup.

Moreover, it deserves emphasis that this case presents no question of the admissibility in evidence of anything Wade said or did at the lineup which implicates his privilege. The Government offered no such evidence as part of its case, and what came out about the lineup proceedings on Wade's cross-examination of the back employees involved no violation of Wade's privilege.

The fact that the lineup involved no violation of Wade's privilege against self-incrimination does not, however, dispose of his contention that the courtroom identifications should have been excluded because the lineup was conducted without notice to, and in the absence of, his counsel. Our rejection of the right to counsel claim in *Schmerber* rested on our conclusion in that case that "[n]o issue of counsel's ability to assist the petitioner in respect of any rights he did possess is presented." 384 U.S., at 766. In contrast, in this case it is urged that the assistance of counsel at the lineup was indispensable to protect Wade's most basic right as a criminal defendant—his right to a fair trial at which the witnesses against him might be meaningfully cross-examined.

. . .

. . . our cases have construed the sixth amendment guarantee to apply to "critical" stages of the proceedings. The guarantee reads: "In all criminal prosecutions, the accused shall enjoy the right . . . to have the assistance of counsel *for his defense."* (Emphasis supplied.) The plain wording of this guarantee thus encompasses counsel's assistance whenever necessary to assure a meaningful "defense."

As early as *Powell v. Alabama, supra,* we recognized that the period from arraignment to trial was "perhaps the most critical period of the proceedings . . . ," *Id.* at 57, during which the accused "requires the guiding hand of counsel . . . ," *Id.* at 69, if the guarantee is not to prove an empty right. That principle has since been applied to require the assistance of counsel at the type of arraignment, for example, that provided by Alabama— where certain rights might be sacrificed or lost: "What happens there may affect the whole trial. Available defenses may be irretrievably lost, if not then and there asserted. . . ." *Hamilton v. Alabama,* 368 U.S.52, 54. See *White v. Maryland,* 373 U.S.59. The principle was also applied in *Massiah v. U.S.,* 377 U.S.201, where we held that incriminating statements of the defendant should have been excluded from evidence when it appeared that they were overheard by federal agents who, without notice to the defendant's lawyer, arranged a meeting between the defendant and an accomplice turned informant. We said, quoting a concurring opinion in *Spano v. New York,* 360 U.S.315, 326, that "[a]nything less . . . might deny a defendant 'effective representation by counsel at the only stage when legal aid and advice would help him.' " 377 U.S., at 204.

In *Escobedo v. Illinois,* 378 U.S.478, we drew upon the rationale of Hamilton and Massiah in holding that the right to counsel was guaranteed at the point where the accused, prior to arraignment, was subjected to secret interrogation despite repeated requests to see his lawyer. We again noted the necessity of counsel's presence if the accused was to have a fair opportunity to present a defense at the trial itself.

Finally in *Miranda v. Arizona,* 384 U.S.436, the rules established for custodial interrogation included the right to the presence of counsel. The result was rested on our finding that this and the other rules were necessary to safeguard the privilege against self-incrimination from being jeopardized by such interrogation.

Of course, nothing decided or said in the opinions in the cited cases links the right to counsel only to protection of fifth amendment rights. Rather, those decisions "no more than reflect a constitutional principle established as long ago as *Powell v. Alabama. . . ." Massiah v. U.S., supra,* 377 U.S., at 205. It is central to that principle that in addition to counsel's presence at trial, the accused is guaranteed that he need not stand alone against the state at any stage of the prosecution, formal or informal, in court or out, where counsel's absence might derogate from the accused's right to a fair trial. The security of that right is as much the aim of the right to counsel as it is of the other guarantees of the sixth amendment—the right of the accused to a speedy and public trial by an impartial jury, his right to be informed of the nature and cause of the accusation, and his right to be confronted with the witnesses against him and to have compulsory process for obtaining witnesses in his favor. The presence of counsel at such critical confrontations, as at the trial itself, operates to assure that the accused's interests will be protected consistently with our adversary theory of criminal prosecution. Cf. *Pointer v. Texas,* 380 U.S.400.

In sum, the principle of *Powell v. Alabama* and succeeding cases requires that we scrutinize any pretrial confrontation of the accused to determine whether the presence of his counsel is necessary to preserve the defendant's basic right to a fair trial as affected by his right meaningfully to cross-examine the witnesses against him and to have effective assistance of counsel at the trial itself. It calls upon us to analyze whether potential substantial prejudice to defendant's rights inheres in the particular confrontation and the ability of counsel to help avoid that prejudice.

The Government characterizes the lineup as a mere preparatory step in the gathering of the prosecution's evidence, not different—for sixth amendment purposes—from various other preparatory steps such as systematized or scientific analyzing of the accused's fingerprints, blood sample, clothing, hair, and the like.

We think there are differences which preclude such stages being characterized as critical stages at which the accused has the right to the presence of his counsel. Knowledge of the techniques of science and technology is sufficiently available, and the variables in techniques few enough, that the accused has the opportunity for a meaningful confrontation of the government's case at trial through the ordinary processes of cross-examination of the government's expert witnesses and the presentation of the evidence of his own experts. The denial of a right to have his counsel present at such analyses does not therefore violate the sixth amendment; they are not critical stages since there is minimal risk that his counsel's absence at such stages might derogate from his right to a fair trial.

But the confrontation compelled by the state between the accused and the victim or witnesses to a crime to elicit identification evidence is peculiarly riddled with innumerable dangers and variable factors which might seriously, even crucially, derogate from a fair trial.

The vagaries of eyewitness identification are well-known; the annals of criminal law are rife with instances of mistaken identification.

A major factor contributing to the high incidence of miscarriage of justice from mistaken identification has been the degree of suggestion inherent in the manner in which the prosecution presents the suspect to witness for pre-trial identification. . . . Suggestion can be created intentionally or unintentionally in many subtle ways. And the dangers for the suspect are particularly grave when the witness' opportunity for observation was insubstantial, and thus his susceptibility to suggestion the greatest.

Moreover, "[i]t is a matter of common experience that, once a witness has picked out the accused at the lineup, he is not likely to go back on his word later, so that in practice the issue of identity may (in the absence of other relevant evidence) for all practical purposes be determined there and then, before the trial."*

The pre-trial confrontation for purpose of identification may

---

* Williams and Hammelmann, Identification Parades, Part I, [1963] CRIM.L.REV. 479, 482.

take the form of a lineup, also known as an "identification parade" or "showup," as in the present case, or presentation of the suspect alone to the witness, as in *Stovall v. Denno,* 388 U.S.293 (1967) *supra.* It is obvious that risks of suggestion attend either form of confrontation and increase the dangers inhering in eyewitness identification. But as is the case with secret interrogations, there is serious difficulty in depicting what transpires at lineups and other forms of identification confrontations: "Privacy results in secrecy and this in turn results in a gap in our knowledge as to what in fact goes on. . . ." *Miranda v. Arizona, supra,* 384 U.S., at 448. For the same reasons, the defense can seldom reconstruct the manner and mode of lineup identification for judge or jury at trial. Those participating in a lineup with the accused may often be police officers; in any event, the participants' names are rarely recorded or divulged at trial. The impediments to an objective observation are increased when the victim is the witness. Lineups are prevalent in rape and robbery prosecutions and present a particular hazard that a victim's understandable outrage may excite vengeful or spiteful motives. In any event, neither witnesses nor lineup participants are apt to be alert for conditions prejudicial to the suspect. And if they were, it would likely be of scant benefit to the suspect since neither witnesses nor lineup participants are likely to be schooled in the detection of suggestive influences. Improper influences may go undetected by a suspect, guilty or not, who experiences the emotional tension which we might expect in one being confronted with potential accusers. Even when he does observe abuse, if he has a criminal record he may be reluctant to take the stand and open up the admission of prior convictions. Moreover, any protestations by the suspect of the fairness of the lineup made at trial are likely to be in vain; the jury's choice is between the accused's unsupported version and that of the police officers present. In short, the accused's inability effectively to reconstruct at trial any unfairness that occurred at the lineup may deprive him of his only opportunity meaningfully to attack the credibility of the witness' courtroom identification.

What facts have been disclosed in specific cases about the conduct of pre-trial confrontations for identification illustrate both the potential for substantial prejudice to the accused at that stage and the need for its revelation at trial.

. . . state reports, in the course of describing prior identifications admitted as evidence of guilt, reveal numerous instances of suggestive procedures, for example, that all in the lineup but the suspect were known to the identifying witness, that the other participants in a lineup were grossly dissimilar in appearance to the suspect, that only the suspect was required to wear distinctive clothing which the culprit allegedly wore, that the witness is told by the police that they have caught the culprit after which the defendant is brought before the witness alone or is viewed in jail, that the suspect is pointed out before or during a lineup, and that the participants in the lineup are asked to try on an article of clothing which fits only the suspect.

The potential for improper influence is illustrated by the circumstances, insofar as they appear, surrounding the prior identifications in the three cases we decide today. In the present case, the testimony of the identifying witnesses elicited on cross-examination revealed that those witnesses were taken to the courthouse and seated in the courtroom to await assembly of the lineup. The courtroom faced on a hallway observable to the witnesses through an open door. The cashier testified that she saw Wade "standing in the hall" within sight of an FBI agent. Five or six other prisoners later appeared in the hall. The vice president testified that he saw a person in the hall in the custody of the agent who "resembled the person that we identified as the one that had entered the bank."

The lineup in *Gilbert,* 388 U.S.263, *supra,* was conducted in an auditorium in which some one hundred witnesses to several alleged state and federal robberies charged to Gilbert made wholesale identifications of Gilbert as the robber in each other's presence, a procedure said to be fraught with dangers of suggestion. And the vice of suggestion created by the identification in *Stovall, supra,* was the presentation to the witness of the suspect alone handcuffed to police officers. It is hard to imagine a situation more clearly conveying the suggestion to the witness that the one presented is believed guilty by the police. . . .

The few cases that have surfaced therefore reveal the existence of a process attended with hazards of serious unfairness to the criminal accused and strongly suggest the plight of the more numerous defendants who are unable to ferret out suggestive influences in the secrecy of the confrontation. We do not assume that these risks are the result of police procedures intentionally designed to prejudice an accused. Rather we assume they derive from the dangers inherent in eyewitness identification and the suggestibility inherent in the context of the pre-trial identification.

Insofar as the accused's conviction may rest on a courtroom identification, in fact the fruit of a suspect pre-trial identification which the accused is helpless to subject to effective scrutiny at trial, the accused is deprived of that right of cross-examination which is an essential safeguard to his right to confront the witnesses against him (*Pointer v. Texas,* 380 U.S.400). And even though cross-examination is a precious safeguard to a fair trial, it cannot be viewed as an absolute assurance of accuracy and reliability. Thus in the present context, where so many variables and pitfalls exist, the first line of defense must be the prevention of unfairness and the lessening of the hazards of eyewitness identification at the lineup itself. The trial which might determine the accused's fate may well not be that in the courtroom but that at the pre-trial confrontation, with the State aligned against the accused, the witness the sole jury, and the accused unprotected against the overreaching, intentional or unintentional, and with little or no effective appeal from the judgment there rendered by the witness—"that's the man."

Since it appears that there is grave potential for prejudice, intentional or not, in the pre-trial lineup, which may not be capable of reconstruction at trial, and since presence of counsel itself can often avert prejudice and assure a meaningful confrontation at trial, there can be little doubt that for Wade the post-indictment lineup was a critical stage of the prosecution at which he was "as much entitled to such aid [of counsel] . . . as at the trial itself." *Powell v. Alabama, supra,* 287 U.S.45, 57. Thus both Wade and his counsel should have been notified of the impending lineup, and counsel's presence should have been a requisite to conduct of the lineup, absent an "intelligent waiver." No substantial countervailing policy considerations have been advanced against the requirement of the presence of counsel. Concern is expressed that the requirement will forestall prompt identifications and result in obstruction of the confrontations. As for the first, we note that in the two cases in which the right to counsel is today held to apply, counsel had already been appointed and no argument is made in either case that notice to counsel would have prejudicially delayed the confrontations. Moreover, we leave open the question whether the presence of substitute counsel might not suffice where notification and presence of the suspect's own counsel would result in prejudicial delay. And to refuse to recognize the right to counsel for fear that counsel will obstruct the course of justice is contrary to the basic assumptions upon which this court has operated in sixth amendment cases.

In our view counsel can hardly impede legitimate law enforcement; on the contrary, for the reasons expressed, law enforcement may be assisted by preventing the infiltration of taint in the prosecution's identification evidence. That result cannot help the guilty avoid conviction but can only help assure that the right man has been brought to justice.

Legislative or other regulations, such as those of local police departments, which eliminate the risks of abuse and unintentional suggestion at lineup proceedings and the impediments to meaningful confrontation at trial may also remove the basis for regarding the stage as "critical." But neither Congress nor the federal authorities have seen fit to provide a solution. What we hold today "in no way creates a constitutional straitjacket which will handicap sound efforts at reform, nor is it intended to have this effect." *Miranda v. Arizona, supra,* 384 U.S. at 467.

We come now to the question whether the denial of Wade's motion to strike the courtroom identification by the bank witnesses at trial because of the absence of his counsel at the lineup required, as the Court of Appeals held, the grant of a new trial at which such evidence is to be excluded. We do not think this disposition can be justified without first giving the government the opportunity to establish by clear and convincing evidence that the in-court identifications were based upon observations of the suspect other than the lineup identification. . . . The admissibility of evidence of the lineup identification itself is not involved, a per se rule of exclusion of courtroom identification would be unjustified. . . . A rule limited solely to the exclusion of testimony concerning identification at the lineup itself, without regard to admissibility of the courtroom identification, would render the right to counsel an empty one. The lineup is most often used, as in the present case, to crystallize the witnesses' identification of the defendant for future reference. We have already noted that the lineup identification will have that effect. The State may then rest upon the witnesses' unequivocal courtroom identification, and not mention the pre-trial identification as part of the State's case at trial. Counsel is then in the predicament in which Wade's counsel found himself—realizing that possible unfairness at the lineup may be the sole means of attack upon the unequivocal courtroom identification, and having to probe in the dark in an attempt to discover and reveal unfairness, while bolstering the government witness' courtroom identification by bringing out and dwelling upon his prior identification. Since counsel's presence at the lineup would equip him to attack not only the lineup identification but the courtroom identification as well, limiting the impact of violation of the right to counsel to exclusion of evidence only of identification at the lineup itself disregards a critical element of that right.

We think it follows that the proper test to be applied in these situations is that quoted in *Wong Sun v. U.S.*, 371 U.S.471, 488, " '[W]hether, granting establishment of the primary illegality, the evidence to which instant objection is made has been come at by exploitation of that illegality or instead by means sufficiently distinguishable to be purged of the primary taint.' Maguire, Evidence of Guilt 221 (1959)." . . . Application of this test in the present context requires consideration of various factors; for example, the prior opportunity to observe the alleged criminal act, the existence of any discrepancy between any pre-lineup description and the defendant's actual description, any identification prior to lineup of another person, the identification by picture of the defendant prior to the lineup, failure to identify the defendant on a prior occasion, and the lapse of time between the alleged act and the lineup identification. It is also relevant to consider those facts which, despite the absence of counsel, are disclosed concerning the conduct of the lineup. . . .

We doubt that the Court of Appeals applied the proper test for exclusion of the in-court identification of the two witnesses.

The judgment of the Court of Appeals is vacated and the case is remanded to that court with direction to enter a new judgment vacating the conviction and remanding the case to the District Court for further proceedings consistent with this opinion.

It is so ordered.

PART III

POST-ARREST PROCEDURE

CHAPTER 7

GENERAL ASPECTS OF BAIL

Section I. INTRODUCTION

BASICALLY, "bail" is defined as setting at liberty a person arrested or imprisoned, on security taken which secures his appearance at a subsequent trial or hearing.

"Bail" is also used to refer to the *undertaking* by the *surety* in whose custody the defendant is placed and conditioned on the promise that the surety will produce the defendant in court at the required time and place.

"Bail" may be considered to be the delivery of a person to the sureties of his bond, in whose friendly custody he is to remain in lieu of jail. (The *sureties* are regarded as custodians or bailees of the principal (the accused). They have control of the principal and are bound at their peril to keep him within the jurisdiction for surrender upon demand.)

Furthermore, a man's "bail" are jailers of his own choosing who are bound to keep him under the power of the court.

> Hence a defendant who is delivered to a special *bail* is looked upon in the eye of the law as being constantly in their custody. They are regarded as his jailers, and have him always as it were upon a string that they may pull at pleasure and surrender him in their own discharge. They may take him on Sunday which shows that it is not an original taking, but that he is still in custody. Their authority arises more from contract than from the law, and, as between the parties, neither the jurisdiction of the court nor of the state controls it, and so the bail may take the principal in another jurisdiction or another state, on the ground that a valid contract made in one state is enforceable in another, according to the law there. This shows that the authority need not be exercised by process, but that it inheres in the bail themselves, and they may exercise it personally or *depute* to another to exercise for them (*Worthen v. Prescott*, 11 A.690 (1887)).

Once the defendant is released on bail bond, he is constructively within the custody of the law, and the sureties may require that he not leave the state. Although a surety or bondsman guarantees that the accused will show up in court, he is under no obligation to keep the accused under surveillance.

Although there are many and varied definitions for "bail," in the popular usage of the word, it simply means that security, cash or bond (cash need not be paid into the court to constitute a bail, since any security or bond that is acceptable to the court will suffice) is given for the appearance of the accused in order to obtain his release from prison.

1.1. Bail Bond

A "bail bond" is a contract between the principal and surety on one side and the government on the other, to pay money under certain conditions such as the nonappearance of the accused (the principal) at trial.

This contract is executed by the accused and from its nature requires that sureties or bail, in whose custody he is to remain, be a party to it.

1.2. Recognizance

Although many courts and statutes use the terms "bail bond" and "recognizance" interchangeably, strictly speaking a *recognizance* is an obligation of record, entered into before a court or magistrate so authorized to take it, upon condition to do a certain act.

Some courts and scholars further delineate and distinguish between "bail bond" and "recognizance" by stating that they are the *two* methods of taking bail: a) a *recognizance* is an acknowledgment of a debt already due, and b) a *bail bond* (or bond) is the creation of a new debt.

1.3. Personal Recognizance

Often the prisoner is allowed to obligate *himself* to answer the charge; in other words, the accused is released on his *own* recognizance without the requirement of posting security. Generally, personal recognizance is granted when the offense is minor and the chance of flight from the jurisdiction is slight.

Another term that is sometimes used as a synonym for "bail bond" or "recognizance" is *surety bond*.

1.4. The Right

Although most scholars argue that there is no absolute right to bail, the Supreme Court has said, *in dictum,*

> The right to release before trial is conditioned upon the accused giving adequate assurance that he will stand trial and submit to sentence if found guilty. . . . Like the ancient practice of securing oaths of responsible persons to stand as sureties for the accused, the modern practice of requiring a bail bond or the deposit of a sum of money subject to forfeiture serves as additional assurance of the presence of the accused (*Stack v. Boyle,* 342 U.S.1 (1951)).

1.5. Authority

At common law, all crimes were bailable, however, today the application of bail is modified or replaced by statutes and constitutional provisions. Thus the power under which the court fixes bail must either be inherent in the judicial office or granted by statute, for if it is not, the power does not exist.

1.6. Object and Effects

The object of *bail* is to relieve the accused of imprisonment and the state of the task of keeping him pending trial, while concurrently securing the appearance of the accused at the trial.

The effects of *bail* are as follows: a) to allow the accused to remain at large and thus uphold the presumption of innocence until proven guilty, and b) to allow the accused the opportunity to confer with his attorney and prepare his defense. Note that during the time the accused is released on bail, he is considered under the power of the court.

1.7. Jurisdiction

A motion to be admitted to bail is made to the court which has primary jurisdiction over the accused, and only when the trial court has refused to grant bail, should the accused bring the matter of bail before a court of appeal.

When an arrest is made in a jurisdiction that is different and removed from that in which the crime was committed, the court in whose jurisdiction the accused is apprehended should not fix bail, but rather return the accused to the court which has original jurisdiction over the offense, for a determination of bail.

1.8. The Power to Grant Bail

If there is no statutory authority, neither a *sheriff* nor a *police officer* has the power to grant or to fix the amount of bail. However, some state statutes provide that the sheriff has the right to take bail in misdemeanor cases. In such cases, the accused should not be detained for a long period of time just because the sheriff has not set bail.

In police courts when a warrant is issued by the *police judge* for a person's arrest, the judge must fix the amount of the bail bond at the time of issuance of the warrant.

Where statutes allow, the *magistrate* has the power to set and grant bail, but such power is lost when the defendant is bound over to the trial court and the magistrate loses jurisdiction over the defendant.

Clerks of the court may only fix bail when they are given statutory power to do so. However, the clerk of a court, under the direction of the judge and at the request of the defendant, may do the necessary work in taking a recognizance.

The *judge* of any court which has primary jurisdiction over the accused may grant bail upon proper application to the court.

1.9. Habeas Corpus

The defendant who has petitioned the court for a writ of habeas corpus may be granted bail by the court having jurisdiction over the habeas corpus determination. Conversely, where a person is held on an extradition warrant, such as a fugitive from justice, he should not be admitted to bail while awaiting the outcome of a habeas corpus proceeding.

It has been held that a person appealing an adverse judgment from a habeas corpus proceeding may be admitted to bail by the appellate court pending the appeal.

Section 2. CRITERIA

2.1. The Eighth Amendment

"Excessive bail shall not be required . . ." *Eighth Amendment.* The quoted provision of the amendment applies to Federal

Courts only, however, this does not mean that the individual state constitutions cannot contain such a clause.

> The bail clause was lifted with slight changes from the English Bill of Rights Act. In England that clause has never been thought to accord a right to bail in all cases, but merely to provide that bail shall not be excessive in those cases where it is proper to grant bail. When this clause was carried over in our Bill of Rights, nothing was said that indicated any different concept. The eighth amendment has not prevented Congress from defining the classes of cases in which bail shall be allowed in this country. Thus in criminal cases it is not compulsory where the punishment may be death. Indeed the very language of the amendment fails to say all arrests must be bailable (*Carlson v. Landon,* 342 U.S.524 (1952)).

2.2. Admission of Bail

In some state court jurisdictions, the granting of bail is a matter of discretion of the court to be exercised within the guidelines of established principles and case law. However, the majority of jurisdictions make the admission of bail mandatory on the court in all cases except those involving capital crimes, as set forth in constitutional and statutory provisions. Note that if the right to bail is absolute, the court must grant bail when proper application is made.

When a person is being held for treatment of a social disease, and not for a crime, he is not entitled to bail since he is not being held as a criminal, charged with a crime. Conversely, when a person is held for an alleged criminal offense, he cannot be denied bail on the grounds that he is suspected of having a social disease.

2.3. Factors in Determining Bail

If the offense is bailable, the primary question for *any* court is, will recognizance or bond assure the appearance in court of the accused. In determining the answer, the court takes into consideration: a) the seriousness of the offense, b) the type and degree of punishment for the offense, c) the previous conduct of the accused (i.e. if he has been out on bail before, has he shown up for trial), d) the present conduct of the accused (did he turn himself in for the present offense), and e) the health of the accused.

If the accused is in bad health and imprisonment would aggravate his condition, he probably would be granted bail. However, if prison medical authorities can adequately care for the accused, the health factor will not be given much weight in the determination.

Yet another element in the consideration of the feasibility of bail is the willingness of the public prosecutor to allow such, for if he agrees to it, the court will give weight to the acquiescence.

2.4. Capital Cases

Depending on the particular state constitution and statutes, if the presumption of guilt of the accused is not great, bail may become a matter of right in capital cases. Those states that do not have such provisions in their constitution, follow the common law rule which leaves the question of bail to the discretion of the judge, who decides in view of the facts and circumstances of the particular case. (By *capital offense,* it is meant those crimes which are punishable by death.)

Usually, *first degree murder* is the only type of homicide that is considered a capital offense and as such, one must consider the various elements of murder in the first degree, in determining whether or not bail should be granted. For example, if neither premeditation nor malice aforethought is shown (elements of first degree murder), the person must be admitted to bail. Conversely, if it appears likely that the jury will convict the defendant of murder in the first degree, bail should be denied.

2.5. Conviction and Appeal

Whether an individual can be admitted to bail in a state court after conviction and pending appeal, varies from state to state. Some states provide that bail is a matter of right after conviction if the offense is a misdemeanor and the appeal arises from a judgment imposing imprisonment. Statutes of other states provide that where the sentence is a fine, bail on appeal is a matter of right. Contrastingly, the denial of bail after conviction and pending appeal has been upheld as a valid statute in those states that have such.

States that allow bail on appeal after conviction make an exception in cases imposing capital punishment. Accordingly, where the penalty could have been death, but a lesser sentence was imposed, bail has been denied.

If any of the following four conditions are present, admission to bail will be denied on appeal: a) The defendant is a threat or danger to an individual or the community; b) the appeal is frivolous; c) the appeal is merely taken for delay; or d) the conditions of the release are not sufficient to assure that the defendant will not escape. After an individual has been convicted, the probability of his receiving the punishment is greatly increased, and correspondingly the chance of his flight is increased. Also, since the presumption of innocence no longer exists after conviction, the chances of the defendant committing a crime similar to the one he was convicted of are greatly increased.

There are two views in the state courts as to availability of bail on an appeal from an adverse judgment in a *habeas corpus* proceeding: One view holds that the petitioner is entitled to bail on appeal in habeas corpus proceedings and the other view is that he is not. The states that deny bail in such a case, do so on the basis that habeas corpus proceedings are not criminal proceedings and thus bail statutes do not apply.

2.6. Revocation of Bail

Some statutes provide that the court may revoke bail at its discretion during the trial, or recess, to assure an orderly proceeding. Similarly, when the defendant, on bail, is found to be involved with jury tampering, the trial court may revoke the bail.

Section 3. PROCEDURE

3.1. Application and Hearing

Application for bail is made to the court which has custody of the defendant. In those states where bail is not a matter of right, the defendant must show that he is entitled to bail. Generally, if the court has a reasonable doubt as to the guilt of the defendant, bail should be granted.

When the granting of bail is a matter of discretion, a hearing must be had before bail may be granted. Unless the statutes so provide, the defendant need not appear before the judge setting the bail. However, at such a hearing, if the defendant does appear, he should be allowed to cross-examine the witnesses for the state.

The defendant is entitled to a hearing wherein the trial court sets the amount of bail according to its discretion. Bail should be of such an amount so as to assure the appearance of the defendant in court, however, bail must not be set at an amount in excess of a sum which will guarantee appearance.

3.2. Approval

Although exact requirements vary according to the statutes of the particular jurisdiction, a bail bond or recognizance must be approved or accepted by an authorized officer or judge to be valid. After the approving official signs and files a bond or recognizance, he cannot render the instrument invalid by withdrawing his approval.

To *become* an obligation of record, the bail bond or recognizance must be filed and recorded in the court which approved it.

3.3. Requirements

Although statutory requirements for bail bond, in the state system, vary from state to state, generally speaking, the bail bond should describe the offense charged. One need not describe the crime, however, if the bail bond refers to the indictment which describes it. If the offense described in the bail bond is different from the offense charged, the bail bond is invalid.

3.4. Review

Decisions regarding bail may be reviewed by habeas corpus, appeal, certiorari, or bill of exceptions, depending on the statutes of the particular jurisdiction.

On review from a refusal of the trial court to grant bail, the defendant must show an abuse of discretion by the trial court of a change in the fact situation since the matter was last before the trial court.

3.5. Requirements for Bond or Recognizance

When the law is silent regarding the form an obligation is to take, a bond or recognizance may be given. Unless the statute requires a particular wording on the obligation, either bond or recognizance, the instrument may simply contain the contractual essentials:

1. The *name* of the accused needs to be included for purposes of correct identification.
2. The *amount* in which the accused is held in bail.
3. The *date* of execution is a necessary element in every bond or recognizance.
4. It is good practice to include the *name of the county* and the *state* in which the recognizance was taken.
5. In state courts a recognizance or bail bond should run *in favor of* the state, and in federal courts in favor of the United States.
6. The bail bond or recognizance should *recite* that the accusation was legally made.
7. Generally the *offense* must be set out with sufficient clarity to disclose the charge to be answered. (If the charge is a named offense, merely giving the technical name is sufficient without setting forth the facts of the situation. If the offense has no specific name, the elements of the crime must be clearly set out. If the charge of indictment is different in substance from that stated in the bail bond or recognizance, the instrument will be considered invalid, in the absence of statutes to the contrary.)
8. Finally, the bond is *conditioned* that the accused will appear at the proper time and place to answer the charge against him.

3.6. Execution of Bond or Recognizance

As the undertaking of bail is a contractual agreement between the obligor (the accused) and the state, the following requisites should exist:

1. The obligor must be *legally competent* to execute it.

2. The obligation must be in *writing,* unless excused by statute.

3. A bond is considered executed when it is *signed.* (Note that if the date of execution and the date of approval are different, the date of execution controls.)

4. A bail bond becomes binding upon *delivery* and *acceptance,* as with any other contractual obligation.

5. A number of statutes require a recognizance to be *acknowledged* before the court or authorized officer taking it. However, if the statutes are silent with respect to acknowledgement, it need not be included.

6. If a recognizance is taken in court, *signatures* of the parties thereto need not be affixed if such is not required by statute.

3.7. Amount

The amount of bail is product of the exercise of discretion of the court and is determined by considering: the nature of the offense, the strength of the evidence to support the charge (s), the criminal record of the accused, his financial ability to give bail, his health, his character, if he was a fugitive from justice or not when arrested, and the probability of escape. No set rule can be fixed to determine the amount of bail required, since each case must stand on its own facts and circumstances.

When the statutes specify certain amounts of bail for certain offenses, a lesser amount than specified voids the obligation.

If a person is charged with several different and distinct offenses, each of which requires bail, generally he may *not* give one bond or recognizance for the aggregate amount.

Once the accused has been released on bail, the court may not alter the amount of bail by arbitrary order, but must show good cause if there is an alteration.

Upon proper application to the court and showing of good cause, a reduction in the amount of bail may be obtained. Good cause might include the following: a) where the accused is unable to raise the bail after an honest effort, b) where the amount is unreasonably large, c) where the public interests will be better served, or d) where other legal reasons exist.

3.8. Sureties

Under most statutes two sureties are sufficient to fulfill the obligations on a bail bond or recognizance. The accused must consent to those persons who propose to act as sureties as he cannot be compelled to accept bail from persons that he does not want to act as such.

The court has the power to require a cash deposit as collateral to the surety's undertaking.

If provided for by statute, some states may accept cash deposits in lieu of a bail bond. If the defendant fails to appear when required, the cash deposit may be forfeited.

Unless there is a statute to the contrary, anyone that is legally competent to contract and has the pecuniary ability, may act as surety.

A surety cannot be rejected merely because he is a friend or relative of the accused. It should be noted however, that the judge has the final say as to who shall or shall not be a bondsman in his own court.

Generally, to qualify as a bail bondsman one must: a) execute a bond with sufficient sureties, b) never have been convicted of a crime of moral turpitude, and c) obtain a license or a permit.

The sureties on recognizance or bail may take the defendant into custody and surrender him to the authorities to exonerate their liability. If the defendant is not delivered into court by the surety as required by the bond, the bond will be forfeited unless the surety can prove excuse.

When a person appears at the time and place provided for in the bail bond and the terms of the bail bond are fulfilled, the sureties are exonerated.

A void indictment will exonerate a surety, however, a mere defect in the indictment or information, that does not render it void, will not exonerate him. Also, if the prosecuting attorney moves for vacating a valid indictment, the liability of the surety is terminated.

Unless there is an additional agreement or the defendant fails to appear for trial, payment by the defendant to the bondsman and the execution of the bond ends the transaction between the two parties.

3.9. Forfeiture

To enforce liability on a forfeited bond, one institutes a civil proceeding by issuance of a *writ of scire facias*. The purpose of the writ is to give notice to the principal and sureties of the forfeiture and to give them adequate time to show the court why judgment should not be entered. The action is usually brought in the name of the state.

As a defense in such a civil proceeding, one must show a valid excuse for nonperformance of the bail bond; in other words, why the accused did not appear at the required time and place. Some of the defenses are the following: a) sickness, b) insanity, c) acts of God, or d) involuntary induction into the armed forces.

If a *writ of scire facias* is defective on its face, the writ may be quashed or dismissed upon proper appearance and motion.

Where a *writ of scire facias* has been issued and served but lost before its return to the clerk of the court, an *alias writ* is issued.

Depending on the state, relief may or may not be granted when a bail bond has been forfeited. Usually the courts will remit the penalty of a forfeiture of bond or recognizance upon the surrender of the accused.

Acquittal, pardon, or discharge of the accused before default, generally will discharge the bond or recognizance when the terms of the obligation so provide.

3.10. Waiver

In some jurisdictions the accused waives his right to bail, a) when he waives a preliminary examination in a capital case, or b) when he accepts executive clemency and waives his right to appeal.

3.11. "Jumping Bail"

Some state statutes provide that if a person who has been admitted to bail, in connection with a charge of felony, willfully fails to appear as required, he incurs a forfeiture of bail and is guilty of a felony if he subsequently does not appear or surrender himself within a specified time period.

Statutes may provide that "jumping bail" is an offense which is either a misdemeanor or a felony. Generally, if the offense for which the bail was given is a felony, the jumping of bail will be classified as a felony.

Usually, an individual convicted of "jumping bail" may appeal the conviction in the appellate courts.

Section 4. FEDERAL COURTS

4.1. Federal Rules of Criminal Procedure, Rule 46

Thirty years ago an advisory committee was appointed to prepare the Federal Rules of Criminal Procedure for the United States District Courts. The purpose of such a vast undertaking was to simplify procedure and eliminate technicalities in criminal pleadings. Although sixty rules were prepared, this present study is concerned only with Rule 46, *bail,* as amended in 1966.

4.1.1. RIGHT TO BAIL BEFORE CONVICTION. A person arrested for a noncapital offense *shall* be admitted to bail. However, a person arrested for a capital offense *may* be admitted to bail at the discretion of judge or court after considering: a) the evidence, b) the nature of the offense, and c) the circumstances of the offense. Federal Rules of Criminal Procedure, Rule 46 (a) (1).

4.1.2. RIGHT TO BAIL UPON REVIEW. Bail *may* be allowed pending appeal or certiorari unless it appears that the appeal is frivolous or taken for delay.

Bail may be allowed by the trial judge, court of appeals, or by any circuit judge thereof to run until the final termination of the proceedings in all courts.

Any court, judge or justice authorized to grant bail, may at any time revoke the order admitting the defendant, on appeal, to bail (Rule 46 (a) (2)).

4.1.3. BAIL FOR A WITNESS. If a person is a material witness in a criminal proceeding and it is impracticable to secure his presence by subpoena the court may require him to give bail to secure his appearance (Rule 46 (b)).

4.1.4. AMOUNT. When the accused is admitted to bail, the amount is determined, at the discretion of the court or judge, which will

Figure 7-1

APPEARANCE BOND

In the United States District Court for the ....
District of ...., ... Division.

We, the undersigned, jointly and severally acknowledge that we and our personal representatives are bound the pay to the United States of America the sum of .... Dollars ($ ....).

The condition of this bond is that the defendant ....
is to appear in the United States District Court for the ....
District of .... at .... in accordance with all orders and directions of the Court relating to the appearance of the defendant before the Court in the case of United States v. ....,
File number ....; and if the defendant appears as ordered, then this bond is to be void, but if the defendant fails to perform this condition payment of the amount of the bond shall be due forthwith. If the bond is forfeited and if the forfeiture is not set aside or remitted, judgment may be entered upon motion in the United States District Court for the ....
District of .... against each debtor jointly and severally for the amount above stated together with interest and costs, and execution may be issued or payment secured as provided by the Federal Rules of Criminal Procedure and by other laws of the United States.

This bond is signed on this .... day of ...., 19.... at
....

........................, ...,
Name of Defendant.   Address.

........................, ...,
Name of Surety.   Address.

........................, ...,
Name of Surety.   Address.

Signed and acknowledged before me this ...... day of ....,
19.......

                                   ....
Approved: ....

Justification of Sureties

I, the undersigned surety, on oath say that I reside at ....;
and that my net worth is the sum of .... Dollars
($ ....).

I further say that ....
....
........................,
                                   Surety.

Sworn to and subscribed before me this .... day of ....
19.... at ....

                                   ....

As amended Dec. 27, 1948, eff. Oct. 20, 1949.

ensure the presence of the accused, taking the following into consideration: a) the nature of the offense, b) the circumstances of the offense charged, c) the weight of evidence against the accused, d) the financial ability of the accused to give bail, e) the character of the accused, and f) the policy against unnecessary detention of defendant pending trial (Rule 46 (c)).

4.1.5. FORM AND PLACE OF DEPOSIT. When a person gives bail, he must execute a bond for his appearance. The court may a) require one or more sureties, b) authorize acceptance of cash, bonds, or United States notes, or c) authorize the release of the defendant without security, upon his written agreement to appear at a certain time and place upon the conditions necessary to insure his appearance (Rule 46 (d)).

4.1.6. JUSTIFICATION OF SURETIES. Every noncorporate surety must justify by affidavit and possibly be required to describe in the affidavit the property he proposes to justify, list the number and amount of other undischarged bonds entered into by him, and list all other liabilities. No bond will be approved unless the surety appears to be qualified (Rule 46 (e)).

4.1.7. DECLARATION OF FORFEITURE. If a condition of the bond is breached, the district court declares a forfeiture (Rule 46 (f) (1)).

4.1.8. SETTING ASIDE FORFEITURE. If justice does not require the enforcement of a forfeiture, the district court may set the forfeiture aside upon such conditions as the court may impose (Rule 46 (f) (2)).

4.1.9. ENFORCEMENT OF FORFEITURE. When a forfeiture has not been set aside, the court may enter a motion of judgment of default and execute thereon.

By entering into a bond, the obligors appoint the clerk of the court the agent for service of process, with respect to their liability thereon (Rule 46 (f) (3)).

4.1.10. REMISSION OF FORFEITURE. After entry of judgment of default the court may remit such judgment in whole or in part (Rule 46 (f) (4)).

4.1.11. EXONERATION. When the conditions of the bond have been satisfied or the forfeiture remitted or set aside, the court will release bail and exonerate the obligors.

A surety may be exonerated by a deposit of cash in the amount of the bond or a timely surrender of the accused into custody (Rule 46 (g)).

4.1.12. SUPERVISION OF DETENTION PENDING TRIAL. The court must exercise supervision over the detention of defendants and witnesses within the district for purposes of eliminating all *unnecessary* detention. Biweekly, a report must be made by the attorney for the government, listing each person who has been held in excess of ten days, with accompanying reasons for said detention (Rule 46 (h)).

4.2. Crimes and Criminal Procedure*

Title 18 of the United States Code contains laws of a general and permanent nature, which are *complemented* by the Federal Rules of Criminal Procedure discussed *supra*.

4.2.1. POWER OF COURTS AND MAGISTRATES. Any court authorized to arrest and commit offenders may take bail, however, only a United States court having original jurisdiction in criminal cases may admit to bail a person charged with a capital offense (18 U.S.C. 3141 (Title 18, United States Code, Section 3141)).

4.2.2. SURRENDER BY BAIL. Any person released on execution of an appearance bail bond with one or more sureties may be arrested by his surety and delivered to the marshall and brought before any officer having power to commit for such an offense. Furthermore, at the request of the surety the individual may be recommitted and held in custody, concomitant with the discharge and exoneration of surety (18 U.S.C. 3142).

4.2.3. ADDITIONAL BAIL. When proof is made to any judge of the United States, that the accused, released on bail bond with surety, is about to abscond, and that his bail is insufficient, the judge will require him to give better security or have him committed (18 U.S.C. 3143).

---

* United States Code: Title 18.

4.2.4. CASES REMOVED FROM STATES COURTS. Whenever a judgment of a State Court in a criminal proceeding is brought to the Supreme Court of the United States for review, the defendant cannot be released from custody until a final judgment is rendered upon said review, or, if the offense is bailable, the defendant may be released from custody upon giving a bond in a reasonable sum, with sufficient sureties (18 U.S.C. 3144).

4.2.5. RELEASE IN NONCAPITAL CASES PRIOR TO TRIAL. Any person charged with a noncapital offense may be released on his personal recognizance or upon an unsecured appearance bond, pending trial, unless the judicial officer (judge, magistrate or justice) determines that such a release will not assure the appearance of the accused. Furthermore, the judicial officer may impose any or all of the following conditions in addition to, or in place of the aforementioned bond or recognizance, if such conditions will *reasonably* assure the appearance of the accused: a) place the accused in the custody of a third party; b) place restrictions on travel, association or abode; c) require execution of an appearance bond of a specified amount; d) require execution of a bail bond with sufficient sureties; or e) impose any other condition reasonably necessary to assure the appearance of the accused.

In determining the conditions of release the judicial officer considers the following factors:
1. Nature and circumstances of the offense charged.
2. The weight of evidence against the accused.
3. The family ties of the accused.
4. Employment.
5. Financial resources.
6. Character and mental condition.
7. Length of residence in the community.
8. Record of convictions.
9. Record of appearance at court proceedings or of flight to avoid prosecution.

If a person has conditions of release imposed, but continues to be held in custody for more than twenty-four hours because of his inability to meet the conditions, he may have a judicial officer review the conditions of release. Upon such review, if the judicial officer does not amend the conditions of release, he must set forth in writing, the reasons for the conditions imposed.

When the accused is ordered released by a judicial officer, he may amend his order at any time, imposing additional or different conditions of release (18 U.S.C. 3146).

4.2.6. BAIL REFORM ACT OF 1966. The purpose of the Bail Reform Act of 1966 (18 U.S.C. 3147-3152), as amended in 1970, is to revise the practices relating to bail to assure that all persons, regardless of their financial status, will not be needlessly detained pending their appearance to answer *charges,* to *testify,* or pending *appeal,* when detention serves neither the ends of justice nor the public interest.

4.2.6.1. *Appeal from Conditions of Release.* A person who is detained or released on conditions which require him to return to custody after specified hours, may move the court having original jurisdiction over the offense, to amend the order imposing the conditions of release.

When a person is detained after the court denies a motion to amend the conditions of release, or the conditions of release have been imposed or amended by a judge of the court having original jurisdiction over the offense charged, the person detained may appeal the conditions of release to the appellate court (18 U.S.C. 3147).

4.2.6.2. *Release in Capital Cases or after Conviction.* A person charged with a capital offense, or a person who has been convicted of an offense and is either awaiting sentence or sentence review, or has filed an appeal, will be treated according to 18 U.S.C. 3146 (release in noncapital cases prior to trial, discussed *supra*), unless the court or the judge has reason to believe that no one, or more, of the conditions of release will reasonably assure that the person will not flee or pose a danger to any other person or to the community. The person will be ordered detained if the following apply: a) a risk of flight or danger exists, b) the appeal appears frivolous, or c) the appeal was taken for delay (18 U.S.C. 3148 (1970)).

4.2.6.3. *Release of a Material Witness.* If it appears by affidavit that the testimony of a person is material in a criminal proceeding, and it is shown to be impracticable to secure his presence by subpoena, a judicial officer may impose conditions of release as provided for in 18 U.S.C. 3146.

4.2.6.4. *Penalties for Failure to Appear.* Any person released pursuant to Title 18 of the United States Code, that willfully fails to appear before the court as required, will incur a forfeiture of any security which was given or pledged for his release. In addition, if he was released in connection with a charge of felony, waiting sentence, or pending appeal after conviction, he may be fined not more than 5000 dollars, or imprisoned not more than five years, or both. If he was released in connection with a charge of misdemeanor, he may be fined not more than the maximum fine for said misdemeanor or imprisoned for not more than one year, or both. If he was released for appearance as a material witness, he may be fined not more than 1000 dollars or imprisoned for not more than one year, or both (18 U.S.C. 3150).

4.2.7. FEDERAL STATUTES 18USC 3146-3152

4.2.7.1. *Release in Noncapital Cases Prior to Trial.* Any person charged with an offense, other than an offense punishable by death, shall, at his appearance before a judicial officer, be ordered released pending trial on his personal recognizance or upon the execution of an unsecured appearance bond in an amount specified by the judicial officer, unless the officer determines, in the exercise of his discretion, that such a release will not reasonably assure the appearance of the person as required. When such a determination is made, the judicial officer shall, either in lieu of or in addition to the above methods of release, impose the first of the following conditions of release which will reasonably assure the appearance of the person for trial or, if no single condition gives that assurance, any combination of the following conditions:

1. Place the person in the custody of a designated person or organization agreeing to supervise him.
2. Place restrictions on the travel, association, or place of abode of the person during the period of release.
3. Require the execution of an appearance bond in a specified amount and the deposit in the registry of the court, in

cash or other security as directed, of a sum not to exceed 10 percentum of the amount of the bond, such deposit to be returned upon the performance of the conditions of release.

4. Require the execution of a bail bond with sufficient solvent sureties, or the deposit of cash in lieu thereof.

5. Impose any other condition deemed reasonably necessary to assure appearance as required, including a condition requiring that the person return to custody after specified hours.

A judicial officer authorizing the release of a person under this section shall issue an appropriate order containing a statement of the conditions imposed, if any; he shall inform such person of the penalties applicable to violations of the conditions of his release; and he shall advise him that a warrant for his arrest will be issued immediately upon any such violation.

A person for whom conditions of release are imposed and who after twenty-four hours from the time of the release hearing continues to be detained as a result of his inability to meet the conditions of release, shall, upon application, be entitled to have the conditions reviewed by the judicial officer who imposed them. Unless the conditions of release are amended and the person is thereupon released, the judicial officer shall set forth in writing the reasons for requiring the conditions imposed. A person who is ordered released on a condition which requires that he return to custody after specified hours shall, upon application, be entitled to a review by the judicial officer who imposed the condition. Unless the requirement is removed and the person is thereupon released on another condition, the judicial officer shall set forth in writing the reasons for continuing the requirement. In the event that the judicial officer who imposed conditions of release is not available, any other judicial officer in the district may review such conditions.

A judicial officer ordering the release of a person on any condition specified in this section may at any time amend his order to impose additional or different conditions of release: *Provided,* that, if the imposition of such additional or different conditions results in the detention of the person as a result of his inability to meet such conditions or in the release of the person on a condition requiring him to return to custody after specified hours, the provisions listed above shall apply.

Information stated in, or offered in connection with, any order entered pursuant to this section need not conform to the rules pertaining to the admissibility of evidence in a court of law.

Nothing contained in this section shall be construed to prevent the disposition of any case or class of cases by forfeiture of collateral security where such disposition is authorized by the court.

4.2.7.2. *Appeal from Conditions of Release.* A person who is detained, or whose release on a condition requiring him to return to custody after specified hours is continued, after review of his application pursuant to subsection 4.2.7.1. by a judicial officer, other than a judge of the court having original jurisdiction over the offense with which he is charged or a judge of a United States court of appeals or a Justice of the Supreme Court, may move the court having original jurisdiction over the offense with which he is charged to amend the order. Said motion shall be determined promptly.

In any case in which a person is detained after a court denies a motion to amend an order imposing conditions of release, or conditions of release have been imposed or amended by a judge of the court having original jurisdiction over the offense charged, an appeal may be taken to the court having appellate jurisdiction over such court. Any order so appealed shall be affirmed if it is supported by the proceedings below. If the order is not so supported, the court may remand the case for a further hearing, or may, with or without additional evidence, order the person released pursuant to subsection 4.2.7.1. The appeal shall be determined promptly.

4.2.7.3. *Release in Capital Cases or after Conviction.* A person who is charged with an offense punishable by death, or who has been convicted of an offense and is either awaiting sentence or sentence review or has filed an appeal or a petition for a writ of certiorari, shall be treated in accordance with the provisions of subsection 4.2.7.1. unless the court or judge has reason to believe that no one or more conditions of release will reasonably assure that the person will not flee or pose a danger to any other person or to the community. If such a risk of flight or danger is believed to exist, or if it appears that an appeal is frivolous or taken for delay, the person may be ordered detained. The provisions shall not apply to persons described in this section: *Provided,* that other rights to judicial review of conditions of release or orders of detention shall not be affected. As amended Pub.L. 91-452, Title X, §1002, Oct. 15, 1970, 84 Stat. 952.

4.2.7.4. *Release of Material Witnesses.* If it appears by affidavit that the testimony of a person is material in any criminal proceeding, and if it is shown that it may become impracticable to secure his presence by subpoena, a judicial officer shall impose conditions of release pursuant to the preceding subsection. No material witness shall be detained because of inability to comply with any condition of release if the testimony of such witness can adequately be secured by deposition, and further detention is not necessary to prevent a failure of justice. Release may be delayed for a reasonable period of time until the deposition of the witness can be taken pursuant to the Federal Rules of Criminal Procedure.

4.2.7.5. *Penalties for Failure to Appear.* Whoever, having been released pursuant to this chapter, willfully fails to appear before any court or judicial officer as required, shall, subject to the provisions of the Federal Rules of Criminal Procedure, incur a forfeiture of any security which was given or pledged for his release, and, in addition, shall, if he was released in connection with a charge of felony, or while awaiting sentence or pending appeal or certiorari after conviction of any offense, be fined not more than 5,000 dollars or imprisoned not more than five years, or both, or if he was released in connection with a charge of misdemeanor, be fined not more than the maximum provided for such misdemeanor or imprisoned for not more than one year, or both, or if he was released for appearance as a material witness, shall be fined not more than 1,000 dollars or imprisoned for not more than one year, or both.

4.2.7.6. *Contempt.* Nothing in this chapter shall interfere with or prevent the exercise by any court of the United States of its power to punish for contempt.

4.2.7.7. *Definitions.* As used in subsections 4.2.7.1. through 4.2.7.8. of this chapter:

1. The term *judicial officer* means, unless otherwise indicated, any person or court authorized to bail or otherwise release a person before trial or sentencing or pending appeal in a court of the United States, and any judge of the District of Columbia Court of General Sessions.
2. The term *offense* means any criminal offense, other than an offense triable by court-martial, military commission, provost court, or other military tribunal, which is in violation of an Act of Congress and is triable in any court established by an Act of Congress.

CHAPTER 8

PRE-TRIAL DETENTION

IN HIS first public statement on crime control, President Nixon, on January 31, 1969, called for legislation to permit temporary pre-trial detention of criminal defendants whose pre-trial release would present a "clear danger" to the community. Pursuant to the President's directive, the Justice Department sent a proposal to Congress which would amend the Bail Reform Act of 1966. The proposal would permit federal courts to detain those criminal defendants, up to sixty days prior to trial, who are charged with certain crimes of violence, whose release would constitute a danger to the community, and who have been afforded a hearing with certain procedural sageguards. Furthermore, it would authorize the courts to consider the potential dangerousness of the defendant to the community and in light of such determination, set the conditions of pre-trial release. New sanctions would be provided for "bail jumping" and for crimes committed while on release.

Senator Joseph D. Tydings proposed a similar bill for Washington, D.C. which would permit the judge the option of ordering an immediate trial within thirty days and detaining those criminal defendants, who if released, would pose a serious danger to the community.

The impetus for such bills is found in the goal of reducing the amount of crimes committed by those released on bail or personal cognizance pending trial.

The question of pre-trial detention raises constitutional issues with respect to procedural safeguards, the presumption of innocence, the due process clause of the fifth amendment, and the bail clause of the eighth amendment. The aforementioned issues will be discussed and analyzed in section 3.

Section I. CRIME COMMITTED WHILE ON BAIL

1.1. Violation of Release

The Judicial Council Committee to Study the Operation of the Bail Reform Act in the District of Columbia, reported in

Figure 8-1

INCIDENCE OF REINDICTMENT IN CALENDAR 1968 FOR
OFFENSES ALLEGEDLY COMMITTED WHILE ON BAIL
AWAITING TRIAL IN THE UNITED STATES DISTRICT COURT
FOR THE DISTRICT OF COLUMBIA

| | Incidence of Reindictment While on Bail | | |
Time	*Number of Persons Indicted for Offenses Allegedly Committed on Bail*	*Number of Persons Indicted*	*Percent Indicted for Offenses on Bail*
1968 (12 mos.)			
Incl. riot cases	153	2557	5.9
Excl. riot cases*	147	2098	7.0
1967 (10 mos.)	143	1513	9.4

Source: Dockets and criminal case files of the United States District Court for the District of Columbia.

* Charges of Burglary II and rioting.

1969 that crime charged against persons released on bail continues at a significant level in Washington, D.C. The estimates of crime allegedly committed by defendants on bail range from 6 percent to 70 percent. The wide variance is explained by the use of different statistical bases. For example, the lower percentages are obtained when rates of reindictment are measured among persons released on bail in all felony cases; the higher percentages are obtained when the rates of rearrest among persons indicted for robbery are measured.

During 1968, data collected by the Department of Justice on each person indicted in the United States District Court for the District of Columbia showed that 6 percent to 7 percent of the persons indicted allegedly committed the offense for which they were indicted while on bail awaiting trial for another offense. Specifically, about 150 persons who were already under indictment allegedly committed another offense which resulted in indictment in Washington, D.C. in 1968.

It is noted that the reindictment figure does not measure the full range of crime on bail. It excludes many incidents which do not result in indictment; it does not measure crime allegedly com-

Figure 8-2

LAPSE OF TIME BETWEEN INDICTMENT AND ALLEGED
COMMISSION OF FELONY OFFENSE WHILE ON BAIL AWAITING
TRIAL IN THE UNITED STATES DISTRICT COURT FOR
THE DISTRICT OF COLUMBIA IN CALENDAR 1968

Days Between Indictment and Second Offense	Number of Persons Reindicted	Percent of Persons Reindicted	Cumulative Percent
0-30	40	26.1	
31-60	21	13.7	39.8 (0-60 days)
61-90	20	13.0	52.8 (0-90 days)
91-120	17	11.1	63.9 (0-120 days)
121-210	28	18.3	82.2 (0-210 days)
211-over	27	17.6	99.8 (over 210 days)
Total	153	99.8	

Source: Dockets and criminal case files of the United States District Court for the District of Columbia.

mitted by misdemeanants who are on bail; and it does not measure the many undetected and unsolved crimes which may be committed by persons on bail. It is the view of many that the 6 percent to 7 percent figure measures only the most serious and probably the lowest incidence of crime on bail.

1.2. Offender's Characteristics

The President's Commission on Crime in the District of Columbia reported that accused felons tend to commit felonies of the same type as the original offense while out on bail. Specifically, thirty-one of sixty robbery offenses allegedly committed by persons on bail were attributed to persons originally charged with robbery, thirty-two of fifty-seven housebreaking to accused housebreakers, eighteen of thirty auto thefts to persons accused of auto theft, and nineteen of twenty-eight narcotics offenses to persons accused of narcotics offenses (see Fig. 8-3). More than 80 percent of the persons studied committed crimes as serious or more serious than the original offense.

Available data reveals a high incidence of prior arrests and convictions among persons who allegedly committed offenses while on bail. Of the persons arrested for allegedly committing offenses while released on bail, 88 percent had adult arrest or conviction records prior to release on bail.

The average age of the persons arrested while on bond was 26½ years; 51 percent of them were twenty-four years of age or younger.

1.3. Reduction of Crime on Bail

Pending passage of legislative bills providing for pre-trial detention, the Judicial Council Committee to Study the Operation of the Bail Reform Act in the District of Columbia has recommended five types of action which could be taken by courts and prosecutors to reduce crime on bail: a) Use of conditions of release designed to reduce the risks of flight and crime on bail; b) Imposition of sanctions, including contempt, whenever a defendant violates conditions of release; c) Expedited proceedings for persons deemed likely to commit offenses when on bail; d) Denial of bail on appeal in certain cases; and e) Consecutive prosecutions and sentences in cases where crime is committed while on bail.

1.4. Fault of the Bail Reform Act of 1966

The Bail Reform Act of 1966 was the first basic change in federal bail law since 1789, in that it markedly reduced reliance on money bail. The suspect's promise to return for the next court appearance (personal recognizance) is the rule of Act. In exceptional cases the judge can attach conditions to the release if he determines that the suspect is likely to flee. Such conditions, for example, might be to restrict defendant's travel, his association, his place of abode or to require the execution of an appearance bond by a refundable deposit.

What the judge cannot do under the Act, however, is to consider danger to the community as criteria for release. Under the Act, the sole standard of granting or denying bail is the defendant's likelihood of flight. Jerry V. Wilson, Chief of Police, Washington, D.C., has said, ". . . the significant fault of the Bail Reform Act was its specific omission of danger to the community as criteria for determining conditions of release."

Figure

CORRELATION BETWEEN FELONY
OBTAINED AND FELONY

Most serious felony pending for which release on bond was obtained*	Total	1st degree murder	Rape	Kidnapping	2d degree murder	Robbery	Attempted robbery
Total	†253	6	2	1	5	60	1
1st degree murder	1					1	
Rape	5	1					
Manslaughter	1				1		
Robbery	58	4	1		1	31	1
Attempted robbery	2					1	
Aggravated assault	12					2	
Housebreaking	60				1	13	
Abortion	7					2	
Grand larceny	9	1					
Carrying deadly weapon	2				1	1	
Counterfeiting	1						
Forgery	8		1			1	
Auto theft	37			1	1	4	
Narcotics	33					3	
Other theft, possession	4						
Perjury	1						
Fraud	2						
Operating a still	1						
Gambling	9					1	

* Felony totals in this column are higher than the actual than one felony during the same release on bond are counted
† Committed by 207 persons.
Source: Commission Bail Study.

8-3

FOR WHICH RELEASE ON BAIL WAS CHARGED WHILE RELEASED

Aggravated assault	Housebreaking	Abortion	Grand larceny	Carrying deadly weapon	Counterfeiting	Forgery	Auto theft	Narcotics	Other theft, possession	Bail jumping	Bribery, obstructing justice	Operating a still	Gambling
19	57	4	11	5	1	7	30	28	4	1	4	1	6
	2						1				1		
4	6		2	2	1		2	3					
								1					
5	4						1						
3	32		2	1			6			1	1		
		3									2		
	1		2				2	2	1				
	1												
	2					4							
3	4		2	2			18	1	1				
3	3		1			2		19	2				
1	2		1										
						1							
		1	1										
												1	
								2					6

number of releases on bond since offenders charged with more
more than once.

Figure 8-4

PRIOR ADULT CRIMINAL RECORDS OF PERSONS ALLEGEDLY COMMITTING OFFENSES WHILE RELEASED ON BAIL

Type of prior adult record	Total number of prior offenses	Offenders with one or more		Offenders with two or more	
		Number	Percent of all offenders	Number	Percent of all offenders
Felony:					
Arrests	499	156	75.4	106	51.2
Convictions	145	89	43.0	29	14.0
U.S. misdemeanors:*					
Arrests	370	131	63.3	83	40.1
Convictions	253	108	52.2	57	27.6
D.C. misdemeanors:†					
Convictions	583	140	67.6	91	44.0
Total		182	88.0	167	80.7

* Misdemeanors prosecuted by the United States Attorney for the District of Columbia. See 23 D.C. Code § 101 (1961).

† Misdemeanors prosecuted by the Corporation Counsel of the District of Columbia. See 23 D.C. Code § 101 (1961).

Source: Metropolitan Police Department criminal records.

Under a personal recognizance release system and possibly under a money bond system where the judge is prohibited from considering danger to the community in determining release conditions, three situations may develop. These are the following: a) incentive is added for the defense attorney to pursue *delay,* for the longer the trial can be delayed with the defendant out of jail, the better are his chances of remaining out of jail; b) with the defendant out on the street he can influence witnesses against him by threats; and c) when the criminal finds himself released almost immediately after arrest, and subsequently learns that regardless of the number of times he is arrested, he will be released, an atmosphere may be produced that will lead the criminal to believe that nothing will happen to him, regardless of how many crimes he commits or how often he is arrested.

Some other deficiencies of the Act are continued setting by many judicial officers of money bail in an amount that is completely beyond the defendant's economic means to meet, and consequently a large number of defendants in jail awaiting trial due to high money bail and/or failure of counsel to apply for twenty-four-hour review.

To alleviate the deficiencies of the Act the following amendments to the Act have been suggested: a) authorize judges to consider danger to the community in setting nonmonetary conditions of bail; b) allow revocation of release on bail with expedited trial for violation of conditions of release or after indictment for a felony allegedly committed while on bail if no condition of release will protect the public; c) provide an additional one-year penalty for persons convicted of crimes committed while on bail, and d) conform standards for appellate review of bail decisions under 18 U.S.C. 3148 and 3146 (b) (see Chap. 7) and direct affirmance of District Court decisions where they are supported by the proceedings in the court below (Report of the Judicial Committee to Study the Operation of the Bail Reform Act in the District of Columbia, May, 1969).

Section 2. PREVENTIVE DETENTION

2.1. Proposed Legislation

In the Senate of the United States, October 15, 1969, Mr. Tydings introduced the following bill, which was read twice and referred to the Committee on the District of Columbia.

To provide for thirty-day pre-trial detention, in lieu of bail, for certain dangerous persons in the District of Columbia . . . *Be it enacted by the Senate and House of Representatives of the United States of America in Congress assembled. . . .*

The following procedures shall apply with respect to persons charged in the District of Columbia with the commission of an offense.

At the time of a person's appearance before a judicial officer in the District of Columbia for release in accordance with the provisions of section 3146 of title 18, United States Code, or at any time after the person's release pursuant to said section 3146 by one such judicial officer, the Government may request a special evidentiary hearing for the purpose of imposing the conditions of release or commitment to custody provided for by subsection (e) of this section. The Government's application for such a hearing shall be granted only if:

1. The person is charged with the commission of a felony involving the infliction of or threat to inflict serious bodily harm on another while released pending trial of a prior felony charge or pending appeal from a conviction of a felony.

2. The person is charged with the commission of a felony involving the infliction of or threat to inflict serious bodily harm on another and the Government, by affidavit, alleges that, if released, the person will inflict serious bodily harm on another or pose, because of his prior pattern of behavior, a substantial danger to other persons or to the community.

3. The person is charged with the commission of an offense relating to robbery or burglary.

If the Government's application is granted, the person shall be committed to custody until after the special hearing and appellate review thereof have been concluded.

If the judicial officer grants the Government's application for a special evidentiary hearing, such hearing shall be held within two days, unless the person or his attorney requests a delay of the hearing.

Upon granting the Government's application, the judicial officer shall notify the person and his attorney of the time and place of the hearing. If the person is without funds to provide for the assistance of counsel for the hearing, the judicial officer shall appoint counsel to represent the person at the expense of the United States, when the offense is to be tried in the United States District Court for the District of Columbia, or at the expense of the District of Columbia, when the offense is to be tried in the Superior Court of the District of Columbia.

In conducting a hearing under this section, the judicial officer shall receive and consider all relevant evidence and testimony which may be offered. The person shall have the right to present evidence, and to present and cross-examine witnesses. The testimony of the person at this hearing may not be used against him in any other judicial proceeding, nor shall the person waive his privilege against self-incrimination in any future judicial proceeding by testifying at this hearing.

If the judicial officer conducting the special evidentiary hearing under this section determines, upon clear and convincing evidence, that there is substantial likelihood that the person if released will seek to intimidate witnesses, or otherwise unlawfully interfere with the administration of justice, or cause the death of, or inflict serious bodily harm upon, another, or participate in the planning or commission of any of the offenses enumerated, the judicial officer shall impose upon the person any condition or combination of conditions of release set forth in section 3146 (a) of title 18, United States Code, which will reasonably protect against the dangers set forth in this section. If the judicial officer finds that a conditional release of the person under section 3146 of title 18, United States Code, would not provide the necessary protection against the dangers set forth in this subsection, the judicial officer shall order the person committed to custody for a period not to exceed thirty days prior to his trial. The judicial officer shall state on the record his reasons for imposing any order of commitment to custody or the conditions of release. The judicial officer shall make any determination pursuant to this subsection, and shall impose any order of commitment to custody or condition of release, within twenty-four hours after the conclusion of the special evidentiary hearing.

Any person committed to custody or conditionally released under subsection (e) of this section shall have the rights of review and appeal, as provided in section 3147 of title 18, United States Code, and any other rights to judicial review as provided by law: *Provided,* that any appeal arising pursuant to this subsection must be disposed of within ten days of the entry of the order appealed from.

Any judicial officer who conducts the special evidentiary hearing provided for in this section, or who reviews the outcome of said hearing, shall not sit in any trial of the person for an offense which was the basis for or pending at the time of said hearing.

Any person committed to custody under subsection (e) of this section shall have his case placed on an expedited trial calendar, and the handling of motions and other preliminary matters pertaining to the case shall also be expedited. Continuances shall be granted only upon a showing of compelling circumstances. A continuance granted upon motion of the defense shall extend commitment to custody ordered pursuant to this section for the additional period of such continuance. If the trial of the person has begun but not been completed before the expiration, after the order of commitment to custody, of thirty days plus the period of any such continuance, the person shall remain subject to the commitment order until the conclusion of the trial.

Any hearing under the provisions of this section shall be taken down by a court reporter or recorded by suitable sound recording equipment. A copy of the record of such a hearing shall be made available, at the expense of the United States, when the offense is to be tried in the United States District Court for the District of Columbia, or at the expense of the District of Columbia, when the offense is to be tried in the Superior Court of the District of Columbia, to a person who was the subject of the hearing and who makes affidavit that he is unable to pay or give security therefor; and the expense of such copy shall be paid by the Director of the Administrative Office of the United States Courts, when the offense is to be tried in the United States District Court for the District of Columbia, or by the Executive Officer of the District of Columbia Courts, when the offense is to be tried in the Superior Court of the District of Columbia.

No person committed to custody pursuant to this section shall be denied the right to communicate with counsel or any other person at any reasonable time. Also, upon the application of counsel on behalf of any such person in custody, a judicial officer shall order, for a strictly limited and necessary period of time, the release of such person in the custody of and at all times to be accompanied by a designated public law enforcement officer, if the judicial officer determines that, notwithstanding the rights secured by this section, the person cannot otherwise prepare his defense.

2.2. Justification

In the 1969 Report of The Canadian Committee on Corrections, "Towards Unity: Criminal Justice and Corrections," it was said that pre-trial detention can only be justified where it is necessary in the public interest to ensure the appearance of the accused at trial, and to protect the public pending trial of the accused.

In short, pre-trial detention is necessary to prevent criminal activity by the accused pending trial. The offenses that one wishes to prevent are those similar to that charged and/or offenses relating to the trial, such as destruction of evidence, tampering with the witnesses, or otherwise obstructing the course of justice.

Pre-trial detention cannot be used to obtain guilty pleas or inflict punishment on a person whose guilt has not yet been determined.

It is desirable that every accused pending trial be released on bail, unless release is outweighed by the public interest. It is acknowledged that the accused awaiting trial may be unfairly damaged by pre-trial detention if he is subsequently acquitted. Incarceration prior to trial may cause loss of job by the accused and make it impossible for him to fulfill societal obligations such as support of his family. Even if he does not lose his job, the loss of income during the period of pre-trial detention, may have similar effects. In view of such possibilities, the accused should not be incarcerated pending trial unless the protection of the public requires it.

2.1.1. BAIL RELEASE PROBLEMS. (Address by Chief Jerry V. Wilson, Metropolitan Police Department, Washington, D.C., for the 76th Annual Conference, International Association of Chiefs of Police.)

Our association is assembled here at a time when society's problem with those who will not obey the law has never loomed larger in our national life; when serious crimes increase annually at a rate far in excess of the growth of our population; when, in the words of the National Crime Commission, crime has "eroded the quality of life in America." Last year, for example, according to our Uniform Crime Reports, crime increased 17 percent to a total of 4.5 million crime index offenses. Two people out of every hundred in America are victims of crime each year. As a matter of statistical probability, no person can count on reaching fifty years of age without being the victim of a crime.

These are troubling times indeed, and we need not be ashamed or embarrassed if, as policemen, as Americans, we have difficulty in explaining our crime problems or in devising simple remedies.

Indeed, one of the major pitfalls we professionals must guide our constituent citizens and our legislators away from is the trap of reliance on simple remedies. For the simple remedy is what is generally asked for but it is never likely to be effective.

Think how often you have been before a legislative body, a city council, or even a citizens association and have been asked "What can we do to help the police stop crime?" Each of you has heard that question numerous times, I am sure. And what your questioners would like to have is some simple straight-forward answer—some panacea, some magic thing which can be done to control crime.

But 150 years of searching by criminologists has uncovered no simple answer—indeed, application of scientific analysis has only increased the complexity of the questions; so we—who know from experience that law enforcement is far more art than science—cannot be expected to rely on or to give simple solutions.

It would be comforting if we could believe that crime in America is the vice of a handful of people. Many people today believe that and would attribute spiraling rates of crime to a small number of lawbreakers. But as police officials, we know that, although the proportion of lawbreakers among us is small, the number is quite large. In the United States today, about one boy in six is referred to the juvenile court. In 1965 alone more than 2 million Americans were received in prisons or juvenile training schools or placed on probation. And the unhappy fact is that most of these offenders will commit other crimes after they are released.

Of offenders released to the street in 1963, 63 per cent were rearrested within five years, 43 per cent within one year of their release.

Of persons under 25 released in 1963, 70 per cent were rearrested within five years.

As police chiefs, we know and judges know and corrections officials know, and the general public knows: that society has corrections processes that practically never correct nor rehabilitate. Available evidence points to a conclusion that, as a general rule, the principal rehabilitation factor affecting a criminal is that he simply grows too old for the active life of a criminal.

As police officials, we know also that what the public speaks of as "crime" is not a narrow range of behavior. An enormous variety of acts make up the "crime" problem. Crime is not only a tough teen-ager snatching a woman's purse, not only a professional thief stealing cars "on order," not only a well-heeled loan shark taking over a legitimate business, not only a pusher selling drugs to addicts, not only student demonstrators wrecking school buildings and rifling deans' files . . . it is much more. Indeed, as you well know, even in periods when serious crime—robberies, burglaries, even murders—are at a peak, the clamor from citizens may be for control of truants and disorderly street gangs of youths. As policemen, we understand this. We know the complexity of the problem, but we have not always adequately conveyed to the public the fact that no single formula, no single theory, no single generalization can explain the vast range of behavior called "crime."

We know, too, that many Americans believe that controlling crime is the task of the police alone. Many Americans do not understand our dependence on the effectiveness of the other segments of the criminal justice system—prosecutors, courts, and corrections. As police officials, we know that unless the man on the beat is backed up by a system of vigorous prosecution, prompt trials, and rehabilitation programs that produce results, the criminal will sooner or later be back on the street to cause more problems for society and for us.

The fact is that making police more effective is wasteful if society continues to permit the overburdening of judges and the clogging of courts. *And* increasing the number of judges is futile if courtroom administration is not modernized and the number of prosecutors and defense attorneys remains inadequate. *And* an expanded judiciary cannot take advantage of realistic sentencing alternatives if new correctional facilities and programs are not provided. *And* the best correctional programs will fail if reformed offenders cannot be assimilated into the community.

It is no overstatement to conclude that our criminal justice system is a failure. *Our Criminal Justice System is a failure.* We are not preventing crime; we are not apprehending and convicting enough offenders; we are not rehabilitating enough convicts.

As Chief Justice Warren Burger has said: "Many people . . . will be deterred from serious crimes if they believe that justice is swift and sure. Today no one thinks that."

We, as police officials, certainly share in the responsibility for this state of events. We are part of this ineffective criminal justice system. We can do more. And we are doing more—more to improve ourselves, more to professionalize ourselves, more than ever before. Others in the criminal justice system must do more also. Courts and corrections, in particular, must improve their effectiveness. Unless each agency of the criminal justice system works to improve itself, and unless all of the agencies of the criminal justice system work together to improve the total system, we will never begin to reverse the rate of crime increase in our country.

One area where the system needs desperately to work together is in regard to bail, in regard to the releasing of suspects on cash bond or personal recognizance prior to trial or conviction. In my city, the District of Columbia, the problem of pre-trial release has become particularly acute because our system is governed by the Federal Bail Reform Act of 1966, but I am sure that many of you are experiencing similar difficulties in your own jurisdiction or will begin to have these problems if pre-trial release practices continue towards relaxation, a trend indicated by current reports on the subject.

For many of you, perhaps even for most of you, my comments on the problems of liberalized bail release policies may be a forewarning of future problems you may face, if the release policies of the Federal Bail Reform Act of 1966 are not soon rewritten and should subsequently spread to state judicial procedures, as the Federal rules regarding search and seizure and regarding questioning of suspects have been extended to the states over the past decade.

Although specific practices vary, the typical operation of the bail system in the United States can be simply described. An arrested person is brought by the arresting officer before a committing magistrate or judge. The judge fixes an amount of money as security for the suspect's appearance for trial. In some courts, there is a bail list which sets an amount for each offense, for example, 5,000 dollars for robbery, and if the defendant can post bail for this amount, the committing magistrate seldom considers the facts of his case individually. In either event, if the defendant can pay a bondsman and can convince the bondsman that he is a good risk, the bondsman posts security and the accused is given his freedom until trial. If he cannot pay, or if the bondsman sees him as a poor risk, he remains in jail until trial—commonly a long period of time, in my own jurisdiction, an average of nearly one year in a felony case.

The standard rate of premiums paid to bondsmen varies from 5 to 10 per cent, and occasionally is higher. A study in New York, where the bondsman's fee is 5 per cent, showed that 25 per cent of arrested persons were unable to furnish bail of 500 dollars, that is pay a premium of 25 dollars, and nearly 50 per cent failed to raise the 75 dollars needed when bail is set at 1,500 dollars. Another study revealed that in some large counties, such as Cook and Hennepin, over 70 per cent of all felony defendants did not make bail, and in smaller counties, the figure was as high as 93 per cent.

This system of bail generates the problem that a defendant, no matter how heinous the crime charged or how strong the evidence against him, can go free if he can pay the premium. Conversely, the defendant unable to pay may languish in jail for months—not because he is found guilty, not because he is under sentence, not because he is likely to flee but simply because he is without money to pay.

In some types of cases, this system of bail serves no purpose except to enrich the bondsman at the expense of some working man's family. An example of this type case is the arrestee is a domestic quarrel, an arrestee who, we all know, is unlikely to flee; an arrestee who, we all know, need not be held in custody longer than it takes for tempers to cool. An arrestee who pays money to the bondsman to insure his appearance at a hearing at which, we all know the charges will be dropped.

President Johnson, in signing the Bail Reform Act of 1966, cited three examples of how the traditional bail system inflicted arbitrary hardships.

"A man was jailed on a serious charge brought on Christmas Eve. He could not afford bail and spent 101 days in jail until a hearing. Then the complainant admitted the charge was false.

"A man could not raise $300 bail. He spent 54 days in jail waiting trial for a traffic offense, for which he could have been sentenced to no more than 5 days.

"A man spent two months in jail before being acquitted in that period, he lost his job, and his car, and his family was split up. He did not find another job for four months."

All of us here could cite many similar examples. We are as familiar with the inequities of the bail system as anybody in the country. As policemen, we have seen its imperfections many times.

In this context, and from this perspective, the Bail Reform Act of 1966 was a promising development. The first basic change in federal bail law since 1789, the Act drastically reduced reliance on money bail. Release on personal recognizance—the suspect's promise to return for the next court appearance—was to be the rule. In exceptional cases, the judge could attach conditions to the release *if he determined that the defendant was likely to flee*. He could, for example, restrict the defendant's travel, his associations, his place of abode, or require the execution of an appearance bond by a refundable deposit. He could even place the defendant in partial custody, releasing him during the day so that he could work and support his family and confining him at night. These things he could do *if he determined that the defendant was likely to flee*.

What he *could not* do, however, is consider danger to the community as a criterion for release. Under the Act, the sole standard of granting or denying release is the defendant's likelihood of flight. Money bond or other restrictions may be required only "to assure the appearance of the person for trial."

Under these circumstances, there is little the judge can do to detain the dangerous offender; for example, a holdup man who has been arrested on three prior occasions for armed robbery but who has always showed up for scheduled court appearances; or a convicted narcotics addict who needs a hundred dollars a day to support his habit but who has a record of regular court appearances. Such crime-prone individuals have demonstrated under the terms of the Bail Reform Act that they are "reliable," that is, that they will show up for the hearings, motions, rehearings, and appeals, the seemingly endless series of judicial events that are necessary to conclude a criminal case in this country. Indeed, experience has shown that very few defendants fail to appear on schedule.

But too many such defendants have also demonstrated something else, something more than a mere ability to return to the courthouse on cue. They have demonstrated that, given their freedom before trial, they are likely to threaten the safety and freedom of others.

My own department conducted a survey of individuals released on personal recognizance, prior to trial, after being indicted on charges of armed robbery—our survey showed that 35 per cent of these individuals released in one year were rearrested and reindicted on subsequent felonies, mostly armed robberies, before coming to trial. Some were *rearrested* and *reindicted* as many as three times in one year.

Let me make one point clear. The money bail system in general use in the American system of criminal justice, the money bail system used in the District of Columbia before the Bail Reform Act of 1966, had no provision authorizing a judicial officer to set terms of bail on a basis of likelihood that the accused might commit additional crimes before trial. Indeed, even under the money bail system, if the defendant is arrested for a second offense while on pre-trial bail, he is nonetheless entitled bail on the second offense. And the magistrate is supposed to set that bail without regard to the fact that a second offense has occurred.

But, it is generally recognized that in the money bail systems, the magistrates *do* consider the defendant's danger to the community in setting high bonds, despite the traditional purpose of bail to insure the defendant's appearance for trial. (For example, the District of Columbia Crime Commission found that the average amount of bond set by the Court more than doubled in cases where a defendant was arrested while out on bail.)

And, what happens under a personal recognizance release system (and what could happen under a money bond system) where the magistrate is *prohibited* from considering danger to the community in determining release conditions is that, first, further incentive is added for the defense attorney to pursue the classical method for defense of a criminal case—*delay;* the defendant is out of jail, the longer the trial can be delayed, the better the chance he will remain out of jail; secondly, the defendant is out on the street where he can influence witnesses against him, either by direct threats from himself or by threats from friends of his—and our experience has been that this can be a considerable problem in a free release system; and, thirdly, as the criminals find themselves released almost immediately after arrest, and learn that this release process prevails regardless of the number of times they are arrested, we produce an atmosphere in which criminals feel that nothing will happen to them, regardless of how often they commit crimes, regardless of how often they are arrested.

Because of these reasons, I support the development of a visible constitutional, highly selective system of pre-trial detention for the dangerous offender.

Now, when I speak of the need for a just and permissible system of pre-trial detention, I must also add that if our courts were doing their job of providing speedy justice instead of seemingly interminable delays, a system of detention would not be as urgently needed. Today, many individuals arrested for felonies are not given their day in court for months, sometimes years. We all know that delay—dead time during which the criminal justice system is motionless, or perhaps is moving, but without gaining any headway—can only hurt the government's case and aid the defense. Overcrowded calendars and inefficient court procedures permit the defense to manipulate the scheduling of the myriad proceedings for their own benefit. Delay *is* a classic defense tactic. During prolonged waiting periods witnesses disappear and evidence grows stale.

In my own jurisdiction, as I indicated earlier, the average time between arrest and trial for a suspected felon is nearly one year, sometimes longer. If during this period the suspect is free on bail, he has no incentive to develop roots in the community, to get a job, to reconcile with his family, to further his education, especially if the evidence is strong against him. On the contrary, his natural impulse may be to live high in the interim period by committing additional crimes, perhaps more than he would have committed had he never been apprehended by the police in the first instance. Perhaps most distressing, there is no evidence that the period of delay between arrest and trial and between arrest and final appeal will grow shorter. Indeed, as crime rates increase, as more policemen are added to the department, as more arrests are made, the already clogged court systems will be more ineffective than ever.

In addressing himself to this problem, the Chief Justice of the United States has said:

"The celebrated case which takes five to ten years to complete is common talk in the best clubs and the worst ghettos. If lax police work and lax prosecution will impair the deterrent effect of the law, repeated reversals and multiple trials in the highly publicized cases will likely have a similar effect. . . . Is a society which frequently takes five to ten years to dispose a single criminal case entitled to call itself an organized society? Is a judicial system which consistently finds it necessary to try a criminal case, 3, 4, 5 times deserving of the confidence and respect of decent people?"

Judicial processes must be improved by the application of modern management techniques and provision of greater resources to the courts. The prompt and fair processing of arrested individuals is our primary goal. But it is unrealistic to assume that this goal will be achieved soon. Court processes will not suddenly become prompt and efficient no matter how hard all of us strive, as we should, to make them so. We will still be faced with the problem of fashioning standards for the pre-trial release or detention of the dangerous offender.

Fortunately, the Federal Administration has sent to the Congress a bill which will amend the Bail Reform Act to provide for the detention of certain defendants who are dangerous. In broad outline, the proposed new bill contemplates detention in four categories. First, if a defendant is charged with what is designated a "dangerous crime" he may be subjected to a pre-trial detention hearing based on this charge alone. A "dangerous crime" is restrictively defined to cover offenses with high risk of additional public danger if the defendant is released. These include bank robbery and the sale of a narcotic drug. The second category covers a group of repeat offenders who have been charged with at least two crimes of violence. The third category covers narcotic addicts who are charged with any crime of violence. (Probably no more predictable person exists than the addict who must find dollars to maintain his habit.) While the bill permits the addict to be held on the first charge, that charge must be a crime of violence. Thus, the addict supporting a habit by petit larceny or prostitution is excluded. Only when the addict appears to have "graduated" to crimes of violence can he be subjected to pre-trial detention. A final category covers those persons, who irrespective of the offense charged, obstruct justice by threatening witnesses or jurors.

The Act provides many safeguards for the accused. No one falling within the specific categories can be ordered detained unless a detention hearing is held. At this hearing the judicial officer must find that the person falls within one of the above categories, that a substantial probability exists that the person committed the offense charged, and that no condition or combination of conditions of release will reasonably assure the safety of any other person or the community. In addition, so that a defendant who is detained will be able to effectively assist in the preparation of his case, the Act provides that he may even secure release for limited periods to obtain evidence or witnesses. Finally, once ordered detained, the person will be entitled to an expedited trial and to release within sixty days unless the trial is in progress or the trial is being delayed at his request.

I should make it clear that in supporting these amendments, I am not advocating a return to the system existing before passage of the Bail Reform Act. Then, we were holding too many people for too long; then we did have a system of preventive detention, a de facto one that held only poor people. A poor, dangerous man would automatically be detained by a high bond. A wealthy dangerous man or a professional holdup man who could produce a fee would go free. Dangerousness, not wealth or poverty should be criteria for detaining individuals.

I should also emphasize that, in my opinion, to make the bail system effective, we need detain prior to trial only a small number of individuals, a very small number *if* we detain the right ones—the hardened recidivists, the individuals too dedicated to crime to turn back, and the addicts who cannot live a law-abiding life.

I prefaced my remarks about bail by observing that the criminal justice system must work together as a system if we are to bring crime under control. The reason I have emphasized this point here is because I believe that bail is an example of the many systemic problems to law enforcement that the police cannot solve by themselves. The basic responsibility for the formation and implementation of bail policies, after all, lies with the legislatures and the courts. But as officials whose success or failure depends on the total system, we have a right and duty to give advice and judgment on this subject. We need to make our influence felt to develop an effective and fair system of bail, one that is designed to protect society as well as the the accused, and one that reflects the needs of the policeman as well as the prosecutor, the judge, and the correctional officer.

I would not want to leave the impression in anyone's mind that by tightening up or revising existing laws and practices on bail we will have won the war on crime. I think we will have taken a step, perhaps a large one, in the right direction, but I would stress again that the complex problem of crime cannot be reduced to any single dimension. There are many causes of crime, for example, slum conditions, parental irresponsibility, unemployment, and racial discrimination, over which the criminal justice system has no control and little influence.

Those "factors" within the control of law enforcement are, however, important ones, and as we move toward professionalization. more and more will be asked of us as policemen. The last decade has been in a real sense the decade of the policeman in America, a decade marked by an emphasis on training and education, new recruiting methods, improvements in communications and technology, application of computers to the patrol function and the utilization of modern management techniques. There will undoubtedly be greater change in the next decade. Certainly there is no reason to believe that the enormous burdens that have been ours will be lightened, or that public expectations of police performance will be lowered. On the contrary, there is every reason to believe that more will be asked of us in the decade ahead.

We know that we have a long way to go toward a true police

profession, but we also know and should be proud of the fact that we have made so much progress. As we continue to progress, as we continue to improve the quality of police services to the community, we will, I believe, receive ever-increasing public recognition and support which will be based on our achievements.

2.3. Grounds for Denying Bail

It has been argued by some that there is no accurate way of predicting the behavior of the accused pending trial. Notwithstanding, some reasonable assessment of the probable behavior of the accused pending trial is possible.

As a rule of thumb, if the prosecution does not make a reasonable case for denial of bail, it should be granted.

Some standards that have been suggested for denying bail are the following: a) if the accused has previously been convicted of an indictable offense while on bail, and is presently charged with an indictable offense; b) if the accused has previously been convicted of absconding bail; or c) if the accused has been charged with the commission of an indictable offense while on bail charged with another indictable offense.

The above enumerated standards are not to be considered controlling in denying bail, but rather as factors to be weighed in its consideration.

It is recognized that for such standards to have practical value, a central record section maintaining data of those persons charged with indictable offenses would have to be readily available to judges, magistrates, and police, in order to preclude a person from avoiding the standards by moving to a different jurisdiction. It should be noted that the Department of Justice Law Enforcement Assistance Administration (LEAA) has proposed and is implementing computerized files for use at all levels in the criminal justice system, including courts, probation and police. The network of computer files store criminal histories and would seem to be readily adaptable to storing data for use in pretrial detention determination.

Section 3. CONSTITUTIONAL QUESTIONS

3.1. Protections for the Accused

Certain procedural safeguards would be available to the accused under a pre-trial detention bill.

No one would be ordered detained unless a detention hearing was held. At such a hearing the judicial officer must find the following if he is to detain the accused: a) that the person falls within one of the categories of person described by the pre-trial detention legislation; b) that substantial probability exists that the accused committed the offense charged; c) that release will endanger the safety of a person or the community; d) that the accused may be able to assist in the preparation of his case if detained; and e) that once detained the person will be entitled to an expedited trial and to release within 30 (or 60) days unless the trial is in progress, or has been delayed at the request of the accused. The proposed bill should also include a provision that the accused, if detained, should be confined in facilities separate from convicted persons.

3.2. Presumption of Innocence

The presumption of innocence is a basic concept of the criminal law in this country. Technically, it is a legal rule of evidence that places the burden of proof on the government. Nevertheless, there are those who give it a much broader interpretation. They argue that pre-trial detention assumes the guilt of the accused and consequently is in conflict with the presumption of innocence.

Apart from the dictum of the Supreme Court in *Stack v. Boyle,* 342 U.S.1, 1951 ("Unless this right to bail before trial is preserved, the presumption of innocence secured only after centuries of struggle, would lose its meaning.") there is no basis for thinking that the presumption of innocence has any application to pre-trial proceedings. If it did, the firmly established practice of pre-trial detention of those charged with capital crimes would be unwarranted.

There is no presumption of innocence at the *pre-trial* inquiry, as there is at the *trial* itself. If we were to presume that everyone was innocent, no one should be charged until an extensive investigation has taken place resulting in strong evidence against them. Chief Metropolitan Magistrate, Frank Milton, of London, England has said that 97 percent of the people that appear in his Magistrate's courts either plead or are found guilty as are 85 percent of those who appear in the high courts.

If the presumption of innocence applied to the *pre*-trial period of a criminal proceeding, it would be wrong to detain *anyone;* even a homicidal maniac who had confessed to a dozen murders, would have to be released on bail.

3.3. Due Process and the Fifth Amendment

In determining whether or not pre-trial detention comports with the due process requirements of reasonableness, one must consider the following: a) the degree of harm or danger to be anticipated from a particular defendant, b) that appropriate procedural safeguards are devised so that *only* those who actually pose a danger to the community will be detained, and c) the burdens imposed on law enforcement and the judiciary by a pre-trial detention plan must be minimized.

It is argued by some that pre-trial detention of an individual, based on the likelihood of his committing additional crimes, is said to violate the fifth amendment because it discriminates against the person detained. Specifically, it is said: a) to hamper in the preparation of his defense, b) to induce him to plead guilty instead of seeking a trial, c) to adversely affect a jury because he is seen in the custody of the law, and d) to minimize his chances of probation. Furthermore, it is contended that pre-trial detention denies him due process of law contrary to the fifth amendment, in that he is deprived of liberty because of possible future conduct.

In answer to the contention that pre-trial detention precludes preparation of a proper defense, the President's Commission on Crime in the District of Columbia, maintains that the inequity can be eliminated by changes in the judicial process. Specifically,

1. If it is shown in a hearing that the detention is interfering in the case preparation, the court can liberalize visitation privileges or grant daytime release.
2. Liberalized sentence crediting provisions in the Bail Reform Act and other safeguards which include limitation on the length of detention would guard against the possibility of a guilty plea induced by detention (*sentence crediting* is the deduction of time served, while awaiting trial, from the sentence eventually handed down).

3. Mechanical and administrative safeguards can be made available to avoid the appearance of criminality as the defendant enters the courtroom from the cell block.
4. Denial of probation will be based on the nature of the crime and the character of the defendant, not merely the fact of pre-trial detention.

Some arguments for pre-trial detention, vis-à-vis alleged violations of the fifth amendment, presented by the President's Commission mentioned, *supra,* are as follows:

1. The present bail system authorizes pre-trial detention in capital cases and in those cases where the defendant cannot meet the conditions of bail. In setting terms of bail, a prediction of future conduct is made, i.e. will the defendant appear at trial.
2. In certain situations, deprivation of liberty is constitutional, such as the mental incompetent who is confined prior to a determination of guilt; the mentally ill person that is civilly committed; and the defendant who is being deported who may be detained because of possible future dangerous conduct.
3. The public interest in protection against crime is just as important as the public interests protected by the present bail system. Furthermore, the difficulty in identifying those who are a risk to the community is no greater than identifying those who may flee justice.
4. Procedural safeguards can be established whereby a judicial hearing will be had to determine the question of future conduct and to prevent the unnecessary detention of those who are not a risk to the community.

In summary, the due process clause of the fifth amendment does not prohibit pre-trial detention in criminal cases. The test is one of reasonableness which involves the weighing of the individual's interest in freedom against societies just demand to be free from criminal interference while the accused is awaiting trial.

The Right Honorable Lord Denning, Master of the Rolls, London, England, has said, ". . . due process of law requires fundamental fairness, not perfect accuracy."

3.4. The Eighth Amendment

Although the eighth amendment set up the guideline that "excessive bail shall not be required" (see Chap. 7), it does not contain words which confer a right to bail. Two years before the amendment was ratified, the right to bail was separately legislated in the Judiciary Act of 1789. The Act provided that "upon all arrests in criminal cases bail shall be admitted, except where the punishment may be death."

Arguments which rely on the literal words of the amendment, which do not specify a right to bail, contend that the English Bill of Rights of 1689, from which the amendment came, never contemplated an absolute right to bail. Further, it is argued that the almost simultaneous drafting of the Judiciary Act and the eighth amendment indicate an intention to leave bail in the legislative domain. Even if the constitutional right to bail does exist, it is dependent upon the legislatures definition of capital crimes, for which bail may be denied.

Section 4. RECOMMENDATIONS

The Bail Reform Act of 1966 should be amended a) to permit a judicial officer to determine the danger of the defendant to the community if released on bail, and b) to authorization revocation of release of any defendant who is charged with a crime while released on bail upon the showing or probable cause that the defendant committed the offense last charged.

Persons who are potentially dangerous to the community should be tried within thirty days after indictment.

Legislation should be adopted which would double the maximum penalty for any offense committed by defendants while released on bail pending trial or appeal in a criminal proceeding.

Legislation should be passed to authorize the pre-trial detention of those defendants who are a danger to the safety of the community.

Section 5. NEW LEGISLATION

To date, the only national legislation, which embodies the element of dangerousness of the defendant in considering his pre-trial release in capital cases or after conviction, is a 1970 amendment to the Bail Reform Act of 1966, 18 U.S.C. 3148:

5.1. Release in Capital Cases or After Conviction

A person (1) who is charged with an offense punishable by death, or (2) who has been convicted of an offense and is either awaiting sentence or sentence review under section 3576 of this title or has filed an appeal or a petition for a writ of certiorari, shall be treated in accordance with the provisions of section 3146 unless the court or judge has reason to believe that no one or more conditions of release will reasonably assure that the person will not flee or pose a danger to any other person or to the community. If such a risk of flight or danger is believed to exist, or if it appears that an appeal is frivolous or taken for delay, the person may be ordered detained. The provisions of section 3147 shall not apply to persons described in this section: *Provided,* that other rights to judicial review of conditions of release or orders of detention shall not be affected. As amended Pub.L. 91—452, Title X, § 1002, Oct. 15, 1970, 84 Stat. 952.

The amended section quoted, *supra,* corrects the significant fault of the Bail Reform Act which Chief of Police Wilson referred to (see "Fault of the Bail Reform Act of 1966," this chapter). However, the amendment only considers the element of dangerousness in a *pre-trial* situation with respect to capital offenders. Furthermore, it does not consider or provide: a detention hearing (see "Protections for the Accused," this chapter), an expedited trial, or separate confinement from convicted persons.

Although this amendment does not implement the proposed concept of pre-trial detention, it is a small step in the direction of the protection of the community at the expense of the detained, dangerous, accused capital offender.

CHAPTER 9

THE STRUCTURE OF THE COURTS

Section I. CRIMINAL JUSTICE SYSTEM

IN the administration of justice in legal systems, one immediately encounters a dilemma: on one hand, the system must preserve and protect lives, property, and civil order; on the other hand, when the criminal process is invoked against an individual, it is one of the surest means of guaranteeing oppression of the citizen. The system should be capable of retaining the criminal while allowing the innocent suspect to go free.

The Constitution provides a framework for the administration of criminal justice, with safeguards being afforded the individual accused. The application of safeguards in procedure is one of the major distinctions between our federal and state systems.

1.1. Legal Systems and the Constitution

Constitutional safeguards contained in the Bill of Rights have always applied to *federal proceedings,* namely, to protect the accused from unfairness and oppression by law enforcement officials. Until recently, such safeguards did *not* apply to the states. In the field of criminal justice, each state has received an undisputed sovereignty to make its own laws and determine rules of procedure and evidence in criminal matters. Decline of state sovereignty in the criminal procedure area began with an 1868 Constitutional amendment—the fourteenth.

In 1927, a conviction was set aside at the state level on the grounds of unfairness of procedures which were employed to obtain the conviction. During the past half century, the court has relied more and more on the requirements of due process and the incorporation of certain of the Bill of Rights by the fourteenth amendment. However, the reader must understand that neither the court, nor Congress has ever imposed upon the states the *duty* of including within their criminal procedures all of the protective features which the fourth, fifth, sixth, and eighth amendments make mandatory in Federal proceedings.

Beginning in the 1940s, the court began announcing guidelines as to what due process required of the states. In more recent years, the court has departed from strict traditional due process requirements in its decisions, for example, holding that due process standards extend to evidentiary standards.

1.2. Division of Judicial Power

Governments' judicial power, whether state or federal, is vested in a system of courts which are divided into several specific categories, all of which perform a different function. Each division of the court system has special and limited authority to hear certain cases.

The federal court system is more complex than that of any state, and, although larger, the federal framework follows basically the same pattern as the state systems.

There are certain courts where proceedings are initiated within the federal system. United States District Courts are said to have *original jurisdiction* in a majority of criminal actions. From the District Court, a case may proceed to the Court of Appeals, and finally to the United States Supreme Court.

The authority for the federal court system is found within Article III of the Constitution. Section (1) establishes that the "judicial power of the United States shall be vested in one Supreme Court and such inferior courts as Congress may from time to time order and establish."

Section (2) defines the scope of federal judicial power to adjudicate cases. "The judicial power shall extend to all cases in law and equity, arising under this Constitution, the laws of the United States, and treaties made, or which shall be made, under their authority; to all cases affecting ambassadors or other public ministers and consuls; to all cases of admiralty and maritime jurisdictions; to controversies to which the United States shall be a party; to controversies between two or more states, between a state and citizens of another state; between citizens of different states; between citizens of the same state claiming lands under grant of different states, and between a state, or the citizens thereof, and foreign states, citizens, or subjects." Figure 9-2 presents a block diagram representing the federal court structure.

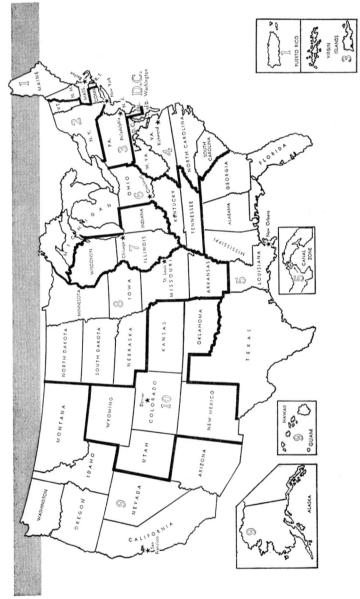

The Eleven Federal Judicial Circuits

See 28 U.S.C.A. § 41

Figure 9-1. The United States is divided into eleven judicial districts, including the District of Columbia. Courtesy West Publishing Company.

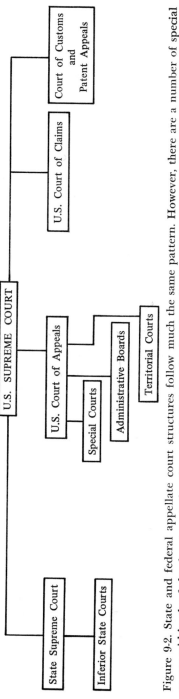

Figure 9-2. State and federal appellate court structures follow much the same pattern. However, there are a number of special courts within the federal system to handle quasi-judicial and administrative matters.

1.2.1. JUDICIAL DISTRICTS. The United States is divided into eighty-eight judicial districts to facilitate law enforcement and administration. Within each state there is at least one district, served by a district court.

A criminal case begins at the district court level, which has general jurisdiction to hear criminal cases. The first appellate court in the federal system is the U.S. Court of Appeals. There are eleven such courts. The Court of Appeals is said to be an intermediate appellate court, the final decision in the appellate process being made by the Supreme Court of the United States. The Supreme Court, which is said to be the court of last resort in the federal system, has original jurisdiction in certain limited proceedings. The greatest portion of its work is to review decisions taken from the lower federal courts and from state courts of last resort. In order for the Supreme Court to review decisions from state courts, however, a substantial issue of federal law must be raised.

There are three methods by which the United States Supreme Court may review a case. The most common is by application for a writ of *certiorari*. Such a petition is granted where, in the Courts discretion, there are special and important reasons to review the case. Because of the volume of petitions, the Court only decides those cases which present questions whose resolution will have an immediate impact and import beyond the particular facts of the case.

A case may also reach the Supreme Court by *direct appeal*. An appeal will be taken when a state court declares a statute to be unconstitutional, or when a federal court finds a state statute contra to the treaties, laws, or constitution of the United States. In such cases, the Court will only review questions of federalism which have been raised in the appeal.

Finally, a case may be brought to the Court upon a certification by a United States Court of Appeals, asking instructions on procedure with respect to a point of law. Certification of a case to the Supreme Court is rarely granted.

In addition to the district court, appellate courts, and supreme court, the federal court system is comprised of numerous specialized courts which have been established to hear particular

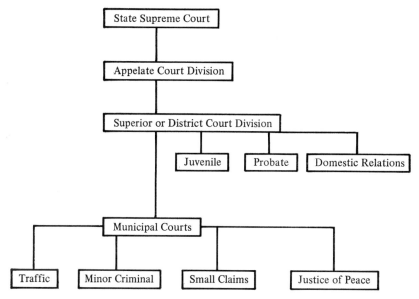

Figure 9-3. Typical state court organization.

classes of cases: for example, there is a United States Customs Court to hear cases arising from the imposition of custom duties on goods brought into the United States; there is a United States Court of Claims to hear cases brought against the United States; and there is a United States Tax Court to hear cases relating to the levying of federal taxes.

There are also a number of *quasi judicial* boards or commissions, which have special and limited authority with respect to specific federal statutes, for example, the Federal Communications Commission has limited authority in the area of radio, television, and wire communications.

1.2.2. STATE COURT SYSTEMS. As noted previously, the state court systems follow the same general structure as the federal systems, in that there are both lower courts of general and original jurisdiction and a series of appellate courts.

On the local level, courts having original jurisdiction may be called municipal courts, traffic courts, or justice of the peace courts. Usually the jurisdiction of these tribunals is limited to misdemeanor offenses, and controversies involving small sums of money.

The next step that one encounters in a state court system might be the county court of the state court of a given district. These courts are usually competent to hear both misdemeanor and felony cases, in addition to civil cases where the disputed amounts may run into the thousands of dollars. Usually the more serious cases will be commenced on the county or district court level.

From the district court, cases may travel through one or more appellate courts, until finally reaching the state supreme court. Authority for the state court system is usually derived from the individual state constitutions. As mentioned in our discussion of the federal court system, if the case involves special constitutional problems, it may proceed on to the United States Supreme Court for review.

1.3. Criminal Proceedings

Generally, there are seven recognized stages to any criminal proceeding. These seven stages are listed below and discussed in the following pages.

1. Bring the accused before or within the power of the tribunal.
2. Conduct a preliminary investigation to insure that the cause is one which should be prosecuted.
3. Give notice to the accused of the offense charged.
4. Allow an opportunity to prepare for trial, procure witnesses, and make needed investigations.
5. Insure a speedy trial.
6. Insure a fair trial before an impartial tribunal.
7. Grant one review of the case as a whole by a suitable appellate tribunal.

1.3.1. POWER OF THE TRIBUNAL. In order for a court to hear and decide a case, it must have jurisdiction over both the subject and the subject matter. In other words, the court must not only have the litigants, or plaintiff (and usually defendant) within its territorial boundaries, but also have the power to hear the case.

Any one court does not have the power to hear all types of

cases. For example, a divorce petition may not be heard by the Supreme Court, by reason that it does not have competent jurisdiction to hear such cases.

1.3.2. JURISDICTION OF THE SUBJECT MATTER. Subject matter jurisdiction refers to the authority or competency of the court to adjudicate or try certain types of cases. As noted earlier, each court in the judicial system, whether state or federal, has been granted power to decide particular kinds of cases. For example, a state district court may hear all felonies committed within its territorial jurisdiction, which may be a county, while a Justice of the Peace or municipal court, situated within the same area, would be allowed to hear misdemeanors, but not felonies. The power to decide cases is usually determined by state constitutions and/or statutes, while in the federal system, by the United States Constitution and/or Congress.

A court *must* possess the *legal* authority to hear a case. The lack of jurisdiction ordinarily cannot be waived by any party to an action, regardless of the expediency of doing so. Note that failure of jurisdiction will render void any decision by the court.

A second requirement to hear a case is that the court must be located within the political subdivision wherein the action or the crime was committed. Thus, the court of one district would lack power to hear a case resulting from a crime committed in an adjoining district. However, when a change in *venue* is applied for and granted by the court, a party may then be tried in a different jurisdiction than that wherein the crime occurred.

Venue refers to the geographic location of the crime, the bringing of charges, and elements of proof required for a particular jurisdiction. Jurisdiction, as contrasted with venue, refers to the *power* of the court to try the case.

By appropriate legislation, the criminal jurisdiction of a state may be extended to meet the following situations:

1. Crimes committed in part within the state of jurisdiction. Under this category, crimes committed partly in one state or jurisdiction and partly in another area may be punished by *either* jurisdiction. For example, X, standing on the border between Nebraska and Colorado, fires a fatal shot at Y, who is standing across the state line, in Colorado. X

may be tried for homicide either in Colorado *or* Nebraska.

The one requirement of the "partial commission" doctrine above is that to be tried in either state in the above example, X's actions must have been criminal *in the state where tried*.

2. Crimes committed entirely outside of jurisdiction. States may punish for crimes committed outside their boundaries, where the acts affect the state, persons, or property *within* the state.

A co-existent requirement to subject matter jurisdiction is *jurisdiction over the subjects* to an action. Subject jurisdiction refers to bringing the litigants or defendants physically before the court, at the time of trial. The defendants must be before the court during trial when the charge involves a felony or high-grade misdemeanor. A defendant may, however, be adjudged guilty of certain misdemeanors without being present during the proceeding. The guarantee that a trial will not be conducted in the absence of the accused is specified by the United States Constitution, and by many state constitutions, in addition. It should be noted that the Supreme Court has modified the "presence" requirement in felony cases where the defendant consistently attempts to disrupt the proceedings, in that he may be removed from the courtroom, or appropriately silenced while the proceeding continues.

There are a number of ways that jurisdiction of the person may be obtained when the accused must be brought within the jurisdiction of the court to stand charges:

1. Arrest.
2. Summons or citation.
3. Voluntary appearance.
4. Waiver of personal jurisdiction (although jurisdiction of the offense cannot be waived).
5. Posting of bail.

Arrest is the taking of a person into custody so the accused will be available to answer for the commission of a criminal offense. Necessary elements of arrest include the following:

1. Intent of arresting officer to bring person into custody to answer charges.

2. Submission of arrestee to arrest.
3. Authority to arrest, either real or pretended.
4. Actual or constructive *present* seizure or detention of person.
5. Understanding by arrestee that he is under arrest.
6. Communication by officer of present intent to arrest.

An arrest may be made by authority of a warrant. Upon a showing of probable cause by affidavit, information, or declaration, an arrest by warrant may take place. The warrant will describe the offense charged, the name of the accused, if known, and some type of description to aid in reliable identification (blank or John Doe warrant may be held void for a lack of definiteness). A warrant may be executed by any officer within the issuing jurisdiction. (It is not necessary for the arresting officer to have the warrant in his possession at the time of the arrest.) An arrest warrant is only good within the jurisdiction or state where issued. Execution of arrest warrants for *felonies* usually may be made at *any time,* while misdemeanor arrests are usually restricted to daylight hours. Arrest warrants remain valid until executed or cancelled. In contrast, search warrants are usually only good for ten days.

Summons or citations are orders to appear, usually issued for minor offenses. Nonetheless, they still require a sworn complaint by the officer. See Figure 4-8.

A person may *voluntarily submit to the jurisdiction of the court by making an appearance.* Once before the court, the accused may not invoke want of personal jurisdiction as a defense.

By entering a plea, or *posting of bail,* the accused thereby submits to the courts' jurisdiction.

1.3.3. Illegal Arrest. Once the defendant is before the proper court, the legality of his arrest need not be questioned, for due process requirements are satisfied by a fair trial (see Chap. 3). The Supreme Court has held that jurisdiction to try a person for a crime is not impaired by the fact that the accused is forceably brought before the court from another jurisdiction (*Frisbie v. Collins,* 342 U.S.519 (1952)). The rationale behind allowing a court to try the accused once within its jurisdiction, regardless of how obtained, is that as long as the accused is held under valid process, the illegality of events preceding detention are immaterial, so long as *present detention* is valid. The defendant's wrong against the state cannot be excused by the means employed to gain his custody.

1.3.4. EXTRADITION. Extradition is the surrender of a person within the jurisdiction of one state (asylum state) to a sister state for the purpose of a criminal prosecution or imprisonment.

The purpose of extradition laws or agreements is to insure that one may not avoid justice by merely running outside the jurisdiction of the court. The United States Constitution allows for the extradition of fugitives between states (Article 4, Section 2).

Requirements for extradition are as follows:

1. It is necessary to show that the accused has committed a crime within the demanding state.
2. It is not necessary to show that the accused was physically within the state during the commission of the crime, as long as he is responsible.
3. Extradition, or rendition, may be invoked whether the defendant left the requesting state voluntarily or involuntarily.
4. *Any crime* will form a basis for extradition, as long as it is a crime in the demanding state.
5. The guilt or innocence of the accused is immaterial in judging the validity of an extradition.
6. Once extradition is accomplished, the accused may be tried for any offense, not just the one he was extradited for. This does not apply when the extradition is between foreign nations as a person may only be tried for the offense forming the basis of the extradition. A person extradited will usually be held immune to civil suit in the demanding state.

The governor of the demanding state requests the chief executive of the asylum state to turn over the accused. The executive may or may not grant the extradition request, at his discretion.

It must be pointed out that once jurisdiction is acquired over a person, it is not lost or defeated by the accused subsequent flight to another location. In addition, if the defendant flees during the course of his trial, he may be held to have waived his right to be present at trial.

1.3.5. PRELIMINARY INVESTIGATION AND EXAMINATION. Both the police and prosecutor have the responsibility of determining whether criminal conduct has occurred, and if it has, who is responsible. The cooperation of both law enforcement officers and the prosecutor is in the best interest of justice.

Once a person has been arrested for an offense, whether by warrant, complaint, or other means, he must be brought before a magistrate without unreasonable delay, to be advised of the charge, to conduct a preliminary examination and have bail set (if it is a bailable offense) (see *McNabb-Mallory* decision). If the person was arrested on a warrant, he must be taken before the court that issued it.

Where conferred by statute, the defendant must be afforded the opportunity for a preliminary examination. The purpose of the hearing is to allow a judicial inquiry to determine whether probable cause exists for the accusation. In essence, the preliminary hearing attempts to ascertain whether, in fact, a crime has been committed, and if there is cause to believe that the defendant has committed it. Secondary functions of the hearing are the following:

1. Perpetuate testimony.
2. Determine bail.
3. Eliminate groundless prosecutions.
4. Discover evidence.

The preliminary hearing is not a trial, although its rulings are binding.

1.3.6. MISDEMEANOR CASES. If the defendant is charged with a misdemeanor, he must plead to the charges at the time of the hearing.

If the charge involves a felony, the defendant must be afforded a reasonable time to secure counsel before pleading to the charge.

The evidence presented at the Preliminary hearing will give defense counsel some insight into the prosecution's case, and the defense may cross-examine witnesses. Any testimony elicited during the hearing may be used at trial to impeach the credibility of witnesses. Also, if agreeable to both sides, transcripts of the hearing may be used in the course of the trial.

In the Federal system, if an indictment has been returned by a grand jury, no hearing is required, as the grand jury proceeding in effect determines probable cause of the charges brought (see Chap. 5).

The accused may waive a preliminary examination by:
1. Pleading not guilty.
2. Voluntarily giving a bond or recognizance.
3. Pleading guilty.

A waiver operates as an admission by the accused of sufficient evidence to justify the examining officer in holding the accused for trial. Unless given under duress, the waiver will be an effective bar to later claims of no hearing.

The preliminary hearing must be conducted in accordance with Constitutional guarantees of due process. The state need only produce enough witnesses to satisfy probable cause requirements.

1.3.7. NOTIFY THE ACCUSED. As a result of the preliminary hearing, the accused will either be bound over for trial, or released.

Our legal system has developed on the theory that everyone accused of a crime must be informed of the charge against him. The offense must be spelled out in clear and precise language to enable the accused to prepare a defense and to be protected from double jeopardy.

Thus, the next step in the criminal process involves the advising of charges against the accused. An *arraignment* usually serves this function. The precise functions of the arraignment are the following:
1. Identify the accused.
2. Inform him of the charge.
3. Give him an opportunity to plead.
In felony cases, arraignments are regarded as essential, although they may be waived by the defendant. In the case of misdemeanors, the arraignment stage may be omitted, according to local requirements.

After a complaint, affidavit, or information has been filed, the defendant must be called into the court having jurisdiction, to have the charge read, and to give him an opportunity to plead. Usually, all that is required is that the defendants be called before the bench, the accusatory pleading is read to him, and a plea demanded.

1.3.8. ARRAIGNMENT. The defendant is required to be present at arraignment for a felony; contrastingly, counsel may appear in lieu of the accused in misdemeanor cases. As the arraignment is considered a *critical stage,* the right to counsel exists.

The accused must be arraigned prior to the impanelling of the jury, and within a reasonable time after being taken into custody.

An arraignment may be waived in the following ways:
1. Express waiver in open court by defendant.
2. Entry of plea.
3. Failure to object to a defect in procedure at the proper time.
4. Announcing readiness for trial.
5. Filing a *demurrer* or special plea.

1.3.9. PLEADING. A pleading by the defendant is a requisite to a proper trial, in felony cases, to define the issues. A plea usually is entered between arraignment and trial.

At common law only the defendant could plead; however, today an attorney acting for the accused may usually enter both pleas of innocent and guilty. The record must indicate that the defendant had the opportunity to plead, and what the plea was.

If the defendant stands mute, a plea of *not guilty* will be entered for him.

1.3.9.1. *Not Guilty.* This plea puts in issue every material allegation made by the prosecution. The plea will allow every defense including the following:
1. Statute of limitations.
2. Lack of jurisdiction.
3. Justification, excuse, and self-defense.
4. Entrapment.

In other words, pleading "not guilty" allows every possible avenue to remain open to refute the charges brought.

1.3.9.2. *Exception.* Certain defenses must be specifically pleaded, these include the following:

1. Double jeopardy.
2. Insanity.
3. Diminished responsibility.
4. Alibi.

1.3.9.3. *Demurrer.* A demurrer is a written pleading challenging the *legal* sufficiency of a charge, and it is restricted to defects on the face of the accusation. Grounds for demurrer include the following:

1. Want of jurisdiction.
2. Charge not amounting to an offense.
3. Legal justification is shown.
4. Misjoinder of offenses.

A demurrer is usually filed at the time of arraignment. What the demurrer does is to admit the accusation (s), yet deny the legal conclusions.

1.3.10. MOTIONS

1.3.10.1. *To Quash.* The accused may make a motion at arraignment to quash or dismiss the indictment for lack of evidence or procedural defect. The motion to quash differs from the demurrer in that grounds for this motion are not evident on the face of the charge.

The motion to quash is usually made at the arraignment. If granted, the defendant is either released or the complaint is amended.

1.3.10.2. *To Dismiss.* After a certain statutory period, the defendant may be released if no indictment or information has been filed.

1.3.10.3. *Change of Venue.* Where the court does not have proper jurisdiction to hear the case, venue may be invoked. In addition, a change of venue, or court, may be asked for and granted where the ends of justice will be furthered. A change of venue may be granted based on the following:

1. Lack of jurisdiction in the court.

2. Local prejudice, excitement, or inability to obtain a fair trial.

3. Bias or prejudice of the judge.

Generally, a change of venue request should be made prior to trial.

1.3.10.4. *Motion to Suppress.* The motion to suppress must be made prior to trial. Its purpose is to challenge and eliminate disputes relating to police conduct with respect to the evidence gathered.

1.3.11. GUILTY PLEAS. Guilty pleas must be entered voluntarily, knowingly, and intelligently. The court may or may not accept the guilty plea from the defendant. If it be shown that a plea of guilty was not made voluntarily, then due process of law is deemed to have been violated. The *presumption* is that the plea is involuntary. If the "voluntariness" standard is not met, the proceeding will be held invalid. The reader is directed to a discussion of the *Miranda* decision.

When the guilty plea is accepted, it, in effect admits every element of the offense charged. The plea waives any defects in prior procedure, e.g., arrest, search, and incarceration, but does not waive jurisdictional defects. The plea is conclusive, so the court has nothing to do but give judgment and sentence.

1.3.11.1. *Withdrawal of Plea.* The withdrawal of a plea of guilty may be made prior to sentencing, if it is for good cause. If entered after judgment, the plea will only be set aside for grounds such as duress and fraud.

1.3.11.2. *Nolo Contendere.* The plea of nolo contendere may be entered at the discretion of the court and in effect says, "yes, I am technically guilty of the charge and I do not wish to go into further details of it." Such a plea is a device whereby the defendant: a) need not make admissions which may be used as the basis for other prosecutions, b) avoids trial, c) avoids publicity, and d) avoids the stigma of a guilty plea.

1.3.12. CONDITIONAL PLEAS. Conditional pleas such as "I will plead guilty only if a fine will be levied," are not accepted.

1.3.13. NOLLE PROSEQUI. A nolle prosequi is a formal entry by the prosecutor stating his unwillingness to prosecute the case. The effect of a nolle prosequi plea is to immediately dismiss the defendant, and bar a subsequent prosecution of the same charge.

The power to issue the plea usually rests solely with the prosecutor, regardless of the attitude of the court. Once such a plea has been entered, the court is powerless to continue the prosecution. Note that if two courts have concurrent jurisdiction of a case, an entry of nolle prosequi or dismissal in one will *not* bar the other from proceeding on the case.

1.3.14. WRITS OF RELEASE. Two other methods employed in an attempt to release persons in custody and accused of a crime are those of *habeas corpus* and of *prohibition*.

1.3.14.1. *Habeas Corpus.* The writ of habeas corpus is a means of questioning and reviewing the lawfulness of detention of a prisoner. It is an immediate remedy for false imprisonment as guaranteed by the Constitution of the United States. It assures and secures personal liberty by simple and direct process available to all citizens, and is considered the greatest writ of the common law. The writ allows a *collateral attack* on a criminal judgment or charge.

When issued by the court, the writ says to a custodian, "You have the prisoner in your possession. You must produce this person before the court and show cause why he is held in custody."

Habeas corpus is a *writ of inquiry* used to determine if the person is being denied his liberty, as required by due process. The writ may be used prior to trial to challenge the showing of probable cause and/or the constitutional validity of a statute. The writ may also be employed to obtain release on bail when the amount of bail is excessive. Habeas corpus may also inquire into the following:

1. Failure to indict.
2. Defects in indictment.
3. Denial of speedy trial.
4. Denial of right to counsel.
5. Use of involuntary confessions.

6. Denial of right of appeal.
7. Denial of jury trial.
8. Denial or exclusion of members of petitioners race from jury.
9. Insanity or mental incompetence.
10. Former jeopardy.

1.3.14.2. *Writ of Prohibition.* A writ of prohibition is a means of challenging the jurisdiction of a court to try a case. The writ, usually issued by a superior court to an inferior court, is a remedy designed to prevent another court from acting beyond its power. Prohibition is a means of preventing a tribunal from proceeding with a case. The writ will only issue to prevent a future act, and will not lie subsequent to a final judgment made by the court in question.

The writ of prohibition is an extraordinary writ, and will only issue with a showing of great necessity—not in cases which are merely doubtful. It is a *preventative*, rather than corrective measure used to prevent injustice.

1.3.15. PLEA BARGAINING. Plea bargaining occurs frequently and its purpose is to avoid extensive and timely litigation. The prosecutor makes "a deal" with the accused, that if the accused will plead guilty to a lesser charge, the prosecution will amend the charge and/or drop other possible charges.

Justification for plea bargainings is as follows:
1. Defendant's willingness to accept guilt.
2. Several uncleared cases may often be closed by confessions of the defendant, thereby eliminating future investigative effort at solving the crimes.
3. Decrease in court cases.

1.3.16. TRIAL PROCEDURE. Criminal trials are conducted following a standard procedure or format. Generally, there are ten recognized stages to the trial subsequent to the impanelment and selection of the jury. Brief comment will be made regarding juror selection, which will be followed by a discussion of the criminal trial proceeding.

1.3.17. JURY SELECTION. Theoretically, jurors are selected from a representative sampling of our population. In reality, however, many competent persons are excluded from jury duty because of their occupations, family associations, or backgrounds. Although our jury system is considered the best that man has devised for the determination of guilt or innocence, it has been argued that our system of justice often excludes many segments of our population who should serve. Often lawyers, doctors, teachers, policemen, clergy, and other occupations are customarily excused from jury service, leaving, many times, the unexperienced and uneducated to sift through difficult and confusing evidence. Notwithstanding, trial by jury has been recognized as the fairest means to determine criminal responsibility.

A master list is usually prepared by each political subdivision, often based on tax rolls, of the persons eligible to serve on jury duty. A cursory records check is usually conducted on each prospective juror, and if he or she is then considered qualified, he or she will be notified to appear for a prescribed period for possible selection as a juror.

On the appointed day, all of those persons selected will appear at the prescribed court. A certain number will then be sworn in and directed to the appropriate courtrooms. There they will be questioned by both the prosecution and defense as to matters pertaining to the forthcoming trial: this may include biases, ability to be impartial, relatives on trial, familiarity with witnesses, thoughts on punishment, and knowledge of the case.

Both the state and the defense have a certain number of *challenges,* which may be used to exclude persons from sitting on the jury: *challenge for cause* and *peremptory challenges.* Challenges for cause may be invoked where there is a legitimate or legal reason why a person should not be a juror; for example, a person would be removed for cause if the defendant was a relative.

A peremptory challenge is one which is based more on the whim of counsel than on reason or fact. Accordingly, peremptory challenges are limited in number. In cases involving capital offenses, the number of challenges is usually greater.

After all of the jurors and alternatives have been selected, they are impaneled or sworn in as a body and the trial may begin.

1.3.18. THE TRIAL. The trial is a judicial hearing to bring forth factual issues from the evidence, and to apply the law to such facts. The United States Constitution lays the foundation for the right to a jury trial in four amendments:

Amendment V
. . . "nor (shall any person) be deprived of life, liberty, or property without due process of law . . ."

Amendment VI
"In all criminal prosecutions, the accused shall enjoy the right to a speedy and public trial, by an impartial jury of the state and district wherein the crime shall have been committed . . ."

Amendment VII
"In suits of common law, where the value in controversy shall exceed twenty dollars, the right of trial by jury shall be preserved, and no fact tried by a jury, shall otherwise be reexamined in any court of the United States, than according to the rules of the common law."

Amendment XIV
Section 1 . . . "nor shall any state deprive any person of life, liberty, or property, without due process of law . . ."

The Constitution does *not require* a jury trial in any case, but merely provides the right in all criminal and some civil cases. The right to a trial by jury may, in any event, be waived.

Trial by jury usually means a jury of twelve, and in the absence of statutory provisions, requires a unanimous decision by all twelve. (For a more detailed treatment of the constitutional basis of the right to trial, see Chap. 6.)

The trial is conducted in a manner developed out of custom and practical considerations. The following stages occur in the order presented, and will be explained to a limited extent:

1.3.19. STAGES OF TRIAL

1.3.19.1. *Reading of Charges and Plea.* The charge against the defendant(s) is read in open court, along with the pleas entered.

1.3.19.2. *Opening Statements.* Upon the commencement of the trial, the judge will ask both the State and the Defense if they are ready to proceed. After receiving an affirmative answer from both sides, the prosecutor will "open" the trial with a statement to the jury of the crime charged and how the state intends to prove the defendant is responsible.

The defense will follow by making an opening statement which will attempt to refute the allegations made by the prosecutor. The defense will tell the jury, generally, why the accused should not be found guilty. After the opening statements have been made, the state presents its case.

1.3.19.3. *Prosecution Presents Case.* The state presents its case to the jury by proving all of the necessary elements of the crime charged. In proving the *corpus delecti,* witnesses will be called, and evidentiary exhibits admitted. All items brought before the court must conform to certain established rules of evidence. For example, all confessions must adhere to *Miranda* and *Escobedo* requirements.

All of the witnesses called by the prosecution are subject to cross-examination by the defense. Likewise, all defense witnesses may be examined by the prosecution.

At the conclusion of the prosecutions' case, the defense presents its case.

1.3.19.4. *Defense Presents Case.* The defense now presents evidence to refute what the prosecution has shown, and to place a *reasonable doubt* in the minds of the jurors as to the guilt of the accused. If there does appear to be a reasonable doubt, the defendant must go free.

1.3.19.5. *Rebuttals.* At the close of the defense, the prosecution and then defense may be allowed to rebut certain evidence presented by the other side.

1.3.19.6. *Arguments to the Jury.* The prosecution and defense will make closing arguments to the jury, summarizing the evidence most favorable to their side, and asking the jury to decide in their favor.

1.3.19.7. *Instructions to Jury.* After closing arguments are presented to the jury, the judge will instruct the jury on the applicable laws. The jury's function is the determination of facts presented, leaving the proper application of the law to the judge.

Often, counsel will prepare jury instructions, which the judge may or may not allow to go to the jury.

1.3.19.8. *Jury Deliberations.* After receiving instructions on how to proceed, the jury will go into deliberations to weigh and discuss all of the evidence presented.

There are strict rules regarding the secrecy and inviolability of the jury during deliberation. Any attempt to learn how the deliberations are proceeding, or to influence the decisional process may result in criminal charges or a mistrial. The jury will deliberate until reaching a unanimous verdict; however, if they cannot all concur in their verdict, the jury is said to be "hung" and a new trial will be ordered.

1.3.19.9. *Return of Verdict.* Once the jury has reached a verdict, they will return to the court to present their findings. Usually, the bailiff of the court reads the decision aloud, after which the judge will ask if all concur. At this point, counsel has the right to "poll the jury," asking each of them if they agree to the verdict. If the jury is unanimous, they will be dismissed.

1.3.19.10. *Judgment and Sentence.* After the verdict of guilty has been returned, the judge will pass sentence, according to the law. It may take the form of a fine, jail sentence, imprisonment, or probation. If incarceration is prescribed, the sentence may be for a definite or indefinite period. The imposition of sentence must occur without unreasonable delay from the time of verdict.

1.3.20. REVIEW OF CASE BY APPELLATE TRIBUNAL. The accused is entitled to one complete review of his case by an appellate court. This is accomplished by the superior court examining the transcript of the lower court proceeding. The United States Supreme Court has ruled that if a person cannot afford the costs of an official transcript for purpose of appeal, one must be provided by the state.

1.3.20.1. *The Role of the Judge.* The role of the judge in the criminal trial is that of an overseer who insures: a) fairness prevails, b) rules of evidence are strictly adhered to, and c) due process requirements are met. The judge is responsible for making all *legal* rulings, i.e. those pertaining to law, as contrasted with factual questions weighed by the jury. The judge alone is the one to make the determination as to sentence, if the defendant is found guilty.

1.3.20.2. The Role of the Advocate. The lawyer appears as an advocate before the court to present, as persuasively as is possible, the facts of the case as seen from his client's point of view.

The lawyer owes a duty of loyalty both to his client and the court. At times, it is somewhat difficult for the attorney to know where his first duty does lie.

An English Lord, during the middle of the 1800's, somewhat exuberantly exclaimed, of the lawyers role and responsibility to his client,

> . . . an advocate by the sacred duty which he owes his client knows in the discharge of that office but one person in the world, that client and none other. To save that client by all expedient means, to protect that client at all hazards and costs to all others, and among others to himself, is the highest and most unquestioned of his duties; and he must not regard the alarm, the suffering, the torment, the destruction which he may bring upon any other. Nay separating even duties of a patriot from those of an advocate, and casting them if needed be to the wind, he must go on reckless of the consequences, if his fate it should be unhappily to invoke his country to confusion for his clients' protection.

(Lord Brougham, in defense of Queen Caroline before the House of Lords, nineteenth century.)

More seriously, one eminent jurist of the United Kingdom, in discussing a lawyers responsibilities, said . . .

> Sometimes there may seem to be a nice conflict between the duty to the court and a duty to the client . . . but our supreme loyalty always is to our profession and in the cause of justice; our overriding duty to the court. . . . We are entitled to put our client's case, we are his representative, with courage and with vigour. We have no right to invent a case for him. A clear distinction has to be drawn between suggesting the facts which it would be desirable to prove, in order to establish some particular case, which is something we may never do, and indicating what is the proper line of defense or claim available on the facts as we are told them by our client. We can point out the nature of the evidence which is required to estab-

lish facts as the client states them to be, but it is manifestly not for use to concoct a case. It is axiomatic that the advocate must never knowingly mislead the court. Whether in a criminal or civil case, subject to rules as to onus, the duty is to present to the court the whole truth . . . and just as with the facts, so with the law. It sometimes happens that one's researches lead to the discovery of some authority adverse to the case for which one is contending, but that neither opposing counsel nor the judge is aware of it. Occasionally a barrister will hear the court misdirecting itself on some point of law. It is always the duty of the advocate to assist the court and bring all cases to the notice of the court.

(Sir Hartley W. Shawcross, 17th Annual Benjamin N. Cardozo Lecture, May 28, 1958, New York City, Bar Association.)

What does the lawyer precisely do? Basically, he is responsible for the preparation of a client's case. This includes the counseling function, wherein he seeks to advise alternate courses of legal action which may be taken.

At the trial stage, he must develop strategy for the presentation of evidence, and must be able to anticipate and refute evidence brought forward by the state.

In effect, the advocate gives his client the use and benefit of his learning, experience, and judgment.

Although the attorney is acting for the client, he must not be identified with him. He is merely a representative. The lawyer must not forget his allegiances, to the client, court, and justice. He must always remember that a lawyer has a prior and perpetual obligation to truth and justice, which can never be discharged in favor of an individual.

Often when an attorney has undertaken a very unpopular case or client to represent, the public cannot understand how the lawyer can act for such a person or cause. The simple response is that the justice or injustice of the cause is to be decided by judge and jury, not attorney. The purpose of our courts is to allow every man to have his cause fairly tried. Though a lawyer must not tell what he knows to be false, also he must not usurp the prerogatives of the judge and jury, which is to determine what should be the effect of the evidence.

If lawyers were to undertake no cause until they were sure they were just, a man might be precluded from a trial, even though he might have been found to be in the right upon judicial examination.

It may be fairly stated, in conclusion, that the integrity of the adjudicative process itself depends in large measure upon the participation of the advocate.

GLOSSARY

Alias Writ. A second writ issued after the first writ was returned without being effective.

Arraignment. The initial appearance of the accused in district court after an indictment or information has been filed.

Bill of Exceptions. A formal written statement of exceptions taken to a decision or direction of the judge, delivered during the trial, which sets forth the proceedings of the trial, the opinion and exception thereto, signed by the judge.

Capital Offense. An offense which may be punished by the death sentence.

Certiorari. A method of bringing the record of inferior courts before the court for purposes of ascertaining whether the inferior court had jurisdiction and whether the proceedings were authorized.

Competent. Legally fit and duly qualified.

Credibility. The conviction, certainty, and truthfulness of a witness.

Cross-Examination. A leading and searching inquiry of a witness for further disclosure of matters detailed by him under direct examination.

Defendant. One against whom a cause of action or a charge is brought.

Defense. That which is offered and alleged by the defendant as a reason why the plaintiff (or the prosecution) should not establish what he alleges.

Dicta. Statements by the court which are not essential to the determination of the case at hand.

Direct Examination. The first interrogation of a witness.

Disbarment. The act of a court to take away an attorney's license to practice law.

Double Jeopardy. The doctrine that one cannot be tried or prosecuted a second time for the same offense.

Due Process. A combination of history, reason, and past deci-

393

sions which demands that the law shall not be arbitrary, capricious or unreasonable; and in criminal procedure is found in the Federal Bill of Rights as applied to the states through the "due process" clause of the fourteenth amendment.

Exculpate. To excuse or justify.

Exemplar. A specimen.

Exonerate. To free from a charge.

Ex Post Facto. After the fact.

Felony. A criminal offense for which the accused may be imprisoned or executed in the state prison.

Grand Jury. An investigatory body which determines from evidence whether any crimes have been committed. At least twelve grand jurors must concur in the finding of a particular indictment.

Habeas Corpus. A writ which challenges the continued confinement of an individual.

Hearsay. An out-of-court assertion used in court to prove the truth of a matter asserted.

Holding. The conclusion of law reached by a court in a particular case.

Impeach. To attack the credibility of a witness and cast doubt on his testimony.

Indictment. An accusation by a grand jury that reasonable grounds exist to believe that a crime has been committed.

Information. A formal charge which informs the defendant that he has been charged in order that he might prepare his defense.

Infra. Below.

Injunction. A judicial process whereby a party is required to do or refrain from doing a particular thing.

Intent. The purpose for which an act is done.

Jurisdiction. The authority, capacity, power or right of a court to act.

Jus Tertii. The right of a third party.

Juvenile. Generally, a child under the age of eighteen.

Magistrate. A judicial officer of a lower court.

Magna Charta. A constitutional enactment made by King John of England in 1215, which is now regarded as the foundation of English constitutional liberty.

Mandamus. A *writ of mandamus* is a command in the name of a state or sovereign, issued by a court of law having jurisdiction to an inferior court, corporation, or person, requiring the performance of some duty.

Misdemeanor. All those crimes and offenses for which the law has not provided a particular name. It is distinguished from a "felony" in degree by reason of place and severity of punishment.

Nexus. A connection or link.

Preliminary Hearing. An examination of the accused and witness for the accused to ascertain whether the crime charged has been committed. It is not a trial and accordingly, the guilt or innocence of the accused is not determined at such a hearing.

Prosecute. To carry on a judicial proceeding against a person to its ultimate conclusion.

Putative. Supposed.

Quasi. Seemingly.

Recidivism. The continued commission of crimes by an individual.

Scrire Facias, Writ of. A writ founded upon some matter of record.

Supra. Above.

Venue. The geographical division in which an action or prosecution is brought for trial.

Waiver. A relinquishment of a known right.

Witness. One who gives evidence in a cause before the court.

Writ. A formal document prohibiting or ordering some act.

BIBLIOGRAPHY

American Jurisprudence: San Francisco, Bancroft-Whitney Publishing Company, 1972.

American Law Reports: San Francisco, Bancroft-Whitney, 1972.

Berman and Greiner: *The Nature and Function of Law.* Brooklyn, Foundation Press, 1966.

Cleary and Strong: *Evidence.* St. Paul, West Publishing Company, 1969.

Corpus Juris Secondum: St. Paul, Minn., West Publishing Company, 1972.

Graham, F. P.: *The Self-Inflicted Wound.* New York, Macmillan, 1970.

Hall, J.: *Criminal Law and Procedure.* Indianapolis, Bobbs-Merrill, 1949.

Hearings before the Committee on the District of Columbia United States Senate: 91st Congress, First Session on S.3034, Pre-Trial Detention, Part 6, Crime in the Nations Capital, Washington, D.C., Government Printing Office, 1972.

Introduction to Advocacy: Mineola, Board of Student Advisors, Harvard Law School, 1970.

Louisell, Kaplan, Waltz: *Principles of Evidence and Proof.* Mineola, Foundation Press, 1968.

Miller, J.: *Criminal Law.* St. Paul, West Publishing Company, 1934.

Packer, H. L.: *The Limits of the Criminal Sanction.* California, Stanford Univ. Press, 1968.

Penofsky, D. J.: *Guidelines for Interrogation.* Rochester, Acqueduct, 1967.

Perkins, R. M.: *Criminal Law and Procedure.* Brooklyn, Foundation Press, 1966.

Schafer, William J.: *Confessions and Statements.* Springfield, Thomas, 1968.

Weinreb, L. L.: *Criminal Process.* Mineola, Foundation Press, 1969.

West's Law Finder: St. Paul, West Publishing Company, 1967.

Wright, C. A.: *Law of Federal Courts.* St. Paul, West Publishing Company, 1970.

INDEX